CHILTERN
ARCHAEOLOGY
RECENT WORK
A Handbook for the Next Decade

Edited by Robin Holgate
Foreword by Professor Keith Branigan

This book is dedicated to J.F.Dyer, MA, FSA and C.L.Matthews, FSA, who have both contributed significantly to our understanding of the archaeology of the north Chilterns.

First published November 1995
by
The Book Castle
12 Church Street
Dunstable
Bedfordshire LU5 4RU

This book is published with financial assistance from Hertfordshire County Council.

ISBN 1 871199 52 2

Printed by Progressive Printing (UK) Ltd., Leigh-on-Sea, Essex.

Cover: Aerial view of Barton Hill Cutting showing the excavation of three earlier Bronze Age ring ditches undertaken by the Bedfordshire Archaeology Service in summer 1989. Photograph taken and reproduced by courtesy of Bob Wood.

CONTENTS

LIST OF CONTRIBUTORS

Keith Branigan	Head of the Department of Archaeology and Prehistory, University of Sheffield
Stewart Bryant	County Archaeologist, Hertfordshire County Council
Gil Burleigh	Keeper of Field Archaeology, North Hertfordshire Museums Service
Stanley Cauvain	Field Officer, Chess Valley Archaeological & Historical Society
Royston Clark	formerly Senior Archaeological Field Officer, Bedfordshire County Archaeological Services
Mike Daniels	County Archaeologist, Cumbria County Council
Michael Dawson	Senior Archaeological Field Officer, Bedfordshire County Archaeological Services
Nicholas Doggett	Assistant Conservation Officer, South Oxfordshire District Council
Michael Farley	County Archaeologist, Buckinghamshire County Museum Service
Robin Holgate	Museums' Curator, Luton Museum Service
Renwick Hudspith	Assistant Site Director, Manshead Archaeological Society of Dunstable
Jonathan Hunn	Project Manager, Tempus Reparatum, Oxford
Tom McDonald	Senior Projects Officer, Hertfordshire Archaeological Trust
Roger Miles	Field Director, St Albans & Hertfordshire Architectural & Archaeological Society
Mike Morris	City Archaeologist, Grosvenor Museum, Chester
Rosalind Niblett	District Archaeologist, St Albans District Council
Andrew Pike	formerly Sites & Monuments Records Officer, Buckinghamshire County Museum Service
Angela Simco	formerly County Heritage Officer, Bedfordshire County Council Heritage Group
Anna Slowikowski	Artefacts Manager, Bedfordshire County Archaeological Services
Paul Smith	County Archaeologist, Oxfordshire Museums & Archives & Centre for Oxfordshire Studies
Bambi Stainton	formerly Chairman, Chess Valley Archaeological & Historical Society
Angus Wainwright	Archaeological Field Officer, The National Trust, Hughenden Manor, High Wycombe
Carolyn Wingfield	Senior Museums Officer (Central Services), Doncaster Museum & Art Gallery

PREFACE AND ACKNOWLEDGEMENTS

This book stems from a day conference on the archaeology of the Chilterns held at the John Dony Field Centre in Luton in September 1990. The conference was organised by Luton Museum Service in conjunction with the Institute of Archaeologists' South Midlands Group. Stewart Bryant and Mike Morris helped the Editor plan and organise the conference. Thanks are due to Val Bryant, David Hillelson, Vivienne Holgate and Lis Salmon for their help in running the conference.

Eleven of the sections in this book are based on talks given at the 1990 day conference. The remainder have been commissioned for the book in order to give a comprehensive overview of the current state of knowledge of Chiltern archaeology and how archaeological work in the region is organised. The papers were submitted by 1993 and the Editor is grateful for the enduring patience of all the contributors in seeing this book through to publication. The Editor is also grateful to Mark McCall, Documentation Officer with Luton Museum Service, for his assistance with lay-out and format work on the book and to Karen Worrell, Melinda Spelman, Alison Tigg, Helen Hill and Michaela Knight who helped type parts of the text. The Editor would like to acknowledge the generous financial support of Hertfordshire County Council towards the cost of publishing this book, Bob Wood for granting permission to reproduce his photograph on the front cover and Hertfordshire Record Office for permission to reproduce two illustrations from the Buckler Drawings, volume 1.

Stewart Bryant is grateful to Gil Burleigh, Chris Saunders and John Collis for their helpful comments on earlier drafts of his section. The views expressed therein are, however, entirely his responsibility.

Carolyn Wingfield would like to acknowledge the help of colleagues from the following organisations who have discussed their recent excavations with her and provided information, although the interpretations offered in her contribution are her responsibility: Bedfordshire County Council Archaeology Service: E. Baker, M. Dawson, H.B. Duncan, A. Slowikowski; Hertfordshire Archaeological Trust: D. Hillelson; North Hertfordshire Museums Service: G.R. Burleigh; Buckinghamshire County Museum Service and the Milton Keynes Archaeological Unit: M. Farley, A. Pike, R.J. Williams.

Royston Clark and Michael Dawson's section draws heavily upon the work of Bedfordshire County Archaeological Services up to 1989. The opinions expressed by them are their own and do not necessarily reflect any aspect of the Services' policy. Their drawings are by Michael Dawson and Mike Trevarthen.

Mike Morris and Angus Wainwright wish to ackowledge the support of the National Trust, the Hertfordshire Archaeological Trust and English Heritage. Their contribution is the product of the work of many individuals and they would like to record their debt to Alex Thompson, Alan Wyatt and the other members of the Berkhamsted and District Archaeological Society who undertook most of the fieldwork at Cow Roast and to the members of the Community Programme team who helped with the survey at Ashridge. Thanks are also due to Martin Millett for his helpful comments on the paper and to Stewart Bryant, Mike Cantor, Juliet Clutton-Brock, Nicola Godwin, Julia Green, Jonathan Hunn, Gerry McDonnell, Caroline Malone, David Neal, Mike Parker-Pearson and to John Wilson and his staff at Ashridge. Figure 24 was drawn by Frances Chaloner.

Jonathan Hunn wishes to record his thanks to David Neal and Malcolm Wagstaff for their comments on earlier drafts of his contribution on the study of the Romano-British settlement around Verulamium.

Rosalind Niblett is indebted to G.B. Dannell, V. Rigby, I.M. Stead and I. Thompson for their interim comments on the material found at Folly Lane. The drawings are the work of Alex Thorne and the photographs were taken by Kate Warren.

Andrew Pike is grateful to Mike Farley for commenting on a drart of his contribution on medieval enclosures and for his suggestions.

The archaeological investigations described by Tom McDonald in advance of the construction of the A41 Kings Langley and Berkhamsted By-passes were funded by English Heritage. The Trust also acknowledges the assistance of the Department of Transport, Brian Colquhoun and Partners (Consulting Engineers), Ameys and Budge (the Contractors).

Bambi Stainton, on behalf of the Chess Valley Archaeological and Historical Society, is grateful to all the landowners, without whose permission and support none of this work could have taken place, and to Mike Farley, the Buckinghamshire County Archaeologist, who has given us unfailing support and advice over the years. Stanley Cauvain, Field Officer, and Pauline Cauvain, Editor, have kindly vetted this contribution.

Renwick Hudspith expresses thanks to the landowners and farmers who have granted permission to fieldwalk their land, to the hardy fieldwalkers of the Manshead Archaeological Society, to J. Hitchcock for the mapwork and to Dr R. Holgate for helping with the preparation of his contribution.

Stanley Cauvain is grateful to the Buckinghamshire County Museum and the Central Excavation Unit for providing some of the samples used in this study, to M.J. Hughes of the British Museum Research Laboratory for providing standards, to Dr. Paula Curtis for the multivariate statistical analyses, and to Dr. L.R. Day and J. Evans of the Polytechnic of East London for guidance with the practical work.

The illustrations of the pottery for Anna Slowikowski's contribution were drawn by Mike Trevarthen, to whom she is grateful for the time and effort he put into them. She also wishes to thank Bedfordshire County Archaeological Services for the use of the above material prior to its publication. All the views expressed, however, are her own.

THE ARCHAEOLOGY OF THE CHILTERNS - AN EVERYDAY STORY OF COUNTRY FOLK

Keith Branigan

"In this tiny palimpest
All the roots of England rest"

Edward Bucknell

It is customary to begin an introduction to any book, but particularly a book about archaeology, by claiming that it will be of interest to a wide, if not universal, audience. The 'interested laymen' of this world will be queuing up to buy it. But the editor of this book is an honest man, and he rightly makes no such claim. This book is written by, and intended for, all those who are actively involved in the archaeology of the Chilterns. Its genesis was a conference held at the John Dony Field Centre in Luton in 1990 - a conference where the papers were read by archaeologists to an audience of archaeologists. Where did they all come from?

They came of course from the County and Town Museums, from the Council Planning Offices and various Archaeological Units, and (a few) from the Universities. But they also came from the towns, villages and farms of Bedfordshire, Buckinghamshire Hertfordshire and Oxfordshire, members of county, town or area archaeological societies, or in some cases of no society at all. Professional and amateur, full-time and part-time alike, they packed the lecture theatre - an audience of infinite variety.

Variety is indeed the key-word both to this volume and its subject. Those who do not live in the Chilterns and rarely if ever visit them tend to think of them as those chalk hills north of London. Chiltern folk know better. Even a glance at the map and a casual acquaintance with the area quickly reveals the variety of landscapes - the clay vale, the steep scarp, the dipslope scored with the valleys of half a dozen rivers, the Thames valley and its gravel terraces, and the peaty marshland of the Colne valley. Little wonder that throughout history, people have had to adapt to these different environments in different ways and that they have left behind such a wealth and variety of archaeological remains.

Within the area encompassed in this book one can find examples of most, though not all, of the principal prehistoric, Roman and medieval monuments of lowland Britain. From the neolithic and Bronze Ages we have examples of long and round barrows, ring ditches, causewayed enclosures, henges, pit and ditch alignments, flint mines, and 'ridgeways'. From later prehistory we have hillforts and oppida, cremation cemeteries and rich 'Welwyn' burials, and dykes and other land boundaries. The 'Romans' have left towns and posting stations, villas and temples, potteries and tileries and - of course - their roads. From the medieval era we have chapels and churches, and the monumentality of abbeys and castles. And these monuments are really no more than the tip of the iceberg, the most visible or most easily identified human remains in the landscape, put there by generations of Chiltern dwellers who lived in far simpler buildings, long since vanished, but whose endless toil created the landscape palimpsest that is the Chilterns of today.

To rediscover many of these remains, and to analyse and attempt to understand all of them and how they relate one to the other, is a task requiring not only many hands but also a wide variety of methods and techniques. That variety is well represented in this book. We have descriptions of research excavations and of 'rescue' operations, we have examples of long-term fieldwalking schemes and of short-term linear bypass surveys. There are analytical reports and artefact studies, and there is a variety of documentary approaches described. Some of the sections which present overviews of particular periods or topics bring together the results of excavations, field survey, artefact studies, documentary research, geophysical investigations, aerial photography and a wide variety of environmental evidence. With so many varied skills being called upon it is hardly surprising that the two dozen sections in this book represent the joint efforts of several hundred archaeologists.

Each section offers variety too. First we have a valuable series of period overviews, beginning with Holgate's review of the early prehistoric settlement which demonstrates that *occupation* of the Chiltern valleys only really began in the later mesolithic period. Bryant and Farley concentrate on the relatively sparse evidence for later prehistory in the Buckinghamshire and north Chilterns, rightly questioning whether the present evidence is spatially biased by a variety of geological, archaeological and economic factors. In considering

Anglo-Saxon settlement, Wingfield sensibly avoids a historical bias to interpretation by allowing the archaeological evidence to stand on its own merits. Hunn's overview of the medieval landscape of the dipslope highlights the similarities and differences between the later Iron Age and Roman landscape of the area and that of the late Saxon period.

A second group focuses on specific pieces of landscape within the region. Clark and Dawson in contrasting the evidence from the Ouse Valley and the Bedfordshire Chilterns emphasise the intensity of agricultural activity here in the later Iron Age and Roman periods. Morris and Wainwright, looking at the upper Bulbourne valley, record the invaluable discovery of Romano-British small farmsteads within what is normally taken to be a villa-dominated landscape, whilst in a second contribution Hunn presents an interesting discussion of villa estates and their populations in the vicinity of Verulamium.

Another group looks at specific monuments or types of monument. Bryant and Burleigh examine the later prehistoric dykes and conclude there are three types which are related to a probably complex succession of land divisions constructed during the first millennium bc. Niblett describes the conquest-period burial and subsequent ritual monument at Folly Lane, St Albans, and assesses its significance, whilst Burleigh's second contribution argues for the recognition of an oppidum at Baldock. Moving into the post-Roman era, Doggett examines the overlooked but fascinating evidence for manorial chapels and chapels-of-ease in south-west Hertfordshire, and Pike reviews the enigmatic woodland enclosures of the Buckinghamshire Chilterns, proposing they belong to the medieval period.

Four of the contributions present the results of survey and fieldwork. McDonald's description of the A41 By-Pass project is a good example of how the enforced study of a previously neglected zone (Clay-with-flints valley slopes) can open new windows on the past, in this case by revealing unsuspected, and long awaited, neolithic and Bronze Age settlement sites. Stainton's description of the work of the Chess Valley Archaeological and Historical Society is an encouraging story of how initially casual fieldwork by a team of three enthusiasts developed into a carefully planned long-term project and finally became integrated into the County Museum's overall strategy. In contrast, Hudspith's report on fieldwalking in south Bedfordshire is an account of work done by an individual in co-operation with a local society, and is written with a commendable awareness of the

problems of interpreting archaeological distribution maps. Miles' contribution is different again, describing the results of fieldwalking in a very restricted area which has allowed him to make some interesting suggestions about the significance of burnt flint recovered in field survey.

Two further sections are concerned with artefact material, in both cases pottery, but from very different perspectives. Cauvain's description of chemical analysis of medieval ceramics from south Buckinghamshire is a neat example of a carefully planned local study which has produced results which should lead to a better understanding of local trade and communications in the later Middle Ages. In contrast, Slowikowski's section uses more traditional methods of pottery analysis to provide new information about the much neglected local potters who supplied so much of the pottery used in late prehistoric, Roman and medieval rural settlements.

The final group is concerned in their various ways with the organisation of archaeology in the region. Pike provides an interesting potted history of archaeology in Buckinghamshire, and Daniells and Smith explain how professionals, amateurs and developers are learning to work together in Hertfordshire and Oxfordshire respectively to their mutual benefit. Simco's section, though focussed on Bedfordshire, addresses strengths and weakness in present legislation which are of importance throughout the region, and indeed throughout the country, and suggests how the realities of development and the requirements of archaeology might be better accommodated, if not integrated, during the next decade.

In a sense this book might be said to be the regional archaeologists' handbook for the next decade. It sets out our current state of knowledge, and ignorance, and in doing so it points to the directions in which our efforts should be channelled. There is clearly a lot of work to be done, but the message of this book is that there is an army of well-trained, capable and enthusiastic archaeologists in the region - professional and amateur alike - to do the job. Enjoy reading this book by all means, but then - back to work!

EARLY PREHISTORIC SETTLEMENT OF THE CHILTERNS

Robin Holgate

Introduction

The main aim of this section is to present an overview of the nature and development of settlement on the Chiltern Hills from the earliest times to the early second millennium bc. Initially, the palaeoenvironmental background and the nature of the evidence for early prehistoric settlement of the Chilterns is considered. This is followed by a review of palaeolithic to earlier Bronze Age settlement patterns. Finally, priorites for future work are discussed.

Palaeoenvironmental background

The Chiltern Hills form a well-defined geographical region, consisting of a Chalk scarp slope on its north-eastern flank and an undulating Chalk dipslope extending as far as the middle Thames valley and the London basin to the south and south-west. The dipslope is capped extensively with Clay-with-flints and other superficial deposits, and is divided into blocks of rolling downland by south and south-west flowing tributaries of the Thames. The lower stretches of most tributary valleys contain Pleistocene gravel and Flandrian alluvial, peat and tufa deposits. To the north lie the south-west to north-east running Gault Clay vale and the Greensand Ridge; the middle and lower Thames gravel terraces are situated to the south.

Palaeoenvironmental information for the region is patchy. Pollen analysis of interglacial deposits has been undertaken by Richard Hubbard at Caddington, Beds. (Campbell & Hubbard 1978), whilst early post-glacial peat deposits have been studied at Iver in the Colne valley, Bucks. (Lacaille 1963, 206), at Broxbourne in the Lea valley, Herts. (Warren *et al.* 1934) and, more recently, in the lower Colne and Lea valleys (Lewis *et al.* 1992). No other work on pollen assemblages of note has taken place and the nearest site to the Chilterns which has produced a pollen sequence spanning the early post-glacial period is Hampstead Heath, Greater London (Girling & Greig 1977; 1985; Greig 1989). Although this pollen sequence lacks a radiocarbon chronology, very high tree pollen values occur at the beginning of the sequence, which probably date to the sixth-fourth millennia bc, suggesting that there was a thick forest cover growing locally. Lime was dominant, followed by oak and elm; pine and birch, along with shrubs such as ivy, were also present. Alder was probably growing extensively in wet areas by the site and hazel may have formed a forest understorey. Some disturbance of the forest is shown by the presence of traces of ribwort plantain (Girling & Greig 1977, 47; 1985, 348). In the late fourth and early third millennia bc, there are significantly lower elm pollen values. Associated changes include falls in the levels of oak, lime and hazel, accompanied by the appearance of cereal pollen and a rise in ruderals such as ribwort plantain (Girling & Greig 1977, 47; 1985, 349; Greig 1989, 96). The importance of this pollen sequence is the association of the beetle *Scolytus scolytus* (F.), which is the main carrier of the fungus which causes Dutch Elm Disease, immediately below the elm decline horizon (Girling & Greig 1985, 349). Later, probably in the second millennium bc, the lime and oak pollen values fall dramatically and beech appears (Greig 1989, 97).

Analysis of snails from deposits in dry valleys and features associated with earlier Bronze Age ditches has been undertaken for a few sites near the Chiltern scarp. Dry valley deposits from the Chiltern escarpment at Pitstone, Bucks. yielded snails which suggested a woodland environment that, on the basis of a radiocarbon date of 1,960 $\pm$ 220 bc on associated charcoal fragments, was cleared in the early second millennium bc (Evans & Valentine 1974, 350-1). The ring ditches at Barton Hill Farm (Dyer 1962) and the Waulud's Bank henge (Dyer 1964a), both in Beds., overlay a number of irregular subsoil hollows which can be interpreted as tree hollows resulting from the pre-Bronze Age woodland cover. Snail assemblages from the ditch fills of the ring ditches at Bartonhill Cutting showed that they had been constructed and maintained in a tall, lush grassland environment indicative of low land-use pressure with perhaps a slight grazing of rough pasture (Allen 1991). It is thus likely that this part of the north Chilterns was used for low intensity seasonal pasture in the early second millennium bc.

Extrapolating from the Hampstead Heath pollen sequence and the Pitstone snail analysis, it is likely that mixed deciduous woodland covered the Chilterns in the sixth-fourth millennia bc, with

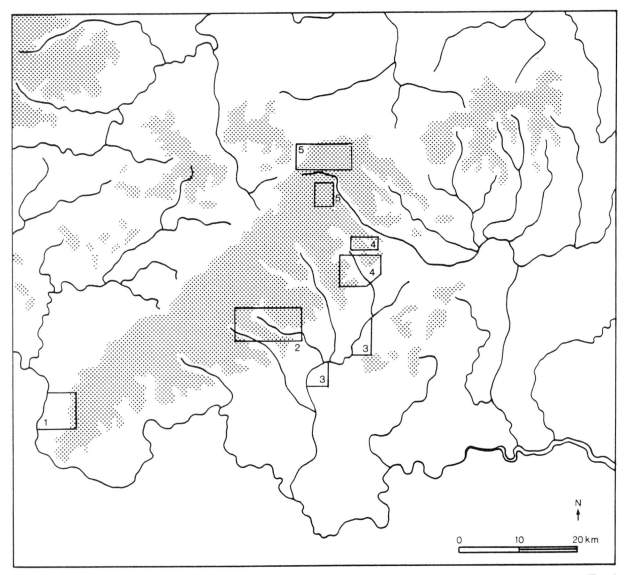

Fig. 1. Location of surface collection survey work in the Chilterns. 1, east of North Stoke, Oxon. (Ford 1987); 2, Chess and Misbourne valleys, Bucks. (Stainton this volume); 3, Dunstable environs, Beds. (Hudspith this volume); 4, St Albans environs (Miles this volume); 5, Colne valley, Herts. (Phil Jones pers. comm.; Roger Jacobi pers. comm.).

clearings certainly appearing on the Chiltern scarp and south of the Chilterns by the early second millennium bc. Further pollen and snail analysis, notably on colluvial and post-glacial valley deposits, is a priority for future work in order to fill out this rather sketchy picture.

The nature of early prehistoric settlement

Evidence for early prehistoric settlement consists of earthworks and flint artefact scatters. Earthworks mainly comprise long and round barrows, causewayed enclosures and henge monuments; surface traces of the majority of these have been obliterated by later activity, mainly ploughing. In recent decades, aerial photography has helped increase the known distribution of these sites. Domestic sites, since they went out of

use, have been either buried under superficial deposits, for example brickearths and colluvium, or disturbed by ploughing and other activity. Examination of brick pits in the Luton district by Worthington G. Smith in the 1880s - 1910s yielded four undisturbed palaeolithic sites (Roe 1981), whilst fieldwalking and rescue excavations on later period sites have led to the recovery of palaeolithic - Bronze Age flint assemblages. Usually, flint artefacts are the only items resilient enough to survive weathering and other processes that early prehistoric sites have been subjected to since their abandonment. Paradoxically, whilst ploughing and other ground disturbance activities can destroy these sites, they also expose flintwork and thus aid the discovery of these sites.

The search for palaeolithic - earlier Bronze Age

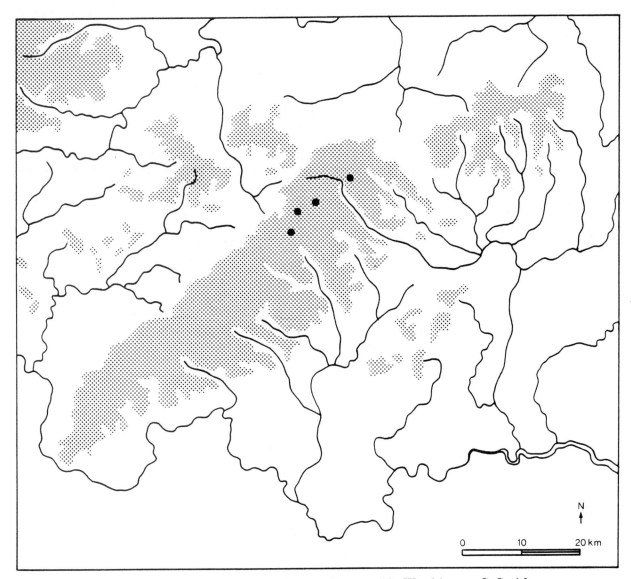

Fig. 2. In situ *lower palaeolithic sites discovered by Worthington G. Smith.*

domestic sites has vexed archaeologists in recent decades (*cf.* Holgate 1988a, 104). Recent work on the interpretation of flint scatters recovered by surface artefact collection survey (e.g. Brown & Edmonds 1987; Holgate 1988b; Schofield 1990) has focussed on the identification of domestic and other activity sites. Certainly, discrete concentrations of flint artefacts can be located on the surface of cultivated land; those which consist of dense concentrations with a substantial number and range of implements can be interpreted as representing the remains of domestic sites. The flint artefacts recovered in this way can be dated by studying the technological and typological characterists of the artefacts themselves (Holgate 1988b, 51-61). Only a small proportion of the Chilterns has been surveyed by surface artefact collection (Fig. 1), limiting the extent to which the distribution of early prehistoric settlement can be mapped. Of those surveys which have taken place, the work of Worthington Smith on lower

palaeolithic settlement in the Dunstable-Luton area, Beds., Phil Jones and Roger Jacobi in the Colne valley, Herts. and recent survey work by Stephen Ford (1987), the Manshead Archaeological Society (Hudspith this volume), the Buckinghamshire County Museum Archaeological Group and the Chess Valley Archaeological and Historical Society (Stainton this volume) and St Albans Museums Service and the St Albans and Hertfordshire Architectural and Archaeological Society (Miles this volume) have all recovered evidence of early prehistoric settlement.

Lower and middle palaeolithic settlement

The palaeolithic period in Britain, the start of which dates back to at least 500,000 years bp, is largely represented by artefact findspots and a number of both cave and open sites (Roe 1981, 9). However, the advance of the Anglian, Wolstonian and Devensian ice sheets into southern England has destroyed an unknown proportion of open sites. Worthington Smith's fieldwork at the turn of this century led to the discovery of four intact lower palaeolithic flint-working areas in brick pits at Caddington, Gaddesden Row, Whipsnade and Round Green, Luton, all in Beds. (Fig. 2: Roe 1981, 184-200; Smith 1916; Smith 1919). Given the paucity of *in situ* open sites in Britain, Smith's discoveries are significant for the information they provide on the location and nature of British lower palaeolithic sites. All four sites were situated on the edge of ponds on the upper Chiltern slopes in the vicinity of the headwaters of the river Lea. Such a location would have provided an attractive camping site in the palaeolithic period, especially since flint was abundant in the local chalk.

Smith recovered over 2,000 flints from one discrete area at Caddington between April 1890 and December 1895 (Sampson 1978; Roe 1981, 191-8). Reinvestigation of the brick earth deposits at Caddington in the early 1970s by Garth Sampson (1978) did not produce further flintwork, suggesting that the original flint-working areas were relatively small and discontinuous. However, Sampson recovered faunal remains and pollen which suggested an Ipswichian Interglacial date (*c*.125,000 bp) for occupation of the site (Campbell & Hubbard 1978, 48-9). At the time, the site comprised rough grassland which gave way abruptly to dense forest dominated by oak but also containing elm, ash, hazel and juniper. A reassessment of the flint assemblage showed that two or possibly three individuals spent a few hours making at least 13 bifacial implements using flint obtained from the Chalk escarpment *c*.450 m away (Sampson 1978, 146-8). This indicates that Caddington was a manufacturing site rather than a living or butchery site. It is likely that contemporary living sites existed close by: otherwise, why else bring flint to this site for making tools if they were not to be used in the vicinity of the site? However, although in 1903 Smith located another undisturbed flint-working area containing flakes and cores worked using the Levallois technique *c*.100 m away in a virtually identical setting, the relationship between the two sites is unknown.

Round Green and Gaddesden Row were similar in nature to the Caddington site. Round Green produced nearly 300 flints, including 21 hand axes, whilst Gaddesden Row yielded at least 50 hand axes, as well as an unspecified number of flake tools and debitage (Roe 1981, 184-8). In addition to debitage, Whipsnade produced at least six hand axes (Smith 1918). Smith also recovered lower palaeolithic flint artefacts from the brick pits at Ramridge End, Luton, Beds., probably rep-

resenting the remains of another flint-working area (Roe 1981, 209).

Significant quantities of lower palaeolithic flintwork, mainly hand axes, have also been recovered from gravel deposits at Rickmansworth (notably at Croxley Green and Mill End) and Hitchen, both in Herts., and Limbury, Luton, Beds. (Roe 1981, 189, 176-7 & 209). A series of gravel terrace sites in the middle Thames valley on the southern edge of the Chilterns has also yielded substantial numbers of lower palaeolithic flint artefacts. These include Highlands Farm, Rotherfield Peppard, Oxon. and Burnham, Farnham Royal, Iver and Taplow, all in Bucks. (Roe 1968; Wymer 1968). None of these sites produced *in situ* flintwork, as the gravels from which they derive have been redeposited during interglacial periods. However, the condition of the flints from Croxley Green, Hitchen and Highlands Farm suggests that they probably represent remnants of working areas that have not moved too far from their original location. Originally, these sites would have been situated close to stream or river channels. Whilst they cannot be dated with accuracy, they are likely to date somewhere between the Hoxnian and Ipswichian Interglacial periods (Roe 1981, 200; Gibbard 1985).

On present evidence lower palaeolithic sites in the Chilterns, as is common elsewhere in southern Britain, appear to have been located near rivers or other water bodies such as small lakes (Roe 1981, 279). Occupation could date back to at least the Hoxnian Interglacial period (*c*.250,000 bp). There is scant evidence for settlement during the ensuing middle palaeolithic period (*c*.70,000-30,000 bp), possibly because Britain offered too hostile an environment for settlement throughout the first stages of the Devensian Glaciation. Middle palaeolithic flint artefacts, in the form of round-butted cordate hand axes, have been recovered from sites on the middle and lower Thames gravel terraces, for example Iver, Marlow and Taplow, all in Bucks. (Roe 1981, 254-5). However, it is still uncertain whether or not the Chilterns were occupied during this period.

Upper palaeolithic settlement

The upper palaeolithic period, corresponding broadly to the Devensian Glaciation, can be divided into two periods: the earlier upper palaeolithic, dating between 36,000 and 25,000 bc and the later upper palaeolithic, dating between 9,500 and 8,300 bc (Jacobi 1980, 15). The only material from the Chilterns dating to the earlier upper palaeolithic period consists of leaf points or leaf-shaped spearheads recovered from two sites

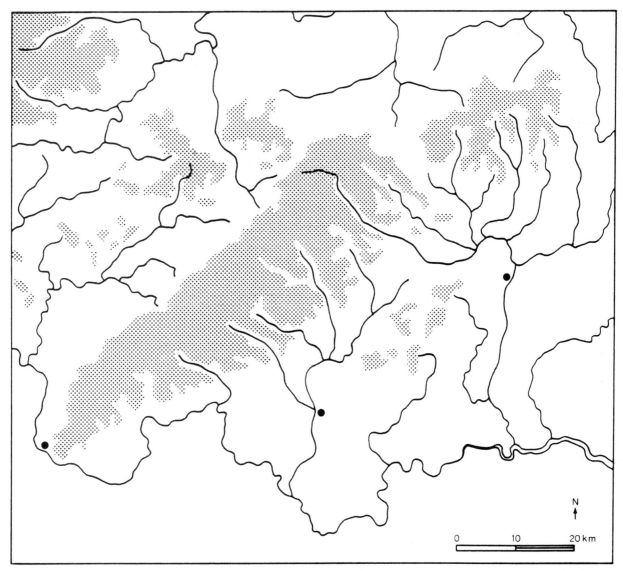

Fig. 3. Later upper palaeolithic sites.

at Broxbourne, Herts. (Jacobi 1980, 18-19). These two findspots could represent the remains of camp sites situated near the river Lea. Settlement in Britain at this time appears to have been episodic, leading to a period without human occupation in *c*.16,000 bc, at the time of the maximum development of the Devensian ice sheets when glaciers covered half of England and most of Ireland (Jacobi 1980, 28). Resettlement occurred after the Devensian maximum in the tenth millennium bc, at a time when birch woodland was becoming established, and is represented in the Chiltern region (Fig. 3) by Broxbourne Site 106 (Jacobi 1980, 80-1), Three Ways Wharf, Uxbridge (Cotton 1991, 151; Lewis *et al.* 1992, 238-9) and Gatehampton Farm, Oxon. (Graham Kerr 1988). Excavations at the Uxbridge site in the late 1980s produced two major *in situ* flint scatters and associated animal bones, the earlier of which consisted of a long-blade flint assemblage with *c*.700 pieces and *c*.100 fragments of horse and reindeer

bone. Two samples of the horse material produced radiocarbon dates of 8,320 ± 100 bc (OxA-1778) and 8,050 ± 120 bc (OxA-1902). The second scatter comprised *c*.7,000 typologically earlier mesolithic flints and *c*.2,000 pieces of mainly red deer bone; burnt flint from the scatter produced a thermoluminescence date of 6,050 ± 800 bc (OxTL-772f). These sites can be interpreted as the remains of short-stay food processing camps (Lewis *et al.* 1992, 239), where animals were butchered by the river before transporting the meat joints to more permanent camps (Merriman 1990, 17).

Mesolithic settlement

Mesolithic flint assemblages fall into two categories (Jacobi 1973, 237-8): assemblages with broad-blade microliths, mainly obliquely-blunted points, which date to the earlier mesolithic period (8,300-6,500 bc), and assemblages with narrow-

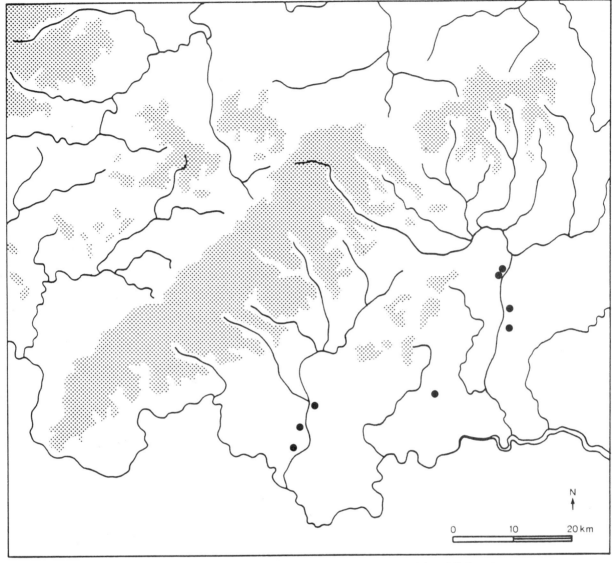

Fig. 4. Earlier mesolithic sites (after Jacobi 1975 with additions).

blade or geometric microliths dating to the later mesolithic period (6,500-3,500 bc). The earlier mesolithic period is associated with the post-glacial establishment of birch and pine woodland across the north European Plain, of which Britain was a part. Sites of this date in the Chilterns region occur mainly in the lower stretches of the rivers Colne and Lea, in similar locations as later upper palaeolithic sites (Fig. 4). Two of these sites have been excavated recently: Three Ways Wharf, Uxbridge (see above) and West Heath, Hampstead (Collins & Lorimer 1989), the latter yielding c.61,000 flints, a few pits and post holes and a thermoluminescence date on burnt flint of 7,641 ± 900 bc (OxTL-238).

By c.6,500 bc Britain was separated from the continent and the Boreal birch-pine forest had developed into the Atlantic climax deciduous forest. Apart from changes in environment and flint industries, the main difference between the

earlier and later mesolithic periods is the very large number of later sites (Fig. 5). These sites are located mainly along river valleys, notably the rivers Colne, Misbourne, Chess, Ver and Lea. Excavations at five of these sites (Stratford's Yard, Chesham; Redbourne; Low Farm, Fulmer; Gerrard's Cross; Tolpit's Lane Site B, Moor Park: Fig. 5; Holgate 1988b, 215-6, 376 & 388), have produced substantial *in situ* flint assemblages containing a variety of implements, for example scrapers, truncated blades, cutting blades, tranchet axes and axe-sharpening flakes, geometric microliths and microburins. They can be interpreted as either base or short-stay camps. At Tolpits Lane Site B, Moor Park, Herts. excavations in 1968 (Jacobi 1975; Holgate 1988b, 216) yielded over 2,100 flints, wild cattle and deer bones, carbonised hazelnut shells and charcoal, a sample of the latter producing a radiocarbon date of 4,380 ± 80 bc (Q-1099). Excavations at Stratford's Yard, Chesham, Bucks. in 1969 and

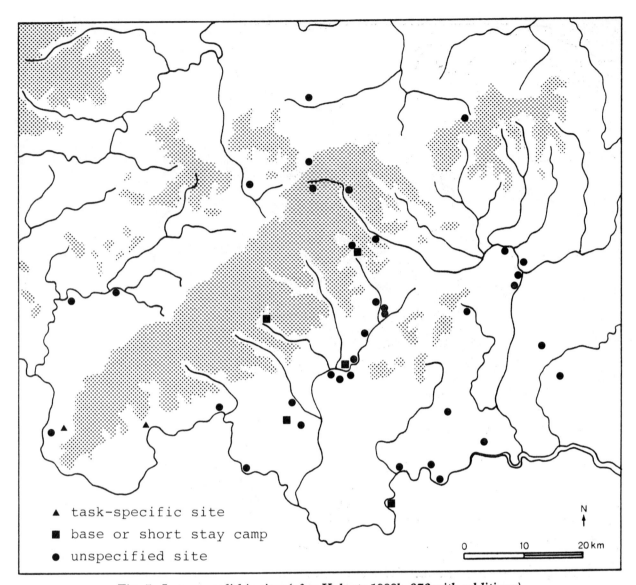

▲ task-specific site

■ base or short stay camp

● unspecified site

N
↑

0   10   20 km

Fig. 5. Later mesolithic sites (after Holgate 1988b, 376 with additions).

1982 (Stainton 1989) produced over 4,000 flints, four possible post holes, animal bones and carbonised hazelnut shells. The most important of the animals represented amongst the bone assemblage were wild cattle, followed by red deer and pigs in roughly equal numbers and then by a few roe deer (Grigson 1989, 68). Frog, rodent and small bird bones were also recovered. The presence of meat-eating bones suggests that meat was prepared on site, whilst the presence of other limb and foot bones suggests that bone was used as a raw material for making artefacts. Cut marks on some of the bones could indicate that skinning and leather processing also took place. Wild cattle bones from the site gave a radiocarbon date of 3,940 ± 100 bc (BM-2404). There were no positive indicators of seasonal occupation but the damp conditions to which the site was subjected at times during the year make it unlikely that occupation was permanent. Recent fieldwork by St Albans Museums Service at Wheathampstead

(Saunders & Havercroft 1982a; 1982b) and Aldwickbury (West 1993a) in the upper Lea valley and Redbourne (West 1992) and Friar's Wash (West 1993b) in the upper Ver valley, along with reevaluation of the mesolithic flintwork recovered from the Park Street Roman villa excavations (O'Neil 1945, 63) in the lower Ver valley (housed in Verulamium Museum), indicates that almost the entire lengths of these valleys were exploited during the later mesolithic period.

Apart from the apparent increase in site numbers during the later mesolithic period, there is also an apparent expansion in the area of land being exploited, with the upper stretches of the rivers Colne and Lea, along with the main tributaries of the river Colne, being occupied. Sites are also beginning to appear on the upper slopes of the Chilterns, notably at the headwaters of the river Lea (Fig. 5). Furthermore, the lower stretches of the rivers Colne and Lea where sites were located

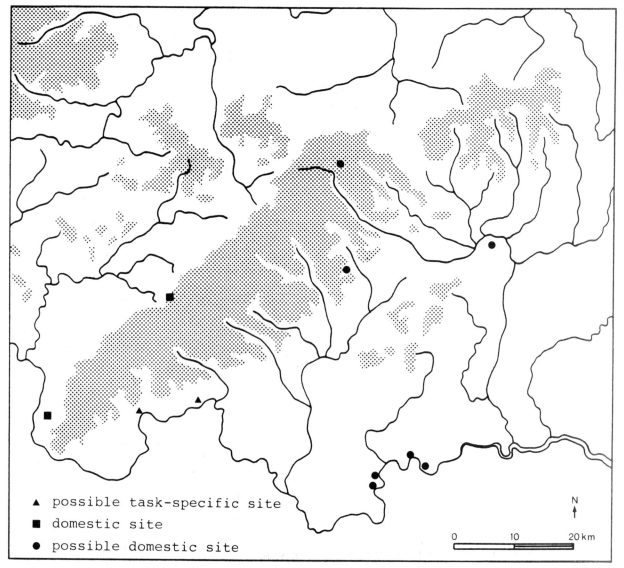

Fig. 6. Earlier neolithic domestic sites (after Holgate 1988b, 377 with additions).

▲ possible task-specific site
■ domestic site
● possible domestic site

N

0   10   20 km

in the earlier mesolithic period are no longer occupied, although sites occurred further downstream on the Thames floodplain. This change in settlement pattern could, in part, be associated with the rise in water table and the accumulation of peat and tufa deposits that took place in response to a rise in sea level and changes in the availability of plant, animal and riverine resources during the late sixth-early fourth millennia bc (Holgate 1988b, 23-4: discussed below).

Neolithic settlement

The neolithic period is divided on the basis of differences in flint industries, pottery styles and classes of monument into earlier (c.3,500-2,700 bc) and later (c.2,700-2,000 bc) neolithic periods (Smith 1974). Traces of earlier neolithic activity in the Chilterns (Figs. 6 & 7) have mainly resulted from the investigation of post-neolithic sites: for example, the ditch sections associated with the

causewayed enclosure at Maiden Bower, Beds. were recorded below the Iron Age plateau fort by Worthington Smith (1904) and the remains of a building at Gorhambury, Herts. came to light during the excavation of a Roman villa (Neal et al. 1990). Earlier neolithic monuments in the Chilterns include the Maiden Bower causewayed enclosure and two long barrows, Pegsden and Therfield Heath, both in Herts. Earlier neolithic monuments are all located on the periphery of the Chiltern hills, either on the scarp or in the middle Thames and Stort valleys (Fig. 7).

Known domestic sites of earlier neolithic date are few in number (Holgate 1988b, 238 & 377); those discovered to date are situated on the scarp or dip slope (Fig. 6). These sites are represented by pottery and flintwork recovered from the old land surface below the two earlier Bronze Age barrows at Whiteleaf, Bucks. (Childe & Smith 1954, 216-17) and Five Knolls barrow 5, Beds. (Dyer 1991)

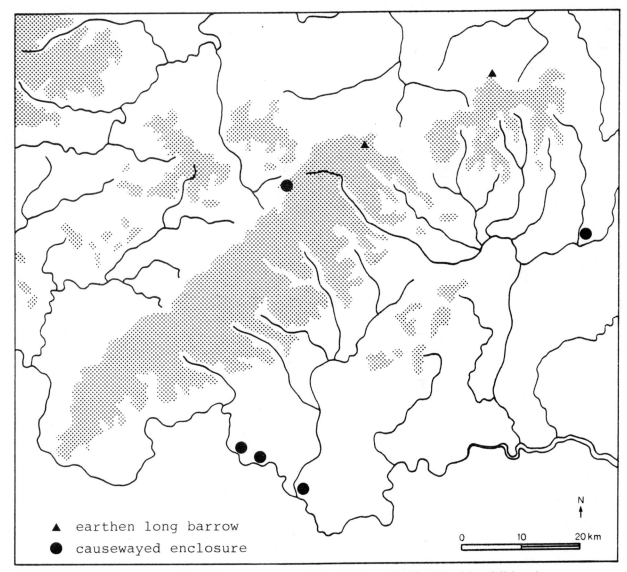

Fig. 7. Earlier neolithic monuments (after Holgate 1988b, 378 with additions).

and by flint scatters. Recent surface collection surveys have recorded dense concentrations of flintwork that, in some instances, probably represent the remains of domestic sites. However, most of the associated flintwork dates to the later neolithic period or the Bronze Age (Hudspith this volume; Stainton this volume). Pits containing earlier neolithic plain bowl pottery have been located near Maiden Bower (Matthews 1976, 8), Old Parkbury, Herts. (Niblett 1990a) and Foxholes Farm, Herts. (Partridge 1989, 8). These could result from domestic activity although ceremonial activity, for example votive offerings, should not be discounted (*cf.* Herne 1988). The features at Gorhambury, although interpreted as dating to the later neolithic period (Neal *et al.* 1990, 7-8), would appear from the pottery and other material associated with them to be earlier neolithic in date. Two sets of gully-like features, both rectangular in plan, produced fragments of plain bowl pottery (Neal *et al.* 1990, 175-6), burnt

daub and charcoal from which a radiocarbon date of 2,860 ± 80 bc (HAR 3484) was obtained. Further fragments of plain bowl pottery were recovered from a nearby Romano-British feature, along with four flint blades. Unless the pottery and charcoal are, like the pottery from the Romano-British feature, all residual the gully-like features can be interpreted as the footings for an earlier neolithic structure. Whether this was a domestic structure or, given the absence of an internal hearth and other traces of domestic activity, a form of 'cult house' (*cf.* Holgate 1988a, 104) is uncertain. Although few earlier neolithic domestic sites are presently known, it would appear on present evidence that domestic sites were mostly sited on upper slopes on the Chiltern scarp or dipslope and not in the valleys (Fig. 6).

Later neolithic remains from the Chilterns include two round barrows, a henge monument and a number of domestic sites (Figs. 8 & 9). The bar-

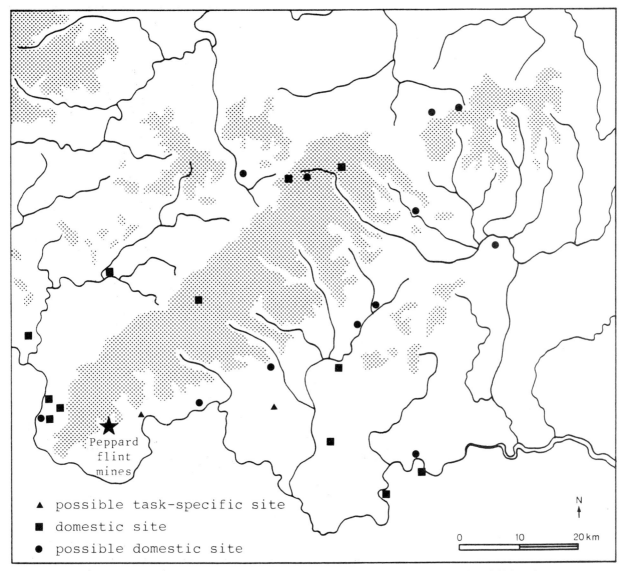

▲ possible task-specific site

■ domestic site

● possible domestic site

Fig. 8. Later neolithic domestic sites (after Holgate 1988b, 379 with additions).

rows, Whiteleaf and Five Knolls barrow 5, both covered single adult inhumations and are situated, like the two earlier neolithic long barrows, on the Chiltern scarp. Waulud's Bank, the henge monument, abutts the river Lea at one of the springs which feeds the river near its source (Dyer 1964; Selkirk 1972). As a henge, it is unusual in having the bank inside the ditch; excavations in 1953, 1971 and 1982 produced Grooved Ware pottery from the lower ditch silts. It is located in a central position in the north Chilterns near the point where the Icknield Way fords the river Lea. Cursus monuments and other henge monuments are situated on gravel terraces in the neighbouring river valleys, notably in the upper Thames, middle Thames and Great Ouse valleys (Fig. 9).

Later neolithic domestic sites (Fig. 8) outnumber earlier neolithic domestic sites and are situated on the dip slope or in valleys (Holgate 1988b, 237 & 379). Some sites have produced subsoil features containing pottery, flintwork and animal bone, e.g. Old Parkbury, Herts. (Niblett 1990a), Foxholes Farm, Herts. (Partridge 1989, 8), Codicote, Herts. (Greenfield 1961), Baldock, Herts. (Stead & Rigby 1986), Blackhorse Road, Letchworth, Herts. (Moss-Eccardt 1988 and Puddlehill, Beds. (Matthews 1976, 3-18). At Blackhorse Road, Letchworth ten pits, a post hole and a gully produced Peterborough Ware, Grooved Ware and beaker pottery, along with flintwork and animal bone. Excavations at Puddlehill located eight pits containing Grooved Ware pottery, flintwork and animal bone; the residual flintwork recovered from post-neolithic contexts, for example the flints from the Saxon sunken-featured buildings now housed in Luton Museum, suggest that a substantial domestic assemblage would probably have been retrieved had the site not been investigated under rescue conditions. At both Blackhorse Road and Puddlehill, the animal bone assemblages included wild cattle, domesticated cattle, pig,

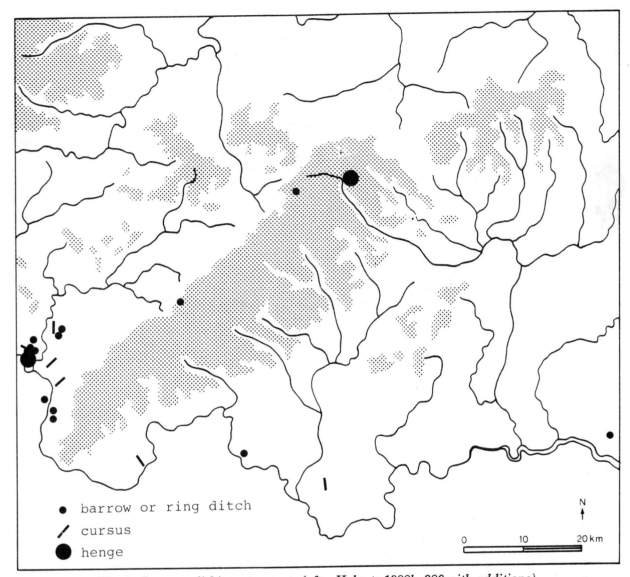

Fig. 9. Later neolithic monuments (after Holgate 1988b, 380 with additions).

sheep/goat and red deer; a brown bear mandible was also recovered from Letchworth.

The majority of domestic sites, though, are represented by flint scatters recovered by surface collection survey. Recent surveys (Hudspith 1993b; this volume; Stainton this volume) and trial-trenching in advance of large-scale earthmoving activities (McDonald this volume) have located a number of previously unknown sites, mostly on ridges capped with Clay-with-flints. These sites are represented by substantial quantities of hard hammer-struck debitage with a multiplicity of implement types, mostly worked on locally-available nodules from Clay-with-flints deposits. These deposits would have supported loess-based soils with high nutrient levels and good water retention properties (Catt 1978, 14) which would have been ideal for farming. Furthermore, cultivation of areas cleared of forest on these soils would have brought flint nodules to the surface

which could then have become the raw material for flintworking.

The flint-mining site at Peppard Common, Oxon. (Fig. 8) produced a number of discoidal knife and thin-butted axe roughouts (Holgate 1988b, 336-7) of a similar nature to those recovered at Grimes Graves (Saville 1981), suggesting a later neolithic date for the site. Further investigation of neolithic domestic sites on the Chilterns might provide information on whether or not the implements produced at Peppard Common were intended for local consumption or 'export' to neighbouring areas. The remains of neolithic flint mines have also been recorded at Pitstone Hill and High Wycombe (Holgate 1988b, 336-7). Hoards of later neolithic edge-ground flint axes have been recovered from the floodplain of the river Lea at Hertford, Herts. and Temple Mills, Stratford, Greater London (Holgate 1988b, 285) and probably represent votive deposits.

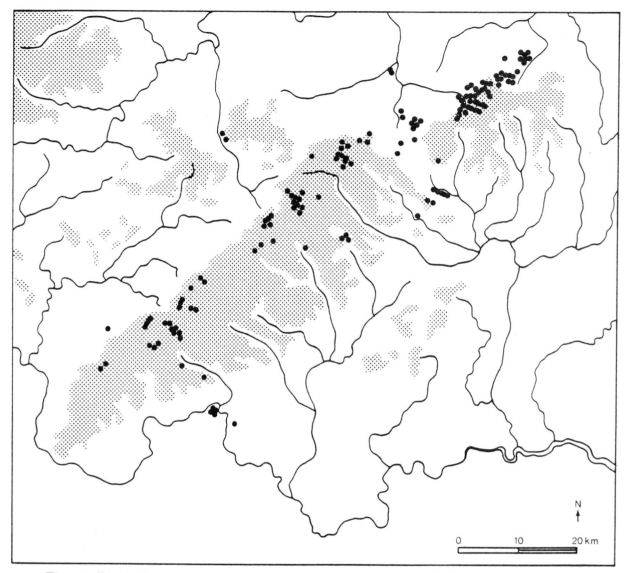

Fig. 10. Earlier Bronze Age round barrows and ring ditches in the Chilterns (after Dyer 1964 with some additions in the Luton area).

Earlier Bronze Age settlement

The most prolific earlier Bronze Age (c.2,000-1,400 bc) sites surviving in the Chilterns are round barrows and ring ditches (Fig. 10). These appear to cluster in five main areas on the Chiltern scarp (Dyer 1960): at the head of the Wye valley around Bledlow, Bucks.; around Ivinghoe at the headwaters of the Bulbourne valley, Bucks.; on Dunstable Downs (Dyer 1991) and Barton Hills (Dyer 1962; 1974; Clark 1991) at the headwaters of the river Lea; and east of the Hitchen Gap near Royston, Herts. Aerial photography has revealed the location of more ring ditches since Dyer's study and further work could extend the known distribution of these sites.

A number of later neolithic domestic flint scatters also contain flint implements commonly found in beaker contexts, for example barbed and tanged arrowheads, invasively-retouched scrapers and pressure-flaked knives, suggesting that they continued to be occupied into the earlier Bronze Age. Analysis of snail assemblages from the ditch silts of the ring ditches at Bartonhill Cutting, Beds. suggests that the land surrounding them was used for seasonal grazing (Allen 1991). Domestic sites might not have been located far away, a practice which has been demonstrated elsewhere near the Chilterns: for example, investigation of a group of ring ditches at Roxton in the Great Ouse valley indicated that these ring ditches were located both on a site of earlier settlement and probably close to a contemporary domestic site (Woodward 1986). Thus the location of clusters of barrows and ring ditches, together with the discovery of flint scatters containing material of earlier Bronze Age date, in a band on the Chiltern dipslope parallel with and immediately south of the scarp along the line of the Icknield Way suggests that this zone could have been the main focus of settlement on the Chilterns during this period. Similar foci of settlement occur in the Great Ouse valley to the north, in the upper Thames valley to the west and in the middle Thames valley to the south.

Summary of changes in settlement pattern in the early prehistoric period

Only a small proportion of the Chilterns has been surveyed. However, the location of domestic sites and monuments in those areas which have been surveyed, notably in the Luton-Dunstable area, in the Chess valley and in the St Albans-Rickmansworth area, enables some conclusions to be drawn concerning the nature and extent of settlement in the early prehistoric period.

Occupation of the Chilterns was episodic throughout the lower, middle and earlier upper palaeolithic periods. Sites that have been discovered were located near rivers or small lakes. In the early Holocene period, sites associated with hunting and processing horse and deer were located in the lower stretches of the two main rivers draining the Chilterns. A major change in settlement pattern occurred after the 7th millennium bc. Following the severence of Britain from the continent and the development of mixed deciduous forest, wild cattle and other woodland animals were hunted and woodland plant foods, for example hazelnuts, were gathered. Hunting and other short-stay camps continued to be sited near rivers but now the middle and upper stretches of the rivers Lea and Colne, as well as tributaries of both rivers, were occupied. With the exploitation of woodland resources, camps were also located on the Chiltern Hills overlooking river valleys.

This shift in settlement away from the lower stretches of the rivers Colne and Lea might have been related to the gradual rise in sea level that took place between c.4,500 and c.3,450 b.c. (Devoy 1980, 137). During this marine transgression the water table in the tributary valleys draining into the lower stretches of the river Thames rose, resulting in the accumulation of peat and tufa deposits which would have made these localities less attractive for settlement (Holgate 1988b, 24 & 129). However, exploitation of wetland resources in these valleys could have continued (cf. Lewis et al. 1992, 245). With the establishment of mixed deciduous woodland throughout the Chilterns by the 6th and 5th millennia bc, rivers and valleys might have been settled and exploited intensively throughout the spring, summer and autumn months, when plant and riverine resources were abundant, with deer and other

large ungulates being hunted throughout the Chilterns in the winter months when the reduced foliage would have made woodland hunting easier than in the summer months.

The start of the earlier neolithic period was associated with another apparent change in settlement pattern. Although few sites are known, settlement appears to have been focussed on the Chiltern Hills away from the river valleys occupied in the later mesolithic period, possibly because easily cultivable soils occurred here in places which were not being intensively exploited for natural resources. Water could have been supplied by creating dew ponds.

During the later neolithic period settlement continued on the Chiltern Hills, with new sites appearing in the river valleys. A similar expansion in settlement during the later neolithic period took place in the London area (Merriman 1990, 24). This increase in the number of settlements and apparent expansion into areas that were unsettled in the earlier neolithic period could be due, as suggested for the Thames basin as a whole, to changes in farming practice involving the development of an infield-outfield farming system, although there is no direct evidence for this on the Chilterns (Holgate 1988b, 135). Monuments, notably cursus monuments and henges, are now situated in the valleys in positions central to these freshly-settled areas. The earlier Bronze Age probably saw the continuation of occupation in the areas settled during the later neolithic period, with the "Icknield belt" and the upper Thames, middle Thames and Great Ouse valleys being the main foci for settlement.

Future work

There is still much work to be done to locate and investigate further sites of early prehistoric activity. The surface collection surveys undertaken by the Manshead Archaeological Society (Hudspith this volume), Buckinghamshire County Museum, the Chess Valley Archaeological and Historical Society (Stainton this volume), Verulamium Museum and the St Albans and Hertfordshire Architectural and Archaeological Society (Miles this volume) have located previously undiscovered traces of mesolithic, neolithic and earlier Bronze Age activity, showing that survey work of this kind is a useful and relatively inexpensive way of locating sites of early prehistoric activity. It might be worth undertaking survey work and sample excavation in the vicinity of dew ponds or places where dew ponds might have existed to determine how far back they can be dated and whether or not any are linked directly to domestic sites. Excavation of dense flint artefact scatters recovered by survey work, though, is unlikely to yield much more information other than a greater quantity of flintwork and possibly the occasional subsoil feature which could contain fragments of pottery and other artefacts.

In recent years a number of aerial photograghs has been taken, notably in Hertfordshire and Bedfordshire. The careful plotting of the features recorded on these photographs which could be interpreted as prehistoric sites needs to be undertaken to give a more complete picture of the distribution of neolithic and Bronze Age monuments and field systems. Features of particular interest could then be sampled by excavation, perhaps as part of a research project to investigate all sites recorded on aerial photographs which are of unknown date and function.

There is a need to recover palaeoenvironmental information that can be used to record both the vegetational sequence and the intensity of land use throughout the prehistoric period. Postglacial peat deposits have been recorded in some of the river valleys draining the Chilterns, for example the Bulbourne, Colne and Lea valleys, and a detailed lithostratigraphic and palynological study of these valleys would yield information on fluctuations in water table and vegetational history throughout the Flandrain period. Such a study would make a good topic for postgraduate research. Should the opportunity arise to excavate the ditch fills of barrows or ring ditches, samples should be taken for molluscan analysis (*cf.* Allen 1991) in order to provide a picture of the degree of woodland clearance and intensity of land use at the time when the monuments were constructed. Similarly, the sampling of colluvial deposits for molluscan analysis should be undertaken either when these deposits are encountered in the course of fieldwork (*cf.* Clark 1991) or as a specific research project (*cf.* Waton 1982).

The excavation of later prehistoric or Romano-British sites has often revealed traces of earlier prehistoric activity, e.g. Gorhambury (Neal *et al.* 1990), Herts. Thus any large-scale excavation of sites of Iron Age or later date should also seek to recover evidence of earlier activity, either in the form of residual artefacts, sub-soil features or old land surfaces sealed in underlying deposits. Wherever possible, the opportunity to recover environmental information either from the site itself or from alluvial or colluvial deposits in the vicinity of the site should be taken (*cf.* the A41 Bypass project: McDonald this volume).

The condition of most palaeolithic to earlier Bronze Age sites in the Chilterns that have been excavated to date is variable. Sites on upper slopes are often plough-damaged and sites discovered under rescue conditions have been either badly truncated or only partially investigated due to insufficient resouces being available for a thorough investigation. Well-preserved sites which contain a wealth of *in situ* archaeological and environmental deposits are likely to exist in valley locations under layers of alluvium, colluvium or tufa, e.g. Three Ways Wharf, Uxbridge (Lewis *et al.* 1992). Whenever the opportunity arises, either in the form of an archaeological evaluation in conjunction with proposed development or as a specific research project, fieldwork must be focused primarily on valleys in order to recover substantial artefact assemblages from securely-datable contexts from which palaeoenvironmental data can also be obtained. Realistically, it is only with information of this quality that knowledge of the Chilterns in the earlier prehistoric periods can be transformed.

Note on the maps

References for the sites plotted on the maps are referred to in the captions. Where references have not been included or there are additions, the sites in question are mentioned in this paper.

THE LATE BRONZE AGE TO THE MIDDLE IRON AGE OF THE NORTH CHILTERNS

Stewart Bryant

Introduction

The aim of this survey is to provide a brief overview of the current state of knowledge of later prehistoric settlement in the North Chilterns area. The period covered is from the beginning of the late Bronze Age (c.1,000 BC) to the beginning of the late pre-Roman Iron Age (c.100 BC).

The survey area comprises the narrow band of calcareous upland known as the 'Icknield Belt', as well as the extensive Chilterns dipslope to the south east, parts of the adjoining Boulder Clay plateau and the river systems of the Colne and Lea. It is intended that the survey will complement the surveys of the later prehistoric period which have been undertaken in the neighbouring counties of Essex (Couchman 1980; Drury 1980), Bedfordshire (Simco 1973) and Cambridgeshire and Northamptonshire (Knight 1984). It will also to some extent serve to update the survey by Saunders (1972) of the Chilterns evidence.

This contribution is divided into two sections. The first is a survey of the settlement evidence, which is divided chronologically into three periods: the late Bronze Age and the late Bronze Age/early Iron Age transition (1,000-600 BC), the early Iron Age (600-300 BC), and the middle Iron Age (300-100 BC). This is followed by a discussion of the evidence, which will include a discussion of future research priorities.

The settlement evidence

The value of the settlement evidence under examination is limited considerably by the lack of sites which have been excavated adequately by modern scientific standards. Most of the available evidence consists of unstratified pottery and animal bone with few associated datable artefacts. It is thus difficult in many instances to make even the most basic assumptions about the date, size and duration of occupation of sites. Nevertheless, it is possible to discern some generalised patterns in the settlement evidence, and a rudimentary threefold chronological division can be made on the basis of pottery and metalwork, along the same lines as Saunders (1972). However, because of the uncertainty over the duration of occupation for many sites, the dates which are given below should be treated as only an approximation of the earliest date; it should also be borne in mind that, in most cases, this is unlikely to be representative of the full time scale of occupation.

1. The late Bronze Age and the transition to the early Iron Age (1,000-600 BC)

Pottery. This is equivalent to Phase One of Saunders' (1972) sequence for the Chilterns, including the Ivinghoe-Sandy, West Harling-Staple Howe and Darmsden-Linton pottery style zones as defined by Cunliffe (1978, 35-9). The pottery is characterised by flint-gritted shouldered jars and bipartite bowls with rounded and angular profiles. Most of the bowls and some of the jars have smoothed or burnished surfaces and some are decorated with finger impressions around the shoulder and rim.

Dating assemblages is hampered by the general conservatism of pottery fabrics and styles in the region, particularly for the coarser wares. The likelihood, as Barrett (1978, 272) has pointed out, that long-lived settlements were the norm during this period could also reduce the value of many of the unstratified or ungrouped pottery assemblages for dating, as they are likely to represent long periods of accumulation. The situation is not helped by the lack of absolute dates and datable artefacts associated with pottery assemblages. Ivinghoe Beacon hillfort and Turnford are the only sites in the survey region for which radiocarbon dating has been used (Green 1981; Kiln 1986, 8) and most of the datable metalwork finds are confined to a relatively short period at the end of the late Bronze Age (Needham & Burgess 1980).

A broad chronological division of the pottery into two groups has been proposed by Barrett (1978; 1980). The first group dates from the tenth to eighth centuries BC and is made up of assemblages which are consist predominantly of plainware jars and bowls with rounded profiles (Fig. 11, 1). The pottery from this period also characteristically contains high densities of flint inclusions, particularly around the base of the vessels. Site assemblages from within the survey area which fall into this group are those from Ivinghoe Beacon hillfort (Cotton & Frere 1968), Tottenhoe (Hawkes 1940a), the earliest phase at Puddlehill (Matthews 1976, 48-59), and probably

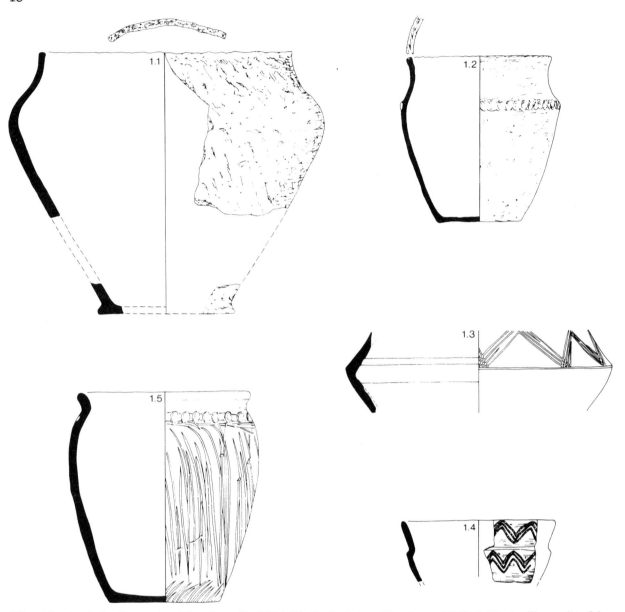

Fig. 11. 1: plain flint-gritted jar from Puddlehill, Beds. (after Matthews 1976, 141); 2, flint-gritted jar with a single band of finger decoration from Foxholes Farm, Hertford (after Partridge 1989, 163); 3, bipartite, carinated bowl from King Harry Lane, St. Albans, Herts. (after Longworth 1989, 54); 4, carinated bowl with inlaid geometric decoration from Puddlehill, Beds. (after Matthews 1976, 143; 5, sand-gritted jar with finger-tipped and scored decoration from Gatesbury Track, Braughing, Herts. (after Partridge 1980b, 119).

Whiteley Hill (Bryant 1994). Also probably belonging to this group are several recently discovered sites which have produced quantities of plain, flint-gritted jars of late Bronze Age type, including Gadebridge, Hemel Hempstead (Herts. SMR 6900); and Crawleys Lane, Bottom House Lane and Pea Lane from the A41 project (McDonald this volume). Most of the pottery from this group falls within Cunliffe's (1978, 35) Ivinghoe/Sandy style zone, although some of it is likely to be earlier than the seventh and sixth centuries BC dates which he proposes.

The second group of assemblages dates from the eighth to sixth centuries BC and shows increasing use of finger decoration (Fig. 11, 2 & 3). There is also a tendency for the inclusions used for tempering the pottery of this period to be sparser and finer than before, allowing the shaping of thinner-walled vessels and sharper, carinated forms (Longworth 1989). The rest of the datable site assemblages fall into this group, including Blackhorse Road, Letchworth (Birley 1988), Thunderidge (Kiln 1970), Ware (Kiln 1973), St Albans (Longworth 1989), Berkhamsted (Herts. SMR, 0038), and Half Hide Lane, Turnford (Stewart 1983). Other assemblages containing pottery which probably belongs to this group are Wilbury Hill hillfort (Applebaum 1949); Wood End; the A41 sites mentioned above; Cole Green,

Hertford (Herts. SMR 6898); and Foxholes, Hertford (although Foxholes also has a high proportion of plain wares which have many parallels with the early, plain ware assemblage at Runnymead Bridge: Partridge 1989, 12 & 163-8). Some of these assemblages, such as Blackhorse Road, probably fall within Cunliffe's (1978) West Harling-Staple Howe and Darmsden-Linton style zones but others, such as Thunderidge, lack carinated bowls and are closer to the Ivinghoe/Sandy style zone.

Metalwork. This period is also characterised by bronze metalwork finds, both from hoard and settlement contexts. Typical finds include socket axes and spear heads, pins, razors, chisels and the occasional sword or sword fragment. The hoards also frequently contain large amounts of scrap material. Settlements which have produced metalwork in the survey area are Wilbury Hill (Applebaum 1949; Needham & Burgess 1980, 464), Totternhoe (Hawkes 1940a, 491), Ivinghoe Beacon (Cotton & Frere 1967, 204-213), Raffin Green (Herts SMR ref. 6312), Lordship Lane, Letchworth (Moss-Eccardt 1988, 38), Blackhorse Road, Letchworth (Moss-Eccardt *op cit.*, 87), Arbury Banks (Needham & Burgess 1980, 464), Baldock (Stead & Rigby 1986, 141-3) and Abingdon Piggots (Fox 1924).

Evidence of bronze manufacturing has come from two sites. Fragments of clay moulds, crucibles and hearths, possibly indicating a rare example of *in situ* bronzeworking, associated with an eighth century pottery assemblage, have been found at Half Hide Lane, Turnford (Stewart 1983). A group of Ewart Park axes, together with copper bun ingots which reportedly came from pits with 'blackened stones and sooty earth', have also been found at Prior's Wood, Hertford (Partridge 1980a). That the axes and ingots were associated with a contemporary occupation site is also suggested by the late Bronze Age/early Iron Age occupation evidence found at the eastern edge of Prior's Wood in 1956, approximately 200 m from the metalwork finds (Holmes & Frend 1957; Hussen 1983).

The finds of late Bronze Age metalwork from settlement contexts have recently been analysed by Needham and Burgess (1980). They have shown that virtually all metalwork finds from settlements of this period belong to the Ewart Park technology phase at the end of the Bronze Age, and many objects date from a relatively short period at the end of the phase in the eighth century BC. The reason for the sudden appearance of relatively large quantities of metalwork on settlements is not fully understood, although

Needham and Burgess (1980, 456) consider that it may have been associated with widespread social and political changes at the end of the Bronze Age. Ewart Park metalwork land finds in general, which include hoards and stray finds, also appear to be a good indicator of areas which were favoured for settlement during the late Bronze Age/early Iron Age (Burgess & Needham 1980, 457-466) and within the survey area concentrations of Ewart park metalwork do seem to correspond with clusters of settlements, particularly around the Hitchin Gap and in the Lea valley (see Fig. 13).

Structural evidence. Only a few sites in the survey area have produced meaningful structural evidence and there is little to add to Saunders' (1972, 7-9) survey of the evidence. Circular structures with post-hole foundations appear to have been the main form of dwelling; examples are known from Puddlehill (Matthews 1976, 48), Ivinghoe Beacon (Cotton & Frere 1967, 194-6), Foxholes (Partridge 1989), Cole Green (Herts. SMR 6898), Pea Lane and Bottom House Lane (McDonald this volume). Four- and six-post rectangular structures, which are conventionally interpreted as granaries, are also known from all of the extensively excavated sites of this period (Puddlehill, Ivinghoe Beacon, Foxholes, Letchworth and the A41 sites mentioned above). As Saunders (1972, 7-9) pointed out, storage pits are relatively rare compared with succeeding periods. From the small number of excavated sites there are examples of both open and enclosed settlements. The huts at Puddlehill and Foxholes were both unenclosed, but a D-shaped ditched enclosure is known from Totternhoe (Matthews 1976, 152-3) and a group of unusual rectangular enclosures without any internal structures from Blackhorse Road, Letchworth are assigned to this period by Moss-Eccardt (1988, 67). Other palisade enclosures, which were probably for the control of stock, are also known at Foxholes (Partridge 1989, 71). The defences of the hillfort at Ivinghoe Beacon probably belong to this period, comprising a single ditch 2.4 m deep by 2.5 m wide enclosing an area of 2.4 ha, with an internal box-rampart 1.9 m wide probably standing 2.7 m high (Cotton & Frere 1968). Likewise, the first phase of the defences at Wilbury Hill hillfort probably date to this period on the basis of the small quantity of late Bronze Age/early Iron Age pottery found in the lower silts of the ditch (Applebaum 1949, Fig. 8, 15), although the pottery was mixed with later material which included a La Tene I iron ring-headed pin (*op cit.*, Fig. 15, 8). The defences at Wilbury comprised a single ditch 6 m wide by 2 m deep and an internal box-framed rampart (Applebaum 1949, 21).

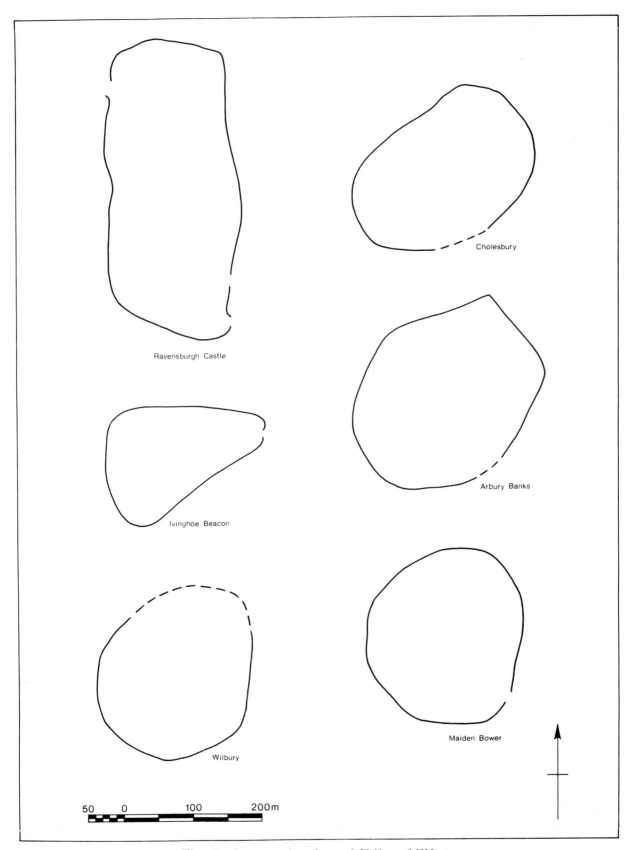

Ravensburgh Castle

Cholesbury

Ivinghoe Beacon

Arbury Banks

Wilbury

Maiden Bower

50   0   100   200m

Fig. 12. Comparative plans of Chiltern hillforts.

2. The early Iron Age (600-300 BC)

Pottery. The pottery is equivalent to phase two of Saunders' (1972) sequence and Cunliffe's (1978, 39) Chinnor-Wandlebury style zone. The pottery is characterised by its fine-ware bowls, which typically have angular profiles, flaring rims and shoulders, burnished exteriors and decoration in the form of geometric patterns (Fig. 11, 4). The decoration is often incised after firing and inlaid in white, whilst the bowls frequently have foot-ring or pedestal bases. The course wares of this period are similar to those of the preceding period with a high proportion of flint-gritted, shouldered jars decorated with finger impressions on the rim and shoulder.

Sites which have produced major assemblages of pottery are Jacks Hill, Wymondley (Tebbutt 1932), Pitstone (Waugh 1967), Puddlehill (Matthews 1976, 143) and Holwell (Applebaum 1934). In addition, small quantities of fine-ware bowls are known from Ravensburgh Castle (Dyer 1976, 157), Maiden Bower (Matthews 1976, 161), Park Street (O'Neil 1945, 73) and Wilbury Hill (Applebaum 1949, 42).

The distribution of the decorated fine-ware bowls is restricted to the Chilterns. In the Thames valley plain, angular bowls of the Darmseden-Linton style zone appear to continue into the 4th century BC (Cunliffe 1968, 39-40; Barrett 1978, 287), although no such assemblages are known from the survey area. A long currency for the decorated bowls is indicated by development of the style over more than one phase of occupation at two sites outside the survey area, at Wandlelbury, Cambs. (Hartley 1957) and Chinnor, Oxon. (Richardson & Young 1951), and the association of a decorated bowl with a La Tene Ib brooch, dated to c.350BC, at Ravensburgh Castle (Dyer 1976, 157).

The origins and dating of the distinctive, decorated fine-ware bowls has been the subject of some debate. Harding (1974, 157-73), developing an argument originally put forward by Hawkes (1962), has suggested that the similarity between the angular pottery of the south east and early La Tene *vases carenes* pottery from the Marne area of France marks a clear chronological horizon of continental influence during the fifth and fourth centuries BC. He has also argued that the angular pottery formed part of a wider cultural assemblage of continentally influenced artifacts, which included the La Tene I Thames daggers, and the La Tene Ia safety pin brooch (Harding 1974, 157-73). Barrett has challenged the chronological integrity of the 'angular horizon' by pointing out that angular bowls also occur in assemblages which date from at least the eighth century BC, but he does consider that the introduction of the pedestal base and the consistent use of scoring as a means of decoration, which have a more restricted geographical distribution, probably date from the fifth and fourth centuries BC (Barrett 1978, 286-7). The high frequency of

these two traits in the decorated bowls from the Chilterns, both of which are also common on the continental *vases carenes* pottery, suggests that Harding's theory of continental influence during this period is probably valid, although it is likely to have been confined to the Thames valley and Chilterns area, rather than the whole of the south east. A connection between the Thames valley/Chilterns and the Marne/Champagne during this period is also supported by Collis (1984a, 118), who considers that the similarity between their pottery, brooches and daggers indicates that significant inter-regional contact was occurring between the two areas, probably in the form of trade.

Metalwork. Metalwork finds on settlements are much rarer for this period. The only notable finds are the fine La Tene Ib brooch at Ravensburgh Castle, which is of insular construction (Dyer 1976, 423), a small, tanged knife from Puddlehill (Matthews 1976, 71-2) and a small bronze pendant from Jack's Hill (Burleigh 1976).

Structural evidence. Again, there is very little to add to Saunders' (1972, 15-16) survey of the evidence. Puddlehill is the only site which has produced significant structural evidence, consisting of an open settlement with three circular huts and a number of storage pits (Matthews 1976, 67-93). The huts were defined by ring-gullies rather than the post-holes of the preceding phase. Good parallels for this type of dwelling are known from the Iron Age site at Little Waltham in Essex (Drury 1978): Drury (1978, 118-24) also provides an extensive discussion of the structural details of ring-gully houses. The earliest defences at Ravensburgh Castle and Maiden Bower hillforts have both produced small quantities of early Iron Age decorated pottery. In the case of Ravensburgh Castle the period 1 defences comprised a single flat-bottomed ditch 3 m deep by 6.7 m wide with a Hollingbury-type box rampart 4 m wide (Dyer 1976). Those of Maiden Bower also comprised a single ditch approximately 8 m wide by 3.5 m deep with an internal box rampart (Matthews 1976, 160).

3. The middle Iron Age (300 BC-100 BC)

Pottery. The middle Iron Age is marked by a change in pottery forms and fabrics throughout the survey area, from the flint-gritted jars and bowls of the preceding periods to rounded, globular or barrel-shaped bowls with sand, shell or vegetable tempering and short, everted or beaded rims (Fig. 11, 5). External decoration of the pottery is rare and, where it occurs, as at Puddlehill (Matthews 1976, 145), Barley (Cra'ster 1961),

Gatesbury Track (Partridge 1980b, 119) and Wilbury Hill (Applebaum 1949, 39), consists of irregular scoring.

Seven sites in the survey region have produced middle Iron Age assemblages: Puddlehill (Matthews 1976, 94-139), Wilbury Hill (Applebaum 1949, 40-41), Barley (Cra'ster 1961), Cholesbury (Kimble 1933), Foxholes (Partridge 1989, 166-170), Gatesbury, Braughing (Partridge 1980b, 119; 1981, 27) and Blackhorse Road, Letchworth (Birley 1988, 80-3). In addition, small quantities of handmade, middle Iron Age pottery occur mixed with later material at Crookhams (Rook 1968b, Fig. VII, 13), Brickwall Hill (Rook 1970a, 30) and Grubs Barn (Rook 1970b, Fig. III, 1), all situated in the Welwyn Garden City area.

Metalwork. Finds of metalwork are also rare from the middle Iron Age. A small quantity of iron agricultural implements and small bronze objects including a pruning or reaping hook, a saw, a ring and a needle are known from Barley (Cra'ster 1961, 33-5) and a La Tene II brooch was found associated with a group of transitional middle Iron Age/late Iron Age pottery at Brickwall Hill (Rook 1970a, Fig. III). It is also likely that some of the bronze and iron objects from Blackhorse Road which are listed as from 'Iron Age contexts' probably date to the middle Iron Age (Moss-Eccardt 1988, 87-8).

Structural evidence. Storage pits appear to be more common in this period, with large numbers recorded at Puddlehill, Foxholes and Barley. A series of four successive, rectilinear enclosures are also known from Puddlehill (Matthews 1976, 95-139), one of which contains three circular, posthole houses (Matthews *op cit.*, 115). In addition, a circular house defined by a pennanular ring-gully is known from Barley (Cra'ster 1961, 25-7).

The defences at Cholesbury hillfort probably date to the middle Iron Age on the basis of pottery found in the ditch. They comprise a single ditch and an internal rampart of 'glacis' type dump construction (Kimball 1933). It is also possible that the ramparts' dump construction which replace the box ramparts at Ravensburgh Castle, Wilbury Hill and Maiden Bower date to the middle Iron Age (Dyer 1976, 155; Applebaum 1949, 20-36; Matthews 1976, 160), although no middle Iron Age finds are known from either Ravensburgh or Maiden Bower.

Discussion

1. Settlement distribution. In Fig. 13 all of the known sites in the survey area are shown against a background of drainage, physical relief and environmental zones. Each site name, with its principal reference, is given in the key to Fig. 13. The division of the survey area into six, broad environmental zones was undertaken to take account of the variety of environments and landscapes which it contains and also because of the fact that environmental considerations, particularly the agricultural potential of land, are likely to have played a significant role in determining the location of settlement. The division of the survey area into six zones was achieved by taking into account a combination of physical factors including soils, soil properties, solid geology and surface topography. The principal source used was the Agricultural Research Council Soil Surveys (King 1969; Thomasson 1964; Thomasson 1969; Thomasson & Avery 1970).

Considering the overall distribution of sites in relation to the environmental zones shows a broad division into two groups, with a cluster of settlements and linear ditches along the calcareous upland zone of the Chiltern Hills and a smaller group of settlements on the river terrace zone at the south-east corner of the survey area. This distribution is not surprising, as the calcareous upland and river terrace zones contain some of the most fertile and easily worked soils in the survey area and also these have a history of almost continuous exploitation and settlement which dates from at least the fourth millennium BC (Holgate this volume). It is, however, likely that the settlement distribution has been biased towards these areas to some extent by artificial factors which have favoured the discovery of sites, most notably urban development, mineral extraction, archaeological fieldwork by individuals and local societies and the high responsiveness of the dry chalk and gravel soils to aerial photography. The extent of later prehistoric settlement on the heavier clay areas, particularly the Boulder Clay zone, is therefore likely to be underrepresented. This view is supported by the results of systematic archaeological fieldwork which has been carried out on two areas of the Boulder Clay plateau outside the survey area, at north-west Essex (Williamson 1984, 125-134) and at Stanstead Airport (Brooks & Bedwin 1989). Both areas have produced evidence of extensive later prehistoric settlement, some of which dates from the late Bronze Age, and it seems clear that some clearance and colonisation at the edges of the Boulder Clay plateau for farming was taking place by this time. A recent excavation at Thorley, Herts. on the Boulder Clay plateau just to the east of the study area has revealed an extensive complex of later prehistoric settlements and field systems. The Boulder Clay soils are inherently fertile and once cleared provide good arable land

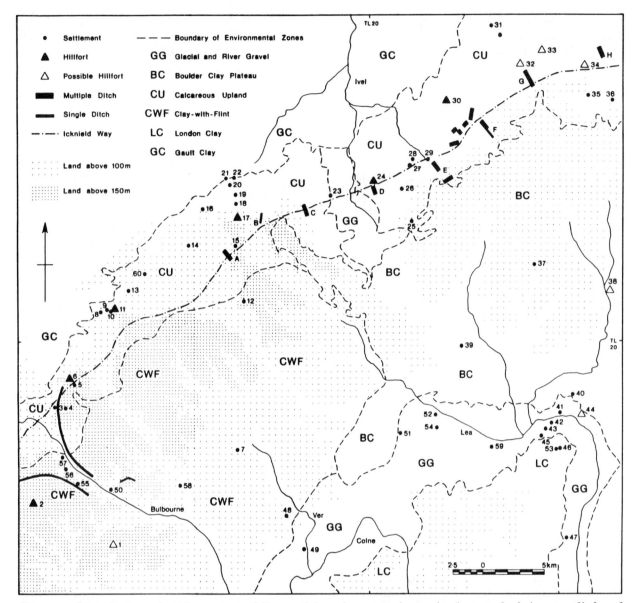

Fig. 13. Distribution of settlements and linear dykes shown against a background of rivers, relief and major environmental zones. Key: 1. Ashley Green (Bucks. SMR 0022); 2. Cholesbury (Kimble 1933); 3. Pitstone (Waugh 1968); 4. Pitstone (Dyer & Hales 1961); 5. Ivinghoe (Dunnett 1973); 6. Ivinghoe Beacon (Cotton & Frere 1968); 7. The Aubreys (Herts. SMR 0025); 8. Totternhoe (Hawkes 1940a); 9. Totternhoe (Matthews 1976, 153); 10.Totternhoe (Matthews 1976, 154); 11.Maiden Bower (Matthews 1976, 160-2); 12.Ramridge End, Luton (Beds. SMR 0367); 13.Puddlehill (Matthews 1976); 14.Sundon (Hall 1991); 15.Maulden Firs, Barton (Dyer 1964); 16.Sharpenhoe Clappers (Dix 1983); 17.Ravensburgh (Dyer 1976); 18.Barton (Hall 1991); 19.Barton (Hall 1991); 20.Barton (Hall 1991); 21.Barton (Hall 1991); 22.Barton (Hall 1991); 23.Holwell (Applebaum 1934); 24.Wilbury (Applebaum 1949); 25.Jack's Hill (Tebbutt 1932); 26.Lordship Lane, Letchworth (Moss-Eccardt 1988, 38); 27.Blackhorse Road, Letchworth (Moss-Eccardt 1988); 28.Norton Road, Letchworth (Moss-Eccardt 1988, 72-73); 29.Baldock (Stead & Rigby 1986); 30.Arbury Banks (Beldam 1859); 31.Abington Piggots (Fox 1924); 32.Limlow Hill (Cambs. SMR 03293A); 33.Moles Farm (Cambs. SMR 02396); 34.Hyde Hall Farm (Cambs. SMR 03241); 35.Whiteley Hill (Wilkerson & Cra'ster 1959; Bryant 1994); 36.Barley (Cra'ster 1961; 1965); 37.Wood End, Ardley (Herts. SMR 6174); 38.Gatesbury (Partridge 1981a, 27); 39.Raffin Green (Herts. SMR 6312); 40.Thunderidge (Kiln 1970); 41.Glaxo Site, Ware (Partridge 1989, 3); 42.Ware (Kiln 1973); 43.Rush Green, Ware (Day 1980); 44.Widbury Hill, Ware (Herts. SMR 2012); 45.Foxholes (Partridge 1989); 46.Prior's Wood (Partridge 1980a); 47.Turnford (Herts. SMR 6484; Stewart 1983); 48.King Harry Lane, St Albans (Longworth 1989); 49.Park Street (O'Neil 1945, 73); 50.Berkhamsted (Herts. SMR 0038); 51.Brickwall Hill, Welwyn Garden City (Rook 1970, Fig. III); 52.Crookhams, Welwyn Garden City (Rook 1968a, Fig. VII, 13); 53.Hertford Heath (Holmes & Frend 1959; Hussen 1983); 54.Grubs Barn, Welwyn Garden City (Rook 1970b, Fig. III, 1); 55.Pea Lane, Berkhamsted (McDonald this volume); 56.Crawleys

which can support a wide range of crops, provided there is sufficient drainage; they soon repay the initial investment needed to clear the land.

The three known sites on the Boulder Clay plateau at Wood End (Fig. 13, 37), Raffin Green (Fig. 13, 39) and Gatesbury (Fig. 13, 38) are situated in river valley locations or on the edge of the plateau and would therefore seem to fit this general pattern of early colonisation of the clay areas. It is to be hoped that further field- work on the Boulder Clay plateau, particularly systematic fieldwalking of the type carried out at Stanstead and North West Essex, will in the future give a clearer picture of this important phase of early settlement.

The low density of sites on the large Clay-with-flints zone on the dip-slope of the Chilterns and the London Clay zone is probably a more accurate reflection of the extent of later prehistoric settlement in these areas, as both are less suited to agriculture than the Boulder Clay soils. However, the same general bias against the discovery of sites on the Boulder Clays also applies to these areas and the examples of the Ashridge survey, which has produced evidence of extensive late Iron Age occupation on the Clay-with-flints zone (Morris & Wainwright this volume) and the high density of prehistoric sites found on the A41 project (McDonald this volume) suggests that exploitation of the heavy clay areas was taking place in the prehistoric period, particularly in areas within or adjacent to river valleys.

The bias in the distribution of settlements in favour of the calcareous upland and glacial gravel zones makes any overall assessments of the survey area problematic. It is also likely that the true extent of settlement in these two areas was more extensive than is known at present, particularly as both contain large numbers of undated cropmark enclosures. However, a closer examination of the evidence does reveal several patterns which are likely to be at least of local significance, which are outlined below.

2. Hillforts. A possible total of twelve hillforts is known from the survey area. Six definite hillforts are situated along the calcareous upland zone of the Chilterns and a further six possible sites are known at Ashley Green (Fig. 13, 1), Widbury Hill, Ware (Fig. 13, 44), Gatesbury, Braughing (Fig. 13, 38), and there is a group of three sites at the

north-east corner of the survey area, which are probably natural features (Fig. 13, 32-34). Two other possible sites are not included in the group as they are not hillforts of the classic type. The large multivallate, defended enclosure at the Aubreys, Redbourn (Fig. 13, 7) is situated on a lowland location and is an enigmatic site which so far has not produced any conclusive evidence of its date or function. Also, the double ringwork at Whiteley Hill, Royston, at the far north east of the survey area (Fig. 13, 35), was thought until recently to be a hillfort (Wilkerson & Cra'ster 1959), but a reassessment of the evidence (Bryant 1994) suggests that it is more likely to be late Bronze Age ringwork. Similar double ringwork enclosures are known at Mucking South Rings, Essex (Jones & Bond 1980), Thwing, Yorks (Manby 1980) and Carshalton, Surrey (Champion 1980, 233-43) and they belong to a distinctive class of late Bronze Age circular enclosures, first identified by Champion (1980). Excavations at Mucking, Thwing and the single interrupted ringwork enclosure at Springfield Lyons, Essex (Buckley & Hedges 1987) have produced evidence for specialist activities including the manufacturing of swords and possible ritual feasting and it is reasonable to assume that these sites, like the riverside metalworking sites along the Thames valley, were at the top end of the late Bronze Age settlement hierarchy (see below: the late Bronze Age).

The six Chiltern hillforts can probably be treated as a group. Their distribution at regular intervals of between 7 km and 12 km along the narrow Icknield Belt of the Chilterns is apparent in Fig. 13, suggesting that they probably formed part of a unitary system. A comparison between the plans of the six hillforts also reveals that there are many similarities between them both in terms of their size and form, particularly in the cases of Maiden Bower, Wilbury Hill and Arbury Banks, all three of which are remarkably alike (Fig. 12). Excavations at four of the six, namely Ravensburgh, Wilbury Hill, Maiden Bower and Ivinghoe Beacon, have also shown that these were all initially provided with a single ditch and a box-framed, timber-laced rampart (Dyer 1976; Applebaum 1949; Matthews 1976, 160-2; Cotton & Frere 1968). The dates for the initial construction of the defences of the six do not on the face of it appear to be uniform, ranging from Ivinghoe Beacon at the end of late Bronze Age to Cholesbury in the middle Iron Age. However, Ivinghoe Beacon is the only hillfort of the six for which a sufficiently large sample of the interior and defences has been excavated under modern conditions to provide a reasonably secure date for its occupation and the construction of the defences. It is therefore probable, given the other factors outlined above, that the Chilterns hillforts formed a broadly contemporary group with the possible exception of Cholesbury.

Most of the other known settlements along the calcareous upland of the Chilterns occur as a series of clusters around the hillforts. This is particularly noticeable around Ivinghoe Beacon, Wilbury Hill, Maiden Bower and Ravensburgh Castle and, of the total of 23 settlements along the Chilterns, thirteen are situated within 3 km of these four hillforts. Any attempt to assess the significance of the clustering is, however, hampered by the difficulties outlined above of accurately dating the occupation of sites of this period, which makes attesting contemporary periods of occupation for groups of sites such as this, problematical. The dating evidence from the hillforts, apart from Ivinghoe Beacon, is also not reliable enough to date their principle phases of occupation (see above). An additional factor to be taken into account is that the cluster around Ravensburgh Castle is likely to be biased to some extent by one of the few systematic fieldwalking surveys which have been carried out in the survey area (Hall 1991; Hudspith this volume). Therefore, while it is probably safe to assume that the clustering is significant and that the majority, if not most, of the settlements were occupied at the same time as the hillforts, it is also possible that some may have been abandoned or may even represent a movement of population from the hillforts to the surrounding countryside.

The function of hillforts in Iron Age society has begun to be better understood in recent years, largely as result of a number of excavations of hillfort interiors (see bibliography in Gent 1983 for a list of excavated sites). Explanations have in the past tended to emphasise the role of hillforts in warfare (Hawkes 1940b; Avery 1976; Harding 1974, 54-76) or have seen them as defended towns or villages (Stanford 1974; 1981; Cunliffe 1978, 260). These have, by and large, proved to be unsatisfactory as unitary explanations and more recent theories have concentrated on the role of hillforts in the regional social and economic system, particularly as centres for the storage and redistribution of grain (Stopford 1987; Gent 1983). Gent (1983) in particular has shown from an analysis of the frequency of four-post granary structures within excavated Iron Age sites that hillforts, particularly those dating from the early

Iron Age, have a relatively higher grain storage capacity than other settlements. He has also shown by looking at the relationship between the grain storage capacity of hillforts and the agricultural productivity of land within a 7.5 km radius that they were probably dependant upon an area which was larger than could be farmed directly from the hillfort. These observations suggest that one of the primary functions of hillforts was to serve as secure tribal or territorial centres for the storage and redistribution of grain, rather than as defensive sites for the local population.

The distribution of settlements along the Chilterns would appear to be consistent with the storage/redistribution model outlined by Gent (1983). The regular spacing of the Chiltern hillforts at intervals of between 7 km and 12 km suggests that the size of the area upon which each of the hillforts was dependent was larger than could reasonably be farmed directly from the site. In addition, if it is assumed that the farmsteads which cluster around the hillforts are contemporary with them, it would indicate that the hillforts were probably not primarily concerned with agricultural production, as this function could have been carried out more efficiently by the farmsteads. The close proximity of the farmsteads to the hillforts is also consistent with the hillforts performing a function as centres for the secure storage of grain.

There also appears to be some relationship between the size of the Chiltern hillforts and the agricultural productivity of their territories, if it is assumed that the territorial boundaries lie at points equidistant between the hillforts along the Icknield Belt. The agricultural potential is reasonably uniform along the Icknield Belt, which is consistent with the small difference in size between five of the six hillforts; the one exception, Ivinghoe Beacon, which is by far the smallest hillfort of the group, has a territory which is both the smallest and also contains a high proportion of the less fertile Gault Clay and Clay-with-flints soils.

3. The late Bronze Age. The late Bronze Age of the study area is characterised by the appearance of several significant features and trends which make the period worthy of particular note. Some of these have already been touched upon: the construction of hillforts and ringwork settlements, the appearance of metalwork in settlement contexts, and a possible expansion of settlement on to the clay plateau areas. Added to this is a fundamental change in the manufacture and use of pottery, with vessels such as bowls and jars which were used for the consumption and storage of food and drink, appearing to be used in significant quantities for the first time (Barrett 1980). The general importance of this previously neglected period has also been recognised in recent years (see, in particular, Barrett 1980; Barrett & Bradley 1981; Bradley 1984) and the work of Barrett in particular has led to the reclassification of a number of early Iron Age sites to late Bronze Age period, e.g. Whiteley Hill above.

Another important group of sites which have been dated to the late Bronze Age are riverside and water-associated settlements, some of which have produced evidence for metalworking and ritual activities. These include the important site at Flag Fen (Pryor et al. 1986) and a group of riverside sites which have been identified along the Thames valley and its tributaries. Excavations at Aldermaston, Egham and Runneymead Bridge along the middle Thames valley have produced evidence of specialist activities including bronze manufacturing and possible ritual deposits (Bradley et al. 1980; Longley 1980; Needham & Longley 1980) and Bradley (1984, 121-4) considers it likely that these sites were involved with the manufacturing and trading of bronze at both a local and inter-regional level, as well as other activities which indicate a high social status for the sites. The two late Bronze Age sites which have produced evidence for bronze manufacturing at Turnford and Prior's Wood in the Lea Valley, within the study area, have some parallels with the Thames valley sites and would seem to fit in with the pattern of late Bronze Age metalworking along the Thames valley. Similarities between the pottery from Turnford and that at Runneymead Bridge (Stewart 1983), in addition to the similarities between the nearby site at Foxholes and Runneymead pottery already mentioned (Partridge 1989, 12 & 162-7), also point to links between the middle Thames Valley and the Lea Valley.

Parallels between some of the Turnford pottery and Urnfield pottery from the Continent (Stewart 1983; Saunders, pers. comm.) suggests that the pattern of inter-regional contact along the Thames Valley also holds good for the Lea Valley.

4. *Linear ditch systems.* The principal linear ditches or 'dykes' have been plotted on Fig. 13. These comprise two reasonably distinct groups of monuments. The first group lies at the south-west end of the survey area and consist of several long, 'contour' dykes which flank the Bulbourne valley and are known collectively as 'Grims Ditch'. These form part of an extensive series of linear dykes or which extend over the chalk areas of Oxfordshire, Berkshire, Buckinghamshire, Wiltshire and Hampshire (see Bradley 1969; Dyer 1963;

Ford 1982; Hinchcliffe 1975; Davis 1981; Davis & Evans 1984). They are conventionally dated from finds and associations with other monuments to the later Bronze Age and early Iron Age, and are thought to represent territorial boundaries, although their precise function is not entirely clear. The second group of dykes are found at the eastern end of the Chilterns, and comprise shorter lengths of single and multiple dykes situated along the Icknield Belt. These appear to be more complex monuments than the contour dykes in terms of their function and form, and the excavated examples have a date range which spans the middle Bronze Age to the Roman period. (For a fuller discussion of the Chilterns linear ditches see Bryant & Burleigh this volume).

5. *The late pre-Roman Iron Age (100 BC to AD 43).* The late pre-Roman Iron Age is marked by increasing contacts between the Iron Age tribes of Southern England and the Roman Empire, both directly from Caesar's expedition in 55 BC and indirectly from traders and immigrants fleeing from Belgic Gaul. These had the effect of bringing about a period of relatively rapid social, political and economic change which is represented by several significant developments in the archaeological record.

Firstly, the quantity of evidence available increases markedly, both in terms of the number of sites and the quantity and range of finds. Approximately two hundred sites are known from the late pre-Roman Iron Age (information from Herts., Bucks. & Beds. SMRs). This compares with 23 sites from the late Bronze Age/early Iron Age, seven sites from the early Iron Age and ten sites from the middle Iron Age sites (Fig. 13). Part of the reason for the contrast between the small number of middle Iron Age sites and the relatively large number of sites from the succeeding late pre-Roman Iron Age is due to an inherent bias against the identification of middle Iron Age pottery assemblages, which are generally less easy to define than for the other periods and so far all of the known sites have only been recognised as a result of formal excavation. Cunliffe (1978, 46) has pointed out that middle Iron Age pottery groups are frequently mixed in with later Belgic material; at five of the known sites, Gatesbury, Bickwall Hill, Crookhams, Grubs Barn and Wilbury Hill, hand-made pottery of middle Iron Age type has been found in association with Belgic, wheel-thrown wares. It is therefore possible that a significant proportion of the large number of known late pre-Roman Iron Age sites have middle Iron Age phases which are represented only by small amounts of pottery, mixed in with larger, unstratified assemblages.

Secondly, there is an increase in the range of classes of evidence available with the introduction of a new widespread burial rite involving urned cremation, the introduction of coinage and an increasing number of references to Britain in the classical literary sources of the period. Lastly, the settlement evidence itself becomes considerably more complex with the development of a more hierarchical settlement pattern made up of a much wider range of settlement types and structures, including the large settlement and dyke complexes known as 'oppida' represented in the survey area by Verlamion, Braughing and Baldock (Burleigh this volume).

A complementary overview of the late Iron Age of the Chilterns will be published elsewhere (Bryant & Niblett, forthcoming).

Future work

Priorities for future work can be divided into three principal areas. Firstly, systematic fieldwalking surveys of the type already carried out outside the survey area in north-west Essex (Williamson 1984) and Stanstead Airport (Brooks & Bedwin 1990) and inside the survey area around Dunstable (Hudspith this volume) are required to give a more accurate picture of the distribution of settlements on the large blank clay areas. Secondly, selected problem-orientated excavations and field surveys which are more limited in extent need to be undertaken in the gravel and calcareous upland environmental zones to explore the development of the landscape and also to understand more clearly the relationship between key features in the landscape. Examples should include geophysical and fieldwaking surveys of some of the many cropmark complexes, and limited excavation where there appears to be important relationships in the landscape, such as between settlement enclosures and linear boundaries. Lastly, as the summary above has demonstrated, there is a general dirth of independent means of accurately dating settlements within the survey area. Datable metalwork and imported objects are extremely rare, and for the period in question, radiocarbon dating is at its most unreliable. The establishment of local and regional pottery sequences therefore provide the best means of dating sites, and priority should be given to the excavation of well-preserved settlements which have good stratigraphic sequences and also, preferably, those which have an extended timespan of occupation.

THE BUCKINGHAMSHIRE CHILTERNS IN LATER PREHISTORY

Michael Farley

Introduction

It would be satisfactory to report that our knowledge of the Buckinghamshire Chilterns in prehistory has made substantial advance since the publication of the last overview of the region made in 1955 by Jack Head in his book *Early Man in South Buckinghamshire* but this would not be true. The advances which have been made, if they can so be regarded, derive to a limited extent from new discoveries within the Chilterns, derive partly from conceptual changes about prehistory as a whole, but perhaps most importantly arise from work carried out immediately to the north and south of the Chiltern zone.

For the purposes of this article 'later prehistory' is taken to be the period from around 1,000 BC to the Roman Conquest. Once it would have been reasonable to speak of 'the later Bronze Age and Iron Age' but these technological divisions have come to be perceived as something of a straightjacket when dealing with sites of this millennium which may contain neither material.

Geographical and archaeological background

The longer one has to become familiar with a piece of landscape the more attuned one also is to subtle variations in landform which are themselves often linked to underlying micro-geologies. A recent conversation with a sane and sensible Marlow resident elicited the fact that he regarded his home territory as being the Thameside as far upstream as Henley and downstream to Windsor; that High Wycombe - a distance of 6 km north and roughly central to the Buckinghamshire Chilterns certainly lay outside his territory; and that - although he could not quite explain why - he felt that if he strayed out of the Chilterns towards Aylesbury he was entering distinctly alien territory! Such feelings were undoubtedly apparent in later prehistory and are to a degree reflected in the archaeological record.

In simplistic terms the Buckinghamshire Chilterns proper may be considered to be an entity sandwiched between the Icknield Belt to the north which has strong archaeological links both along the south-west/north-east scarp foot and with the Portland limestone ridge to the north on which Aylesbury is sited, and the Middle Thames

alluvial deposits to the south to which our Marlow resident belonged, and which have their own distinct archaeology. If there is a unifying factor to the Chilterns proper - the filling of the sandwich as it were - it is of course the chalk, but this is generally apparent only in the transecting valleys and rarely on the extensive plateau which is frequently mantled with acidic gravels, sands and clays.

The Chilterns are frequently considered to be a heavily (and by inference anciently) wooded area, and in contrast to the present day Icknield Belt to the north this is certainly true. We now realise however looking from an archaeological time perspective that one person's ancient woodland is another's secondary regrowth. The Icknield Belt was extensively deforested during the Roman period judging by the number of small settlements of this period which are present, and indeed much clearance had taken place earlier. In the subsequent centuries some regeneration took place which in turn was again later cleared. Early clearance had also certainly taken place in the Thames alluvial zone, but what of the Chilterns proper?

A definitive answer to this question must await a comprehensive programme of environmental sampling. At the moment the clearest answer seems to come from surface finds of struck flint of later neolithic-mid Bronze Age date which appear to be ubiquitous across all geologies. It is hard not to associate these scatters with the presence of substantial areas of open landscape in the Chilterns at this time howsoever such open areas may have been caused. Problems arise when one tries to form links between these flints, frequently datable only in the broadest terms and even then only rarely attributable as late as the first millennium BC, with finds of metal and pottery from the Buckinghamshire Chilterns which can be dated to these centuries. There appears to be, in short, an artefact gap lying in rough terms between 1,500-950 BC in which period only a handful of bronzes, a few sherds, and perhaps one cemetery, at Stokenchurch, are known.

It would not be unusual in archaeology for such a gap to eventually be seen as artifical. However, on present evidence it should be taken seriously. It would be naive to suggest that the area was deserted in the centuries prior to the first millennium BC but on present evidence it can be suggested that there was very little settlement during these centuries and that substantial reforestation could have taken place. If this was so it would be of great significance to the interpretation of the ensuing millennium when re-colonisation, if that is not too dramatic a word, took place.

The first millennium BC

i. Hillforts. The principal components of the final millennium BC in the area are settlements, forts, boundaries, cemeteries, religious sites and individual artefacts. Of this group the hillforts seize attention and may be roughly categorised into: those which are on the Chiltern scarp, namely Ivinghoe - with perhaps nearby Cheddington, Boddington, and Pulpit Hill; those certainly associated with the Thames, namely Medmenham (Danesfield and States House) and perhaps Seven Ways Plain at Burnham; and the four within the Chilterns, namely Cholesbury, Bulstrode - at Gerrards Cross, Whelpley Hill and West Wycombe (Fig. 13).

It would be foolish to pretend that these are all of one date. Ivinghoe, apparently fairly densely occupied (Cotton & Frere 1968), is probably the earliest, and Boddington Hill may also be early on the grounds of superficial finds of ceramic. Little is known of the date of the others but recent evaluation work at Danesfield, Medmenham by Keevill & Campbell (1991) suggests a mid-Iron Age date. Some, such as States House, Medmenham have associated 'late Bronze Age' metalwork. With the exception of Cholesbury and possibly West Wycombe (see below) there is little to suggest that they still had any role by the first century BC.

It is likely that hillforts, whatever their individual function, were statements about territorial possession and if the earlier argument is accepted, they may have been in particular statements about a relatively new ordering of the landscape. It may be argued that all of the hillforts listed, with the exception of the four lying entirely within the Chilterns, had their principal links either with the Icknield belt to the north or with the Thames zone to the south. Their focus in other words may have lain as much outside as within the Chilterns proper. The four sited within the Chilterns ought therefore to reflect a pure Chilterns interest (Fig. 13). Of these forts Cholesbury may have had links with ironworking (Kimball 1933, 200-202), Bulstrode appears to have been only sparsely utilised if at all (Fox & Clarke 1925), of Whelpley

we have no useful information, and knowledge about West Wycombe derives from a handful of 'sherds from the interior. This does not provide a very promising information base to work from; however, a closer look at West Wycombe may be helpful.

West Wycombe overlooks the junction of two dry valleys in both of which the chalk is exposed. It is highly visible and ideally placed to command a great deal of the traffic which flows from south to north linking the Thames and Icknield belts. This was pointed out some years ago by Jack Head (1974). In recent years metal detector activity in the area has produced at least one La Tene I brooch, and from another site in the area sufficient Iron Age coinage to suggest that a possible religious focus lay in the vicinity. In the case of Wycombe therefore one may argue that, although it is likely to have had some Chilterns hinterland, its existence was dependant on a substantial input from other regions.

The argument is therefore that the Buckinghamshire Chilterns, although no doubt of some as yet undetermined economic significance during the first millennium BC, for several centuries was to form largely a backdrop to activities taking place to the north and south.

ii. Farmsteads. The focus of activities is most clearly seen in the cluster of Iron Age farmsteads along or on the edge of the Icknield belt which stretch from Chinnor on the Oxfordshire border to Puddlehill in Bedfordshire (Fig. 13). Such settlements probably provided the rationale for the adjacent scarp-edge hillforts of the Chilterns proper. Adjacent to this belt on the northern side there is again evidence of intensive Iron Age settlement activity, some of it no doubt focused on the recently discovered hillfort at Aylesbury (Farley 1986a). To the south, on the Thames alluvium, again one sees quite intensive Iron Age settlement activity, much of it known from air photographs, and of course much metalwork of this date has been recovered from the Thames.

The picture may change to a degree in the later pre-Roman Iron Age. There are hints that some of the Roman villa estates which were to develop on the valley floors of the Chilterns, when the Chilterns were again heavily exploited, had late Iron Age precursors. However, the evidence is frequently based either on single coin finds or on pottery of a kind which clearly remains in use into the early post-conquest years and is not closely datable. The largest and most important settlement of this later period known in south Buckinghamshire was at Bierton, just east of Aylesbury

(Allen 1986), where the occupants inhabited classic round houses in a settlement almost large enough to qualify as an oppidum, and enjoyed a range of imported ceramics comparable to that seen at the wealthier Hertfordshire settlements such as Braughing. This was the same wealthy group who buried the young lady with three amphorae, a wine cup, and her mirror at Dorton, 16 km further west (Farley 1983a). Such opulence has yet to be seen in the Buckinghamshire Chilterns.

Future work

So what of the future? It is, of course, quite possible that the argument put forward here for a Chiltern backwater has been overstated. As is well known the area is generally unresponsive as far as aerial photography is concerned, there is still much woodland cover, and Clay-with-flints can be both inimical to the survival of fragile ceramic in ploughsoil and an unfriendly medium to fieldwalkers. The area is also largely an Area of Outstanding Natural Beauty, so that large scale development opportunities (and corresponding opportunities for archaeological investigation) are limited. Serendipity always plays a large part in discoveries and the greater the number of informed people who become involved in peering in holes the better. Pipe trenches in particular, which often appear without warning and once having appeared prove so difficult to monitor, may be a fertile source of new information. There is no doubt that further opportunities should be sought for detailed environmental studies; however, one should not pin too much hope on this approach since suitable deposits to which the full range of techniques can be applied are depressingly few. Finally, at the beginning of this contribution micro-geologies were referred to. Subtle differences in ground topography appear to be of great significance for occupation of all periods and if we want to understand a difficult area such as the Chilterns more fully, we would do well to pay great attention to details of the scenery around us in order to understand past land use.

THE ANGLO-SAXON SETTLEMENT OF BEDFORDSHIRE AND HERTFORDSHIRE: THE ARCHAEOLOGICAL VIEW

Carolyn Wingfield

Introduction

This contribution seeks to fulfill two aims: to provide a general survey of the archaeological evidence for the early Saxon period c.AD400-700 and to indicate how and where future investigations might most usefully be directed. The area under consideration extends from the Ouse valley in the north to the Chilterns in the south, and covers most of the county of Hertfordshire, all of Bedfordshire and the west side of Buckinghamshire bordering the Ouzel valley.

As the title indicates, this contribution is concerned with addressing the archaeological evidence on its own terms and not with attempting a synthesis of archaeological and historical material, nor with confining the archaeology to a framework predetermined by documentary sources. The first section briefly discusses some of the challenges and constraints which must be dealt with in assessing and investigating the archaeology of this period. The main part then discusses the nature and scope of the evidence, and simultaneously extracts potential problems and theories to be addressed by future research. For convenience, this is described under three main chronological phases corresponding approximately to the fifth, sixth and seventh centuries (Figs. 14-16 respectively); however, the difficulties of precisely dating some - especially domestic - material, and the differential rate at which some developments may have taken place in different areas, mean that there is inevitably a degree of overlap between these phases and they should not be regarded as absolute. Finally, the main research priorities are summarised and an appendix lists the sites and finds plotted in the figures.

Challenges and constraints

The archaeologist attempting to survey the early Saxon period for the area in question must contend with two main obstacles. First, the date and manner of retrieval of much of the material for this period has provided relatively little information by modern standards compared to the actual number of objects surviving or known through records; re-analysis in the light of more recent knowledge therefore has certain limimitations imposed upon it. Inevitably, the bulk of early Saxon

finds from the region under discussion (as indeed from anywhere in Anglo-Saxon England) are the products of cemeteries rather than settlements, thus imposing a partial view of early Saxon life through grave-goods, and implying a selective approach to artefactual interpretation, in which objects have tended often to be evaluated in accordance with their ritual, religious and social functions rather than in terms of the domestic and economic context from which they originated. Secondly, studies of Anglo-Saxon artefacts have in the past centred around typological and stylistic studies on the one hand, and the documentary sources on the other. While both these methods are necessary, there is equally a need to interrogate the archaeological evidence afresh on its own terms without being prompted by concerns derived essentially from historical sources. Archaeology now has at its disposal the retrieval and recording techniques to identify a greater range of types of early Saxon site and a wider range of evidence, embracing the whole environment as well as the man-made aspects.

Compared to the abundance of readily identifiable Roman and medieval pottery, finds and habitation sites, the relatively slight artefactual and structural remains of the early Saxon period have been less easy to recognise and only within the last few decades has archaeology developed the techniques to do so. Furthermore, few Anglo-Saxon sites can be readily detected by aerial or geophysical survey and their discovery is often a matter of chance during investigations of other features. Strategies designed primarily to cope with the bulk of recognisable material from a Romano-British or medieval site also need to be flexible enough to cope with the fleeting traces of early Saxon-period occupation which may occur beneath, and partly cut away by later medieval occupation or survive only in the upper fills of Romano-British ditches, as identified recently at Wavendon Gate, Milton Keynes (Williams 1989; pers. comm.). The problem is compounded by the fact that most early Saxon habitations contain residual Roman pottery. Surveys in Northamptonshire (Foard 1978) and at Coldharbour Farm near Aylesbury (Dalwood & Platell 1988) have found that concentrations of as few as three 'sherds can be significant in determining the location of mid-Saxon settlements, but on excavation there are generally very few or no features associated with the pottery (Dalwood & Platell 1988; Farley 1991; Parry & Webster 1991). Similarly, at Odell in the Ouse valley it was found on excavation that mid-Saxon 'sherds from the ploughsoil did not bear any relation to contemporary features beneath (Dix, unpub.). Programmes of fieldwalking designed to positively discriminate in favour of collecting small, hand-made 'sherds of early to mid Saxon wares might help redress the balance, and incidently produce information on prehistoric settlement as well, but such work would be very labour-intensive for units hard-pressed by rescue requirements; maybe the man- and woman-power, and local knowledge of the informed amateur or local archaeological society, have a role to play here (see Hudspith this volume and Stainton this volume). Nor can we assume that pottery is always going to be a reliable indicator, for work on the Saxon site at the Prebendal Court, Aylesbury has suggested a virtually aceramic phase in the eighth to ninth centuries (Farley 1986). Turning to cemeteries, although at first glance there is far more material to work on, a great many of these sites were found as a result of gravel-digging or development and so suffer from the problems referred to above.

The division of the period into three broad phases does allow a general progression to be seen: the first phase, spanning the fifth century and opening of the sixth, is relatively sparse in terms of positively attributable artefacts and structures, and is complicated further by the ineffectiveness of the archaeological record in distinguishing between Saxons and Britons. Nevertheless, out of this relative obscurity shine the well-known early finds from the Kempston and Luton 1 (Argyll Avenue) cemeteries. The second main phase commences in the early sixth century and lasts up to or perhaps a little way into the seventh century. It is the period marked by a notable expansion in both numbers of sites and datable artefacts. Finally, there is the seventh-century group of late cemeteries typified by Chamberlains Barn 2 and Marina Drive, Dunstable. The attribution of sites to each phase could in itself be the matter of a lengthy discussion for a significant proportion of them are known only through antiquarians' reports or chance finds. As explained in the appendix, there is a number of other sites or stray finds recorded but not included in this assessment as there is too little information for them to be dated and evaluated with sufficient accuracy.

Fifth century c.400 - c.525

The cessation in the early fifth century of Roman coinage and the pottery industry may have erroneously created an impression of a more abrupt change from Roman to Saxon period than actually took place. The removal of the late Roman administration and attendant economy would have necessitated a realignment of post-Roman-British society and a return to a largely self-sufficient agricultural economy, fore-shadowing the subsistence economy of the incoming Anglo-Saxons, and therefore not readily distinguishable in the archaeological record (see Esmonde Cleary 1989 for an exposition of this process). Our understanding of the fifth century lies as much in the upper stratigraphy of Romano-British villas (such as Totternhoe) and farmsteads as in the earliest datable Anglo-Saxon graves and sunken-featured buildings. Closer attention to the last phases of Romano-British sites and analysis of the average life-expectancy of late fourth-century artefacts may reveal that the latest phases of some, if not many such sites can be extended to fill the apparent fifth-century lacuna. Since a full picture of society at this date can be achieved only with the integration of the "post-" or "sub-Roman" and "early Saxon" elements, this period can best be defined as the "Anglo-British" phase, although the extent to which each community was "Anglo [-Saxon]" or "[Romano-] British" would differ according to locality and time. However, a clear distinction should be drawn between the site or artefactual assemblage which exhibits "Romano-British" or "Anglo-Saxon" traits and the actual ethnic identity of the people represented by these remains. Sunken-featured buildings, for example, are generally described as "Anglo-Saxon" but may also have been used by the British population, and it may even be possible that other aspects of Anglo-Saxon building traditions derived from late Romano-British timbered structures (see key to Fig. 14: occupation sites). Certain assumptions can or have been made about the natures of the respective post-Romano-British and Germanic societies, but more attention might be paid to the interaction between these societies and the possible mechanisms by which land, food, raw materials (such as metals), finished goods and even humans (slaves; intermarriage) were or were not exchanged. Admittedly, it is not a straightforward matter to deduce such motives and processes from the archaeological record. For instance the location of the fifth-century communities associated with the Kempston or Luton 1 cemeteries could have been due to one or a combination of factors: an original nucleus of settled mercenaries, availability of land and access to local markets and regional trade-routes (whether major river-valley or the Icknield Way) can all be invoked. Nevertheless, a fuller picture of numbers, types and locations of communities extant in the fifth century should in time lead archaeologists to

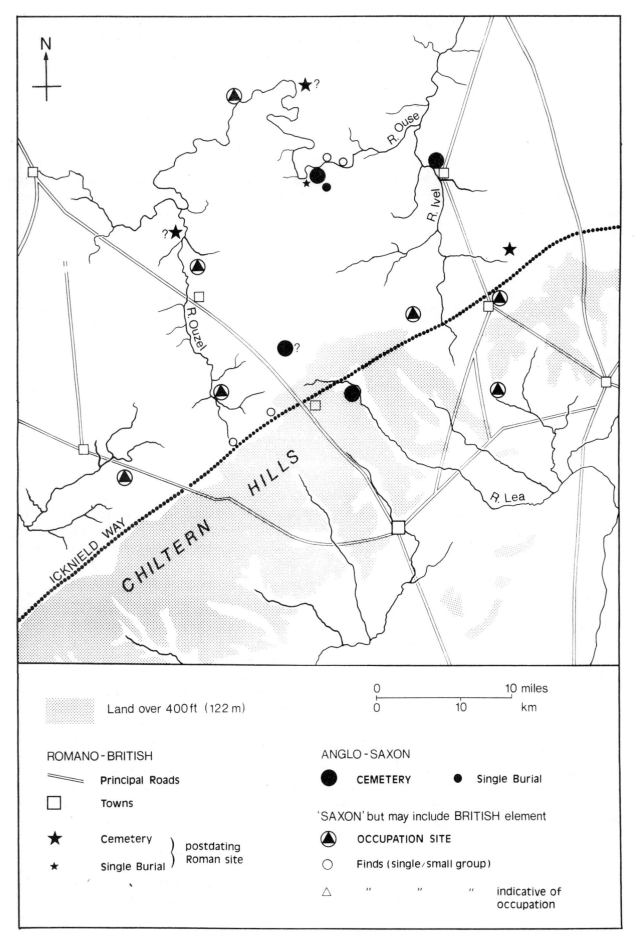

Fig. 14. Principal sites c.400 - c.525.

consider whether "Romano-British" and "Anglo-Saxon" sites led a symbiotic or mutually independent existence. If there is a meaningful degree of coincidence or mutual avoidance between sites exhibiting post-Romano-British and Anglo-Saxon features, it should be possible to detect this as fieldwork gradually adds to the list of sites occupied in the fifth century.

Apparent continuation of use on Romano-British sites into the fifth century can be suggested at Baldock (Upper Walls Common), where traces of sill-beam and post-built structures post-dating the Romano-British period were discovered (G. Burleigh, pers. comm.), and is hinted at by finds of late fourth/early fifth-century bronze buckles with outward-facing horses' heads at sites near Farndish, north-west Bedfordshire (Wingfield 1991, 69-70) and Sandy (H.B. Duncan & M. Dawson, pers. comm.; Clark & Dawson this volume). Another type of late or post-Roman buckle, with a pair of dolphins, has been identified from another Romano-British site in Podington parish (R. Martin, pers. comm.) and both the Farndish and Podington sites have produced late Roman coins of type and quantity to indicate activity at least to the end of the fourth century. This pattern may not be repeated throughout the entire zone under discussion. Neal & Hunn (1990, 96), in their discussion of the Roman villa at Gorhambury, have suggested that villas within a 16 km radius of Verulamium suffered a mid-fourth century decline but their associated farms continued in use on a run-down scale. This was in contrast to the pattern seen further away in Hertfordshire, Bedfordshire and Buckinghamshire, where most villas appear to have continued until the end of the fourth century or later. The question of Verulamium's survival after AD400 has received much attention elsewhere; its potential effect on early Saxon settlement is determined not so much by the number and extent of fifth-century features identified within the walls, but by the possibility that it survived as some form of administrative centre, and its consequent role in the local regulation of land-taking and economy.[1]

The sequence of different uses that many villa and farm buildings were subjected to before their demise may be in itself a sign of economic, social and tenurial transitions. Likewise the "late" burials in the cemetery ditches at Sandy (Dawson 1988; pers. comm.) and Dunstable (Matthews *et al*. 1981, 7-13), the burials in old well-shafts at Dunstable (Matthews *et al*. 1981) and Baldock (G. Burleigh, pers. comm.) and the construction of sunken-featured buildings in soft ditch-silt at Wavendon Gate, Milton Keynes, all may be indicative of a period of changing circumstances,

when previous customs were relaxed or expediency was a main consideration. Ultimately some late Romano-British buildings were reused as burial sites, robbed stone providing material to line the graves at Bancroft Mausoleum, Milton Keynes (Williams 1986; pers. comm.) and Bletsoe (Dawson 1994). If the status and date of these inhumations can be resolved, they may prove to be members of the fifth-century British population. To be considered along with these are a group of sub-Roman inhumations from Slip End, Ashwell (Herts. SMR 0242) and an inhumation dug into Romano-British wall-footings at Kempston on the line of the Southern Orbital Sewer (M. Dawson & H.B. Duncan, pers. comm.; Clark & Dawson this volume); the latter had been interred with a composite bone comb likely to be of fifth-century date. Where diagnostic Anglo-Saxon finds do occur on villa sites, a dislocation rather than continuity of use is apparent. Saxon 'sherds recovered from the Totternhoe villa came from dark soil filling a depression over a dismantled hypocaust in the East Wing, and others were found in the soil accumulated over a late cobbled floor and in the robber trench of a nearby wall of the North Wing. The conclusion is that the villa had been abandoned and the area reverted to arable before the derelict buildings were used as a dump and source of materials by an Anglo-Saxon community who settled nearby in the late fifth or sixth century (Matthews, Schneider & Horne 1992, 65). A similar phenomenon may be observed at Newnham, near Bedford, where early Saxon 'sherds were found among building rubble (Simco 1984, 74).

The list of sites which manifest fifth-century Saxon traits is dominated by Kempston and Luton 1 (Argyll Avenue), to which may be added the earliest phase of the cemetery at Sandy and possibly Toddington B (Warmark). If the "small pots... filled with little bones" (Meaney 1964, 41 quoting *Archaeologia* 27 (1838), 104-6) recorded at Warmark indicate a fifth-century cremation cemetery, this would place the Toddington area alongside Luton and Kempston (and maybe Sandy) as a locality where early Saxon communities took root and flourished at least till the end of the sixth century. Significant among the earliest Kempston and Luton finds are such pieces as an early cruciform and short-armed brooch (Kempston: Kennett 1986, 5) and an equal-arm and a supporting-arm brooch (Luton 1: O'Donoghue 1980, 29-31). Taken in conjunction with the Broadwater site (discussed below) these seem to represent the first tangible traces of Saxon settlement in the region and could represent a distinct first phase within the fifth century. Other sites and objects grouped under this general fifth-to-opening-of-sixth century heading could conceivably belong to a slightly later development. Kennett's (1986, 7) studies of Anglo-Saxon cemeteries in the region have led him to distinguish between the cultural milieu of the early Kempston community, which has regional affinities mainly with Cambridgeshire and Northamptonshire, and that of the Luton community, which - as might be anticipated from its position on the Icknield Way - looks both north-east to Cambridgeshire and south-west to Oxfordshire and the Upper Thames valley. This at least is the impression gained from the metalwork, which represents the most distinctive and portable items and perhaps those likely to be exchanged over greater distances; localised exchange of domestic artefacts, foodstuffs and livestock cannot be so readily discerned. It is regrettable that so much of our knowledge of fifth and sixth century cemeteries in the Toddington/Leighton Buzzard area relies on antiquarian records, for the Ouzel and the Ivel valleys offer links between these two separate early centres and thus a greater knowledge of the finds from the Ouzel and Ivel sites could help establish the date and extent of cultural assimilation between the Ouse valley and the Chiltern zones.

Traces of contemporary settlements are less tangible but may begin to fill out the fifth-century distribution map. The Ouzel valley, north-east of the early site at Walton, Aylesbury (Farley 1976), would have formed a natural route leading to or from the Icknield Way and traversed by Watling Street. Ceramic evidence from Grove Priory suggests that sunken-featured buildings there may date from the fifth and sixth centuries (E. Baker & A. Slowikowski, pers. comm.; Baker 1985). To the north, ephemeral evidence of early sunken-featured structures and potsherds at Wavendon Gate, Milton Keynes point to continuity of settlement in the locality from the Romano-British through to the early Saxon period (Williams 1989, 20). Other traces of fifth to sixth-century pottery are present along the Ouse valley at Harrold (Eagles & Evison 1970, 48-50) and from excavations in Bedford (Baker et al. 1979, 151-4) and at Elstow Abbey (Baker 1971, 55-7), and in south Bedfordshire at Puddlehill (Matthews & Hawkes 1985, 69: Fig. 6 & 102).[2] The discovery at Broadwater, Stevenage in the 1950s of a sunken-featured building with 'sherds of early Saxon pottery and a fragment of an early Germanic belt-buckle may be a tantalizing glimpse of a fifth-century settlement strategically located in the Hitchin Gap (archive in Stevenage Museum).

The positioning of such sites has been viewed principally in the context of the "foederati" and the interests of the Romano-British population, based on references in historical sources. Consideration of the archaeological evidence on its own grounds and of the interests of the Anglo-Saxon immigrants themselves offers an alternative approach. Pressures in Germanic homelands made emigration desirable presumably because it increased chances of obtaining land as the primary means of sustenance, wealth and status. This process could have interacted in some places with a contracted economy and falling post-Romano-British population which affected opportunities for obtaining land or labour. To what extent the take-up of land was regulated, tolerated or resisted by the native population is unclear. Work on populations in sub-Roman and early Saxon cemeteries in Hampshire has had suggestive results - a decline in the proportion of females in the late Roman population was apparent in the cemetery at Lankhills, Winchester, and there was a marked tendency countywide for a higher percentage of Romano-British women to die at a younger age than their Anglo-Saxon counterparts (Arnold 1984, 133-7).[3] Excavations of more late Romano-British and early Saxon cemeteries in Bedfordshire and Hertfordshire, in addition to data already obtained, with all the advantages of modern skeletal and scientific analysis could provide material for similar studies. The demographic data from late Romano-British burials, e.g. the Dunstable cemetery, also needs to be assilmilated with that from the early Saxon cemeteries, e.g. Luton 1 and Marina Drive, to obtain a profile of the whole population from the fifth to seventh centuries for a given area.[4]

Sixth century c.500 - c.625

Those sites which continue to flourish, or begin, in the sixth century are plotted in Fig. 15, and listed in the appendix. There is an element of overlap between this and the preceding phase, as it is not always possible to date domestic pottery and features more closely than "fifth to sixth century". The initial impression is of an intensification and expansion of Saxon influence, if not also population, from the early centres, notably in the Luton/Dunstable area; however, the map is equally a reflection of the opportunities presented by development and gravel extraction for making finds. Complementary evidence from settlement sites is woefully lacking and fieldwork could usefully concentrate on identifying settlements associated with cemeteries known from previous finds. For example, at Toddington A, "Sheepwalk" site, recent finds included plain early Saxon pottery possibly from the cemetery's associated settlement (S.A. Castle, pers. comm.). This of course pre-supposes a one-to-one ratio of ceme-

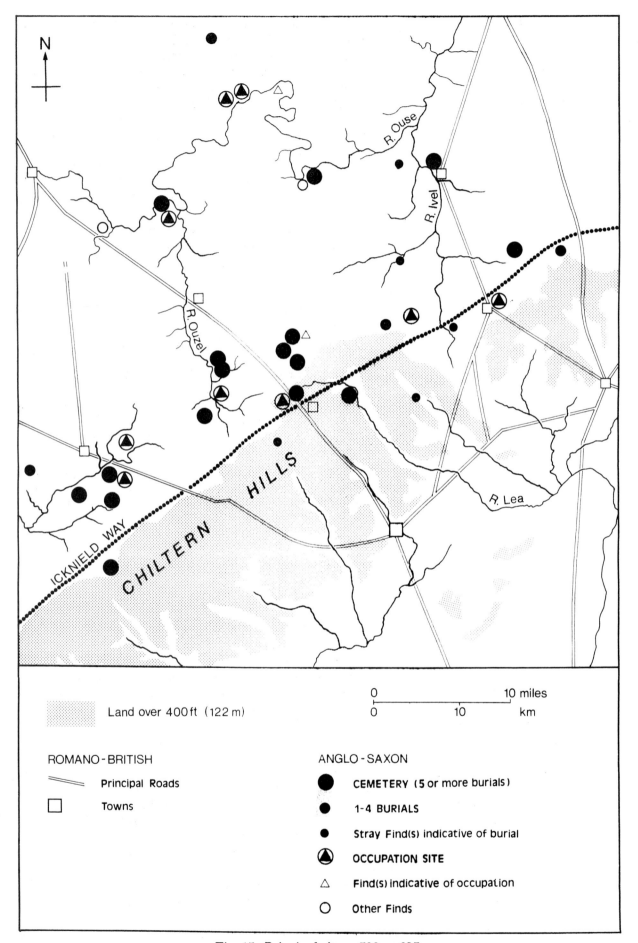

N

R. Ouse

R. Ivel

R. Ouzel

ICKNIELD WAY

CHILTERN HILLS

R. Lea

Land over 400 ft (122 m)

0   10 miles

0   10   km

ROMANO-BRITISH

〰 Principal Roads

□ Towns

ANGLO-SAXON

● CEMETERY (5 or more burials)

● 1-4 BURIALS

• Stray Find(s) indicative of burial

⬤ OCCUPATION SITE

△ Find(s) indicative of occupation

○ Other Finds

Fig. 15. Principal sites c.500 - c.625,

teries to settlements. However, it is quite conceivable that some of the larger cemeteries (e.g. Sheepwalk Hill, Toddington) could have served a number of smaller settlements, or that kinship groups who moved out to new habitation sites would continue to use the old family burial-ground for at least one or two generations. Thus any settlement pattern deduced entirely or mainly from the distribution of cemeteries may conceal subtler fluctuations in the pattern of occupation.

Another problem is dating within the century of grave-goods in the cemeteries as this could be important for understanding the fluctuations in population, that is whether the population steadily increased at an approximately uniform rate or whether after a period of consolidation at a relatively low level, it suddenly increased within one or two generations (whether due to internal or external stimuli). The cemeteries of the Luton area may offer potential here. Kennett's (1986; 1970) work on the cemeteries at Kempston and Sandy has opened the possibility that both continued in unbroken sequence from the fifth through to late sixth (seventh at Kempston), though in each case the amount of material positively attributable to the early sixth was not great. From the later sixth century there is a greater degree of cultural cohesion seen in the finds from these cemeteries which has been equated with political events attributed by the Anglo-Saxon Chronicle to this time. Alternatively one might argue that this cohesion is to be expected if by the late sixth century the development of Anglo-Saxon communities and kinship ties had produced a regional network for trade and exchange, and possibly the emergence of a regional identity later to define these people as the Chilternsaetan.[5]

From the later half of the sixth century into the seventh century there are changes hinted at in the settlement pattern which may or may not be connected with the number of new cemeteries starting at about this time. Two new sites which begin in the sixth and continue through the seventh are Pennylands, Milton Keynes (R.J. Williams, pers. comm.) and Odell (Dix, unpub.); Pennylands has produced structures amounting to two hall-houses and eleven sunken-featured buildings and one timber-lined well, while Odell yielded only vestigial remains of one sunken-featured building, but five timber-lined wells containing much plain, domestic pottery, animal-bones and organic material. If the bone assemblages from the wells and pits at Odell were representational of the site, cattle would appear to predominate and the general picture is not dissimilar to the contemporary settlement on Puddlehill near Dunstable, despite its very different location and idiosyncratic buildings. Of course settlement sites seldom yield finds that are narrowly datable, which hampers correlation of contemporary settlements and burials. At Odell the pottery was dated by dendrochronological analysis of the timbers from the wells, but showed no discernible change in form or fabric over the one-and-a-half centuries that the site was thought to be occupied. The Odell pottery was all made of local clays, blackish in colour and coarse sand was the predominant tempering. A site comparable to Odell and Harrold may have existed at Felmersham by or during the sixth century; parts of two plain, hand-made pots, "some black slime and bones", and two shallow depressions - tentatively interpreted as sunken-featured buildings - were discovered in c.1950 (Jope 1951).

An alternative approach to phasing pottery and associated features on domestic sites has been used on excavations in the Aylesbury area (Farley 1976) and also at Puddlehill, near Dunstable (Matthews & Hawkes 1985). It has been suggested that patterns in the relative percentages of pot fabrics might have chronological significance, the fifth-century features being typified by small amounts of decorated, often hard and relatively good quality wares with some plainer sherds. Coarser wares predominate in the sixth century and grass-tempered fabrics appear to be mainly an eighth- to ninth-century phenomenon. Since early Saxon pottery is so localised, it would be unwise to assume that all sites will show an identical progression. To test the value of such phasing criteria it is necessary to locate and excavate either a single occupation site of unusual longevity (which may in itself be atypical of early Saxon settlements) or a series of small occupation sites of various dates in the same vicinity. A comparable method might be used to examine faunal or floral remains from associated pits to look for changes in the economy and environment over time.

Seventh century c.625 - c.700

Again there is some overlap with the preceding phase (see Figs. 15 & 16), especially in settlements like Odell and Pennylands, which are assumed to continue through this period. However, the criteria used to phase and plot this distinctive group of pre-Christian cemeteries may not be particularly meaningful when applied to domestic sites. The characteristics of these so-called "late" cemeteries have long been recognised and they occur through much of south, central and eastern England (Hawkes 1982). They are almost invariably located on new sites, representing an abandonment of traditional burial-grounds, al-

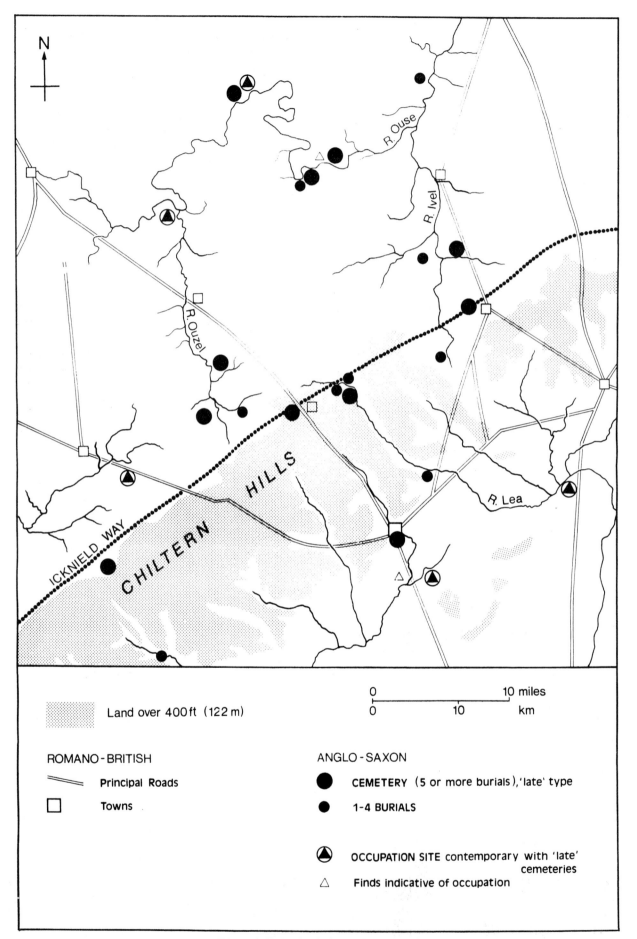

N

R. Ouse

R. Ivel

R. Ouzel

ICKNIELD WAY

CHILTERN HILLS

R. Lea

0   10 miles
0   10   km

Land over 400 ft (122 m)

ROMANO - BRITISH

Principal Roads

Towns

ANGLO - SAXON

CEMETERY (5 or more burials), 'late' type

1-4 BURIALS

OCCUPATION SITE contemporary with 'late' cemeteries

Finds indicative of occupation

Fig. 16. Principal sites c.625 - c.700.

though at Kempston, Mentmore (Meaney 1964, 58) and Luton 1 (if Biscot Mill is accepted as an extension of the Argyll Avenue cemetery: see Hagen 1971), late burials appear to have continued to be made adjacent to tbe old burial-grounds. The graves themselves are all inhumations and accompanied by a few weapons (men) or - in the case of women - by distinctively "late" objects such as workboxes and necklaces, which frequently incorporate pendants, amethyst beads and silver-wire rings; the absence of brooches may be accounted for by a change in dress as much as changes in taste. Small, handmade accessory vessels are also a common feature. Marina Drive, Dunstable (Matthews 1962b); Chamberlain's Barn 2, Leighton Buzzard (Hyslop 1963) and King Harry Lane, St. Albans (Ager 1989) are well-known examples, and the evidence for comparable cemeteries in the Ouse valley has been published by Kennett (1973b). Thus a significant degree of cultural uniformity is evident through both the Ouse valley and Chiltern zone at this period.

The traditional interpretation of these cemeteries is that they represent the period of conversion to Christianity with the accompanying spread of new fashions and influences from Kent. The assumption that the cemeteries are to be explained primarily by religious changes has in turn affected their perceived *terminus post quem*, which is generally held to be around the middle of the seventh century. In relation to the King Harry Lane cemetery, Ager (1989, 225-7) has considered the suggestion first proposed by Welch (1984) for the Sussex cemeteries, that the late cemeteries may simply indicate an expansion of population into previously unsettled areas, at approximately the same time as new ideas spread from southeastern England. If religious causes are no longer seen as the primary motive for the adoption of these new sites, at least some of the late cemeteries could have originated earlier in the seventh century than hitherto supposed. This interpretation does not necessarily exclude a religious element, perhaps as a secondary phase, but it does make greater allowance for a complex of social, economic and political changes which seem to underlie the re-orientation of Anglo-Saxon society in the seventh century. However, continued use of existing sites (and even some expansion onto new ones?) could also have been undertaken by communities who remained conservative in form of dress and burial while their neighbours were adopting new costumes and new sites. If the woman buried on Puddlehill (grave 10) can be dated as the second quarter of the seventh century by the saucer brooches, her traditional West Saxon manner of dress must have contrasted with her contemporaries in the area of Leighton Buzzard, who were abandonning the old style of costume and acquiring the bead-and-silver wire necklaces with which they were eventually buried in their new cemetery (Chamberlain's Barn 2).[6]

The question of to what extent these cemeteries reflect expansion onto new land is not always easy to answer, given the paucity of evidence in some areas and allowing for the possibility that a change in cemetery location could sometimes have taken place without necessitating a change in habitation site (as apparently happened at Kempston). The issue is best addressed on a local basis. At Kempston Church End, a little over 1 km from the main cemetery at Hillgrounds, a small group of inhumations has recently been discovered in the vicinity of a Romano-British villa site. One double inhumation of this group produced a small Saxon accessory vessel and a necklace of silver-wire rings and amethyst beads, with four worn late Roman bronze coins; it therefore appears to belong with "late" period burials (M. Dawson, pers. comm.; Clark & Dawson this volume). Likewise at Luton, in addition to the late extension to the Argyll Avenue site at Biscot Mill, the inhumations at Dallow Road (Luton 2: Morris 1962, 69; Kennett 1973b, 101) and Waulud's Bank, Leagrave (Morris 1962, 68; Meaney 1964, 39), could be seen as representing a possible fragmentation and devolution of the nucleic Saxon settlement, or may even be partly explained by local British communities finally adopting Anglo-Saxon funerary practices (it is tempting to see the "late" burial at Kempston Church End in this light). Further fieldwork in these areas is largely determined by the development of urban housing and related services but opportunities might be sought to investigate potential burial and occupation sites that may represent daughter-settlements of the early Saxon communities. The burials at Blackhorse Road, Letchworth (Moss-Eccardt 1971) could be seen as an incursion of Saxon customs or people from the Ivel valley towards the sub-Roman settlement at Baldock. On the south-east side of the Chilterns, the picture presented by comparison of figures 15 and 16 is indeed one of expansion of Saxon influence and/or population into new areas around St Albans and Hertford. Evidence for occupation from grass-tempered pottery and structural traces at sites such as Foxholes Farm, Hertford (Herts. SMR 2131; Partridge 1989), Old Parkbury, Colney Street (Niblett 1990b, 416) and Bricket Wood, Aldenham (Herts. SMR 0695) all appear to correlate with the seventh-century dates assigned to the beginning of the King Harry Lane cemetery and the burial at Wheathampstead (Meaney 1964, 105; Kennett 1973b, 103).

Another feature of this phase worthy of investigation is the socio-economic status of certain types of burial and the possibility that the types of, and relationships between, buildings and settlements may reflect the same social hierarchy. One aspect is the use of barrows, contemporary or pre-existing, for burials, and in the case of a few Saxon burials, the relative wealth of the accompanying assemblege. It is tempting to see in these burials, marked out by their prominent location or relatively rich assembleges, the inhabitants of the principal hall-house dwelling on contemporary settlements. Barrow-burial was not a new feature of the seventh century, of course, for barrows had always tended to attract burials - for instance the Kempston cemetery was probably located near some earlier tumuli, and the original warrior burial in the barrow on Puddlehill has been dated to the early sixth century. The seventh-century communities of Marina Drive and Puddlehill re-used prehistoric and Anglo-Saxon barrows respectively. Earlier barrows (plotted in Fig. 15) apparently were also used at Pegsden (Morris 1962, 69; Meaney 1964, 39) and Therfield Heath (Meaney 1964, 105; Rutherford Davis 1982, 144) although the few surviving accounts and artefacts from these sites leave their precise dates open to question and they could belong to the late, seventh-century phase. Further potential late barrow-burials, though uncorroborated by archaeological evidence, are hinted at in place-names and documentary sources at Benslow, Hitchin [7] and "Goldenlowe", near Dunstable (Morris 1962, 76). Topographically both these sites would conform with the apparent preferred location, i.e. on high or sloping open terrain, as if overlooking the land associated with the person or community interred. To the southwest, in Buckinghamshire, accounts of burials discovered at the Warren, Bledlow (Meaney 1964, 56) and Castle Hill (Meaney 1964, 59; Rutherford Davis 1982, 141), High Wycombe are further examples and are probably to be dated to about the first half of the seventh century. Barrow-burials are not necessarily distinguished by range or wealth of grave-goods from other burials of the period, although the High Wycombe burial did include a gold-and-garnet pendant of Kentish type, but it could be argued that burial under a visually distinctive monument in itself confirmed the pre-eminence of the person interred. It is also necessary to distinguish between the primary Saxon burial and later secondary burials attracted to the same monument; however, old records of former discoveries do not always allow this distinction to be made. Nowhere in the area under consideration is there a burial known of a local leader or sub-king remotely comparable to that at Taplow unless the "Goldenlowe" treasure was of Saxon

and not Roman or prehistoric date.

The contemporary settlements at Odell and Pennylands have already been described and in the case of Pennylands, the simultaneous use of hall-houses with smaller sunken-featured buildings could be indicative of a social structure in which a community was focussed around an overlord or leading family to whom allegiance was owed. If circumstances permit, the excavation of more late sixth- and seventh- century settlements could then test the hypothesis that this form of settlement, in which type and spatial relationship of buildings reflects the social order, becomes the norm for the Ouse/Ouzel valley zone by c.600, and may also be true of the Chiltern zone. Assembleges of domestic artefacts and environmental remains might also be used as an indication of differences in economic status between one site and another. If problems of dating occupation sites can be overcome sufficiently to identify the contemporary cemeteries, a new range of questions could be applied to the evidence, such as whether the "late" group of cemeteries have an associated group of habitation sites also on previously unsettled ground, or whether - as Odell and Pennylands seem to indicate - a spate of new habitation sites appeared earlier, during the second half of the sixth century. If structural evidence for the size, use and number of buildings in a settlement survives sufficiently well and the duration of its occupation can be assessed, it should be possible to calculate the approximate average number of occupants per settlement, and hence compare the population estimates from the domestic sites with those from contemporary cemeteries.

Conclusions and future work

For the earliest phase of the Saxon settlement, it may be admissible for the time being to set aside questions of ethnic identity or other issues which are either impossible to answer fully from the archaeological record alone or depend heavily on aligning the archaeological evidence to a historical framework pre-determined by other considerations. The analysis from the skeletal record of the population profile from the fourth through to the end of the seventh centuries, coupled with greater attention to the environmental and economic aspects of sites over the same time-span, could provide an overview of transitions or continuing trends in human settlement against which local variations and apparent anomalies could be studied. At Odell, environmental evidence suggested that much the same dry, open grazed landscape was being exploited in the Saxon as in the Romano-British period. Continuity of animal populations and preferred crops from late Romano-British to mid Saxon times might elucidate the extent to which early Saxon communities were conditioned by both local geographic factors and existing Romano-British practices.

The geological background to the Saxon settlement of Bedfordshire has been discussed by Bilikowska (1980) and there is no reason at present to digress from the established view that the heavy claylands (where not overlain by more workable drift deposits) were not favoured for settlement in the early Saxon period, although the extensive use of the rich Boulder Clay soils in the Roman period may suggest these areas are worthy of attention. Work in the Thames Basin, described by Vince (1990, 130-3),[8] supports the view that evidence for early Saxon settlement seems to be lacking from the heavier clay soils. This is not to say that these zones could not have been extensively exploited, e.g. for managed woodland, swine-pasture and hunting, but this aspect of Anglo-Saxon settlement is more easily addressed through study of documentary sources relating to the later Saxon period. However, although the settlement pattern may seem to favour the lighter soils of the river-valley gravels, these are equally the areas which have traditionally offered more opportunities for archaeological discoveries. Priority could be given on the one hand to improving the quality of evidence from the river-valley areas, by targeting developments on sites in the vicinity of previous finds, and on the other hand to examining the various clay areas and greensand belt for signs of occupation. The latter might best be approached by defining a corridor of land that extends over a range of soils and changing environments, and pursuing a programme of intensive fieldwalking and plotting of any finds of early to mid Saxon sherds or other debris. The excavation of occupation sites where local conditions favour survival of evidence for structures and/or waterlogged features with a good environmental record needs to be an especially high priority, and particularly where there is the opportunity to link that settlement to a known or suspected cemetery site. Ironically, it is the remains of the people themselves that were so seldom recovered or survived from earlier discoveries, so there still remains a need to excavate cemetery sites for the information found in the skeletal record alone.

Notes

1. The survival of a predominantly British zone centred on Verulamium and surviving possibly until the seventh century has been discussed most notably by Rutherford Davis (1982). The situation at Verulamium may be contrasted with that at York and Canterbury (summarised in Campbell 1982, 38-9) where there is minimal archaeological evidence for continuing occupation in the fifth and sixth centuries but where both re-emerged as centres of authority to play important roles in the mid and late Saxon periods.

2. Matthews & Hawkes (1985, 69) postulate the existence in the vicinity of the Puddlehill settlement of an earlier pagan cemetery from which the fifth-century urn and miniature razor were looted. However, it is possible that they were used and lost entirely in a domestic context (compare with the miniature comb - another class of object usually associated with burials - found in a sunken-floored building at West Stow).

3. Many of the suggestions discussed by Arnold (1984, 133-7) for studying demographic change between late Romano-British and early Anglo-Saxon populations could be usefully applied to the Chiltern area, particularly in relation to the late- and sub-Roman population of the area centred on Verulamium.

4. An exercise by the author to compare the percentage of deaths occurring among males and females in each age-group for the Dunstable (late Romano-British) and Luton 1, Argyll Avenue (early Anglo-Saxon) cemeteries produced similar patterns for both populations but with a slightly greater proportion of young Anglo-Saxon males dying in the late teens/early twenties age-group. Various explanations could be sought for such a phenomenon: greater incidence of death due to war-injuries, disease or malnutrition (some of which might leave evidence in the skeletal record) or possibly young and able-bodied males at Dunstable tending to move away from the declining Roman settlement. In practice, the results from the Dunstable/Luton 1 analysis are largely invalidated by the small amount of identifiable skeletal material surviving from Luton 1 and the different age-groupings adopted for the two cemeteries, making direct comparison difficult (see Matthews et al. 1981, 18-32 and O'Donoghue 1980, 6-11). However, it has been included as an example of the potential research opportunities presented by cemeteries in this region, if more suitable skeletal data are forthcoming.

5. The Chilternsaetan ("Chiltern-dwellers") are referred to in the Tribal Hidage, a document which may have had its origins as early as the seventh century, although its date, evolution and interpretation have been much debated (see Davies & Vierck 1974). Other readily identifiable

groups in the Tribal Hidage include the Hicce (Hitchin area) and the Gifle (Ivel Valley).

6. Hawkes' relatively late date for the Puddlehill saucer brooches (Matthews & Hawkes 1985, 93-7) rests on the need to derive their design specifically from a group of Kentish brooches which can be dated to after AD600. A re-evaluation of the Puddlehill brooches by Dr. Tania Dickinson proposes that all the elements of the Puddlehill brooches could have been in existence by the turn of the sixth/seventh centuries (T. Dickinson, pers. comm.). This has obvious implications for the *terminus post quem* of the burial, and the degree of contemporaneity with other seventh-century burials, such as Chamberlain's Barn 2.

7. Benslow in Hitchin may relate to a "hlaw" (burial mound), now lost.

8. Vince's (1990, 130-3) comments on the possible reasons for lack of early Saxon settlement on the clays and brickearths of the Thames valley are equally applicable to mid Bedfordshire.

Appendix

The following list of sites distinguishes between two categories: the first group under each phase are those for which the dating evidence is not in doubt, and all or most of the material, or unambiguous records, are extant. The second group are "probables" considered likely to belong at least mostly to that period, although the dating evidence may be less precise and in some cases the finds themselves can no longer be located. Sites in these two categories are plotted on the relevant maps in figures 14 - 16. There are others known, for example stray finds or discoveries listed in SMRs or antiquarian writings, on which there is insufficient information for them to be usefully assessed, or for which the dating evidence is too ambiguous for their inclusion. SMRs for Bedfordshire and Hertfordshire were consulted; other sources used are listed in the notes and references.

C = Cemetery (5 or more burials)
B = Burial(s) (1 to 4 cremations and/or inhumations, may indicate more extensive cemetery)
S = Settlement or occupation site
sf = single or stray find or group of finds
sf/B = as above, presumed to represent a burial
sf/S = as above, presumed to represent a settlement

Fifth century including sites/finds described as "fifth to sixth" but likely to begin before the end of the fifth century. N.B. post-Roman and early Saxon sites are listed without differentiation.

1. Luton 1 (Argyll Avenue) C; Kempston C; Sandy C; Southern Orbital Sewer, Kempston B; Broadwater, Stevenage S; Walton, Aylesbury S; Upper Walls Common, Baldock S; Wavendon Gate, Milton Keynes S; Grove Priory, Leighton Buzzard S; Harrold S: Newnham, Bedford and Totternhoe sf/S [both villa sites which have produced a small amount of fifth to sixth-century pottery]; Elstow B.

2. Slip End, Ashwell C; Bletsoe and Bancroft, Milton Keynes possibly fifth-century C but equally may be mid-Saxon; Toddington B (Warmark) C; Puddlehill sf [fifth-century miniature razor and sub-biconical urn found in sixth-century settlement]; Bedford sf [one sherd from Castle site positively attributed to early fifth century]; Pirton S [Roman-period site investigated by North Hertfordshire Museums Service produced "Dark Age" pottery similar to pottery from post-Roman settlement at Baldock].

Sixth century continuing into first half of the seventh century.

1. Farndish B and sf/B [small-long brooches]; Grove Priory S; Kempston C; King William's Close sf [saucer brooch, sherds?]; Luton 1 (Argyll Avenue) C; Deadman's Slade, Leighton Buzzard C; Moggerhanger B; Odell S; Puddlehill C and S; Sandy C; Toddington A (Sheepwalk Hill) C and sf/S? [domestic pottery recovered 1990-91]; Toddington B (Warmark) C; Whipsnade sf/B [sherd of stamped urn]; Ashwell C; Kings Walden B; Walton, Aylesbury S; Bierton S; Bishopstone (Cursley Hill or Causeway Field) C; Wolverton, Milton Keynes sf [saucer brooch].

2. Chalton C; Chamberlain's Barn 1 C; Felmersham sf/S? [2 pots]; Harrold S; Pegsden B [in barrow]; Shefford sf/B; Baldock (Upper Walls Common)? S; Pirton? S; Grove Hill, Hitchin sf/B; Therfield Heath B [in barrows]; Ashendon sf/B [saucer brooches - however these may be late examples, well into seventh century]; Walton Aylesbury C; The Cop, Bledlow C; Dinton C; Mentmore C [also see below] Tickford Park Estate, Newport Pagnell C; Pennylands, Milton Keynes S.

Seventh century "late" phase of cemeteries mostly on new sites, and occupation sites likely to have been contemporary with them.

1. Astwick C; Bedford sf/S; Chamberlain's Barn 2 C; Clifton (Henlow) sf/B [2 accessory vessels]; Marina Drive, Dunstable C; Harrold C; Kempston C; Church End, Kempston B; Waulud's Bank,

Leagrave B; Biscot Mill, Luton C; Odell S; Bricket Wood, Aldenham sf/S; Old Parkbury, Colney Street S; Foxholes Farm, Hertford S. Blackhorse Road, Letchworth C; King Harry Lane, St. Albans C; Walton, Aylesbury S [occupation possibly continuous from fifth to eighth or ninth centuries].

2. Luton 2 (Dallow Road) B; Tring Road, Eaton Bray B; Eaton Socon B [2 inhumations with scramasax]; Russell Park, Bedford C; Pound Farm, St. Ippolitts B; Wheathampstead B; The Warren, Bledlow B; Mentmore C: Pennylands, Milton Keynes S; High Wycombe B.

THE MEDIEVAL LANDSCAPE OF THE CHILTERN DIPSLOPE: A BRIEF OUTLINE OF THE ADMINISTRATION AND INFRASTRUCTURE OF THE COUNTRYSIDE AROUND ST ALBANS

Jonathan Hunn

Medieval settlement in Hertfordshire

Previous studies of the medieval landscape within the county of Hertfordshire have tended to be limited in the scope of their enquiry. Work has been done on the early medieval period has been done using place-names and archaeological evidence (Rutherford Davis 1982) and on field systems in the Chilterns (Roden 1973). More generalised works are represented by Munby (1977). However, there have been no detailed studies of what might be termed the social infrastructure of a particular locality. This section is concerned with the medieval landscape in one district in Hertfordshire: the St Albans area.

The St Albans area: a case study

The medieval landscape surrounding the abbey and town of St Albans was very different from that of the Romano-British period. In comparison with, for example, the thirtenth century its institutions, population density, settlement and communications pattern bore little resemblance to that which existed a thousand years earlier. Nevertheless, this change was not a sudden development but came about through a series of gradual shifts over the millennia. The most obvious contrast between the two periods was the change from a regional cantonal capital (Verulamium of the Catuvellauni tribe) to that of a market town under the lordship of an eccesiastical authority (the abbot). The location of these two settlements was different and this had arisen through a shift to an intermediate site (Kingsbury) and then deliberate foundation in the mid-tenth century on a third new site closer to the abbey (St Albans).

In the countryside around St Albans the pattern of agriculture was different, though the same reliance on human and animal power remained. The only difference, at a manual level, was that the instructions were spoken in a different language and some of the events recorded on documents that have survived (manorial records). It is principally on these writen sources that this paper is based. A reliance upon the written record, whether of manorial or ecclesiastical origin, necessitates a degree of caution in interpreting the

evidence. Documentary evidence may be reliable after the eleventh century (post-Domesday Book, 1086) but before then the settlement chronology is based on the physical remains within the landscape, e.g. ceramic scatters. Two recent studies concerning dispersed settlement in Bedfordshire (Brown & Taylor 1989) and Worcestershire (Dyer 1990) illustrates the importance of this type of evidence.

The area under examination is the same as that of the section describing the Romano-British settlement around Verulamium (Hunn this volume). In the case study the different elements (administrative, judicial, ecclesiastical, manorial, tenurial and land use) are described that would have been recognisable to someone living in the thirteenth and fourteenth centuries.

The post-Roman to mid-Saxon evidence

The period between the demise of Verulamium and the rise of the precursor of St Albans, Kingsbury, is uncertain. Nevertheless, several points may be made before turning to the question of the change of settlement focus in the locality. Several writers have commented on the comparatively late appearance of Saxon evidence in the Verulamium area and have consequently argued for a continuation of native British independence after the late sixth-early seventh centuries (Garmonsway 1955, 19; Matthews & Hawkes 1985; Morris 1977, 226; Whittock 1986, 30-2 & 209-10). The name of the Saxon settlers was the Waeclingas (Gover 1970, 87). They may be identified by the use of a small mid-seventh-early eighth centuries cemetery outside the Silchester Gate (Stead 1969; Stead & Rigby 1989; Ager 1989). Another cemetery lay 250 m north of Verulamium (TL138078) and consisted of some 56 inhumations (Frere 1983, 287-8). Further away at Redbourn there is an apparent re-use of a Roman barrow in the early seventh century (Wright 1849). Contemporary with the Redbourn burials are those of Wheathampstead (Meaney 1964, 104-5). The cemetery evidence, together with that of place-names, are the only data that exists with which to reconstruct the post-Roman to mid-Saxon period. Research into the origins of St Albans abbey may afford greater insight into this period (Biddle 1986) but until this takes place opinions will remain purely speculative.

The mid to late-Saxon period

At some point in this period there was a change in the location of the principal settlement focus away from Verulamium to the adjacent site of Kingsbury. This new settlement was located on the east bank of the river and was defined by a bank and ditch of which the latter was *c*.12 m wide (Havercroft, pers. comm.) and enclosed 11 ha. Kingsbury was referred to as a 'municipium' in the tenth century (Riley 1867a, 23) but the date of its foundation remains problematical.

There are at least two possibilities for the origins of Kingsbury both of which, as the name suggests, imply royal foundation. Firstly, there is a late ninth century date when, at the conclusion of Anglo-Danish hostilities, a treaty divided the two spheres of jurisdiction along the Thames, northwards up the river Lea to Bedford, then along the river Ouse to Watling Street (Stenton 1971, 260-1). Perhaps it was a strategic necessity that led to the establishment of a burh close to Verulamium and only 7 km from the river Lea boundary. There is a suggestion of a Danish element in the Hundred name of Dacorum which lay to the east and west of St Albans (Morris 1976, note 5, 2).

The second possibility is that Kingsbury was established by King Offa in AD793 when the abbey was 'founded' (Biddle 1977, 30). There is, as yet, no means of proving this connection. However, the fourteenth century inhabitants of St Albans, in their disputes with the Abbot, asserted that their ancestors received their privileges from Offa (Page 1906, 149). This could be dismissed as wishful thinking but there are indications that the inhabitants of the burh did have some form of independent jurisdiction which brought them into conflict with the abbey.

It is possible that the foundation of the abbey in the late eighth century, close to the royal burh, might imply that Kingsbury was a villa regalis and that the abbey was intended to serve in the role of a minster to the local region. Nevertheless, whatever the precise relationship was, it is clear which establishment ultimately triumphed. Kingsbury might have flourished had it continued to have the support of the crown. However, the lack of royal interest combined with the establishment of a market by the Abbot in AD948, led inexorably to its demise and to the development of St Albans (Riley 1867a, 6; VCH 1971b, 67). Between the late eighth century and AD1066 the landed wealth of the abbey grew considerably. Offa endowed his new foundation with a substantial endowment. Most of this land lay to the south of the town up to the borders of Middlesex (Riley 1867a, 39; VCH 1971a, 367-8). This grant, together with those of Offa's son, remained the abbey's only endowment up to the late tenth century. Thereafter more royal grants of land were made (Luard 1882, 13, 16 & 32; Riley 1867a, 39; VCH 1971a, 146). Very little is known as to the precise boundaries of each grant or to the nature of their associated landscape. However, a reference in the Gesta Abbatum (Riley 1867a, 39) and placename evidence suggest that the grants included a high proportion of woodland.

The administrative landscape

Jurisdiction and lordship. Before the Conquest, the area around St Albans appears to have formed part of the Hundred of Dacorum (Morris 1976). At the time of the Domesday inquest (1086) and up to the twelfth century the area was known as the Hundred of St Albans and thereafter the Hundred of Cashio. This coincided with the Liberty of St Albans, and the courts met at two separate locations. The Hundred was divided into three principal and two lesser jurisdictions termed 'sokes'. It is difficult to trace the bounds of these sokes because they do not appear to coincide with any of the manorial jurisdictions of the leet (Levett 1938, 136).

Townships and parishes. In the St Albans area the evidence for township territories is inextricably bound up with the later development of ecclesiastical parishes. It has been argued elsewhere that early parish boundaries can reflect the tenurial landscape of the eleventh century (Roffe 1984, 115). However, due to the lack of direct medieval documentary evidence, it is difficult to prove that the parishes in the St Albans area were composed of township units and not simply an arbitrary imposition. It is, therefore, necessary to be cautious in interpreting what indirect evidence there is for township territories. The only certain township unit is that of St Albans, the boundaries of which were first described in 1327 (Riley 1867b, 166; Roberts 1981, 127-58) and first mapped in 1634 (St Albans Lib.). By the fourteenth century, the vill of St Albans was composed of four parishes (St Andrews and portions of St Peters, St Michaels and St Stephens). Originally, the town itself had consisted of three parishes (St Michaels, St Peters and St Stephens), of which St Peters was by far the largest (Fig. 17). It would seem probable that at least from the early eleventh century, when the parochial system in the area was first laid out,

46

Fig. 17. Medieval parish and township boundaries around St Albans.

that the township of St Albans was included in the rural parishes adjoining St Peters and St Stephens. The only parish which seems to have been based on a single township was Redbourn. The sole mention of a settlement within the parish is of Redbourn itself and, though the medieval evidence is slight, the manorial documents suggest, with two small exceptions, a correlation between the manor and vill boundaries.

In the St Albans area both the early manorial estates and the township boundaries are difficult to

trace. The best that can be attained in terms of reconstruction is to plot those localities that were referred to as 'vills' (townships) from a variety of sources (Fig. 17). Neither the physical evidence nor the historical record suggest that the known medieval settlements existed earlier than the late-tenth century. This does not mean that the landscape was sparsely settled between AD400 and AD1000, only that the means of identifying habitation sites is inadequate. Knowledge of the St Albans area in the post-Roman/pre-Conquest

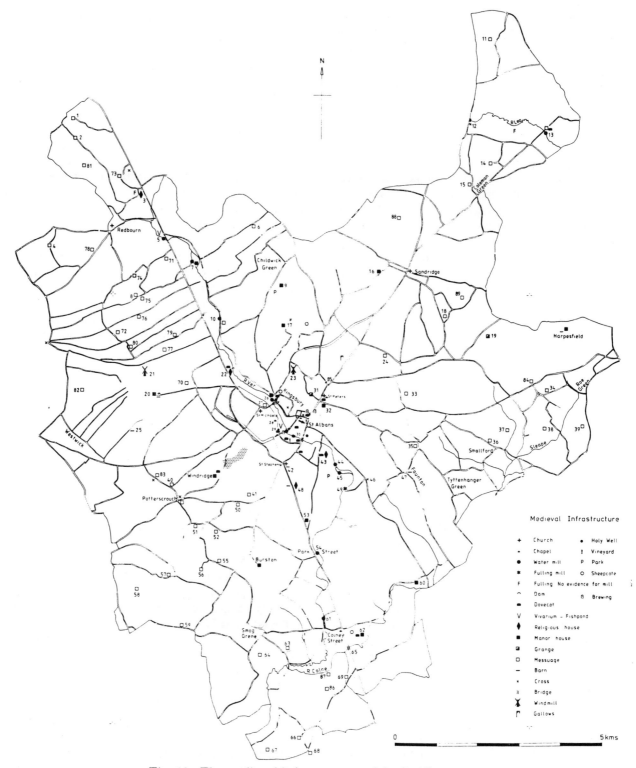

Fig. 18. The medieval infrastructure of the St Albans area.

period is limited to the site of Kingsbury, the indirect settlement evidence of the Anglo-Saxon cemetery south-west of Verulamium and one early Christian site on the north side of Verulamium. The sites of the five parish churches (Redbourn, St Michaels, St Peters, St Stephens and Sandridge, none of which are mentioned in Domesday Book) cannot be safely ascribed to a date earlier than the late-tenth century but may indicate the type of settlements they were built to

serve. The sites of the three earliest churches (St Michaels, St Peters and St Stephens) were located within 1.1 km of the Abbey of St Albans (Fig. 18). It would certainly be unwise to see their concentration around St Albans as evidence for a concentration of population. However, in the case of the churches of Sandridge and Redbourn, the most likely explanation for their siting was their proximity to adjacent settlements. With this relatively late type of evidence the kind of settlement

48

pattern that existed in the pre-Domesday period around St Albans is uncertain. It is possible that the settlement pattern has remained predominantly dispersed from an early period and, therefore, proportionally more difficult to locate than if it had been of a more nucleated nature.

The creation of the parochial system in the St Albans' area does not become apparent until the early-eleventh century. This is due to the presence of the Abbey which probably served in the role of a minster. According to the *Gesta Abbatum* (Riley 1867a, 22) Abbot Wulsin built the three churches of St Michaels, St Peters and St Stephens; this would date the churches to around the mid-tenth century, contemporary with the creation of the market place. However, the site of the church of Kingsbury (St Michaels) was not acquired by the Abbot until at least the very end of the tenth century and an early eleventh century date seems more probable (VCH 1971b, 47). This would be in accord with the architectural evidence (Smith 1973, 26).

The parish of St Peters originally comprised the later medieval parishes of Sandridge, St Andrews, Northaw and Ridge which did not become detached until about the fourteenth century (VCH 1971a, 412). In the mid-nineteenth century the parish contained 5,503 acres. St Peters was based on the combined townships of Thanncton, Harpsfield, Sleape, Thebridge and possibly Sandridge. St Stephens (8,953 acres in the mid-nineteenth century) was based on the townships of Hanstead/Park and there was a detached portion of the parish to the east, possibly Tyttenhanger. The parish of St Michaels (6,443.5 acres) was made up of five townships in the eleventh century: Windridge, Kingsbury, Westwick, Childwick and Redbourn, the latter (4,563 acres) being created a separate parish in the late-eleventh/early twelfth century (VCH 1971a, 368; Riley 1867a, 148). The parishes of Sandridge (5,766 acres) and St Andrews (167 acres) were elevated from the status of chapels in the early fourteenth century, probably as a result of a population increase.

There is no conclusive evidence of parish boundaries but it seems probable that in the St Albans area they were laid out so as to combine several townships. Whether the area of the parish was based on the density of settlements and therefore on allotting equal numbers of communicants is a matter of speculation. This question has been addressed in relation to size of churches and their size of population but not to the area of the parish (Bond 1988, 143; Proudfoot 1983, 241). It should

be pointed out that there is no proof that the delineation of the parish was necessarily contemporary with the construction of the church. It has been argued that it would be unwise to see the parochial system and foundation of church buildings as necessarily contemporaneous (Morris 1985, 51). The church of Kingsbury (St Michaels) was built on the west side of Watling Street, overlying the site of the previous Roman forum. The present day St Michaels street lies directly on the north-east entrance of the forum: other examples of this association may be found at Lincoln, York and London (Rodwell 1984, 1-25). It was situated c.360 m west-south-west of the presumed Saxon burh. The other contemporary church of St Stephens also stood beside Watling Street, near a former Roman cemetery, 1,100 m south-west from the market centre of St Albans. The third church of St Albans was St Peters, situated c.500 m north-north-east from the town centre. Both St Michaels and St Stephens churches stand where the road deviates towards the centre of St Albans, whilst St Peters church stands on a route for the north-east of the county and beyond. The break in the route of Watling Street between St Michaels and St Stephens is often believed to have been the deliberate creation of the Abbot of St Albans to direct traffic through the centre of the town. However, there is the possibility that there was an additional consideration, namely the creation of a deer park in the early eleventh century on the southern half of Verulamium which stretched towards St Stephens; field name elements suggest that it once covered at least 120 acres in the mid-eighteenth century (HRO D/EX 438 T 5) and it may have been larger in the medieval period. It was still possible to avoid the town by using King Harry Lane (which was often referred to as Watling Street: map of 1822 by E. W. Brayley) and proceeding round the outer edge of Verulamium's defences until rejoining the old route of Watling Street beside the Chester Gate.

Manors and manorial estates. For the period between the Norman Conquest and the dissolution of the monasteries the manorial land belonged, with certain minor exceptions, to the Abbot of St Albans. However, most of the manors were administered by various officers of the Abbey: cellerer, kitchener, almoner, refectory and prior. Certain manors were normally leased out by the Abbey (Burston, Windridge and possibly Newland Squillers and Harpsfield) but the manorial lord remained the Abbot. Almost nothing is known of the various manors prior to their acquisition by the Abbey. The relationship between the late Romano-British villa estates and the subsequent development of Anglo-Saxon holdings is lost and only a pairing of estates can be postulated.

Table 1. Dates of properties when first acquired by the Abbey of St Albans.

Late 10th-c.793	c.796	Late 10th	Pre-Early 11th	Mid-11th	Conquest
Hanstead	Sandridge	Westwick	Verulamium Burston Kingsbury Childwick	Redbourn Thwantune	Windridge Napsbury

Table 2. The acreage of manorial and non-manorial estates in the Medieval period around St Albans.

	Area (acres)	Date of source
Batchworth/Childwicksay	92	14th century
Burston	702	16th century
Childwick (584.25 acres in C14th: possibly demesne)	900	estimate
Grange of St Peters	260	14th century
Harpsfield (included under the manor of Park)		
Kingsbury	1,520	estimate
Markeyate (St Margarets cell)	72	16th century
Napsbury	540	16th century
Newland	212	16th century
Newland Squillers (included under Park)		
Park (923 acres in demesne)	11,106	estimate
Redbourn (including St Amphibals)	4,563	estimate
St Juliens	100	16th century
St Mary's Sopwell	796	16th century
St Mary de Pre (home farm)	360	14th century
Sandridge (1,355.8 acres in late C14th in C18th covered parish)	5,766	
Westwick (331 acres in C14th: probably demesne)	2,292	16th century
Windridge (probably only the demesne the remainder under the Manor of Park)	344	16th century

There is uncertainty as to the extent of these individual grants of land. Domesday Book mentions certain lands that were not wholly part of the Abbey estates. For example, the Bishop of Lisieux held 1 virgate and the Count of Mortain half a hide in Redbourn (Morris 1976, 6.1, 15.3) and Geoffrey of Bec held 1.5 hides in Windridge (*op cit.*, 34.1). Of the 12 manors listed in Table 1, five were not mentioned directly. However, of these Batchworth was a subdivision of Childwick, Park the later name for Hanstead, Newland and Newland Squillers were new estates carved out of land previously granted to the Abbey and Harpsfield was possibly included with Hanstead. The donation of Sandridge by Ecgfrith in AD796 may not have included the property of Bridehall, which lay within the manor of Sandridge, since it was later granted by Thurfleda to St Albans Abbey in the early ninth century (VCH 1971a, 434; Riley 1867a, 507). Even in the early thirteenth century it was still possible for individuals to grant land fairly close to the Abbey of St Albans, e.g. St Mary de Pres (B.Lib. Charters 19,962).

It is difficult to establish the size of the manorial estates around St Albans because only a few complete extents survive from the medieval period (Park and Westwick). However, other documents allow us to gain a reasonable estimate of the size of each estate. Table 2 lists the size of manorial and non-manorial estates around St Albans based on documentary and estimated figures.

The management of the Abbey Estates. Most of the area in which the manors lay was on the dipslope of the Chilterns, which has been described as a 'region of fairly advanced agricultural practises during the Middle Ages. This was best exemplified by the quality of the demesne farming, with elaborate manuring, the early appearance of a three-course rotation and controlled grazing within large enclosed fields' (Roden 1969a, 9). The impression gained by examining manorial records of the Chiltern area is that there is not much to distinguish between lay and ecclesiastical manors in terms of their land use and field systems.

A combination of factors influenced the development of the landscape in the medieval period. It has been suggested that inheritance by more than

Table 3. Settlement hierarchy around St Albans according to probable status.

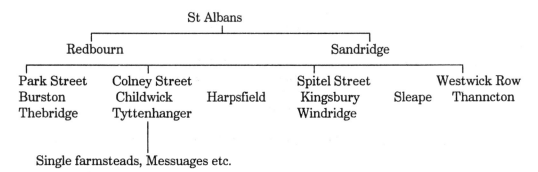

one heir could 'through the dismemberment of compact holdings produce a field pattern of unenclosed strips held by different tenants' (Roden 1969b, 225). There is good evidence that both free and bond tenants could alienate land from their holdings, provided such actions were recorded in the manorial court rolls. By the mid-thirteenth century such activity led to a more flexible pattern of landholding. 'Some customary units were broken-up by sale from them; others were supplemented by the acquisition of strips and closes on lease or by purchase. Some men were able to build up substantial farms in this way, while others were consolidating their land. Average holding sizes differed considerably from manor to manor, the proportion of small tenants in particular varying according to local opportunities for their supplementary employment as wage labour' (Roden 1969b, 227). The economic decline of the early fourteenth century hardened after the epidemic of 1348-50, which then saw the amalgamation (engrossment) of properties rather than a change in the method of farming the common fields. Land utilisation and organisation seem to have remained fairly static until early in the sixteenth century when the population of London expanded and caused both the extension of arable cultivation and a rationalisation of land units (Roden 1970, 118). One consequence of the amalgamation of property was that more land was concentrated in fewer hands. This does not become so apparent until the Dissolution (1539) when some substantial estates were built up, often composed of several manorial units.

The physical appearance of the medieval landscape

Medieval settlement. The distribution of settlement is shown on figure 18 and is summarised in Table 3. The medieval settlement pattern around St Albans is of a predominantly dispersed nature. It exhibits many of the characteristics of a woodland landscape (Williamson 1988, 5-6). Recent work in Bedfordshire (Brown & Taylor 1989) and Worcestershire (Dyer 1990) warn against simplis-

tic interpretations of the origins of dispersed settlement patterns. On the present evidence it would probably only be safe to claim that the eleventh century landscape was characterised by a relatively large central focus (St Albans) surrounded by hamlets and individual farmsteads. Some of the settlements had developed certain village-type characteristics by the fourteenth century (Redbourn and Sandridge), in the form of having churches and possessing a range of different functions, e.g. smithying, innkeeping, brewing and baking (see Table 3). Despite the fact that Kingsbury had a church, it did not possess sufficient population or range of activities to qualify as a village.

Medieval infrastructure. Figure 18 shows the general outlines of the infrastructure in the medieval period. Not all the objects and activities mapped were necessarily in existence at the same time in the early eleventh-sixteenth centuries. Nevertheless, most of the items on figure 18 were functioning either by or before the mid-thirteenth century (for documentary references see Hunn 1990). Figure 18 also illustrates the earliest locations of messuages (farms); many of these still survive today, while others have been obliterated by urban expansion. The number of messuages represents a minimum rather than a maximum figure. Nonetheless, some comparison can be made with other figures. In Domesday Book the number of 'peasants' who were engaged on the land was 93 Villeins, 18 Cottars and 26 Bordars.

Possible farming units in the late eleventh century. If the Villeins are equated with their own separate farm, as has been sometimes assumed (Hoskins 1967, 43), then a basis for comparison is available. The number of Villeins and Bordars totals 119. This number compares quite closely with the figure for the mid-nineteenth century for those establishments described as farms or homesteads (135) over 8.1 ha (20 acres). There are several interpretations that may be made on the Domesday Book and Tithe Apportionment sources. Either the agrarian units of the late

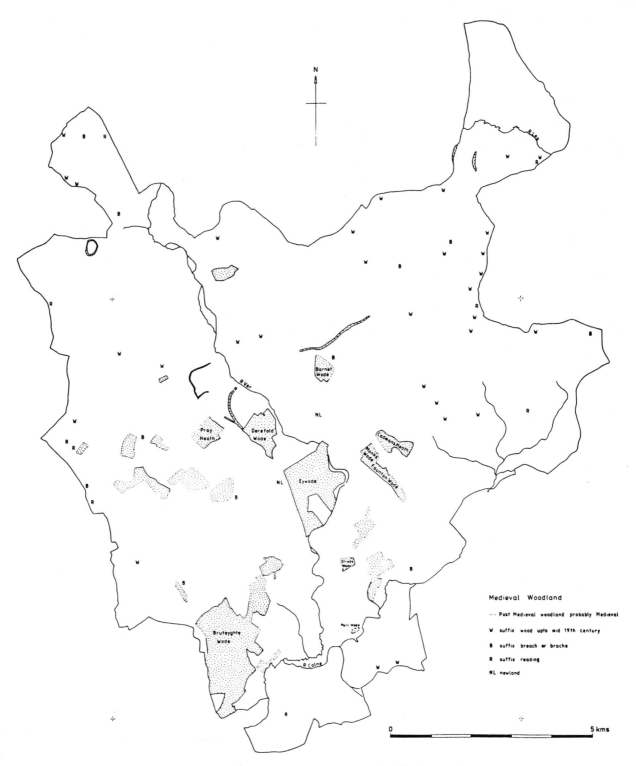

Fig. 19. Medieval woodland in the St Albans area.

eleventh century were larger or there was more land under cultivation in the mid-nineteenth century. The evidence for a greater acreage of woodland in the medieval period has been suggested above. Therefore it would seem that the increase in the number of farm units is more likely due to a diminuation of woodland coverage.

Woodland. Figure 19 plots the known extent of woodland in the Middle Ages. The plan suggests that most of the woodland lay to the south and west of St Albans. This distribution partly coincides with the extent of Boulder Clay soils, e.g. Bruteghte (Bricket) Wood, Fauntons Wood and Cadmans Heath. The remaining woods (Eywode, Derefold, Pray Heath and Barnet Wood) all lay on glacial gravels and pebbly clay and sandy soils. However, since these soil types are common to the area, it is not possible to assert that medieval woodland was located solely on inferior quality

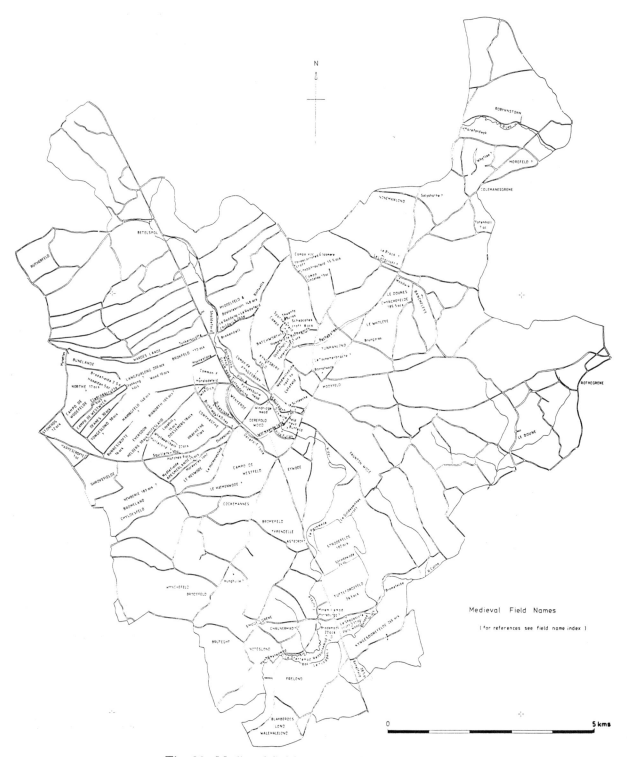

Fig. 20. Medieval field names in the St Albans area.

soil. In the case of Derefold Wood, which was situated over the eastern half of the site of Roman Verulamium, its presence may possibly be due to the uneven and stony nature of the ground which prevented or retarded cultivation in the early medieval period. Most of these woods had vanished by the sixteenth century, though Bricket Wood remained much the same and Pray Heath has expanded to its present day extent. The earliest reference to assarting comes from the late

twelfth-early thirteenth centuries for a 'certain assarto beside the villa de Westwyca' (Westwick), (Chatsworth Cartulary 517/2); Eywode in *c.*1250 (*op cit.*, 301/3); Tydenhangre Wood *c.*1255 (*op cit.*, 298/3); Bricket Wood mid-thirteenth century (*op cit.*, 535).

Fields and field systems. In the St Albans area there is no evidence for any deliberately planned large-scale reorganisation of the landscape prior to the Conquest. This is hardly surprising since the south and east of England never developed a mature open-field system (Williamson 1986, 241; 1988, 5-15). The archaeological evidence from Gorhambury suggests that the two enclosures associated with the Romano-British villa were still a prominent feature in the eleventh/twelfth centuries, albeit now merged into one; its southern boundary was recut at that time (Neal *et al.* 1990, 83). From the manor of Park there is a hint of a possible change in the field system in the post-Conquest period. The former caput of this manor was at Hanstead (Domesday Book), which lay some 1800 m to the west of the fouteenth century site of the manor, and it is possible that the three large demesne fields of Park (Fig. 20) were laid out at the same time as the new manor site was created.

Only a fraction of the total number of field names can be located on a map with the aid of later records and even fewer can be delineated on the ground. Figure 20 shows where the majority of the evidence is located. Virtually no field name material can be plotted for the parish of Redbourn and only some for St Peters parish.

The first impression given by the assembly of the field name evidence is that the field systems in the St Albans area were characterised by open common arable fields interspersed with smaller units, sometimes enclosed with hedges. Most of the information concerning land management is derived from surveys rather than court rolls. For the manor of Westwick the survey of 1306 lists all the land units belonging to the estate. The totals are: 801 acres of arable (90% of the total area), 11.5 acres of meadow (1.29%), 44 acres of pasture (4.9%) and 32 acres of wood (3.6%): a combined total of 888.5 acres. The 90% of the manorial holding in arable consisted of four large fields totalling 690 acres, and nine small fields of some 111 acres. How these fields were managed is not stated. There are only two references to land being enclosed, a 4 acre croft and 10 acres of woodland. To judge by the list of buildings belonging to the manor (which mentions among other items a granary, two cowhouses, two sheephouses and a pig sty) the estate was primarily involved with arable farming, with pastoral activity being of secondary importance.

One of the few large common arable fields that can be delineated on the ground is Brokfeld (170 acres). Brokfeld is first mentioned in the late thirteenth century, though the source is a fifteenth century deed (HRO Gorhambury Deeds XBIA). Apart from its appearance in the 1306 survey of Westwick, there is no further mention of it in the medieval period. In the 1569 survey of Goram-Westwick the 170 acre Brookfield appears as 10 units. Put together these make up the early fourteenth century area of Brokfeld. When the process of dividing up this field took place is not known. The late-fourteenth and early fifteenth century court rolls make no mention of it. Even less is known of the other common arable fields in the manor of Westwick.

The evidence suggests that the field systems around St Albans in the medieval period were characterised by a multiplicity of common fields interspersed with more numerous enclosed fields. The ratio of enclosed to unenclosed fields is difficult to determine. In the parish of St Michaels on the manor of Batchworth the proportion of enclosed fields was as high as 50% of the acreage. The origins of the enclosures of heath and wood is difficult to discern, though according to Roden (1970, 115), the process was established by 1250 further west towards the Chiltern escarpment.

The irregular nature of the medieval field system suggests that it was due to piecemeal enclosure. The physical evidence for this process in the form of the hedgerow ecology has not been studied adequately. However, the location of irregular and sinuous boundaries when plotted suggests they were influenced by their proximity to woodland. This interpretation is further reinforced by field name and documentary sources. Much of this evidence has been gleaned from cartographic references, as much of the hedgerow evidence has been destroyed.

It has been shown that the pattern of inheritance in the Chiltern Hills could influence the configuration of divided fields (Roden 1969b, 225). Partible inheritance produced a pattern of intermixed strips held by different tenants. It has also been shown that impartible inheritance was an important factor in the maintenance of the open field system (Pitkin 1962). Whatever the precise mechanism for this occurrence, the principal impression gained from the field name evidence around St Albans is the multiplicity of tenant holdings in different fields. However, the intermingling of tenant strips in different fields also occurred between the estates of different manors. The manor of Batchworth held 2 acres in the campo de Kyngsbury (B.Lib. Ms Harley 602 fol 40v). The manors of Westwick, Kingsbury and St Mary de Pre all shared land in Morsladefeld (HRO Gorhambury Deeds X.B 31; X.D.0; X.I.2). A similar situation occurred in Westfield, which was apparently held by Kingsbury and Windridge (HRO Gorhambury Deeds X.D.0 and X.E.I.A). The manor of Kingsbury held land near Napsbury

Table 4. The evidence for medieval estates in the St Albans area.

	Manor	Barn	Dovecot	Corn mill	Fulling mill	Windmill	Church	Chapel	Fishery	Fishpond	Vineyard	Park	Warren	Wood	Brick/tile making	Fruit Orchard	Account of stock	Manorial extent	Court roll/book,charter
Batchworth	◉																	○	
Burston	◉																		
Childwick	○		◉									○	○						
Hanstead	◉																		
Kingsbury	◉	◉	◉	◉		○	◉			◉		○							○
Napsbury	◉													○	◉				
Newland	◉																		○
Newland Squillers	◉	○																	
Park	◉		○	◉					◉			○	○			○	○	○	○
Pray	◉	◉	○				◉							◉	◉		○	○	○
Redbourn	◉		◉			◉	○		◉			○							
Sandridge	◉		○	○		◉						○						○	○
Saint Albans		◉	◉	◉	◉		◉	◉	◉	◉	◉	◉	◉	◉		◉			○
Saint Julians	◉	◉						◉											
Sopwell	◉	◉	○	◉				○						◉					○
Westwick	◉	○				◉	○	○				○	◉				○	○	
Windridge	◉		○									○	○						○

Medieval evidence. ● Field evidence. ○ Documentary evidence

◐ Site known but no upstanding remains.

◉ Field and documentary evidence.

(HRO Gor Deeds X.D.0). The manors of Park and Newland held land in Sawalefeld (Bodleian Lib. MS Gough Herts I). Even as late as the mid-eighteenth century there were several lands of the manor of Park intermixed with the demesne lands of Burston (HRO D/EAM T 21).

The field system evidence around St Albans conforms to the previous analysis in the Chilterns (Roden 1966). Roden (1966, 76) states that in most townships 'the typical pattern of arable fields comprised both common arable land (namely, arable land contained in fields cultivated in common and which were open to common grazing after harvest and substantial amounts of enclosed land held in severalty). Some demesne and tenant holdings were completely enclosed, while others included both common and several land'. How early the process of enclosing common arable fields around St Albans occurred is unknown. One of the mechanisms of change from the open field systems to an enclosed pattern was the growth in specialisation, as agriculture became more profitable and increased flexibility became desirable (Baker 1983, 150). The process may have been helped by the changing land ownership pattern of estates and their growth from the mid-sixtenth century onwards. It has been argued that this may have promoted more independence on behalf of tenants and the weakening of manorial control (Yelling 1977, 82). The medieval field name evidence is both dispersed and chronologically discontinuous; it enables a random sample of evidence to be examined and suggests certain trends within the medieval landscape.

Conclusion

Table 4 presents a summary of the evidence for the medieval infrastructure and provides a general assessment of its quality. For the St Albans area, documentary and field evidence accounts for 70% of the information in Table 4 with 30% being documented sites. This compares favourably with the figures for Abingdon Abbey (Bond 1979, 59).

The landscape of the thirteenth to early sixteenth centuries was dominated by a single institution, the Abbey of St Albans. It is thus possible to see the later medieval landscape as essentially unchanging. However, this would be a mistake for there were certain underlying changes which suggest the picture was far from static. Both population and wealth increased. The growth of the Abbey and town of St Albans in parallel with the economic development of London saw new market forces at work (Bolton 1980, 229). Such was the growth of St Albans that contemporaries referred to it as 'Little London' in the thirteenth century (Riley 1867a, 426). The town was surrounded by a defensive ditch (Hunn 1981) and had gateways (Riley 1867a, 426).

In the countryside, the felling of woods and the creation of new manorial estates took place. The appearance of the three course systems on the estates of the Abbey (Park, Tyttenhanger, Sandridge, Childwicksay, Grange of St Peters, probably Westwick and possibly Kingsbury) occurred by the fourteenth century and possibly much earlier. However, the changes to estate management were never as great as on, for example, the estates of Winchester (Levett 1938, 66-7). This may be because estate management was of less interest to St Albans Abbey than to other institutions (Levett 1938, 79-180). Alternatively, it could have been due to the prevalence of local custom and a *laissez-faire* attitude by the Abbey. Whatever the precise reasons, the evidence of field names suggests that continual, albeit gradual, change was taking place before 1539. This change cannot be quantified in the medieval period. The medieval evidence allows a glimpse of an ensemble of the principal elements in the landscape, e.g. settlement, communications and woods, and to recognise their influence in the present day environment.

Future work in Hertfordshire

This contribution has looked at the medieval landscape in one district in west Hertfordshire.

Probably the single most important question to ask about medieval Hertfordshire is concerned with the early settlement of the county: where and in what form did it take place? It would also be implicit in such an enquiry to ask about the present day configuration of the settled landscape. For example, what is the relationship between the earliest existing plans of villages and those of the pre-Conquest period? To what extent has settlement remained static or mobile since the end of Roman Britain? Some of these questions can already be answered in part by studying topography and settlement in relation to fixed institutions such as churches, e.g. Redbourn, Chesfield, Buntingford and Caldecote (*cf.* Doggett this volume). However, within the county there is, as yet, nothing to compare with settlement studies undertaken elsewhere in southern and eastern England (Brown & Taylor 1989; Dyer 1990; Foard 1978; Hall 1985; 1987; Wade-Martins 1980). A classic model for a regional or county survey is the research carried out in West Yorkshire (Faull & Moorhouse 1981), although undertaking such an approach on a county basis in Hertfordshire is unlikely at present. A study of the smaller market towns has great potential to yield evidence for their origins and growth. Very little new research has been carried out on the origins and form of Hertfordshire towns since Page's (1917) work. There is a clear need for work of this nature. There is also no reason why the piecemeal approach to the development of towns should not permit archaeologists to answer questions about settlement origins, provided it is carried out within a coherent research framework. The limitations of such an approach have to be acknowledged; many core areas of towns are in conservation areas which consequently are unlikely to experience major redevelopment. Nevertheless, where potential sites have been noted it is important to record their archaeological deposits prior to destruction in order to increase knowledge of early town formation in Hertfordshire.

THE PREHISTORIC AND ROMANO-BRITISH LANDSCAPE IN BEDFORDSHIRE: RECENT FIELDWORK

Royston Clark and Michael Dawson

Introduction

This section outlines some of the results of recent work conducted north of the Chilterns in Bedfordshire. It will enable settlement patterns on the Chilterns discussed elsewhere in this volume to be viewed in a broader context. By concentrating on fieldwork covering the prehistoric and Romano-British periods in Bedfordshire, it is intended to show how this is contributing to both an environmental history of the county and to the development of a framework for understanding the evolution of the landscape.

The Bedfordshire portion of the northern hinterland of the Chilterns comprises two distinct regions: the southern chalk lands of the Chilterns as far as Chalgrave; and the northern clays which extend north into Northampton. The clays are subdivided by the Lower Greensand Ridge which runs in an intermittent line from Everton in the northeast to Woburn in the west. The valleys of the river Great Ouse, its tributaries the Flit and Ivel and the Hiz, flow from west to east before draining north to the Wash and contribute to the variability of the landscape. Such regional differences are reflected in settlement patterns of all periods.

Recording of archaeology in the Bedfordshire region began as early as John Aubrey's observations at Sandy in 1666 and even by the nineteenth century there had been a considerable increase in understanding and awareness of the ancient landscape. The systematisation of this information in the Sites, Monuments and Buildings Record (SMBR) set up in the 1970s (Baker & Simco 1982) drew not only on the early antiquarian records but on more recent material and now includes extensive cropmark evidence and a diversity of information from sources as disparate as chance finds, the results of rescue archaeology, archaeological assessment and research-based projects. Presently, over 15,500 sites of all periods are known within the county.

The compilation of the SMBR, renamed the Historical Environment Record in 1992, has enabled biases within the archaeological record to be identified more closely. Aerial photography and field survey evidence have begun to indicate the density of settlement, particularly on the lighter soils overlying the glacial drift gravels of the Ouse and Ivel valleys as well as the marl soils of the chalk (Simco 1984, Fig. 5). The current round of modern excavation and survey work is bringing about a reappraisal of the extent to which land-use and settlement patterns are interrelated.

In recent years development pressures have led to some relatively large scale excavations which have introduced new biases in the archaeological record for the county. Gravel quarry sites in particular are concentrated in the river valleys and new building sites tend to be located close to existing towns and areas of development. Large areas such as northern Bedfordshire therefore still remain relatively unknown archaeologically. Limitations in aerial survey techniques are apparent where excavation has confirmed the presence of sites first identified from the air and often cropmarks of indeterminant enclosures under represent the density of settlement. For instance, the recently investigated Iron Age and Romano-British site at Stagsden was evident only as a single open ended sub-rectangular cropmark. Excavation in advance of the new bypass revealed an extensive settlement which included kilns and a deep V-shaped enclosure ditch. Recent work at Warren Villas, Upper Caldecote indicated that perhaps only a tenth of the boundary ditches existing on the site showed up as cropmarks.

Many of the distortions in cropmark evidence are due to the condition of the local water table. But later agricultural activity, such as the formation of medieval headlands, can also bury large sites making them invisible to the ordinary techniques of aerial photography. An example of such burial processes was the discovery of an extensive late Bronze Age and Iron Age settlement complete with a surviving occupational deposit sealed under a later medieval headland at Salford Quarry, on the borders with Buckinghamshire. Similarly, alluvial deposition has masked sites from detection by aerial photography, but has preserved archaeological deposits below layers of silt and clay. The distortion of the archaeological record due to these processes indicates the need for appraisal of techniques such as colour differentiated multi-

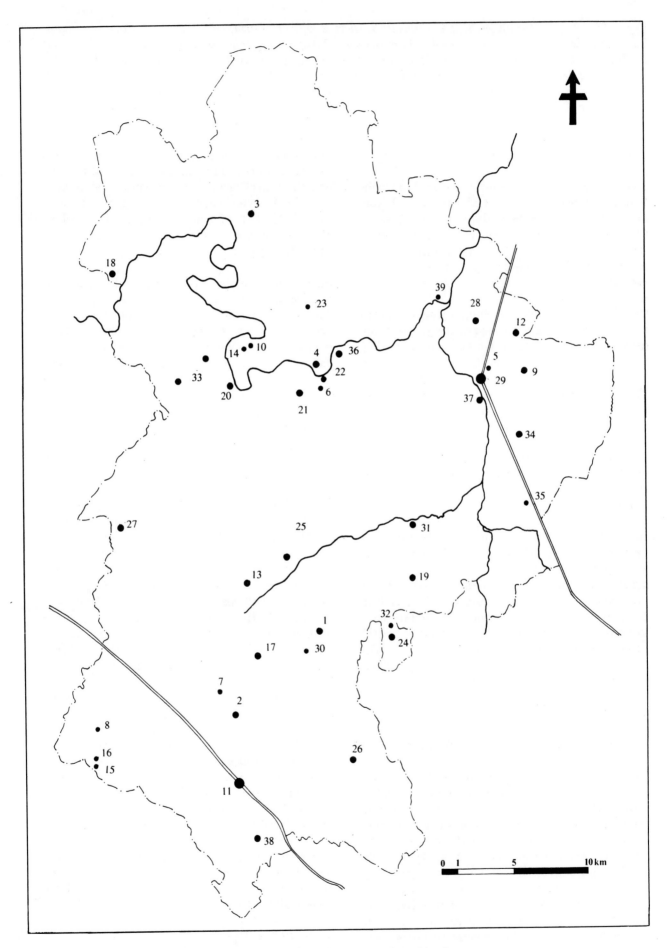

Fig. 21. Location of sites mentioned in the text.

spectral analysis and ground radar.

Lastly a further bias remains. Compared to neighbouring counties, such as Oxfordshire and Northamptonshire, relatively little large-scale fieldwork with adequate environmental sampling has been carried out. As a result an environmental framework for the county is only just beginning to emerge.

The first part of this contribution will attempt to present information on the prehistory of two key areas of Bedfordshire: the Great Ouse river valley and the south Bedfordshire Chilterns. Evidence for pre-Iron Age settlement in the other areas of the county is not addressed as little work has taken place here recently. Also, due to the limitations of space, this paper will not attempt to present the archaeology of the palaeolithic and mesolithic periods, for which there is an increasing amount of information from field survey and the re-examination of the old gravel face at Deep Spinney, Biddenham (Harding *et al.* 1991).

In the second part of this contribution the evidence of later Iron Age and Romano-British settlement is discussed. In this period little modern analysis of the settlement patterns has been undertaken (Hall & Hutchins 1972; Hall & Nickerson 1966). This has not prevented the construction of at least one far-reaching historical model in which, during the late first century BC and first half of the first century AD, the Chilterns and Bedfordshire, possibly as far north as the Nene valley, were combined as part of the tribal area of the Catuvellauni (Branigan 1985).

The Ouse valley: results of recent fieldwork

In many respects recent fieldwork in the Ouse valley is a continuation of the work carried out in the 1970's (Woodward 1978; Taylor & Woodward 1985) as it centres on the large number of ring ditches and associated cropmarks dating to the neolithic period and the Bronze Age. Woodward's fieldwalking suggested that a high density of early to middle Bronze Age lithic material, and the corresponding Bronze Age settlement, was located on the river valley and its gravel terraces. He was also able to suggest that habitation areas were spatially related but did not impinge on the ring

ditch sites, and that the most concentrated habitation areas were located on the junction of the clay and the gravel terraces. Excavations at Roxton (Taylor & Woodward 1985) suggested early Bronze Age dates for many of these ring ditches. More recent work argues for neolithic origins for this landscape.

Since 1987 a series of field projects has added to this picture and it appears that many ring ditches date to the neolithic period. The information presented below consists of preliminary statements as important results such as radiocarbon dates and environmental analysis are still awaited.

Central to the prehistoric landscape east of Bedford is a complex of cropmarks that are of neolithic origin. These include Goldington, the Cardington causewayed enclosure and, to the north of it, a group of cropmarks known as the Cardington cursus complex (Fig. 22).

Excavations at Bury Farm, Goldington (Mustoe 1988) have provided information to suggest that the Ouse valley prehistoric landscape was well established prior to the Bronze Age. A triple ring ditch, immediately north of the river, produced a central burial consisting of two children aged between 7 and 10 years old. Mildenhall pottery was excavated in the primary fill of the earlier ditch. With a date of *c.*2,500BC this puts the earlier phase of Goldington well back into the neolithic period. The burials at Goldington are significant in that out of a total of eight, three were female and the remaining five were children (T. Jackman pers. comm.). An adjacent site at Goldington was a henge type enclosure which contained an inner ring of post holes and cremations in collared urns. As yet no radiocarbon dates are available for these sites, but it would appear that Goldington was used as a funerary/ritual site for a considerable period. Preliminary results suggest that food consumption also took place on site. Goldington, compared to other excavated sites nearby, such as in the Willington Plantation, has produced a relatively larger animal bone assemblage, with a high percentage of meat-bearing cattle bones with clear evidence for butchery.

In the past soil analysis, including that of buried soils, has failed to provide a clear environmental

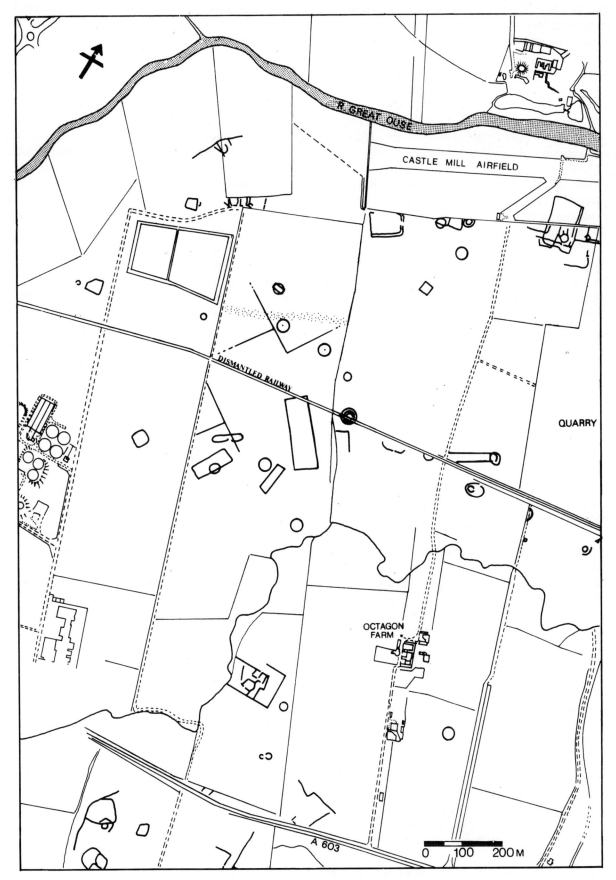

Fig. 22. The early prehistoric landscape of the Bedford area.

history of sites or their context. At Goldington a   Bronze Age buried soil was examined using micromorphological techniques. Preliminary results suggest the local environment had undergone extensive cultivation and that, prior to its burial, the soil was a mature but wet grassland (R. Macphail, pers. comm.). This would support the view taken by the present writers that the well drained terraces of the Ouse were well cleared of trees in the earlier neolithic period. Unfortunately, soil pollen samples failed to provide detail on the vegational history (P. Wiltshire, pers. comm.).

South of the river Ouse, but within close proximity to Goldington, a series of small-scale excavations and field surveys have added further information with regard to prehistoric settlement in the Ouse valley. A group of nearby ring ditches between Bedford and Willington have produced tentative evidence that they date to the neolithic period. At Mill Farm a ring ditch produced a central pit with a double inhumation similar to that found at Goldington. The bones, however, were in very poor condition. At Willington, a square enclosure produced a central pit containing a female inhumation and above the body a red deer antler had been deposited. Potsherds from the associated ditch were undatable, but the association with a red deer antler and other ring ditches in the immediate area could suggest a neolithic date. A second ring ditch in the same group produced a central pit containing poorly-preserved pig skull fragments, together with flint flakes of probable neolithic date and pottery that also dates to the later neolithic period.

The Cardington cursus complex has recently been the subject of archaeological evaluation. The Cardington group of sites occupies an area south of the first river terrace of the Ouse and immediately north of the Elstow brook. Both Goldington and the other ring ditches occupy adjacent land. The cropmarks show a series of rectangular enclosures, a possible cursus and numerous ring ditches, including a further triple ring ditch. The orientation of the cursus and the rectangular enclosures suggests common alignments and archaeological work was conducted over a large area in order to confirm preservation and the date range for the group of sites. Preliminary soil studies suggest that these monuments were located in a relatively wet environment and that some of the monuments appear to have been positioned on natural rises in the otherwise flat topography of the area.

Fieldwalking has produced a relatively large assemblage of neolithic and Bronze Age flint, including leaf-shaped arrowheads and thumb-nail scrapers. Three polished stone axes and a red

deer antler "macehead" were also recovered from the same field by farm workers. The distribution of the lithic material is interesting in that the main concentrations of material are reduced in quantity within the enclosures area. This might suggest that domestic and any other activity associated with flint tools did not take place inside the enclosures. Small-scale excavation provided stratigaphical evidence indicating that one of the large rectangular enclosures was sealed by a later ring ditch. A geophysical survey has also indicated that a smaller rectangular enclosure predates the construction of a later ring ditch immediately above it (J. Gater, pers. comm.). This has been confirmed by recent trial excavations. A further enclosure produced a single 'sherd of pottery. The form of the vessel has affinities with carinated bowls of earlier neolithic date (A. Ap-Simon & D. Tomlin, pers. comm.). The fabric itself is shell tempered and in many ways is similar to the Mildenhall pottery from Goldington.

The main concentration of enclosures has been the subject of a detailed geophysical survey (Geophysical Surveys of Bradford 1991). This produced evidence for further ring ditches and likely enclosures. The possibility of a henge type site within this group was also suggested by a ring ditch with a much bigger and deeper ditch, together with evidence for an internal bank. Recent work has confirmed the presence of internal pit features containing a few flint flakes.

The Cardington complex belongs to a group of neolithic and early Bronze Age sites that have a geographical distribution extending through the Midlands from the Trent valley across to the North Sea and as far south as the Upper Thames. Similar sites include West Cotton, Stratford St. Mary and Lechlade (Loveday 1989). They have been referred to as Barford-type complexes (Loveday 1989) and are often characterised as having a cursus as a central element with large rectangular enclosures and ring ditches. Henges are sometimes directly associated with such groups. Published radiocarbon dates for such sites are limited, but they would appear to centre on the earlier third millennium and extend into the early Bronze Age. This suggests a relatively long tradition of use. The evidence from Goldington indicates that this relatively long term activity was also present on the north bank of the river Ouse where the date range of pottery extends from deposits with Mildenhall pottery to cremations in collared urns in the "hengiform" site. It is perhaps significant that the distribution of Barford-type complexes does not appear to extend into the area of the Chilterns covered by this book and future work should focus on regional variation in monument types. As to their precise function, the enclosures have been considered as possible long mortuary enclosures and, with the proximity of numerous ring ditches some of which contain burials, it is difficult to argue against such an idea. In addition, it has been suggested that sites of a similar date and ground plan, such as Dorchester on Thames and Godmanchester, were aligned with the movements of the sun and moon, e.g. the midwinter sunset or midsummer moonset (Bradley & Chambers 1988; F. McAvoy, pers. comm.). Bradley (Bradley & Chambers 1988) has noted the possibility that during the mid-third millennium BC there was a fundamental change in ideology that saw a shift from beliefs centred on the moon to attention focusing on the sun and that this happened at a similar time to a change from collective to individual burial. Certainly, at Cardington the associated burial tradition would appear to relate to individual burial.

Bronze Age ring ditches and environment at Barton-le-Clay

More central to the main theme of the present volume are the excavations carried out south of Barton-le-Clay on the northern limit of the Chilterns (Clark 1991). In 1989 a group of three plough damaged ring ditches was excavated in advance of road construction. In terms of cultural material the site was relatively poor, although a single cremation in a biconical urn was excavated from a central pit. Fragments of pottery suggest that the earliest phase of ring ditch construction might have dated to the late neolithic period.

The important aspect of the site was the environmental information extracted from the snail samples (Allen 1991). Compared to other areas of southern England only limited environmental work has been conducted in the Chilterns and the Barton snail assemblage has provided important evidence on landscape and vegetational history.

As there was no evidence of relict wooodland snails, it would appear that the ring ditches were constructed in a well-established open hawthorn sere landscape. It is therefore likely that tree clearance occurred sometime in the neolithic period and tree hollows predating the ring ditches support this. Evidence for relict woodland can be seen elsewhere in the Chilterns, for example in Buckinghamshire at Pink Hill and Pitstone, with clearance at the latter site radiocarbon dated to 1,960 ± 220 bc [2,459 cal BC] (Evans 1972). This is a relatively late date compared to the Ouse valley and elsewhere in southern Britain.

The Barton-le-Clay snail histograms indicate two periods of major clearance that have been recorded elsewhere in the Chilterns, but have until now remained undated. The first period can now be confidently dated to the late neolithic-early Bronze Age and it has a similar composition to dry valley deposits at Coombe Bottom and Wing Hall in Hertfordshire (Waton 1982). It is now argued by Allen (1991) that these also belong to the late neolithic - early Bronze Age period. The character of all three snail assemblages suggest non-intensive use of the landscape, possibly light grazing. One question that needs to be addressed, however, is just how widespread this low activity was. Land use might have been very localised, with ring ditch activity on the periphery of more intensive land use associated with arable farming. Indeed a similar pattern can be seen in the Ouse valley where ring ditches appear in what were seasonally very wet areas and therefore on the periphery of drier farm land (e.g. Biddenham Loop).

The second period of post-clearance activity at Barton-le-Clay was initially late Bronze Age and Iron Age in date and the snail evidence suggests open dry grassland with arable activity. It is certain that this intensification of farming continued throughout the Romano-British period. The evidence at Barton was for an increase in colluvial deposits, destruction of possible bank/mound material associated with the ring ditches and the cutting of a negative lynchet across the site. Elsewhere in the Chilterns land snails from Bledlow Cop, Bucks. (Kennard 1938) suggest that this widespread arable activity also had its origins in the Bronze Age, but the main colluvial deposits date from the Iron Age and Romano-British periods when agricultural activity became more intensive.

The Romano-British landscape of Bedfordshire

The limited amount of environmental work so far conducted in Bedfordshire would suggest that the physical environment to which the Romans came in the first century AD was probably similar to that of the present day and that intensive agriculture was being practised throughout the county. However, differential alluvial deposition in the Ouse valley (Keeley 1987, 53) dating to either the end of the Romano-British period at Clapham (Tilson 1973) or the beginning of the third century AD at Warren Villas indicates changes in the hydrological environment which will have influenced local settlement patterns at different times. This view is being refined in detailed excavation. At Kempston Church End, Romano-British ditches and graves were cut through alluvium which had probably been deposited by the

Ouse in the late Iron Age, whilst at Eastcotts assessment trenches indicated alluvial deposition by the Elstow brook in the late third century AD.

Information on the vegetational environment of Bedfordshire immediately before and during the Romano-British period is now being gathered. Analysis of pollen deposits from sites such as Ruxox and Warren Villas and carbonised remains from Sandy and Kempston Church End, although at an early stage, is allowing the development of a tentative framework. At several sites, e.g. Salford, Stratton, Willington and Gold Lane, Biddenham, there is evidence of earlier prehistoric tree clearance on the gravels. Whilst much of this is likely to date to the neolithic period aerial photograph evidence of restricted field systems around some Iron Age and Romano-British sites may indicate the presence of extensive, possibly managed, woodland. At Warren Villas, in the Ivel valley, field systems laid out by the late first century BC may have occupied woodland clearings.

Further local variation is evident. Late Iron Age plough furrows at Warren Villas associated with ditches contain weed flora of such species as *Isolepis setacea* (brittle scirpus) and *Polygonum persicaria* (Red shank) which suggests that ploughing was taking place under very wet conditions. At Ruxox pollen analysis of samples from an old river channel close to the Romano-British site has provided preliminary evidence to suggest that here large scale arable cultivation extended close to the river's edge (R. Scaife, pers. comm.). At Sandy, below Caesar's Camp, the earliest settlement developed in an area of grazed pasture, suggesting Iron Age exploitation of the slopes of the Greensand ridge.

Recent research into late Iron Age and Romano-British settlement patterns has given greater insight into regional aspects of landscape development. As late as 1973 evidence of Iron Age settlement had been dominated by pottery studies (Simco 1973) with few sites excavated. Ten years later Knight (1984, 304) was able to use a wider range of excavation evidence in a study which concentrated on landscape aspects of the Ouse and Nene valleys. Knight, perhaps surprisingly, concluded that settlement density in the hinterland of the two valleys was unaffected by soil differences noting, however, a predilection for sites on south-east facing slopes. At Stagsden two settlement sites have been excavated recently that seem to sustain this view. One on the edge of the clay, west of the modern village, indicates exploitation of the heavier soils (calcareous gley soils of the Hanslope series) had begun by the first century BC whilst the second site actually occupies a

tongue of gleyed brown earth of the Milton series, part of the Ouse drainage. Detailed examination, therefore, of the soil types at Stagsden and Salford suggests that a proportion of sites superficially in clay areas actually occupy islands of brown earth above glacial drift gravels or minor, now dry, embayments of major river valleys.

In the Romano-British period settlement was similarly once thought to be dominated by sites on the lighter soils with only sparse settlement in the Oxford Clay vale and Woburn Park, where the soils are acid on decalcified boulder clay (Simco 1982, 10), and the northern claylands. Recent aerial photographs of increasingly plough-damaged sites on the clay ridges in the northern parishes of Melchboure, Yelden and Little Stoughton indicate a higher density of isolated farms (Fig. 23) which, although unexcavated, may be evidence of occupation from the late Iron Age and into the Romano-British period.

On the lighter soils three settlements of the late Iron Age/early Romano-British period, all occupying rising ground or prominent sites, have recently been excavated: Salford was occupied from the late Bronze Age through to the Iron Age and had over 23 round houses enclosed within a palisade; Gold Lane, Biddenham, occupied in the middle Iron Age, was enclosed within a double ditch; and Stagsden (Site 2) which had possibly five round houses inside a single ditched enclosure was occupied from at least the first century BC probably into the Romano-British period. Dates, for the latter, are based on preliminary pottery spot dates.

Other site types have not been so extensively investigated. On the higher ground of the chalk, the clay scarp and the Greensand Ridge are hillforts but no recent work has taken place on these so that little is known of the occupation of the main sites: Mowsbury; Caesar's Camp, Sandy; Topler's Hill, Arlesey; and Sharpenhoe. It is clear that two of these univallate sites, Sandy and Arlesey, could have remained occupied until the conquest. Arlesey has been postulated as an 'oppida' (Haselgrove 1990), but the site has not been examined in detail.

The interrelationship of Britain and the Roman Empire is evident in the southern part of the county during the late first century BC and first century AD when Roman artefacts are used as the grave furniture of Aylesford-Swarling (Birchall 1965) and Welwyn burials (Stead 1967) at Standfordbury, Old Warden, Felmersham and Hill Grounds, Kempston. The traditions of tribal groups in north-western Europe are seen to in-

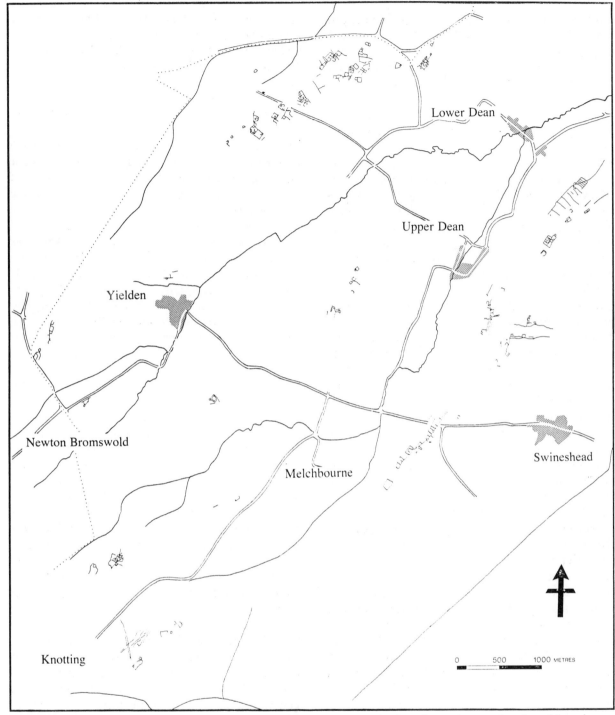

Fig. 23. Cropmark sites which have begun to appear through plough erosion on the clay ridges in parishes in the north of the county. These probably date to the late Iron Age and Romano-British periods.

fluence pottery designs which led to hybrid style now often referred to as 'Belgic' wares. As these Gallo-Belgic forms came to dominate the first century BC, the process has been interpreted not only as indicating the dominance of migrant Belgae, but also with the increasing political influence of Rome itself (Simco 1984, 11-15; Simco 1973, 10-14). Ultimately the development of the so-called 'oppida' and the increasing density of lowland settlement (Knight 1984, Fig. 72) has been interpreted as a response to Roman economic stimulus which, in turn, led to social and

political change. This increasing influence is evident most clearly on settlement sites only when imported pottery appears in the first century AD.

This has led to the development of an historical model for the period which has been most extensively developed by Branigan (1985, 4-31). Branigan linked the Chilterns and Bedfordshire through the distribution of common elements: Gallo-Belgic pottery, the distribution of Allen's LX coinage and the increasing import of Roman artefacts to Caesar's description of the Belgae and the later reference to the civitas Catuvellauni in order to define the geographical extent of the kingdom and what later became the 'territorium' of the Catuvellauni. At its widest this territory, he argues, may have stretched from Essex to Hertfordshire, Buckingham and possibly as far north as the Nene Valley. The general validity of this type of historical model building has been questioned (Millett 1990, 11-28) and there are several weaknesses in Branigan's arguments for the inclusion of the Bedfordshire area in the territory of the Catuvellauni. One major weakness is the lack of excavated evidence (Simco 1984) which left Branigan to concentrate on Hertfordshire and Buckinghamshire, drawing the northern hinterland of the Chilterns only into the territory because of the Welwyn burials.

The territory of the Catuvellauni remains elusive and evidence from the invasion period is sparse. Military operations during the conquest of the eastern part of Iron Age Britain have left little mark on Bedfordshire. The invasion routes may be fossilised in what later became the Ermine Street and Watling Street (Frere 1967, 73) but marching forts indicating the direction of campaigns have not been located in the county, nor any other evidence of offensive military action. Haselgrove (1989) has suggested that several die-linked Iron Age coins from the Sandy area may indicate the presence of a political centre. This raises the possibility that the territory as that of an allied tribe did not merit a strong garrison. Recent excavations at Sandy cemetery have established the presence of a predominantly later Roman settlement but reports of animal and human burial from the nineteenth century, as well as quantities of late Iron Age pottery, suggest the site was preceded by an earlier settlement, not necessarily that at Caesar's Camp (Johnson 1974). Sealed below the later Roman site a small stream bed yielded 36 Iron Age coins, including a gold stater of Tasciovanus, which may indicate a ritual area adjacent to a larger settlement.

The construction of roads in the county may have begun soon after the Conquest. In the west the Watling Street passing through Dunstable was completed by the mid-first century AD. Despite the fact that the major military routes largely bypassed the present area of Bedfordshire, a road built early in the period (Green 1975) from Baldock to Godmanchester passes through Sandy, perhaps indicating the status of Sandy as well as the importance of river-based routeways (Simco 1984, Fig. 66).

Evidence of early Roman influence, possibly predating the construction of the roads, comes from several cemetery sites. There are early cremation cemeteries, e.g. Sandy, Grovebury, Richmond Hill, Shefford, Pegsden Common, Shillington, Silsoe (?and Toddington) and Whipsnade, which are known only through the evidence of chance or antiquarian finds. But at two sites where excavation has recently taken place, Deepdale (Dawson & Slowikowski 1988) and Harlington, the appearence of early local Romanised pottery (Deepdale) and Claudio-Neronian Samian (Harlington) suggest, at least, the adoption of Roman customs soon after the conquest by some groups within the indigenous populations. Early Samian is unusual in rural areas but when found is often associated with burial and Iron Age sites of high status. At Harlington the Iron age settlement was destroyed by quarrying in the 1960s and is evident now only from a large assemblage of pottery which has been recovered from the spoil tips. Even so there is sufficient late pre-Roman Iron Age pottery to postulate a site of considerable status (S. Castle pers. comm.).

There is still only slight evidence to support the contention that 'Iron Age' settlements continued to be occupied into the second century AD. At the second of the sites at Stagsden, east of the modern village, Samian ware has been tentatively interpreted as evidence that settlement continued into the early second century and two semi-sunken kilns (Swann 1984, Fig. III i) and one of more orthodox Roman form suggest continuity of use (Slowikowski this volume). The results of archaeomagnetic dating (Clark 1992) of the kilns which centre on the mid-first century AD suggest the focus of the Romano-British settlement had shifted away from the earliest Iron Age structures.

One class of rural settlement that has been excavated is the villa. The appearence of this type of structure in the landscape of Britain began as early as the late first century AD. In Bedford this generalisation remains to be tested. Newnham Marina (Simco 1984, 26) has Belgic pottery as evidence of early activity at the site but the structure of the villa was only erected in the second century AD.

Cropmarks at the site of the Bletsoe villa and others may indicate that these sites fall into the class of monument characterised by Stanwick and Gorhambury (Neal et al. 1990), where villas succeed earlier Iron Age settlement. At the Kempston Church End villa a circular stone structure nearby, possibly the foundation of a part-timbered roundhouse, may indicate an Iron Age precursor. The lack of associated finds, however, may disguise a concurrent area of habitation.

Perhaps surprisingly our understanding of the development of villas in the county is poor. This situation has arisen either because few excavations have been published or because excavation has been on a small scale. Bidwell has produced box flue tiles and wood pile foundations (Matthews 1989, Pl. 18) from a single trench and at Totternhoe a series of trenches through the main structure of the building was the basis for analysis which suggested two phases of building (Matthews *et al.* 1992). The Newnham Marina villa had been quarried away in the 1950s and only the remains of a bathhouse were excavated between 1972-5 (Simco 1984, 97). More extensive excavations at Kempston Church End in 1991 may illuminate details of the final demise of this villa in the Ouse valley, for amongst the ruins of the villa structure were the remains of burials dating from the fifth to seventh century. This site is only at the preliminary stage of post-excavation analysis.

At other sites villas have been proposed from a combination of evidence, usually the discovery of building materials such as roofing tiles or box flue tiles associated with aerial photograph plots. In two instances excavation has taken place on the periphery of the villa. At Bletsoe the cemetery was excavated during the period 1969-71 (Dawson 1994) and at Ruxox the cemetery was excavated in 1991, both cemeteries dating to the late Roman period.

Recent survey work has shown that more of these site types remain to be discovered: a new site, at Meppershall located on the Petrofina pipeline, was revealed during trenching hidden beneath colluvium. On the Biddenham loop two further sites have been noted recently, one from aerial photographs and the second during building work.

None of the villa sites so far has produced evidence of industry on a scale sufficient to propose an alternative economic base to agriculture (*cf.* Percival 1976, 162-3). There is no evidence of imperial ownership or other forms of tenure which might be responsible for the growth of villas. A factor common to these sites is that they show a preference for lighter, easy to work soils: either the marl soils of the Chilterns area or the river gravels of the Ouse, Ivel and Flit. Thus the soil type may have been fundamentally important to the estate in providing the means to create sufficient agricultural surpluses to afford the new building techniques.

Towns and villas are taken to epitomise the economic changes brought about by Rome which impact most clearly on the landscape. There are two sites commonly referred to as Roman small

towns in the county: Sandy and Dunstable. Dunstable, identified from the Antonine Itinerary as Durocobrivis, has produced little structural evidence, possibly because of extensive scarping in the medieval period. The discovery of an extensive late Roman cemetery beneath the remains of a monastic orchard at Friary Field (Matthews 1981), though, indicates the possibility that more structural evidence awaits discovery.

In the towns the combination of geographical and political factors can be seen most clearly to have led to separate development patterns. Although still lacking detailed evidence, Dunstable (Matthews 1989, 67-70) developed in the second century, nearly two hundred years earlier than Sandy which probably reached its floriut in the fourth century AD.

The early development of Roman Sandy is especially complex as the Roman settlement existed close to the site of an Iron Age settlement as well as the univallate hillfort at Ceasar's Camp. Extensive excavations in the municipal cemetery of the modern town have revealed the remains of a late Roman settlement. This preliminary date, derived from pottery spot dating on imported wares from the 1989 and 1990 seasons, appears to confirm evidence from 1,218 coins of largely third and fourth centuries date recovered from the site. The site, north of the Ermine street loop, occupies an embayment of the Greensand Ridge and the topography, antiquarian discoveries and minor excavations (Johnson 1974) suggest the settlement extended for nearly 10 hectares straddling the Baldock-Godmanchester road. There is no evidence of a fort at the site.

Preliminary results of excavations from 1987-1991 suggest the town had at least three phases during which part-timbered structures were built flanking a minor road adjacent to which areas of craft activity developed. The largest of the structures occupied a site at least 15 m across, whilst the smaller were probably single celled. Expansion of the settlement, or possibly shift within it, was particularly clear in one area where four buildings had been erected over the silted-up course of an earlier stream.

There was sufficient dispersed tile debris, tegula, imbrex and box-flue to suggest that near the area of excavation there was at least one substantial stone building. The position of Sandy on the Roman road network between Baldock and Godmanchester indicates this may have been a *mansio*, the site of the building probably being on the slope between the area of excavation and the Potton Road.

The adoption of Roman architecture at Sandy is not only evident from the buildings which have been interpreted as houses but from a large sandstone relief. This depicts two figures in Celtic costume giving offerings to a third figure which can probably be identified as a local goddess. The relief may have formed part of the pediment of a building, possibly a temple (Appleton & Dawson forthcoming).

The spatial distribution of buildings and craft areas indicated a tendency to create specialised zones which remained in use throughout the occupation of the settlement. Imposed upon this pattern, amongst the excavated buildings, were several areas of burial. These were all inhumations and are broadly dated to the late Roman period. They exhibit a variety of burial forms from simple supine inhumation to complex flexed burial; there were three multiple burials. Several burials were accompanied by pottery vessels used as grave goods. Burial evidence can also be adduced to demonstrate the adoption of Roman practice. Over 18 infant burials were recovered from around the buildings, some quite specifically placed close to or under the eaves of the structures, *subgrundarius* (Watts 1989, 372).

The economic impact of Rome on the landscape, superficially clearest in the towns and villas, is evident in rural areas (Hingley 1989, 21). Some advances have been made in identifying ways of defining relationships between sites beyond spatial distributions. Fineware pottery, including Samian, amphorae and coins are present on many sites and may form the basis for such study (*cf.* Going 1987). The recent excavations at Warren Villas and Stagsden have revealed early kilns which may indicate a response to the creation of new markets. When detailed analysis begins, these may illustrate aspects of broader distribution networks. Using ceramics as a benchmark for economic activity cannot, however, be used alone to express the complexity of the developing economy. In other crafts evidence suggests continuity with activities practised in the Iron Age (Simco 1984, 33-54) but, without detailed analysis of distribution patterns, the small scale of production centres suggests that only local markets were served. Thus increased awareness of the density of settlement in Iron Age and Romano-British Bedfordshire achieved in recent years has yet to be supplemented by an increase in our understanding of the interrelationship of sites. It is in this area that major advances remain to be made.

The end of the Romano-British period in Bedfordshire and the transitional stage to the early mediaeval period, whilst attracting speculation as to a long surviving British enclave (Rutherford Davis 1982), has yielded little specific evidence to define the process of change (Wingfield this volume). At Sandy the decline is evident from a deep build-up of black soil, with only slight evidence for plough damage to the latest structural horizon. At Kempston Church End there is an early mediaeval cemetery with burials dating to the seventh century and earlier burials are known from Luton, Sandy and Kempston but there is no structural sequence yet established to link the two elements. Consequently, this aspect of change in the landscape joins the list of those areas that offer the greatest potential for investigation in the future.

Conclusion

This short report on prehistoric and Romano-British sites in the Ouse valley has attempted to show how work initiated in the 1970s has developed since then. Work on the Cardington cursus complex will add significantly to our knowledge of this type of site, although compared to other parts of Britain, very little work has been conducted on neolithic and Bronze Age ritual sites. In the next few years archaeological work in response to development pressures could add significantly to this growing body of information. For the later prehistoric period, aerial photography and excavation evidence continues to emphasise regional variability and to increase knowledge of the density of settlement.

For the Romano-British period, a general model for developed rural settlement first proposed as a result of the Fenland Survey (Hallam 1970) has, however, not been tested in Bedfordshire. It is clear that there is a gap in excavated evidence between the 'villa' and other rural settlement. Only Ruxox and Limbury, sites which have not been investigated extensively, and the cropmark site at Willington have so far been identified with rural settlement of the type referred to as hamlet/small village (e.g. Hingley 1989, 76). Without further evidence the immediate impact of the Roman invasion on the Iron Age settlement pattern remains elusive.

New sites of all periods are still being discovered in the county although there is a bias to the Romano-British period which yields a higher proportion of recognisable finds (see Hudspith this volume) and to those areas designated for development by modern economic demands. Increased emphasis on field survey has demonstrated human occupation from the early post-glacial period, particularly on land adjacent to the river Great Ouse. In many cases no physical

remains relating to settlement survive and artefact scatters in the plough soil are the only
evidence indicating activities ranging from hunting to permanent settlements.

IRON AGE AND ROMANO-BRITISH SETTLEMENT, AGRICULTURE AND INDUSTRY IN THE UPPER BULBOURNE VALLEY, HERTFORDSHIRE: AN INTERIM INTERPRETATION

Michael Morris and Angus Wainwright

Introduction

The upper Bulbourne valley and adjacent areas have been the focus of sporadic archaeological investigation and survey during the past 15 years. This has revealed considerable evidence for late Iron Age and Romano-British occupation, including a substantial settlement at Cow Roast. Most of the excavation work has been undertaken by members of the Berkhamsted and District Archaeological Society in advance of proposed development. The value of this work has been greatly enhanced by the landscape survey of the adjacent plateau of land between the Bulbourne and Gade valleys. This was carried out by Angus Wainwright for the National Trust between 1985 and 1989 and revealed extensive evidence of late Iron Age/Romano-British settlement and agriculture. Most of the archaeological evidence for the area is as yet unpublished and the following preliminary summary seeks to bring to wider attention its significance for regional and national archaeological research.

The valley forms a major north-west/south-east route through the Chiltern hills, opening onto the Vale of Aylesbury at the Tring gap 4 km to the north-west where it meets the Upper Icknield Way. The predominant soil in the vicinity is a stiff reddish clay with large unworn flints. This lies irregularly over the chalk, which outcrops in places along the east side of the valley. Along the valley bottom alluvium lies over the chalk.

Archaeological fieldwork in the Cow Roast area

Most of the excavated evidence comes from the Cow Roast area (Fig. 36) centered on NGR SP 958102 at OSD 120 m, on either side of the modern A41 and close to the old river course. It can be summarised as follows (Fig. 24.).

A1. Fendley House (the Orchard site, behind the Cow Roast Inn). Excavation of an area of approx. 30 m x 40 m in advance of proposed motorway construction produced evidence dating from *c.*40 BC to the fourth century AD (Rook 1976). Over 80 features were excavated, including several well shafts, pits and beam-slots. Two bowl furnaces with tapslag, hearths and smithing waste were

also located. Small finds included numerous iron objects. A substantial collection of animal bones was also recovered, preliminary analysis of which suggests possible evidence of livestock production for market. A small excavation was also carried out in the car park behind the Cow Roast Inn. The main feature recorded here was a well shaft with several late third century coins in the backfill.

A2. Esso site. Adjacent to site A1 observation of the footings of two bungalows revealed numerous finds from pits, and a possible road surface was recorded. Much iron slag was observed in the fields around this development.

A3. Marina site. This site produced 1½ tons of iron slag along with several timber well shafts and a north-south metalled road probably leading to the masonry structure (site A2).

A4. A41 sewer pipeline. This work demonstrated the probable limits of the settlement to west and east with several furnaces, pits and occupation surfaces occurring in between.

A5. Chapman Garage. Features recorded during evaluation work by Herts. Archaeological Trust on this site included Romano-British pits and ditches.

A6. Cow Roast geophysical survey 1974 and 1976 (position not illustrated). Magnetometer surveys produced evidence for substantial settlement to the south of the modern A41. The line of Roman Akeman Street was also pinpointed (Bartlett 1974; Haddon Rees 1976).

A7. Roman masonry building. This structure is known only from the remains of one wall; the remainder was destroyed during the construction of the railway. Numerous 'sherds and tiles have been found at this location.

A8. Dudswell lock helmet. In 1811, during the construction of Dudswell lock, a Roman military helmet was found. It is now in the British Museum.

A9. Boswick Lane. A detailed watching brief carried out on this site in 1977 revealed 16 pits,

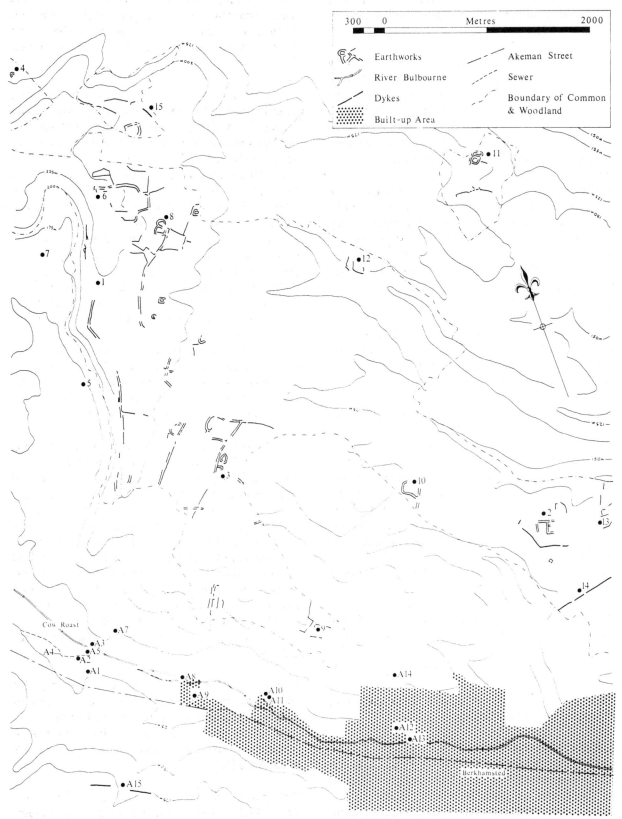

Fig. 24. General plan of the archæological evidence for the upper Bulbourne valley. The modern A41 follows the line of Akeman Street through Berkhamsted but takes a more northerly course through Cow Roast.

including some possible well shafts and the remains of five probable iron smelting furnaces. There was also a Neronian cremation burial with at least two vessels. A range of Romano-British small finds and a quantity of samian ware was also recovered.

A10. Northchurch Roman villa. The villa was excavated in advance of housing development in the 1970s (Neal 1977).

A11. Northchurch circular building. Circular masonry foundations were observed during houseing development adjacent to the villa site. This structure had flint footings and a chalk floor with a central post. About 80 third century coins were found within the floor. It may well have been associated with the villa (site A10 above).

A12. and A13. Easts Woodyard and Billet Lane Gasworks, Berkhamsted. Roman finds were discovered on these sites during watching briefs. The Berkhamsted and District Archaeological Society have also made several other chance discoveries of Roman finds suggestive of ribbon development along the line of Akeman Street through Berkhamsted.

A14. Dellfield, Berkhamsted. Several iron-smelting shaft furnaces and late Iron Age/early Romano-British burials were excavated at this site (Thompson & Holland 1977).

A15. Grims Ditch. This is a dyke system comprising several disjointed segments of earthwork. There are divergent opinions regarding its date, form and function but current opinion is that it was probably a middle Iron Age territorial boundary system, perhaps demarcating upland and lowland spheres of influence. It may have been subject to modifications and additions and there is the possibility that it was still functional in some respects during the lifetime of the Cow Roast settlement (see Crawford 1931; Dyer 1963; Davis & Evans 1984).

A16. Tring Motorway (c.3 km west of Cow Roast: position not illustrated). During the construction of the A41M Tring Bypass an undated shaft furnace with associated slag was observed.

The Ashridge Survey: a late Iron Age and Romano-British Landscape

The Ashridge estate comprises an area of 1,620 ha on the ridge between the Bulbourne and Gade valleys. The estate stretches from Ivinghoe Beacon in the north to Berkhamsted Common to the south. An additional area of Berkhamsted Common not owned by the Trust was also surveyed; this amounted to about 175 ha. Apart from an area of chalk downland at the north extremity, the land is clay with flints with some outcrops of gravel and chalk in the small valleys. Most of the area (c.1,290 ha) was either common or woodland up until the last century. These areas have never

been cultivated in historical times; it is for this reason that the ancient earthworks have survived (note that for the sake of clarity all medieval and later features have been removed from the figures).

Five late Iron Age or Romano-British sites had been identified before the commencement of the survey. Two of these were masonry buildings, one at Moneybury hill (SP 971136) overlooking Aldbury (Neal 1978) (Fig. 24, site 1), the other (TL 004099) on high ground above Berkhamsted (Neal *ibid*.: Fig. 24, site 2). A third site (SP 976123, Herts. SMR 2534) is known from pottery and quern stones turned up by the plough (Fig. 24, site 3). A penannular enclosure (SP 970157) was partially excavated in 1971; this site is on low ground at the head of the Gade valley (Dunnett 1972; Fig. 24, site 4). The last site was a Belgic cemetery in Aldbury (Herts. SMR 4242) excavated by schoolchildren in 1943 (Fig. 24, site 5).

The presence of the first three sites on the heavy and stony soils of the plateau had been something of a puzzle but the survey showed these were not isolated sites but were, in fact, components of a well-developed agricultural landscape.

This landscape is characterised by a surprising number of enclosures and settlement sites, irregularly-shaped fields of various sizes defined by lynchets, sunken drove-ways and occasional dykes. Features have been dated by archaeological excavation in only three cases. Elsewhere dating came from surface scatters of pottery or finds made in the root plates of fallen trees, rabbit holes or other such random natural excavations. Those features which have been dated with certainty were created either immediately before the Roman invasion or during the following century. There is very little material of the third or fourth centuries.

Enclosures and settlements. Taking the enclosures and settlements sites first, fourteen banked enclosures were discovered in the survey area. The enclosures are predominantly sub-rectangular, enclosing areas ranging from 225 m^2 to almost 2 ha.

Dating of all these features has not yet been possible. Only a few features have produced quantities of 'Belgic' pottery (grog-tempered wares which could date from either before or after the invasion) or distinctively Romano-British pottery; the remainder have produced no such material and are unrelated to other dateable features such as field boundaries. Most must be pre-medieval as they lie on common land where manorial custom

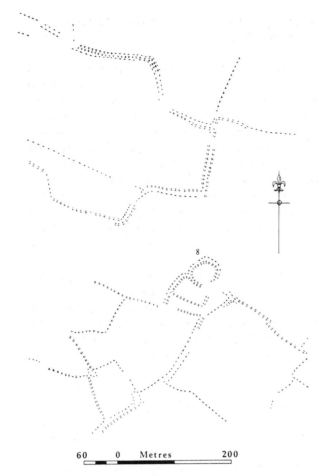

Fig. 25. Part of a field system at SP 978141 showing small irregular fields, meandering droveways and related enclosure (site 8).

did not allow enclosures of any sort.

At least three enclosures are joined to field systems (Fig. 24, sites 8, 10, 11; site 8 is shown in detail in Fig. 25); two of these show signs of adaptation and compartmentalisation of the enclosed area and the degradation of the bank and ditch during the life of the enclosure. Significantly these three have all produced 'Belgic' pottery and one has also produced quantities of distinctively Roman wares. These sites were no doubt farmsteads.

Other enclosures are not obviously related to field boundaries (site 3: Figs. 24 & 26). No dating evidence has been found in these; this may be due to the random distribution of fallen trees and rabbit burrows which were often the only method of obtaining samples from features or because of the use to which these enclosures were put, for example stock pounds. The fact that this category of enclosure is not respected by the field boundaries suggests that they may be later additions to the landscape, created after arable cultivation had ceased. In the absence of dating evidence, this will remain a tentative interpretation of the

evidence. It should be noted that nowhere is a field boundary cut by one of these enclosures.

Including the enclosures just mentioned, ten settlement sites producing 'Belgic' and Romano-British material were identified within the survey area (Fig. 24, sites 1, 2, 3, 4, 6, 7, 8, 9, 10 & 11). Two of these were not defined by any visible earthwork (Fig. 24, sites 2 & 6). These produced predominantly 'Belgic' pottery but site 6 also produced large quantities of Romano-British pottery and tile, suggesting a long history of occupation. Three sites are now wholly or partially under the plough and their original form is as yet unknown (Fig. 24, sites 3, 7 & 10). Two sites are known to include masonry buildings (Fig. 24, sites 1 & 2).

Possible religious buildings. The building at Moneybury Hill (Fig. 24, site 1) was excavated in 1938; unfortunately no records were kept of this work, but coins ranging from one of Cunobelin to one of Allectus have been found on or near the site. The building stands in an unusual and prominent position (OSD 222 m) on the scarp edge next to a large bell barrow and a group of medieval holloways. This position is one of the few places in the area where it is possible to ascend the scarp, making it likely that this route

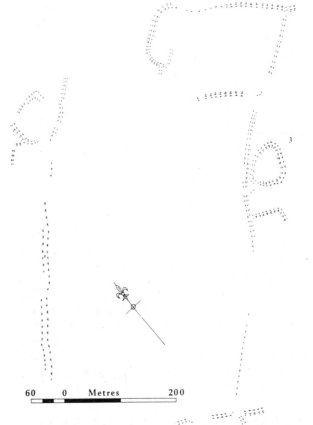

Fig. 26. Part of a field system at SP 976114 showing large sub-rectangular fields with boundary droveways and separate enclosure (site 3).

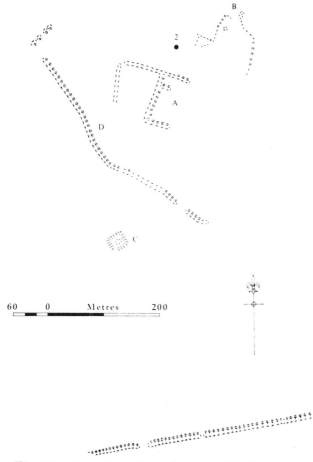

Fig. 27. Location of site 2, a possible Romano-British religious building at TL 004099. A = enclosure, B = possible barrows, C = possible temple or mausoleum, D = dyke.

was also used in antiquity.

The building on Berkhamsted Common (Frithsden) (site 2: Figs. 24 & 27) was discovered in 1927 during the construction of Berkhamsted Golf Course. This building is on one of the highest points in the area (OSD 168 m) and is some distance from the nearest known early fields (Fig. 24, site 13). Next to the site is an incomplete or slighted enclosure (Fig. 27, site A); a few metres away to the east are two small mounds, possibly barrows (site B). A hundred metres to the south on the crest of the ridge is a small square enclosure (900 m²) with a raised area in the centre (site C). This feature has been interpreted speculatively as a temple or mausoleum. The larger enclosure and building are flanked by a considerable dyke, although in the absence of any dating evidence the apparent association may be coincidental (site D).

The original function of the two buildings is puzzling; their extremely prominent but exposed situation seems to argue against a domestic function but the situation combined with the proximity of barrows in both cases might suggest a religious function.

The field boundaries. The main area of fields (centred at SP 975130) stretches from the scarp edge for about 1 km eastwards. To the north and south the earthworks disappear in modern farmland. The fields fall into two categories: the first in the north of this area and around the enclosure (site 8, Fig. 25) is characterised by small irregular shaped fields (*c*.4 ha) bordered by well-defined lynchets and interspersed with meandering droveways. The second type, visible around site 3 (Figs. 24 & 26) appears to be large (perhaps 30 ha) and sub-rectangular; these fields are defined in nearly all cases by slightly sunken droveways and are orientated with the long axis south-west to north-east, parallel to the scarp edge. The fields are bordered along the scarp crest by a roughly surfaced track. It should be noted that these large fields may have been sub-divided by temporary fences which have left no trace.

Similar fields were found in at least five other areas (Fig. 24, sites 9, 10, 11, 12 & 13). These field systems were divided from one another by large tracts of land with no traces of contemporary earthworks. Some of this land, particularly the chalk downland, may have been permanent grazing.

Ironworking. That other areas were wooded is confirmed by frequent finds of iron slag, particularly in the areas nearest the Bulbourne valley. This slag has been found in surface scatters, very often associated with 'Belgic' or Romano-British pottery. Iron smelting requires large amounts of charcoal; this would be derived from woods (possible coppiced) in the immediate area. The source of the iron ore is likely to have been 'Bog Ore' from the Bulbourne valley (G. McDonnell, pers. comm.). Although of similar date it has yet to be demonstrated that this industry was contemporary with the arable exploitation of the area.

The Dykes. The large dykes which are another characteristic of the survey area have not been dated: unfortunately nowhere do the field systems abutt these features. The largest examples are to the south (TL 009092) (Fig. 24, site 14) and north (SP 957157) of the area (not illustrated) and are both known as Grim's Ditch. That to the north on the Downs near Ivinghoe Beacon has been tentatively dated to the Iron Age (Davis & Evans 1984) and is probably associated with a complex of 'Cross Dykes' close by. Two other dykes may be associated with the enclosures which stand nearby; one has been described above (south of site 2, Figs. 24 and 27), the other is close to an undated enclosure in Ringshall Copse (SP 980148: Fig. 24, site 15).

To conclude, the Ashridge survey has demonstrated that the heavy, stony soils of the plateau were well cultivated and well settled at least during the late Iron Age/early Romano-British period. Ashridge is not alone in this respect; the survey had discovered similar field systems and enclosures in comparable situations during its work on other National Trust estates. Particularly good examples can be seen at Bradenham, Bucks. (SU 830981) and at Watlington, Oxon. (SU 708921).

Discussion

Early occupation evidence. Although there have been finds dating from the mesolithic period onwards, little is known about the earlier prehistoric settlement of the area. Settlement in the earlier Iron Age has been demonstrated at Ivinghoe Beacon (Cotton & Frere 1968; Green 1981). More widespread activity is indicated by a scatter of pottery finds across the Ashridge survey area. Continuity of occupation from this period into the Romano-British period may have taken place at the pennanular enclosure in the Gade valley mentioned above (Fig. 24, site 6). Here, unabraded early Iron Age pottery was found in the primary fill of the ditch and late Iron Age and Romano-British cremations were found within the enclosure. The survey also discovered a scatter of Romano-British pottery in a field 100 m to the north-east.

The late Iron Age. The evidence for activity at Cow Roast during this period includes coins, pottery and a burial. Considerable activity in the vicinity can also be surmised: LPRIA burials are also known from Aldbury (Fig. 24, site 5) and Dellfield (site A14). Furthermore, the number and weight of 'Belgic' sherds recovered during fieldwalking and other activities on the adjacent plateau is in fact greater than those definitely attributable to the Romano-British period (although this might merely reflect difficulty in distinguishing between pre- and post-conquest grog-tempered native wares). As has been shown above, several of the landscape features surveyed in this area almost certainly represent farmsteads, field boundaries, droveways and stock enclosures belonging to this period.

What was the character of settlement in the area at this time? This question can perhaps best be approached by reference to the wider changes taking place in Iron Age society. There is growing evidence for increasing differentiation of settlement functions during the late Iron Age in eastern England, perhaps stimulated by a growing competitive market system (Collis 1984b, 182; Haselgrove 1987, 59; 1988, 119-20).

Three broad levels can be identified within the developing regional settlement hierarchy defined by the range and nature of archaeologically visible activities.

1. The major centres at Braughing, Colchester and St Albans stand out as first order settlements.

2. The farmstead enclosures such as those discovered at Ashridge represent a basic unit of settlement.

3. In between the two levels is a spectrum of secondary or subsidiary settlements, tentatively including a possible port and trading centre at Ware (Partridge 1981b), a local chiefly centre at Welwyn and a stronghold at Wheathamstead (Saunders 1982).

It is within this latter, intermediate, level of settlement that Cow Roast can be placed. It appears to have been a substantial centre, despite the lack of structural evidence, a common aspect of late Iron Age sites which have been intensively occupied during the Romano-British period. Significantly, there is no evidence for high status occupation; for example, there would appear to be very few, if any, imports in the ceramic assemblage. There are, however, four tentative indicators for production and market exchange.

1. The possible evidence for pre-Romano-British iron production in this area. Although at this stage it is inconclusive, it is nevertheless plausible. The Dellfield furnaces at Berkhamsted (Fig. 24, site A14) are broadly dated 100 BC to AD100, and it is likely that a proportion of the iron-smelting activity at Cow Roast and the adjacent territory is pre-Roman.

2. The few late Iron Age bronze coins from site A1, Fendley House.

3. The unverified evidence for livestock production from site A1, Fendley House, animal bone assemblage.

4. The economic fluorescence of the site in the early Romano-British period hints that the pre-existing settlement may have been of some economic pretention (see below).

Cow Roast can thus be characterised provisionally at this period as a substantial, ?agricultural village settlement with significant production/market functions, and with several smaller settlements in the vicinity also engaged in agricultural and industrial production. Furthermore, we can speculate that Grim's ditch (e.g. sites A15, 14) retained some significance as a territorial marker between the hilly region and the vale. If this was the case, perhaps Cow Roast lay towards the boundary of two major tribal territories, as defined by Haselgrove's (1987, 56) analysis of the principal regional coin series, serving as a 'gateway' community for the exchange of products between adjacent tribal units.

The Romano-British period. There is some evidence of military activity at Cow Roast in the form of five military bronzes, a pilum head and the Claudian legionary helmet from Dudswell lock (Goodburn 1976) which perhaps relate to a conquest period fort in the vicinity.

Although there is a paucity of building remains from Cow Roast, substantial artifactual evidence and numerous pits, wells and ditches relating to first to fourth century occupation is known. This activity indicates a substantial nucleated roadside settlement acting as one of several subsidiary market centres on the St Albans to Cirencester road (*cf.* Smith 1987, 235). Marketing of agricultural produce is suggested by the unverified evidence for livestock production and, in his analysis of the coin evidence from the site, Richard Reece (1982, 63) concludes that it "is a small rural settlement . . . which prospers early and loses its prosperity or coin use before the rest of the province." The observation of the sewer pipeline (site A4) indicated that occupation spread over perhaps 40 ha. The street aligned at 90 degrees to the line of the Roman road recorded at site A3 may suggest elements of a planned street layout.

At present, however, there is insufficient evidence to determine the status of the site in the Romano-British period. It may have been a semi-nucleated agricultural settlement such as Cople in the Ouse valley and other sites in the Nene valley (Branigan 1985, 131-2). Alternatively, it may have been a more complex centre broadly comparable with sites such as Baldock, Dunstable and Bicester (*ibid.*, 160), although Cow Roast has produced far more evidence for iron working than these other sites.

It is this extensive evidence for iron production which is the most striking aspect of the Romano-British archaeology of the Cow Roast area, both along the valley and on the plateau. That there was a local source of 'Bog Ore' is very likely, although it is conceivable that ore was brought in from Northamptonshire or elsewhere. It is also likely that there was a degree of woodland management such as coppicing to provide the necessary fuel resources (*cf.* Salter & Ehrenreich 1984, 149). A good local parallel for the dispersed iron production recorded at Ashridge can be found at Bradenham, Bucks. (SU 830981), where large concentrations of iron slag have been found along the lynchets of LPRIA/Romano-British fields set on the steep slopes overlooking a dry valley.

Conclusion and Future Research

In conclusion, we can identify three areas of outstanding archaeological significance in the upper Bulbourne valley which can be targetted for further research.

1. Iron Production. The technology and organisation of the iron production is a prime target for investigation. Analysis of the evidence is likely to make a significant contribution to our knowledge of the industrial development of ironworking technology in southern England during the late Iron Age and Romano-British periods (G. McDonnell, pers. comm.). In terms of the social organisation of iron production for both the late Iron Age and Romano-British periods there are perhaps three models which might be investigated through comparative examination of the intensty, scale, location and technique of production and the associated structural and artefact evidence:

a. controlled production. Organised specialised production closely controlled by an elite authority.
b. market production. Specialist production by 'free market' craftsmen.
c. subsidiary production. Iron production as an incidental ?seasonal activity within a predominantly agriculturally based local economy. On present evidence the de-centralised nature of production and its association with agricultural/pastoral activities on the plateau suggests that this is the most likely context. Changing organisation may also be detectable between or within periods.

2. The local settlement pattern. The further examination of the known settlement pattern within its landscape context is required. As yet it is not possible to say whether the area had a mixed economy with elements of arable and pastoral agriculture mixed with woodland management and iron working, whether one or more of these elements dominated at a particular time, or even whether some settlements specialised in a particular activity. It is also necessary to determine what happened in the area towards the end of the Roman period; coin finds from Moneybury Hill suggest a certain amount of rural activity towards the end of the fourth century. The relationship between the rural community, Cow Roast and the nearby villa at Northchurch (site A10: Neal 1977) is also a problematic area. It is hoped to undertake limited excavation of a few features at Ashridge in the near future; close comparison of the finds recovered from this work with those from the Cow Roast and the villa may go a long way towards tackling these issues.

3. *Site status*. There is the question of the status of the Cow Roast site within the regional settlement hierarchy. This might be tackled by examining the structural and finds evidence to outline the range of activities and to compare these with other contemporary sites in the region. The role of the late Iron Age settlement at Cow Roast is of particular importance, especially with regard to the possibility that the site acted as a centre for inter-regional, highland/lowland exchange and also inter-territorial exchange between tribal units. Also, the nature of the changes from the late Iron Age through to the Romano-British period may throw light on broader issues of social organisation in both periods.

It is the rare combination of excavated evidence from a late Iron Age and Romano-British 'subsidiary' settlement, namely Cow Roast, a Roman villa (site A10), and the remarkable survey evidence for the broad agricultural and economic context which makes the upper Bulbourne valley a worthy subject for future archaeological research.

THE ROMANO-BRITISH LANDSCAPE OF THE CHILTERN DIPSLOPE:
A STUDY OF SETTLEMENT AROUND VERULAMIUM

Jonathan Hunn

Introduction

This contribution is part of a wider study of landscape change in the St Albans area as defined by six medieval parishes totalling 126.2 km² (Hunn 1990). The present discussion also includes other sites on the periphery of the study zone. The evidence on which this paper is based has been derived from published sources, aerial photography, fieldwork and topographical observation. However, it is important to be aware of the limitations of this work since only a comparatively small area to the north-west of Verulamium

and on cropmark sites has been fieldwalked adequately (Fig. 28). It is, therefore, not possible to make useful comparisons with more recent archaeological studies (e.g. Gaffney & Tingle 1989; Haselgrove *et al.* 1985; Hayfield 1987; Shennan 1985; Williamson 1984; 1985). Nevertheless, a statement on the present state of knowledge of the Romano-British landscape around Verulamium can be made.

There are four distinct, though interrelated, parts to this contribution. Firstly, there is the question of the nature of the evidence and its quality.

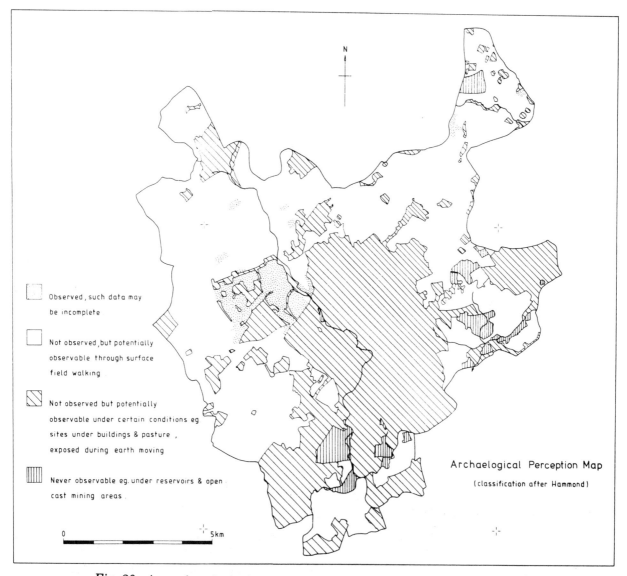

Fig. 28. An archæological perception map of the St Albans study area c.1982.

Table 5. Excavated Romano-British rural sites in the St Albans district.

Villas	Temple/ Mausoleum	Village/ Roadside	Single Farms
Boxmoor (1)	Woodlane End (10)	Cow Roast (12)	Boxfield Farm (15)
Dicket Mead (2)	Rothampstead (11)	King Harry Lane (13)	Foxholes (16)
Gadebridge Park (3)		Ware (14)	Prae Wood En A (17)
Gorhambury(4)			
Kings Langley (5)			
Lockleys (6)			
Northchurch (7)			
Park Street (8)			
Wymondley (9)			

1. Neal 1976;
3. Neal 1974;
5. Wardle 1982;
7. Neal 1974;
9. Westell 1937; Applebaum 1972
11. Lowther 1937;
13. Stead & Rigby 1989;
15. Hunn, forthcoming;
17. Wheeler & Wheeler 1936.

2. Rook 1987;
4. Neal et al.1990;
6. Ward-Perkins 1938;
8. O'Neil 1945; Saunders 1963; Neal et al.1990;
10. Neal 1984;
12. Reece 1982; Smith 1987;
14. Andrews 1900; Day 1980; Holmes 1954; Partridge 1979; 1981
16. Partridge 1989;

Secondly, there is a discussion of the settlement hierarchy of the area. Thirdly, some analysis of the spatial patterning of settlement; this will use geographical models developed in the last 25 years (Bailey & Davidson 1983; Chisholm 1979; Haggett 1965; Hodder 1972; Jarman 1972; Mitchell 1973; Morrill 1970; Vita-Finzi & Higgs 1970). Finally, some suggestions as to the possible direction of future settlement studies in the Chilterns area.

Romano-British settlement in Hertfordshire

At present, Hertfordshire lacks either an overview or any systematic survey of Romano-British rural settlement. County studies are more advanced in Essex (Williamson 1984) and Bedfordshire (Simco 1984). However, in terms of the more Romanised rural sites the county has some important excavations to its credit (see Table 5).

Rural Romano-British settlement has been discussed in relation to the western Chilterns (Branigan 1967), though such an approach may distort the true picture by concentrating on the higher status sites such as villas. With the exception of Gorhambury and Wymondley there has been no attempt to relate individual sites within their territorial framework. The picture can be supplemented by aerial photography, chance finds and fieldwalking. However, in the absence of meaningful fieldwalking strategies and a representative sample of the low status Romano-British rural sites the true nature of the settlement pattern will have little prospect of being understood.

At present, in terms of known sites, the Verulamium area offers the best opportunity for discussing the nature of Romano-British settlement. Other areas around Stevenage may offer a useful comparison to such studies in the future (Hunn, forthcoming).

The St Albans area: a case study

The Celtic social hierarchy seems to have remained essentially the same after AD43 (Niblett this volume). Its energies, however, were channelled differently, since the presence of a Roman field army imposed political stability and stimulated the economy. Both increased the incentive to invest capital in land and Romanised, and therefore more expensive, buildings. Neither implies a change in farming practises, though it might be assumed that a certain degree of intensification of production took place along with the introduction of an improved road and water communication system. The problem of identifying the effects of such a trend in the landscape is that the type of evidence recovered in the form of boundary divisions is only amenable to interpretations of agricultural improvement in specific circumstances. For example, a clear relationship between virgin fenland and 'improvement' can be recognised when drainage ditches appear (Phillips 1970; Hall 1981). Where a landscape has an old established pattern of settled exploitation, it is difficult to identify elements of larger scale change. The evidence of change on an individual 'archaeological site' is not a reliable guide to

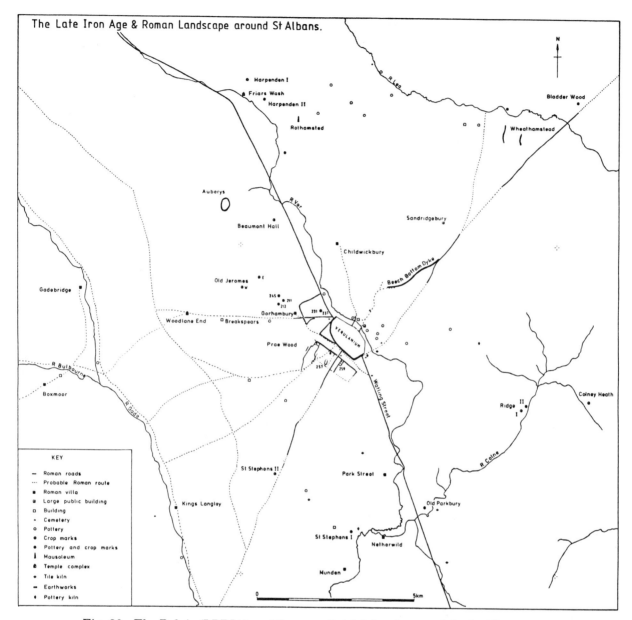

The Late Iron Age & Roman Landscape around St Albans.

Fig. 29. The Belgic (LPRIA) and Romano-British landscape of the St Albans area.

landscape change. While new buildings of different style, function and size may be identified, they can only be used to indicate the social and economic status of the settlement. Even an apparent change in function might be the result of the relocation of previously dispersed buildings in a centralised position. Nevertheless, where rural sites have been excavated fully and a site hierarchy established for a particular locality there are possibilities for identifying general trends in the landscape. However, whilst the morphology of the settlement may be an uncertain guide to change, direct evidence comes from environmental remains, namely seeds, mollusca, pollen and animal bones. The potential of this evidence is great, but recovery depends upon the conditions of preservation, which vary from site to site and from different stratified deposits within an individual site. These are not always favourable in

the Verulamium area.

The principal site: Verulamium

The first Roman occupation of the Ver 'oppidum' area consisted of a fort which overlay the "levelling of a Belgic building" (Frere 1983, 37-8). The position of the fort (of the conquest period) appears to account for the 'oblique line taken by Watling Street across the southern insulae of the city: the road had been laid out to the vicinity of the fort before any city had been founded' (Frere 1983, 33). The first defences of the Roman city are believed to be of pre-Boudiccan date and consisted of a ditch 6.25 m wide and just over 2 m deep below the modern surface, which enclosed an area of approximately 47.6 ha (119 acres); its north-east side was defined by the marshlands of the river Ver. The second Roman defences are believed by Frere to be represented by the Fosse earthwork, though there are grounds for questioning this (Hunn 1993). According to Frere the earthwork was unfinished; it increased the area of the defined town to 93.6 ha (231 acres). The new date proposed for this city circuit falls somewhere between AD140-160 and AD210-230 (Frere 1983, 35). The area of the city was later reduced to 80.9 ha (200 acres) at the time of the construction of the new city wall, c.AD265-270 (Frere 1983, 50).

The suburban landscape

Beyond Verulamium lay an intermediate zone of land use between the urban landscape enclosed by the city walls and the true rural landscape defined solely by its agricultural land use. The principal characteristic of this zone was the presence of cemeteries, kilns and sprawls of insubstantial buildings along the course of the principal roads.

The most extensive area excavated outside the walls of Verulamium was situated in front of the Silchester Gate, on the south-west side of the city (Stead & Rigby 1989). Along the Roman road from the town were found traces of 'ribbon' development as far as the north-west-south-east Belgic (LPRIA) boundary. No house plans were recovered because they had been ploughed away. Occupation ranged from Flavian times, if not earlier, to the end of the third century. Roman burials were found in four separate areas which might possibly have been used for rough grazing around the graves.

Not far from the London Gate, on the south-east side of Verulamium, evidence of industrial activity and burial sites was found (Anthony 1968, 9-65). These consisted of pits and gullies and at least three pottery kilns (others are suspected to exist) and iron-working hearths. There were eight cremations and fifteen burials. As would be expected, burials and industrial sites are absent from Roman Verulamium itself. Further along Watling Street, c.600 m from the London gate, a Roman cemetery has been found at St Stephens Hill (Davey 1935, 243; Rees 1937, 151). About 500 m beyond the north-east gate of Verulamium lay a large public bath-house (Wilson 1975a, 258-9); 175 m to the west lay another building, possibly an inn, though later in date than the bath-house site. The 'inn' building was superseded by a cemetery, probably of the fifth century (Frere 1983, 287). On the north-east side of the Ver, less than 300 m away from the North Gate, there is evidence for a masonry building with crop marks which may be pre-Roman. The evidence is in the shape of two blocks of Oolitic Limestone; one is decorated and has been interpreted as once form-

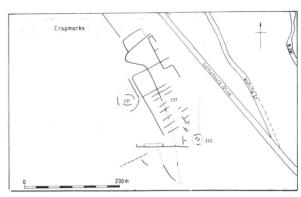

Fig. 30. Allotment strips to the north of the Chester Gate of Verulamium.

ing part of an ornate mausoleum (Hunn & Blagg 1984). More recently, a large mid-first century mortuary enclosure has been discovered on the north-east side of Verulamium, at Folly Lane (Niblett this volume).

Outside the Chester Gate, on the north-west side of Verulamium, there is evidence of burials, settlement and some small-scale allotment of land (Fig. 30). All this activity falls mainly within the area defined by the former LPRIA dykes, with the exception of the royal enclosure at Folly Lane. To judge from the evidence of pottery distribution and other finds, most of the settlement area lies either on or above the 85 m contour. Beyond this area, to the north, the land lies within a dry valley which is subjected to damper and cooler conditions; this might explain why no settlement evidence has been found there. The rectilinear crop mark evidence is, on balance, probably of Roman date. It is unlikely to be medieval, since the area was then common arable land (CAP K17 AM July 5th 1976), whilst quernstone fragments, pottery and Roman coins have been recovered from it. The crop marks consist of what appears to be a rectangular area subdivided by a series of parallel lines lying 10-15 m apart. They all lie at right angles to the alignment of Watling Street, and may have continued towards the road; if so, they have probably been obscured by soil movement down hill. These might best be interpreted as small allotment holdings, associated either with ribbon development or with extra-mural activities of the townspeople. A comparable type of small-scale land division has been revealed at Magiovinium (Neal 1987, 30). The dating of the Verulamium allotments is unknown. However, there is some ceramic and coin evidence to suggest that it may not have persisted beyond the end of the third century. 850 m north-north-west from the Chester Gate, at the point where Watling Street crosses the former course of the Devil's Ditch (TL12560858), three blocks of Oolitic Limestone were found. These were semi-

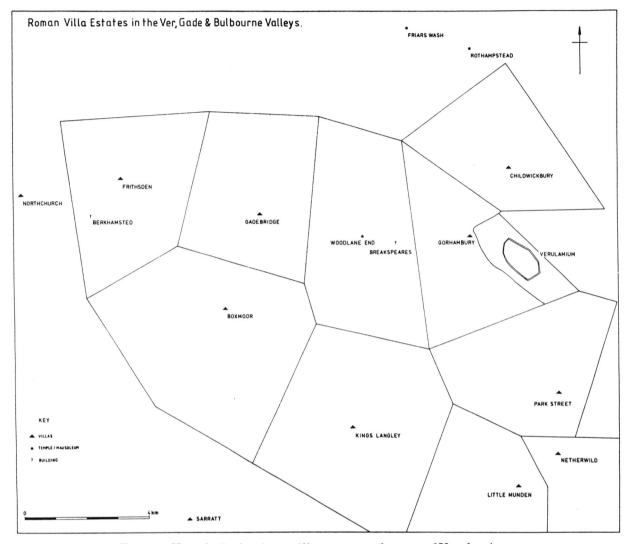

Fig. 31. Hypothetical unitary villa estates to the west of Verulamium.

circular in cross-section and are believed to be coping stones which came from a mortuary enclosure (Hunn & Blagg 1984). The existence of a mausoleum or at least some Roman masonry structure, on a former LPRIA dyke suggests the continuing importance of that boundary, which possibly retained some socio-political significance.

The evidence outlined above indicates the existence of a clear suburban zone around Verulamium. The area is more easily defined on the south-west side of the river Ver than to the north-east, where only the existence of buildings and the royal enclosure can be used to suggest a provisional boundary to a suburban zone extending 300-850 m from the city walls.

The rural landscape

At present the social hierarchy of the rural landscape can be divided into six groups, largely determined by the degree of Romanisation evident on each site. These include villa sites;

religious sites; Romanised farmsteads containing masonry structures of varying sophistication; lesser Romanised farmsteads that exhibit only slight influences of Roman technology but show indications of specialised production for the agrarian market; 'native' sites whose scale suggests a subsistence orientated economy with only minimal vestiges of Roman culture (ceramics and utilitarian objects); and industrial sites. These are discussed below.

1. Villa sites. To what extent the Romano-British landscape around Verulamium was dominated by villa estates is debatable. As the most Romanised of institutions in the province, the villa stands at the apex of the social hierarchy in the rural landscape. There are problems of attempting to equate the variation of villa numbers, or indeed of their size and quality, with any associated estates. It will never be possible to demonstrate whether villas held nucleated, as opposed to dispersed, land holdings. Various models of estate holdings have been proposed

(Applebaum 1972; 1975; Barker & Webley 1977; Branigan 1977; Finberg 1955; Jones 1986; Gaffney & Tingle 1989; Rodwell & Rodwell 1986). However, they can also be enhanced by comparing them with known periods of history. In this way similar or dissimilar patterns of co-variation may become apparent. There are obvious dangers in applying later historical models too uncritically. Questions of social systems, economy, technology and even climate are factors that should not be ignored. However, by offering a comparison between the Romano-British and later periods it is hoped that some insight may be gained into the nature of rural settlement.

Between the Gade and Ver valleys there are at least eight villas (Fig. 31). They have been investigated with varying degrees of intensity. The most complete excavation is that of Gorhambury (TL119080) which begins in the pre-conquest period and declines in the mid-fourth century (Neal et al. 1990). The villa is associated with what looks like a 'home farm' in the form of a large aisled hall and other ancillary buildings. Compared with the villa at Gorhambury, Gadebridge Park (TL145011) looks only partially complete. Villa plans exist for Gadebridge Park (Neal 1974); Boxmoor (TL038056: Neal 1976); Kings Langley (TL078019: Wardle 1982); Park Street (TL146031: O'Neil 1945; Saunders 1963; Neal et al. 1990). The villa at Childwickbury was identified by aerial photography (Verulamium Museum AP 1976 July 12th). Both Netherwild and Munden (TL145011; TL133002) are only probable villa sites (Neal 1976).

Table 6. Height of villa sites above river level.

Site	Contour	Elevation above river
Boxmoor	90m	6m
Childwickbury	125m	45m
Gadebridge Park	80m	5m
Gorhambury	110m	30m
Kings Langley	75m	6m
Munden	75m	10m
Netherwild	70m	3m
Park Street	75m	6m

One of the shared characteristics of the excavated sites from the architectural point of view is the existence of a similar number of rooms, despite the difference of scale of the individual villa buildings (Neal 1976, 123). This may indicate a range of functions, rather than a fixed number of inhabitants. Apart from Gorhambury, only Gadebridge has been sufficiently excavated to

glimpse something of the buildings around the main house block. However, even Gadebridge may not be typical as a villa site because the size of its open-air bath suggests a possible public function. A further characteristic shared by the excavated villas is their location close to rivers, usually above the flood plain: only Gorhambury and Childwickbury are located on the higher ground.

The regular spacing of the villas along the Bulbourne, Gade, Ver, Colne and Chess rivers has been commented on (Branigan 1967; Neal 1976). Recognition of this led to the suggestion of the possibility of 'some form of planning control'. However, the element of planning may be secondary compared with the need for each estate to have a land holding sufficient to sustain it. Regular spacing is less apparent in the land block around Verulamium selected for this study.

It has been estimated that the villa demesne estate may have required between 30 and 40 individuals in order to function as a self-contained unit (Neal et al. 1990, 104). Nevertheless the above population does not include children, with the exception of the proprietor's family. It is probable that only half (15-20) of this number may have lived on the villa site, though there is little prospect of ever demonstrating the amount of living space required for the average Romano-Briton with any confidence. Hingley (1989, 7) proposes a Romano-Celtic family model based on the extended family unit which has two distinct but blood-related households.

An alternative method of assessing the population of a given estate or, indeed, that of an area around Verulamium is to ask what level of population would be needed in order to sustain a given agrarian system. By examining the number of labourers per farm in the mid-nineteenth century census (PRO H.O.107.1713) and comparing it with a medieval source (Levett 1938, 289) a ratio of c.9 ha (22 acres) per agrarian worker is suggested. Given that the level of agricultural technology was broadly similar between the Roman, medieval and even up to the mid-nineteenth century, then if the same land area was being cultivated it would have required a similar number of man-hours (input) to sustain such a system. If the upper limit of 30 individuals (excluding the proprietor's family) were required to maintain the villa demesne, then based on the mid-nineteenth century figures the annual area of cultivation would probably not have exceeded 270 ha (667 acres).

Coincidentally or not, this figure is almost precisely the same for a 1 km area around the

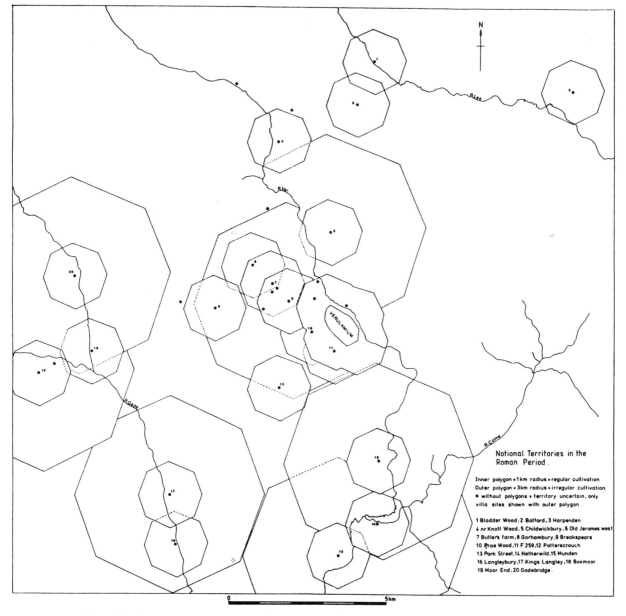

Notional Territories in the
Roman Period.

Inner polygon = 1km radius = regular cultivation
Outer polygon = 3km radius = irregular cultivation
● without polygons = territory uncertain; only
villa sites shown with outer polygon.

1.Bladder Wood,2.Batford,3.Harpenden
4.nr Knott Wood,5.Childwickbury,6.Old Jeromes west
7.Butler's farm,8.Gorhambury,9.Breakspears
10.Prae Wood,11.F.259,12.Potterscrouch
13.Park Street,14.Netherwild,15.Munden
16.Langleybury,17.Kings Langley,18.Boxmoor
19.Moor End,20.Gadebridge.

Fig. 32. Notional territories in the Romano-British period around Verulamium.

Gorhambury villa as denoted by the inner polygon on figure 32. Comparisons with known medieval demesne figures can neither prove nor disprove the hypothesis, though they can afford a means of providing an historically independent yardstick with which to compare the Roman figures (see Table 3; Neal *et al.* 1990, 101).

2. *Religious sites.* Another type of rural site that may have been associated with a landed estate is that with a religious character. So far, excluding the Folly Lane site (Niblett this volume) only two such sites have been identified in the St Albans area, though this could be increased to three if the mausoleum at Rothamstead, near Harpenden is included (TL118138: Busby 1954; Lowther 1937; Neal 1976, 132). The site of Annables Cottages, near Friars Wash (TL10081461) lies within 50 m of the River Ver and consists of two adjacent

Romano-Celtic type temple structures (Fig. 33), with a circular structure beside them and a rounded 'temenos' or enclosure ditch; these structures all stand close to a triple bank of presumably prehistoric date. The site also lies close to Watling Street, less than 400 m away to the southwest. Its proximity to the river may have some special significance and perhaps point to a water cult; it is also conceivable that it marks a point where water was drawn off to feed an aqueduct serving Verulamium, 8 km to the south. Such a system would have consisted of a leet following the contours on the east side of the valley until, opposite the city, it crossed the valley on an arched aqueduct into the town.

The second religious site lay at Woodlane End (TL08200788), *c.*4.5 km to the west of Verulamium. This consists of a group of buildings,

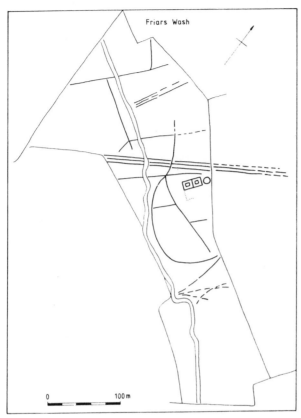

Fig. 33. The Romano-Celtic temple site at Friars Wash, Redbourn.

one of which is a large Romano-Celtic type temple 18 m square. Associated with this were at least five other buildings (a bath-house, a rectangular cellar-type structure, a square shrine, an administrative block and perhaps significantly a possible granary) all enclosed by a wall (Neal 1984). These buildings, though situated on the plateau midway between the Ver and Gade valleys, are on a Roman road linking Verulamium with Akeman Street via Breakspears and Gorhambury. There is no certainty that either Woodlane End or Friars Wash were associated with a self-supporting estate, though the scale of the buildings and the existence of a granary at the former site suggest the possibility that it might have been endowed with its own land holding.

3. Romanised farmsteads. The next level in the settlement hierarchy is the Romanised farmstead. In the area around St Albans, this type can be identified by the presence of Romanised building materials, such as tiles and mortar. Those sites that have such associations are limited to the valley area closest to Verulamium. TF (Topographical Feature) 215 lies 0.5 km north of Gorhambury and Old Jeromes West (Fig. 34). The rectangular enclosure (TF259: Fig. 34) associated with the Prae Wood plateau site lying south of the Silchester Gate contained a Roman barn. However, the conditions under which ar-

chaeological information was retrieved were adverse so that the degree of Romanisation is difficult to assess. The existence of an aisled hall in the LPRIA period at Gorhambury requires a redefinition of the term 'Romanised'. All that can be stated is that the barn inside TF.259 was probably associated with a Romanised farmstead which did not use masonry or develop into a villa. Both TF.215 (TL11200830) and Old Jeromes West (TL107091) have evidence of Roman tile. TF.215, in particular, has a noticeable scatter of tile associated with its rectangular crop marks. There is also a strong suggestion that the tile scatter is associated with the rectilinear crop marks, one of which may be a parallel ditched trackway (Neal *et al.* 1990, 98: Fig. 115). However, the fields could have been laid out in the late Iron Age and remained in use into the Roman period. The site at Breakspears (TL09400775) apparently consisted of a rectangular building and had associated pottery of early-second to late-fourth century date (Anthony 1960, 8). The site was found during the course of constructing the M1 and has subsequently been obliterated. It is not easy to classify it as anything more than a Romanised farmstead because the quality of information was poor. One argument against its being a villa is its position on the central plateau away from the river valleys. Nevertheless, it remains to be demonstrated that villas were not situated on these plateau areas.

4. Lesser Romanised farmsteads. At present, no

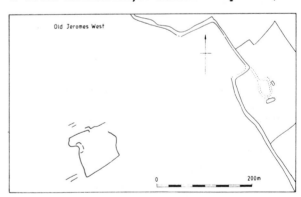

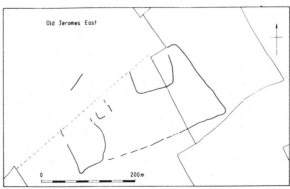

Fig. 34. Romanised farmsteads at Old Jeromes, Redbourn.

N
△

Mid 19th Century Farm Territories .

Central southern area incomplete due to
problems of scale, dispersed holdings
and landscape change.

0   5km

Fig. 35. Mid-nineteenth century farmsteads in the St Albans area.

site of this category has been identified with certainty around Verulamium. However, this type of site is represented by the Boxfield Farm excavation near, Stevenage 22 km north of St Albans (Hunn, forthcoming).

5. *Native sites.* Those sites that have yielded only Roman pottery can be ascribed to the lowest level in the rural hierarchy. This is only a tentative division since the retrieval methods and hence the

quality of information are uneven. Sites that could be assigned to this category would be Harpenden (TL138140: Neal 1976, 132); Redbourn (TL08200050: *op cit.*, 133); Kettlewells (TF.246 at TL11770870) which is associated with a sub-circular enclosure; and Bladder Wood (TL20701450) which is also associated with a LPRIA sub-rectangular enclosure.

6. *Industrial sites.* There are other sites in the

countryside which show associations with industry rather than agriculture. These are principally kiln sites manufacturing tile or pottery. South of Verulamium there are five main sites: a tile kiln at Park Street (TL138039: Rawlins 1970), a second one at Parkbury (TL16620114: SMR 0700) and a third at Radlett (TL16290200: SMR 4838). Both tile and pottery kilns occur at Black Boy Pits (TL12200230: Davey 1932; Rawlins 1970, 62). Another site has been located at Little Munden Farm (TL13851041), where a pottery kiln was found (Saunders & Havercroft 1977).

The tile and pottery kilns are a part of a wider group of kiln sites which lie between Verulamium and Sulloniacis, 13 km to the south. They all lie close to Watling Street, and thus had access to a potentially large market. They are an example of an industry responding to market forces and located in areas which could supply their raw materials, namely clay.

Summary of settlement evidence

The sites described probably represent only a small sample of the settlement evidence that remains to be recovered. There is an obvious preponderance of the larger type of site, particularly villas and more noticeable ones like kilns; the smaller rural sites will always be harder to locate and identify. The scale and nature of the problem is illustrated by comparing the distribution of farms in the mid-nineteenth century, where the total population within the 48 miles^2 around Verulamium was about 15,000, with that of the known rural pattern in the Roman period (Fig. 35). Only the sample area around Gorhambury allows us to have any confidence in the quality of information and permits us to suggest a tentative density of settlement.

The villa and market pattern around Verulamium

It has been suggested by Hodder and Millett (1980, 69-85) that the status of a town, and not its marketing pull, was the determining factor in the distribution pattern of villas. They observe the relative lack of villas within 6 km of towns like Silchester, Verulamium, Colchester, Dorchester and Winchester and contrast it with the villa distribution 8-10 km away from such towns. The pattern led them to interpret the relative absence of villas close to urban centres as a consequence of the town's requirements for land, in the form of 'territorium'. If this is true, then those areas which have an absence of villa estates close to an urban centre are likely to have been cultivated by the urban population. There is some suggestion

of this around Verulamium. Two villas lie within 2.2 km on the north side of the town. Three villas lie 3.5-6.5 km to the south of it. Villas are absent to the east and west, which may indicate that the land there was cultivated by small-scale farmers and town dwellers. Between 8-10 km from Verulamium there are at least three, possibly five, villas in the Gade-Bulbourne valleys. Up to 16 km away the number increases by a further four to seven villas, making a total of between seven and twelve villas in the 10-16 km range band. However, on the edge of the 16 km range to the south, lies the Roman town of Sulloniacis; 15 km to the east lies the probable Roman settlement of Welwyn, with its two to three villas (not included in the previous figures), while 17.5 km to the west lies another Roman settlement or village at Cow Roast (SP195103: see Morris & Wainwright this volume). Just under 18 km to the north lies the Roman town of Durocobrivis (Fig. 36). This spacing conforms well with the model quoted by Hodder (1972, 905) with Verulamium corresponding with London as a higher order site (34 km apart). The settlements of Sulloniacis, Cow Roast, Durocobrivis and Welwyn representing the next level of lower order sites (15-18 km apart). However, there is an absence of the smallest service centres (6.5-9.5 km apart). If this pattern remains true then it may imply that rural settlement could have been organised in a different way: for example, it might suggest that certain classes of villa acted in some capacity as substitutes for service centres. By drawing Thiessen polygons around Verulamium the boundary of the town's 'territorium' would fall midway between the city and Sulloniacis, Welwyn, Durocobrivis and Cow Roast, creating an economic zone of 7.5-9 km or 225-324 km^2. However, the notorious aspect of Thiessen polygons is that they give equal importance (i.e. market pull) to different settlement centres regardless of size (Naroll 1961). It is not just the size of the settlement that determines its 'market pull' but the range of its services and goods. In this respect, Verulamium would be clearly pre-eminent in the region since it was the tribal capital of the Catuvellauni (Frere 1967; 1983). It is therefore probable that Verulamium had direct economic dominance over an area of around 324 km^2 and an indirect dominance of perhaps double that area (Fig. 36). How far its political domination extended is difficult to gauge. Only its economic hinterland may be recoverable by comparing the distribution pattern of ceramic fabrics with those found at Verulamium.

The two villas closest to Verulamium are those of Gorhambury and Childwickbury, both of which stand on high ground, in contrast to the three southerly villas (Park Street, Netherwild, Mun-

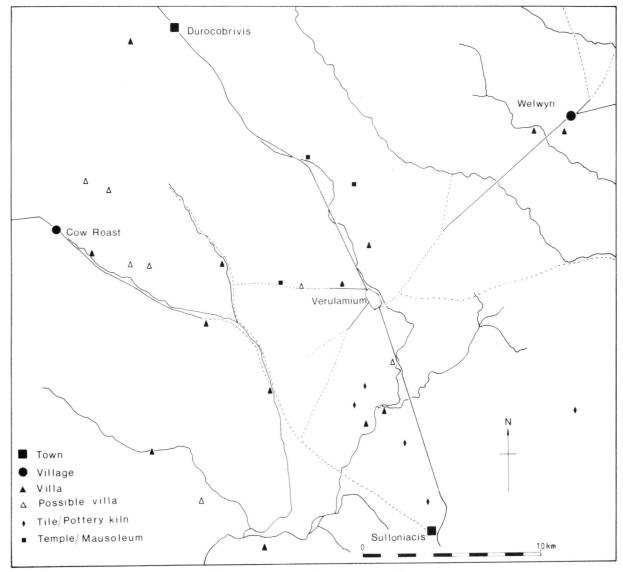

Fig. 36. The economic catchment area of Verulamium.

den) which lie close to the river Ver. It may be no coincidence that the Gorhambury site has been shown to have been laid out between AD 20-43 and that, together with Childwickbury, it probably had a political as well as social significance in its location. Its position in relation to the dyke system of the Ver oppidum has been commented on (Millett 1990; Neal *et al.* 1990). The third closest villa (Park Street) has definite Belgic (LPRIA) antecedents and proves that both the valleys and plateau peripheries were equally favoured for settlement. The site territory/catchment pattern of the Romano-British landscape is shown in figure 32. As with the territorial outline in the LPRIA, there are considerable gaps further away from Verulamium. These may 'fill up' as more information is collected.

Population

What is known of Romano-British settlement in general does not allow for a secure assessment of population. Historically, the 126.2 km² area around Verulamium has supported a fairly low population. This does not mean that in the Roman period it could not have supported figures equal to that of the mid-nineteenth century. It has to be remembered that its social and political organisation was radically different from that of succeeding periods. The evidence for this comes from the status of Verulamium itself, both in terms of its government and its development into one of the premier cities of Roman Britain.

One of the most difficult questions to solve is to what extent Verulamium was dependent on its hinterland and how much it imported from outside its natural catchment area. There are too many variables to permit any confident quantification. It has been shown that there is a relationship between a settlement's range of function and its population. In a western rural society there is a positive correlation of 0.89 coefficient (r) between settlement and functional range (Haggett 1968, 115). However, since the functional range of Verulamium and its surrounding sites can only be guessed at, such an exercise will only produce a comparative size-ratio between sites and cannot, therefore, be of much help in determining population figures.

In the Roman period a general intensification of the exploitation of existing resources, both in terms of woodland, arable cultivation and pasture, must have occurred in order to develop and maintain the urban infrastructure. The resulting landscape would reflect the demands of society and something of its social organisation. Whatever the precise nature of the Roman field system, it would seem that the landscape was not divided by ditched boundaries to any great extent. The Verulamium area is, historically speaking, one of mixed agriculture, with perhaps more emphasis on arable production. The preponderance of this pattern over time is revealed both by records and by early agricultural commentators (Ellis 1732; Young 1804). Most of the pasture and meadow lands are likely to have been confined to the alluvial valleys, in terms of both historical continuity and traditional land utilisation. If the landscape around Verulamium was exploited at the same level of intensity as in the medieval and mid-nineteenth century then it would have required a minimum of 1,402 agrarian workers to have sustained it. The term 'agrarian worker' is here applied to adult males, though both young males and females (particularly in dairying) could also have been employed. To what extent all the agrarian workers (including farmers and bailiffs) were 'heads of household' is difficult to determine. If a lower multiplier of five is taken, and an upper multiplier of ten is used, then a population range of between 7,010-14,020 is quite possible for the rural landscape around Verulamium. This compares with the population figures for the early to mid-nineteenth century (Neal et al. 1990, 104).

Farming Territories

It is a generally accepted axiom that those lands closest to a settlement or dwelling are the ones most intensively cultivated (Jarman 1972). This area constitutes an 'infield' whereas the land further away, because of its relative distance from an occupation centre, was cultivated less intensively. If we accept Chisholm's limits of 1 km for intensive land use and 3-4 km as the absolute boundary (Chisholm 1979, 57), it is possible to reconstruct a hypothetical territorial framework for the vicinity of Verulamium (Fig. 32). Beyond 3 km the increased costs of time and effort are such that dis-

tance acts as an inhibiting factor in the exploitation of agrarian territories. On figure 32 the inner polygon covers an area of 268 ha (662 acres) and the outer polygon covers an area of 2592 ha (6405 acres).

This does not differ widely from that of the LPRIA, except for the existence of a developed urban centre in the valley. In order to assess the validity of hypothetical Roman territories in the landscape it is relevant to look at a period in which attested territories can be plotted on a map and compared to the location of their focus of exploitation, i.e. the farmstead. A comparison of the mid-nineteenth century distribution of farms with their territories provides a reasonable yardstick with which to measure previous zones of exploitation. Figure 35 illustrates the state of tenant holdings c.1840. The area to the east and south of Verulamium has been omitted because of later urban development which destroyed much of the boundary relationship prior to the appearance of the 1st Series OS maps 1878-83. In the 126 km^2 area around St Albans in 1841 there were 135 homesteads or farms over 8.1 ha (20 acres). The equation is not as simple as that since there were lesser units holding smaller portions of land. Nevertheless, the use of the word 'homesteads' or 'farmsteads' is significant and, coincidentally or not, makes a ratio of approximately 1 km per farmstead. If we combine all the land-holdings together we arrive at an average holding of approximately 48.4 ha (120 acres). In historical terms this is a minimum figure. In 1569 there were 30 tenant farmers on the Goram-Westwick estate (992 ha; 2,451 acres). However, as examination of the figures will demonstrate, there is a great variation in the size of tenant holdings. It is most probable that a similar variation in the size of farm units existed in the Roman period. With the absence of distinct boundaries, the principal evidence for the extent of individual farm holdings rests on the size of the settlement site. At present the lack of evidence restricts what can be achieved in the way of landscape reconstruction to the relatively simple identification of settlement hierarchies.

Villa estate models: the example of Gorhambury

One of the main problems in the creation of hypothetical estate models is the question of whether a given territory was primarily centralised, or dispersed. It will always remain impossible to prove, short of the unlikely discovery of inscribed boundary markers. Salway, quoting Jones, has observed that ' Landlords, both great and small, rarely owned a single consolidated estate. Their possessions were usually

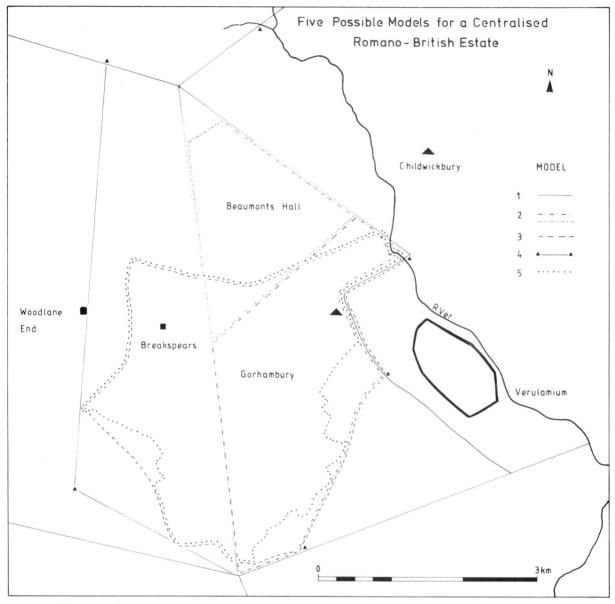

Fig. 37. Possible models for a centralised Romano-British villa estate at Gorhambury.

scattered and consisted of a number of farms, some larger, some smaller' (Salway 1986, 599-600; Jones 1964, 781). Historically, the manor of Westwick (Gorhambury) has never been a single estate since the late Saxon period. At least five possible models for a compact estate territory might be proposed for Gorhambury (Fig. 37).

1. This is based on the assumption that each villa and temple-mausoleum estate held land on an equal basis and that therefore territorial divisions were situated midway between each estate centre, i.e. Thiessen polygons (Haggett 1968, 247-8; Hodder & Orton 1976, 56-60, 78-80, 187). On present evidence there are at least 12 villas in the topographical area of the Bulbourne-Gade-Ver Rivers catchment zone and two temple complexes; of these, eight villas and one temple-mausoleum estate can be ascribed a territory based on the

above premise. The territories listed in Table 7 have been deduced.

Table 7. **Hypothetical territories for each villa and temple-mausoleum estate.**

Location	Area (ha)	Area (acres)
Boxmoor	2,967.7	7,333.2
Childwickbury	1,519.8	3,755.5
Frithsden	1,845.2	4,559.5
Gadebridge	1,799.2	4,445.9
Gorhambury	1,308.1	3,232.4
Kings Langley	2,811.8	6,948.1
Munden	1,494.7	3,693.5
Park Street	1,736.0	4,289.8
Woodlane End	2,125.4	5,251.8

These figures combined would produce an average

territory of 1,956.4 ha (4,834 acres). The Gorhambury villa estate is below average because of its proximity to Verulamium and the dyke systems to the north of the city.

2. This is a combination of the Iron Age estate at Gorhambury with that of the Beaumont Hall territory on the assumption that it may have been amalgamated with the Gorhambury estate in the Roman period, i.e. the river and dyke system to the east of the villa, the Prae Wood boundaries, the median line between the Park Street villa and Woodlane End temple-mausoleum estates and the Childwickbury territory. Together this would create an estate of 1,007 ha (2,489.9 acres).

3. This is based on a combination of the river, dykes, Prae Wood ditch system and the medieval township boundary of Westwick. This pushes the estate further to the west, though it loses land to the north around Beaumont Hall, thereby creating an area of 1,045.9 ha (2,584.4 acres). The lands of St Mary de Pre in the medieval period were concentrated mainly in the townships of Westwick and Kingsbury and conform more closely with the surviving bank and ditch evidence in Prae Wood which could conceivably demarcate the boundary between the two estates. By adopting the estate and later township boundary, which is also the parochial boundary on the western side, this takes the Romano-British estate to within 600 m of the temple-mausoleum complex at Woodlane End.

4. This is based on the premise that the temple-mausoleum site at Woodlane End demarcates the boundary between the Gadebridge Park and Gorhambury villas. The Woodlane End site is situated almost exactly mid-way between the two villas, and could conceivably have been associated with Gadebridge; it was situated on the edge of the estate adjacent to a route between the Gade and Ver valleys. Gorhambury's funerary monument, by contrast, would most probably have been situated closer to Watling Street, as befitted the status of its owner. In addition, by extending the Gorhambury villa boundary to the west up to the River Ver, the combined area would amount to an estate of 2645 ha (6535 acres), i.e. more than double. The attraction of such a hypothesis is that it would greatly increase the Grade 2 agricultural land available to the estate. It is noticeable that there were at least three, possibly four, Romano-British sites situated within this higher quality land area (Jeromes East, Jeromes West, Beaumont Hall and Woodlane End). However, it should be pointed out that the proximity of the higher grade agricultural land to villa sites was probably of secondary consideration compared

with those of other locational factors such as socio-political considerations, communications and terrain. Around St Albans all the Romano-British villas are located on Grade 3 agricultural land and only Gorhambury could be considered to be close to Grade 2 land (i.e. 1 km to the north).

5. This is modelled on the probable medieval estate of the manor of Westwick which was approximately 992 ha (2,451 acres).

The five proposed models create a single consolidated estate of the sizes shown in Table 8.

Table 8. Equivalent medieval/mid-nineteenth century agrarian workers per area.

Area	Agrarian workers
1. 1,308.1 ha	145
2. 1,007.6 ha	112
3. 1,045.9 ha	116
4. 2,645.6 ha	294
5. 992.0 ha	110

Average = 1,399.8 ha (155 agrarian workers)

Of the five proposed models the fifth coincides with the historical data, while the third model conforms more closely to what is known of the historical and archaeological evidence. On this basis a minimum Romano-British estate of about 1,010 ha (2,500 acres) is proposed for the Gorhambury villa with an upper limit (Model 4) of more than double that to 2,645 ha.

The late Roman landscape

The evident decline in the fortunes of the villa settlement at Gorhambury before the mid-fourth century does not necessarily imply a break in the cultivation of its territory. From the time of Diocletian (284-305) villa territories became larger and the 'coloni' may have became increasingly tied to the land. By the fourth century the villa system was beginning to share characteristics of the later manorial organisation in its relationship between proprietor (lord) and cultivator (peasant) (Salway 1986, 606). However, for the survival of an estate from the Roman period into the Middle Ages one has to postulate some degree of social stability. It would be erroneous to compare the villa system at the height of its development with that of the situation a thousand years later, when social conditions were very different. Nevertheless, social 'continuity' may be manifested in the physical remains of the landscape, i.e. the survival of boundaries, locations and place-names. The problem with estate survival, particularly in the

Verulamium area, is that the villa system as personified by the refined country house comes to an end in the mid-fourth century. The reasons lie in a series of interrelated shifts: social, economic, environmental, demographic and political.

In the countryside around Verulamium the fourth century landscape evidence comes mostly from villa sites. There are suggestions that the field system to the north of Verulamium and adjacent to Watling Street in the parish of Redbourn may have been laid out in the LPRIA/Roman periods (Hunn, forthcoming). However, this has yet to be demonstrated archaeologically. A high proportion of villa sites has been excavated around Verulamium and they constitute the most intensively studied group in the country (Neal *et al.* 1990). The archaeological evidence indicates that they did not continue to function much beyond the mid-fourth century. The evidence for this comes from the sites of Boxmoor, Northchurch, Gadebridge, Gorhambury and Park Street (Neal 1974; 1976; 1990; O'Neil 1945). Boxmoor was in decline before the mid-350's, as was Gorhambury which survived to the mid 360's. Gadebridge grew in the fourth century but came to an end *c.*354 when all its buildings were demolished, except for a single building and associated stock enclosures. At Park Street occupation ceased in about 367. Altogether the evidence is fairly unambiguous, pointing to a parallel decline of both town and country in the late Roman period, with those most Romanised of institutions, the villas, having ceased to exist by, or shortly after, the mid-fourth century. In Verulamium, the construction of a corn-drying kiln in about 420 shows that Romanised agricultural methods were still in use, but the kilns were no longer confined to clearly rural sites.

With the decline in the urban population due to the gradual collapse of the market economy, there was less demand for agricultural produce so that a centralised system of large-scale production became unnecessary. Also with a declining urban population there was a reduction in the number of specialist crafts operating. The trades, such as pottery production, would disappear first; tanning and metal crafts would linger on as part-time activities. This is a situation similar to that in the Middle Ages, where many craftsmen held small plots of land and existed with a largely subsistence agricultural system. The effect on the rural economy was to cause contraction, resulting eventually in a subsistence-type agriculture. How would this have affected estate management? Faced with the problems of inflation, declining markets and lower productivity, it would have been quite likely for the estate owner to apportion

land to his 'bondsmen' and receive in return his dues in kind, by labour, service or both.

Traditional agricultural systems may have continued, though on a less intensive scale. As during the agricultural depression of the 1930s, some arable land would have been abandoned and some would become permanent pasture. Analogy further suggests that, though arable production declined, there would not necessarily be a comparable decline in population figures. Between 1870 and 1938 the acreage of permanent grassland in Hertfordshire grew from 86,113 acres to 137,383 acres, an increase of 62.68 % (Stamp 1941). This does not necessarily imply a switch to pastoral farming but rather an abatement of intensive farming practises. Land could remain fallow for longer periods. Possibly after several generations the pace of farming slackened and new traditions of less intensive farming developed.

Future work

1. St Albans area. Recent field survey projects have demonstrated how the quality of landscape evidence in the pre-documentary period may be improved (Gaffney & Tingle 1989; Hall 1987; Haselgrove *et al.* 1985; Hayfield 1987; Reilly 1988; Shennan 1985; Williamson 1984; 1985). There is a need for a similar type of approach in the St Albans area. At present, settlement evidence gradually accumulates on an *ad hoc* basis by means of occasional finds, aerial photography and opportunist development. For example, it is relatively easy, given the will, to visit identified cropmark sites. However, a systematic approach is, by its very nature, both time consuming and expensive. Short of properly funded field surveys the only real chance for an improvement in the quality of landscape studies is the mobilisation of volunteer bodies, e.g. societies and local education organisations. These, together with the co-operation of local landowners, could survey defined field parcels and upstanding topographical features such as earthwork boundaries and hedgerows. What is required are consistently sampled or surveyed areas of landscape with which to make inter-regional or sub-regional comparisons. It is necessary to define the objectives of such a study, for example what is the evidence for activity in different periods, its distribution/pattern, typology and longevity/duration.

After the preliminary stage, questions of varying patterns and influences on data recovery could be considered. What is quite evident is that those questions need to be asked now, and a consistent policy implemented to achieve those objectives.

The landscape around St Albans, as is the case for many other areas in Britain, is continually changing in order to meet the demands of today's society. What is possible today may not be possible in the future. There are changes in the pattern of land exploitation: for example, from arable to pasture, recreation, quarrying, afforestation and construction (mainly roads and housing). Nevertheless, though it is easier to make recommendations rather than to implement them; at least by doing so it is a small step towards their eventual realisation.

2.   *Chilterns dipslope*.   The nature of the Romano-British rural settlement away from the vicinity of St Albans is even less well understood. The apparent absence of villas to the east of Verulamium has been commented upon (Neal *et al.* 1990, 89). There is a need to understand more about the interrelationship between the spatial patterning of villas and small settlements such as Cow Roast (Morris & Wainwright this volume). At present, it is difficult to categorise the Cow Roast site: is it an irregular roadside development that acted as some kind of market focus on the boundary between the Chiltern hills and the Vale of Aylesbury to the north-west? Even the most elementary facts, such as the extent of the settlement, have not been established with certainty. There are Roman masonry structures in the vicinity: what was their function?   There is evidence for a surprising degree of ironworking in the LPRIA: how does the Roman invasion influence this activity?

In north Hertfordshire the cropmark evidence of single and multiple enclosures raises questions as to settlement density, form, function and duration. Many of these enclosures may well originate in the late Iron Age but both this and their continuation into the Roman period has yet to be proven.   There is also the question of the difference in the type of villa establishments in the Ashwell area. Are they of a more institutionalised character than those of the Verulamium villas that appear to be more residential? For example, the Ashwell villa has three large barn-type structures: is this simply a question of scale or are other factors involved?   Further to the south at Wymondley Bury and Stevenage there are indications of contrasting farm types.   What factors determined differences in building tradition, and is this impression being distorted by the unevenness of survival?

In conclusion, there is a need first to improve our understanding of the spatial distribution of enclosure types and other rural sites in the Roman period; and second to obtain adequate excavated samples of different rural sites so that alternative models of the agrarian economy can be developed and tested in the future.

LATER PREHISTORIC DYKES OF THE EASTERN CHILTERNS

Stewart Bryant and Gilbert Burleigh

Introduction

The eastern Chilterns systems of single, double and multiple linear ditched and banked boundaries which, for the sake of brevity, may be called 'dykes' are, of course, only one small area in the later prehistoric landscapes of eastern and central southern England displaying these types of boundary features. In fact such dyke systems have been recorded from many regions of southern and eastern England. Aerial photography has recorded examples from Bedfordshire, Cambridgeshire, Northamptonshire, Leicestershire, Nottinghamshire and Lincolnshire, as well as North Yorkshire and the Yorkshire Wolds where excellent examples survive as earthworks. In the east Midlands aerial photographers have recorded many examples of comparable single, double and multiple dyke sytems of the later prehistoric period. Jim Pickering (1978) published his early results more than a decade ago and more work has been done since, including some excavations. The known systems of the east Midlands seem to be largely related to the 'Jurassic Spine', just as on a smaller scale the systems in the eastern Chilterns are apparently related to the 'Icknield Belt'. However, to some extent this may be reflecting results obtained by soil type rather than reality.

The dyke systems are so extensive in parts of eastern England that they must have been a major element in the landscape of the first millennium BC. They should be able to provide considerable information about contemporary communities and especially about the organisation and farming of the landscape. Apparently some areas, such as the eastern Chilterns, have concentrations of dykes whereas in other areas they are apparently thin on the ground. Where dykes are concentrated it may indicate more intense land use and perhaps a greater population; it may also imply more organisation, possibly with centralised control.

Fieldwork and study of these monuments has so far done little more than scratch the surface: there is clearly a need for more surveys and interpretation and for selective excavation, particularly where there are relationships between dyke systems and other features such as settlements, enclosures, trackways and pit alignments. An in- dication of our current lack of knowledge and understanding of these dykes, pariculary the multiple type, and their functions in the landscape is perhaps given by the lack of discussion of them in the standard textbook for the period (Cunliffe 1991). This is partly explained by the usual problem of a shortage of publication of such work as has been undertaken so far.

Pit alignments

The known national distribution of later prehistoric pit alignments is possibly wider than that known for contemporary dyke systems but the concentration seems also to be in eastern England. In the east Midlands they are frequently recorded as a result of aerial photography. In the Nene and Ouse valleys 114 alignments have been identified and several have been partly excavated; early Iron Age pottery was found in the pits at Briar Hill Farm and at Gretton, Northants. (Cunliffe 1991, 392-3).

There does appear to be a close relationship between the functions and periods of use of pit alignments and dykes in the Iron Age. Where there is evidence, pit alignments seem to originate during an earlier phase of land division, with the elaboration of boundaries into multiple dykes coming in later phases. In the east Midlands variations of the multiple dyke systems include two diches with a parallel pit alignment; two pit alignments and one parallel ditch; three parallel pit alignments; and even four rows of pit alignments. Closer to the Chilterns, at Willington, Beds. in the Ouse valley, a pit alignment forms part of a triple dyke system.

Like single and multiple dykes, pit alignments were constructed to divide the land. Sometimes they were erected to cross several kilometres of landscape, often linking with other boundaries, and sometimes only very short lengths were dug. The physical appearance of pit alignments has caused some debate since most are only known from aerial photography. Several archaeologists have noted that a continuous ditch and bank is a far more efficient boundary to construct than a line of pits. Cunliffe (1991, 393) has suggested that pit alignments were designed to mark the limit of a territory but not to inhibit movement across the line. This is an attractive idea but often, as at Baldock, the pits and presumably their associated banks were spaced so close together that free movement would in fact have been severely restricted. However, it could be argued that it might have been possible for individual beasts and herdsmen to pass through, but not in large groups or, if so, only very slowly. At Baldock there is a further restriction for passage because, at least in certain sections of the alignment, the pits supported posts.

Interestingly, there is evidence that sometimes a pit alignment was replaced by a continuous ditch; in these cases perhaps a more restrictive boundary had become necessary. For instance, this appears to be what happened at Dray's Ditches, Beds. in the late Bronze Age (see below). In Baldock part of a pit alignment was replaced by a ditch dug along the same line at the end of the Iron Age.

The linear dykes of the eastern Chilterns

The linear banks and ditches or 'dykes' which occur along the Chilterns can be divided into two groups. At the south-west end of the survey area (Fig. 13) are several long 'contour' dykes which flank the Bulbourne valley and are known collectively as Grim's Ditch. These appear to be related to the series of linear dykes, often interpreted as ranch boundaries, which extend across much of the chalk areas of Wessex and surrounding regions (see Bradley 1969; Dyer 1961; Ford 1982; Hinchcliffe 1975; Davis 1981). Recent excavation on Grim's Ditch has produced evidence which seems to confirm its Iron Age origins. Generally these 'contour' dykes are conventionally dated from finds and associations with other monuments to the later Bronze Age and early Iron Age. They often form part of complex systems of land allotment which include hillforts, settlements and celtic fields, although the Grim's Ditch does not appear to be directly related to any known settlements or field systems.

The second group of dykes are found at the eastern end of the Chilterns, and comprise varying lengths of single and multiple dykes situated at fairly regular intervals across the Icknield Belt. James Dyer (1961, 39-43) first put forward the idea that these linear dykes divided the eastern Chilterns into a number of territories. In his proposed scheme, the Icknield Belt was divided into six tribal territories in the zone between Dray's Ditches, where Dyer (1961, 32-9) had excavated, and the Bran Ditch, Cambs. The boundaries of the territories were defined by several irregularly spaced single and multiple dykes which ran across the Icknield Way, and by the positions

of the rivers Hiz and Ivel. It was suggested that these boundaries served to block the Icknield Way for purposes of defence or to collect tolls. Each territory also had a prominent settlement which included the hillforts of Ravensburgh Castle, Wilbury Hill and Arbury Banks, all in Herts.

Since Dyer published his article a number of additional single and multiple 'cross ridge' dykes has been revealed in this zone by field survey and aerial photography, notably at Punch's Cross, Wilbury Hill, Baldock and Mitchell Hill, all in Herts. The current distribution of all the multiple dykes and the principal single dykes is plotted on figure 13. This shows a greater number of sub-divisions, perhaps eight or nine, than the model proposed by Dyer, and it is certain that we are looking at more than one phase of division.

The situation is complicated even further by the revelation that there are a significant number of multiple dykes running parallel with the line of the Icknield Way between Baldock and Deadman's Hill, south of Arbury Banks. In effect these constitute a third group of Chilterns dykes (Burleigh this volume).

If the eight cross ridge dykes on figure 13, not counting Mitchell Hill which may be a late sub-division, are accepted as territorial boundaries, they form a system of seven territories between Dray's Ditches (A) and Heydon or Bran Ditch (H), if one also ignores the possibility of the rivers making further sub-divisions. The seven territories are fairly uniform in size, varying between 3.5 km and 5.5 km wide, which compares with a range of between 3 km and 8 km for the system proposed by Dyer (1961).

A comparable but more extensive and better preserved area of later prehistoric territorial boundaries is known from the Tabular Hills of North Yorkshire, which has recently been surveyed in detail (Spratt 1989). There Spratt has suggested that the territorial boundaries were initially marked in the early Bronze Age by round barrows situated along the crests above the valleys. Subsequently, in the later Bronze Age or early Iron Age, a system of continuous dykes was constructed along the crests to replace the barrows as boundaries. These dykes defined a series of self-contained territories, with each territory having access to water, valley lands and upland grazing. In the late Iron Age and early Roman periods, possibly in response to forest clearance and agricultural intensification, the territories were sub-divided into smaller units by the construction of additional dykes across the valley heads. Investigation of several of the dykes was carried out by Spratt (1989, 13-4) which revealed that some of the multiple dykes have more than one phase of construction and, where this occurred, single dykes and pit alignments precede the multiple dykes.

Although considerably less evidence survives of the Chilterns territorial system, comparisons with the Tabular Hills indicate that there are some parallels between the two systems which suggest that the Chilterns territories also had a long and relatively complex history. Firstly, there is a strong association between the Chilterns dykes and Bronze Age barrows. Most of the cross ridge dykes are situated close to barrows, and Dray's Ditches, Baldock, Deadman's Hill and Mile Ditches are all associated with prominent barrow cemeteries sited along ridges. It is possible that these may have been precursors of the linear boundaries in a similar fashion to the early Bronze Age boundary markers in the Tabular Hills.

Secondly, where excavation of the Chilterns dykes has taken place, more than one phase of construction has been apparent. Excavations at the Mile Ditches have suggested that the Iron Age triple ditches were preceded by a single ditch phase (Burleigh 1980). Similarly, at Dray's Ditches the Iron Age multiple ditches wre preceded by two small ditches dated to the middle or late Bronze Age (Dyer 1961, 34-6). It is also possible that at Dray's Ditches the earliest linear boundary consisted of pit alignments which were later converted into ditches. The two Bronze Age ditches were both constructed according to the excavator by joining together a series of square, flat-bottomed pits which were dug at 3 m intervals (Dyer 1961, 33-6). This method of construction would have been particularly inefficient and time-consuming, and could more easily be explained by the conversion of pre-existing pit alignments into ditches.

These examples suggest that there was considerable modification of the Chilterns boundaries over time, indicating a similar construction sequence to that of the Tabular Hills, with a general move from pit alignments and single banks and ditches to larger and more impressive multiple banks and ditches. At Deadman's Hill a multiple dyke system has a single ditch extension which runs for a considerable distance to the south of the multiple arrangement; as at the Mile Ditches, this extension is the largest and western-most ditch. It is possible that these more substantial single ditches represent a phase earlier than the multiple dykes.

The relationship between the dykes and the hillforts first noted by Dyer is still apparent in the proposed territorial system. The nature of the relationship is not clear as each hillfort appears to control two territories. However, it is possible that a sub-division of territories or estates may have occurred in a similar fashion to the sub-division which took place in the Tabular Hills in the late Iron Age, with three large territories, each of which was centred on a hillfort, being sub-divided into six smaller units. Alternatively, but perhaps less likely, there may have been a consolidation of six estates into three larger territories.

It is probable that the hillforts were of most significance as defended sites in the early to middle Iron Age period, and thereafter although still important, perhaps in some cases the main settlements in their territories, were of less importance militarily. In this category it is possible to accept easily both Ravensburgh and Wilbury, although only a limited amount is known about their development.

At Ravensburgh, after a period of abandonment, Dyer has identified a refortification in his Period 3 which he dates on admittedly slender evidence to early in the first century BC (Dyer 1976, 158). It is possible to suggest that this refortification might be slightly earlier in date.

Wilbury Hill, Letchworth seems to have its earliest phase as an undefended settlement and when in the next phase, perhaps in the fourth century BC, it was defended the defences were relatively short-lived before being demolished, allowing the settlement to continue but apparently with little if any military significance. By the late Iron Age structures were being erected over the former defences (Applebaum 1949; Keith Matthews, pers.comm.).

One of the authors (Gil Burleigh) finds it hard to accept Arbury Banks as a hillfort of any great military importance. Its position is not particularly prominent and it is overlooked by slightly higher ground to the south-east. Although it is normally accepted as a hillfort, it is not in the same category as Ravensburgh, and although superficially similar in size and form to Wilbury, it is not in such a defensible position. It appears to be a large defended farmstead enclosure of the Iron Age, of a type represented by other ploughed-out smaller examples within a few kilometres (Fig. 13, nos. 1-4). Unlike these other enclosures in the surrounding area, Arbury Banks appears to have fortuitously survived relatively well-preserved due to its size and later land-use. However, it need not be doubted that Arbury was an important defended settlement in its territory: probably the most important in the early and middle Iron Age. David Wilson (1975b, 63) and Mark Stevenson (1980, 52-5) have convincingly demonstrated that there is no evidence that there were hillforts at either Limlow Hill, Moles Farm (Hoy's Farm) or Hyde Hall Farm (Burlow Hill), all in Herts.

This is not to diminish the importance of Ravensburgh and Wilbury as hillforts with military and territorial significance in the early Iron Age. However, that military phase of the fifth-fourth centuries centuries BC was perhaps relatively short-lived and, in any event, it was not the first phase in the long and complex development of the land divisions created by the pit alignments and single and multiple dykes. Dray's Ditches, for instance, has its origins as a boundary in the middle to late Bronze Age. Ravensburgh and Wilbury may have started as undefended hilltop settlements in the late Bronze Age or early Iron Age. Other examples of such settlements in the early Iron Age are known in the area, such as Jack's Hill south of Baldock, Herts. but which never gained defences.

There is reason to suppose that the regular division of the line of the Icknield Way route by cross-dykes continued north-eastwards beyond the Chilterns proper although still on the chalk bedrock. Travelling north-east from the Mile Ditches these dyke systems are the Bran or Heydon Ditch, the Brent or Pampisford Ditch, the Fleam Dyke near Fulbourn and the Devil's Ditch at Newmarket, all in Cambs. In their final form, they were all constructed as a massive single bank and ditch. At present most of the archaeological and historical evidence suggests that all these Cambridgeshire dykes were either constructed or reconstructed in the late or post-Roman period. If they originate in that period they constitute a remarkable reflection of the Iron Age systems of cross-dykes between Luton and Royston. It is more likely that most of them are Anglo-Saxon reconstructions of Iron Age predecessors but on a more massive scale, thus obliterating most of the evidence for the earlier periods of construction. For instance, excavations at Bran Ditch found evidence for three small ditches beneath the main bank which in character look similar to the Mile and Dray's Ditches (Lethbridge & Palmer 1929). Brent Ditch blocks the Icknield Way 3.5 km north of Great Chesterford and Rodwell (1976, 338-9) considered that the line of the dyke ante-dates the Roman road to Cambridge.

Future work

Cambridgeshire County Council archaeologists are currently implementing a programme of excavation and research on the cross-dykes in their county, and although there are some welcome interim reports, it will be interesting to see the final results (Wait 1991; 1992; Robinson 1992). The Hertfordshire dykes would benefit from a similar programme of research for comparison. It is clear that the territorial boundaries of the Chilterns had a long and complex history of development, although further fieldwork, including selective excavation of some of the dykes, will be needed to support this interpretation.

A NEW SITE AT VERULAMIUM (ST ALBANS)

Rosalind Niblett

During the winter of 1991-92, what at first appeared to be a fairly routine rescue excavation resulted in a major reappraisal of the early history of the Roman town of Verulamium.

The Folly Lane site

The site of the excavation lay on the slope of a prominent hill, on the north-east side of the Ver valley, a short distance outside the northeast gate of Verulamium. In the Romano-British period Stane Street, the road connecting Verulamium with Camulodunum (Colchester), ran along the south side of the site.

Although the site lies within the general area of the pre-Roman oppidum (Fig.38), this was not an area where major traces of pre-Roman occupation had been previously recorded. It was therefore something of a surprise to find that the top of the hill had been incorporated in a large rectangular enclosure, covering nearly 2 ha and surrounded by a substantial ditch, 3 m deep. Central to this enclosure was a large pit, 3 m deep and 8 m square, in the base of which were the remains of an elaborate wooden structure. A rectangular, roofed chamber (3 m x 4 m) had stood in the centre of the pit, surrounded by a sophisticated double revetment with a central clay and gravel packing (Fig. 39). How long this structure stood is uncertain, but it appears to have been used as a funerary chamber prior to the burial of a high status aristocrat whose cremated remains were found buried in an adjacent grave pit. The

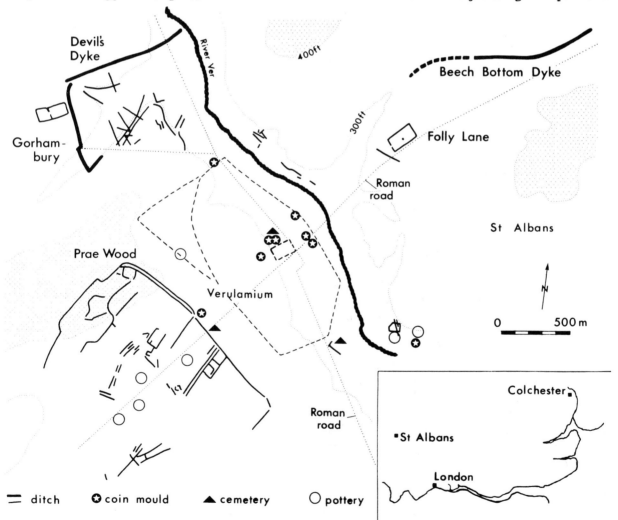

*Fig. 38. The Folly Lane site in relation to the oppidum and the Roman town.
Drawing: after Saunders 1982; copyright - Verulamium Museum.*

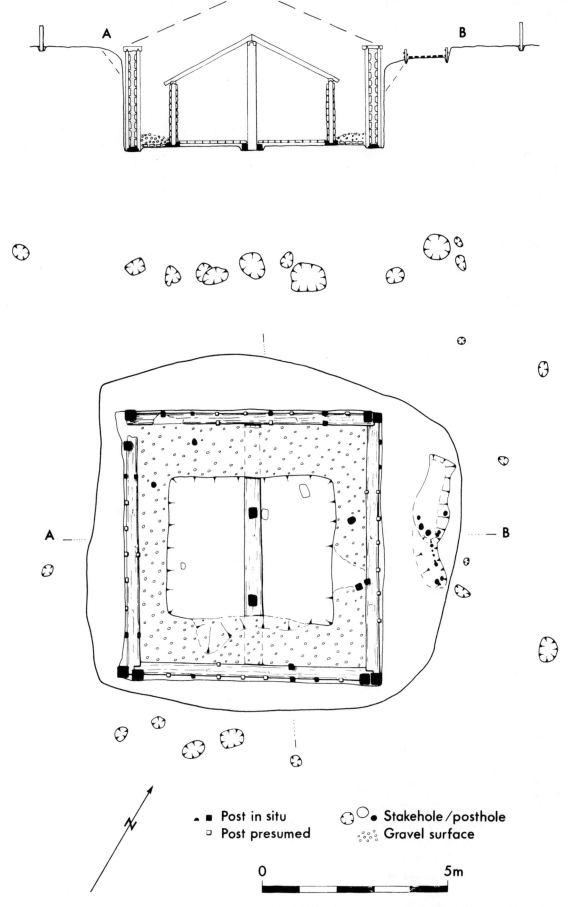

Fig. 39. Plan and suggested cross-section of the funerary structures and grave pit.
Drawing: A. Thorne, copyright - Verulamium Museum.

funerary chamber and the grave pit had been sealed by a single deposit of laid turf which had been placed over the grave and the demolished funerary structures and which had once formed a square mound over both features. This turf had been placed in position immediately after the demolition of the funerary chamber and the filling of the grave pit.

Fig. 40. Folly Lane Burial. Bronze snaffle bit and toggle with enamel decoration. Photograph Verulamium Museum.

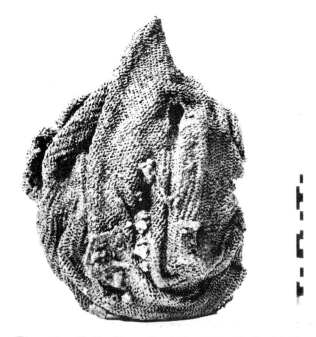

Fig. 41. Folly Lane Burial. The Chain Mail. Photograph Verulamium Museum.

The grave pit contained cremated human bone scattered throughout its fill and a large quantity of extremely rich grave goods. Unfortunately, these had nearly all been burnt on the funeral pyre, so that many of the objects had been damaged beyond recognition. Nevertheless, sufficient survived intact to show that the dead man had been accompanied by a substantial collection of bronze and silver objects, including items of horse equipment decorated with enamel inlay (Fig. 40), silvered bronze vessels, a complete tunic of iron chain mail (Fig. 41), over 400 g of solidified molten silver and remains of an ivory couch. Scattered across the floor of the funerary structure and in the filling of the grave pit were sherds from four Italian amphorae and 30 cups and platters, 15 of these in south Gaulish samian ware and 15 in Gallo-Belgic wares or their local imitations.

The date both of the pottery and the identifiable metalwork is c.AD50. An area of burning 8 m north of the grave pit, associated with amphorae 'sherds, probably marks the site of the funeral pyre.

Apart from the intrinsic interest of the finds and the funerary structures, this discovery is important for several reasons. The custom of burying pre-eminent people in the centre of rectangular or square ditched enclosures was a well-established local practice in the early first century. A series of six of these enclosures were excavated by Dr. Stead at King Harry Lane (Stead 1989) 200 m outside the south-west (Silchester) gate of the later Roman town, whilst 1 km to the south on St. Stephen's Hill parts of what may have been two further enclosures were excavated by the writer in 1989. Nevertheless the scale of the Folly Lane enclosure is out of all proportion to these other enclosures; the size of the ditch alone presupposes some large-scale communal effort for its construction (Fig. 42).

The funerary chamber also implies that additional rituals were demanded for this particular burial which were not normally required even for the comparatively rich central burials in the King Harry Lane enclosures. The closest parallels to the Folly Lane site come from Stanway, a short distance outside Camulodunum. Here, Philip Crummy (pers. comm.) has excavated two funerary chambers both of them in pits within rectangular or square enclosures. Although considerably smaller than the Folly Lane example, these chambers clearly reflect funerary rites very similar to those practised at Folly Lane, and with dates between AD25 and 70 the Stanway chambers span the period of the St. Albans example. On the continent another small mortuary cham-

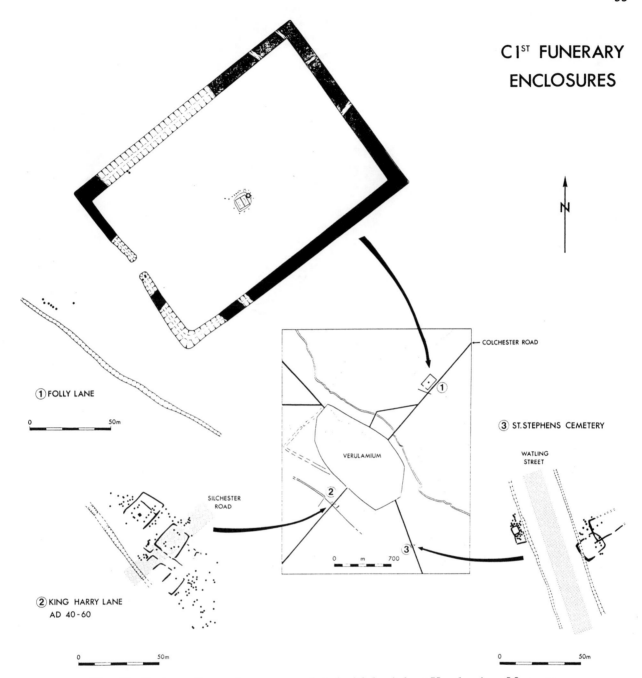

*Fig. 42. Rectangular enclosures associated with burials at Verulamium Museum.
Drawing: A. Thorne, copyright - Verulamium Museum.*

ber at Antran (Vienne) probably belongs to the same category. Here, a square wooden chamber in the base of a shallow pit was associated with rich grave goods dating from the early first century (Pautreau 1991). The Folly Lane site, however, was more than simply a burial place. It clearly had a religious importance that probably persisted for two centuries. At the entrance of the enclosure three inhumations had been laid on the unsilted floor of the ditch. These date from the initial construction of the enclosure and, in an otherwise largely barren ditch fill, clearly had a ritual significance. Indeed, they are reminiscent of the human remains in the enclosure ditches at the ritual sites in northern France, notably at

Ribemont-sur-Ancre, Somme and Gournay-sur-Aronde, l'Oise (Bruneaux 1986).

Conclusive evidence for the long-lived religious importance of the site is provided by the footings for a Romano-Celtic temple, which was built towards the end of the first century a short distance north of the grave pit and funerary chamber, on the possible site of the funeral pyre. This temple faced south-east towards the mound over the grave pit and chamber; it had continued in use at least until the early third century and may only have fallen into decay with the rise of Christianity in the late Roman period. The presence of the Verulamium theatre 850 m away, together with

100

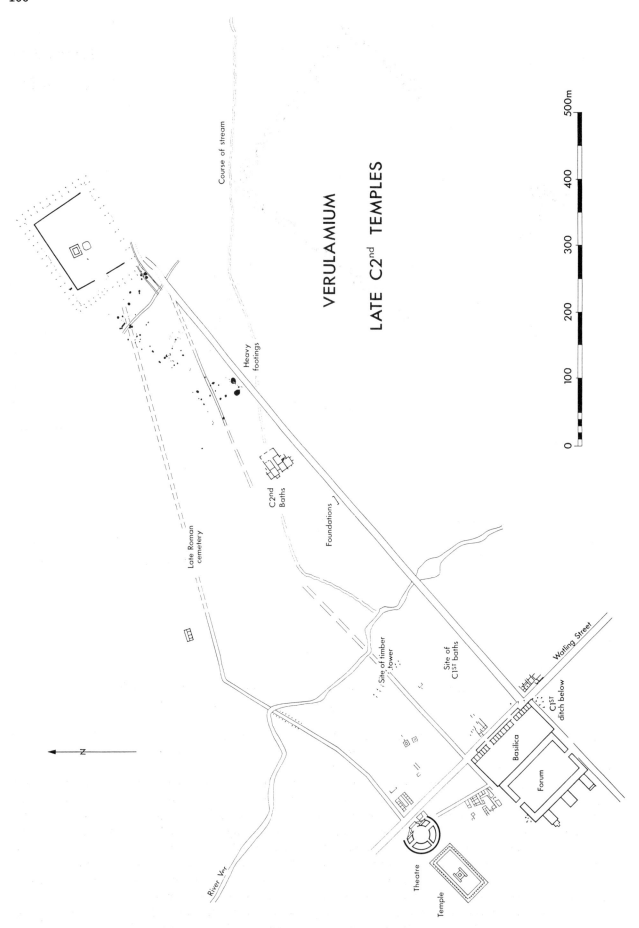

500m

400

300

200

100

0

VERULAMIUM

LATE C2ⁿᵈ TEMPLES

Course of stream

Heavy footings

Late Roman cemetery

C2nd Baths

Foundations

Site of timber tower

Site of C1ST baths

Watling Street

Basilica

C1ST ditch below

Forum

River Ver

Theatre

Temple

N

Fig. 43. The Folly Lane site and the Verulamium theatre/temple in the late second century.
Drawing: A. Thorne, copyright - Verulamium Museum.

the Branch Road bath house, two minor roads apparently connecting the site with the town and numerous wells and cess pits on the lower slope of the site, leads to comparison with non-urban temple/theatre/bathhouse sites, such as Gosbecks, Colchester and Antran and Ribemont on the continent (Fig. 43).

This raises the final point: the identity of the man buried. Although it is impossible to estimate how long the body was kept in the funerary chamber before the final burial, the date of the grave goods suggests that they belonged to a man who died in *c*.AD50. In view of the religious nature of the site, it is possible that both the 'grave goods' and the human remains in the grave pit were all votive deposits, comparable to the sacrificial deposits on the French sites at Gournay and Ribemont. On the other hand, the local tradition of pre-eminent burials within enclosures, and the close parallels with the funerary practices at Colchester, makes it more likely that what was found at Folly Lane was the grave of a local ruler. In this case, this must have been someone who had managed to retain his wealth and status after the Roman conquest of AD43. This in turn implies that he was someone who was ruling under Roman auspices, in other words a client king.

The implications for early Roman Verulamium

The existence of a puppet ruler or client king has far reaching implications as to the attitude of the local people to Rome at the time of the conquest. In the post-invasion period the immediate concern of Rome was not so much to establish 'Roman' towns and 'civilisation' as to create a system whereby native resistance was suppressed and revenue could be collected efficiently. In order to achieve this the Roman administration normally favoured one of two options. One was to garrison an area through a network of forts, each a day's march apart. The other was to set up a client kingdom, in which case a native ruler would be responsible for maintaining peace and order, and for paying tax or tribute to Rome. In return he would exercise a certain amount of self-rule and would retain his traditional status and estate. Obviously, a client kingdom would only be tolerated in an area where the native population was not violently opposed to Rome. As part of the Catuvellaunian/Trinovantian confederacy, whose leaders Togidumnus and Caratacus spearheaded native resistance, it has generally been assumed that the Catuvellaunian territory was garrisoned in the post conquest period, rather than being included in a client kingdom.

As a result of the Folly Lane excavation the following re-interpretation of the earliest years of Roman Verulamium, albeit tentative and provisional, can be put forward. At the time of the Roman conquest in AD43, this section of the Catuvellauni were not violently opposed to Rome and a client kingdom was established. Whether the ruler was some scion of the original Catuvellaunian/Trinovantian dynasty is unknown, but it would not be outside the bounds of possibility that this was Adminius, son of Cunobelin, who had already appealed to Rome for support. Whoever he was, he died in about AD50 and only then was the area incorporated into the Roman province.

This sequence may well explain the absence of a Roman fort. It was noted some time ago that the dearth of early Roman coins from Verulamium makes it unlikely that there was any protracted military occupation here (Reece 1984). The plan of the pre-Flavian timber tower excavated in 1966 on the north-east side of the town does not resemble that of any known fort gate (Anthony 1970; Manning 1979) and it is possible that both it and the early turf rampart found beneath the later town defences in the same insula (Frere 1983, 4-5) relate to an early town defence, rather than a fort. Indeed, the original course of Watling Street suggests that when this road was laid out soon after the conquest, the built up area had already spread as far south as insula III of the later town plan (Frere 1987, 329). The items of military equipment from the town, notably a large fragment of cuirass from a late first century pit south of the London gate, and a helmet allegedly from the river Ver, could derive from a post-Boudiccan garrison posted here to reassure the survivors of the Boudiccan destruction. The very fact that Tacitus tells us that Verulamium was one of the settlements singled out for destruction by the Boudiccan rebels suggests that contemporaries saw it as a settlement of Roman sympathisers (Tacitus *Annales* 14, 33). This is supported by the evidence from Gorhambury (Neal 1990) and King Harry Lane (Niblett & Reeves 1992) for the early and enthusiastic adoption of Roman fashions by local landowners. Perhaps it is not too fanciful to see the occupant of the Folly Lane burial as the original instigator of a local policy of appeasement towards the Roman invaders, a policy which paid off in terms of favourable treatment for this section of the Catuvellauni. What is certainly clear is that the tribal dignitary buried at Folly Lane was remembered by the local people with respect, if not with affection, for several generations.

Postscript. This contribution is an interim account of an excavation that is still in the process of post-excavation assessment. A discussion of recent archaeological discoveries and developments affecting Roman Verulamium is published in the proceedings of the conference on Romano-British towns, held in St Albans in 1989 (Niblett 1993).

A LATE IRON AGE OPPIDUM AT BALDOCK, HERTFORDSHIRE

Gilbert Burleigh

Introduction

Baldock is well-known as a regionally important late Iron Age settlement which developed into a Romano-British small town (Stead & Rigby 1986). Further extensive excavations and surveys over the past fifteen years have added very considerably to our knowledge of the settlement (Burnham & Wacher 1990, 281-8; Burleigh et al. forthcoming). It has been suggested that the pre-Roman settlement may have been significant enough to categorise it as a minor oppidum (Cunliffe 1991, 145). In fact over the years a number of writers have assumed the site should be categorised as an oppidum on the available evidence, for example Stead (1975) and Millett (1990). If one looks at the nature and extent of the late Iron Age settlement, as it is now known, and at the relationship of the settlement to the dyke systems in the surrounding landscape, it is indeed possible to portray Baldock as a minor oppidum (Fig. 44).

Although even now rather less is known about the pre-Roman settlement than about its Romano-British successor, the extensive excavations at Baldock do indicate that the pre-Roman settlement covered an area of at least 20 ha, compared to the later town which perhaps occupied upwards of 40 ha in the second century AD, shrinking back again to c.30 ha during the late Roman period. The Iron Age settlement was delimited on its eastern side by a string of burial enclosures and cemeteries sited along a low south east - north west ridge. This ridge and the use to which it was put in the later Iron Age were defined on the west by a, probably pre-existing, pit alignment which thus marked the eastern extent of the settlement in the earlier first century BC. On the west the settlement area was again defined by burials, although far fewer than on the east, and not including as yet any known extensive cemeteries.

The settlement was founded near the springs forming the source of the river Ivel which flows north to join the Ouse. It is also at the intersection of a number of probable prehistoric tracks linking Baldock with the pre-Roman settlements of Welwyn, Braughing and Sandy, the north-south routes making an important junction with the major east-west route, the Icknield Way. There is archaeological evidence for the existence of these

trackways within the settlement itself; beyond, it is known that there are Roman roads following the routes to the above named settlements, and thus it is hard to accept that the routes were not in use by the late Iron Age. The trackways and cemeteries together delimit the extent and boundaries of the nucleated settlement, roughly in the shape of a triangle. The picture which is emerging so far of the late Iron Age settlement is that although it covered much of the same area as the later small town, occupation and structures were far less dense, suggesting an agglomeration of enclosed farmsteads separated by paddocks, vegetable plots and tracks, rather than an urban environment. This picture matches well that from some other oppida, such as Camulodunon, where there are two major areas of activity: an industrial centre at Sheepen and the major farmstead at Gosbecks, with major cemeteries at Lexden and another at some distance from Gosbecks, and all within the system of dykes (Crummy 1993).

Several of the tracks originating from the Hitchin and Welwyn directions, and ultimately from the western Chilterns and the Verulamium region, which pass through the settlement and beyond either continue to merge with the main line of the Icknield Way or, as in the case of the track from Hitchin, continue as an upper route of the Icknield Way along the higher ground, although the exact line is uncertain. It is interesting that it is where these tracks pass through the settlement to merge with the Icknield Way that the earlier pit alignment was maintained, perhaps to facilitate, but still control, the passage of people, carts and animals. That control may have been made more effective by the excavated evidence which shows that the pits were probably not open, but instead held substantial posts. It is possible that what now appears to be pit alignment originally comprised a barrier of posts and rails with an adjacent bank, and with ingress and egress only permitted by tracks passing through at certain predetermined points.

Baldock's position on the north-eastern edge of the Chilterns, at the head-waters of a tributary of the river Ouse and at an important intersection of local and regional tracks with the major west to east routeway, the Icknield Belt, gives clues as to why it developed and became regionally significant during the late Iron Age. Finds of wealthy

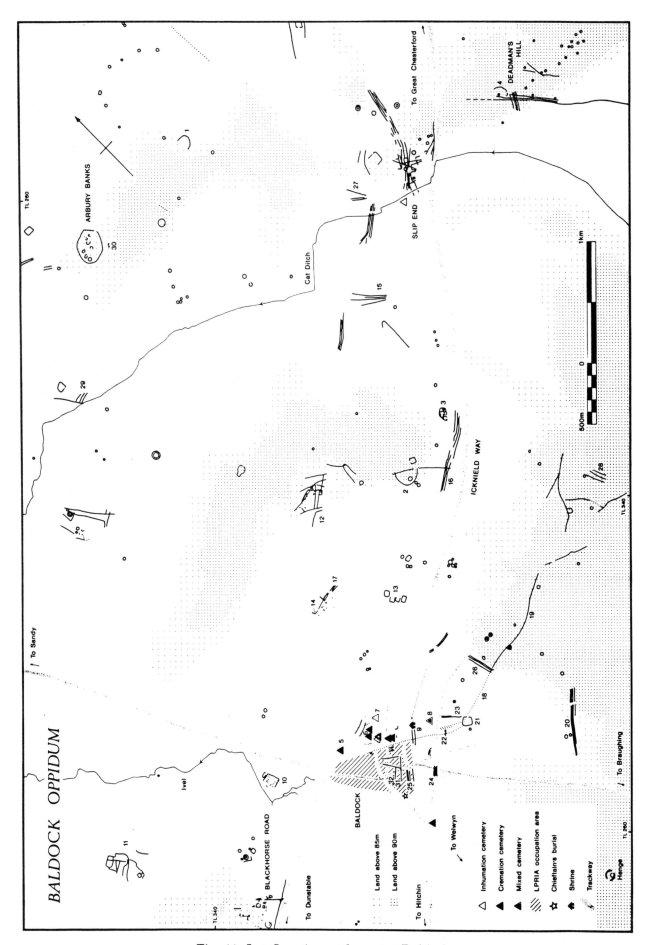

Fig. 44. Late Iron Age settlement at Baldock.

burials, imported pottery, coins and brooches provide some evidence of the settlement's status.

"Chieftain's" burials

Baldock has revealed two important burials of about mid-first century BC date. One was on the south-west side of the settlement, beside the route from the Welwyn/Verulamium region, and contained a large bronze cauldron, two bronze dishes, two bronze-bound wooden buckets, two iron firedogs, an Italian Dressel 1A amphora and part of a pig; the cremated human remains had been wrapped in the skin of a brown bear (Stead & Rigby 1986, 51-61). It is likely that originally the burial was under a mound. Another similar, though less wealthy, burial was excavated on the north-eastern side of the settlement, alongside a continuation of the same route, where it emerges from the settled area before joining the main line of the Icknield Way. The burial, which was probably originally under a mound, was made at the centre of a 33 m square ditched enclosure, and included a bronze-bound wooden bucket with an iron rim, a pedestalled pottery vessel, and parts of three pigs. An adjacent pit apparently contained debris from the cremation pyre which included human and animal bone, burnt and crushed bronze fragments, one with traces of gilt, and several pieces of high-quality iron mail. Within the enclosure there were numerous satellite cremation burials with associated pottery vessels (Rankov 1982, 369; Selkirk 1983, 71-2; Frere 1984, 304; Burleigh et al. forthcoming).

Along the same ridge on this eastern side of the settlement, several other smaller cremation burial enclosures have been excavated. Adjacent to the south-west corner of the 33 m square bucket-burial enclosure was a natural depression in the chalk which had been modified in the Iron Age for a number of ritual activities. This circular hollow was about 18 m in diameter and 2 m in depth, and at its bottom were two late Iron Age inhumations, although there was also evidence for earlier activity involving the deposition of fragmentary human bone going back as far as the fifth century BC. Above the inhumations a small chalk-floored structure was erected, c.4 m by 3 m, containing a hearth. A sequence of associated deposits contained much charcoal, burnt bone and pottery, melted bronze and glass fragments, human bone, brooches, amphora 'sherds, nails, but also fragments of quern, a clay loom weight, spindle whorls, a pottery "counter", daub, and a fragment of painted plaster.

These features were broadly contemporary with the use of the large burial enclosure, although several phases of activity were observed, and they may represent the evidence for ritual involving both high-status as well as domestic activities associated with the adjacent "chieftain's" burial enclosure. It has recently been suggested, in connection with a major late Iron Age ceremonial centre further east along the Icknield Way at Thetford, that weaving was a high status activity, while spinning was a domestic activity (Gregory 1992). At Thetford weaving was represented by finds, but not spinning; in this ritual context at Baldock both activities are in evidence. The structure over the inhumations could be interpreted as a mortuary house, itself of more than one phase, where the bodies of the deceased may have been exposed before cremation and burial. The evidence of the brooches indicates that activity continued from the later first century BC through to just before the Conquest. Early in the Romano-British period the entire hollow was sealed off by a very carefully laid flint gravel surface which followed the contours of the hollow.

Although not representing one event associated with one burial, but several phases of activity, there are possibly similarities here with the mortuary house in a large pit associated with the recently discovered chieftain's burial at Verulamium (Niblett 1992; this volume). It is thus possible that at least some elements of the ritual and structures involved in both the Verulamium burial, and also the similar recently excavated high-status burials at Camulodunum (Crummy 1993), have their origins in precedents which are perhaps partly represented by these discoveries at Baldock (Burleigh 1982, 3-18; forthcoming; Selkirk 1983, 70-4; Rankov 1982, 369; Frere 1984, 304).

Late Iron Age cemeteries

Other burials and extensive pre-Roman cemeteries ran north-west to south-east along this ridge on the eastern side of the settlement area, defined immediately to the west by the pit alignment. To the north, alongside the main branch of the Icknield Way, the partial excavation of a ditched enclosure, c.20 m square, has recovered c.12 cremation burials of Aylesford-Swarling type (Fig. 44, 5). South-east of this enclosure, at the junction of the Icknield Way with the road coming through the settlement from Welwyn, there was another very extensive cremation cemetery (Fig. 44, 6). A few metres south of the junction there existed an exclusively inhumation cemetery (Fig. 44, 7). All three cemeteries just mentioned continued in use into the Romano-British period.

At the southern end of this line of cemeteries a

small late Iron Age inhumation cemetery was succeeded by a cremation cemetery which continued to be used well into the Romano-British period (Fig. 44, no. 8). Interestingly, by the end of the first century BC the pit alignment was breached both by additicnal trackways coming out of the settlement, and by the digging of ditched enclosures that do not seem to be for burial purposes. This suggests that the settlement was expanding and could no longer be constrained by the pit alignment; nor could the ridge to the east of the alignment any longer be reserved exclusively for burial purposes. However, some of the apparently new uses seem to have been burial related. Towards the southern end of the settlement and extending eastwards from the settlement, through the pit alignment and onto the burial ridge, two parallel ditches were constructed, c.20 m apart, creating an enclosure c.120 m long which was open at both ends. At the eastern end of this enclosure a few cremation burials were made around a small circular timber structure, c.5 m across (Fig. 44, 9). It is possible that this was a shrine or mortuary house (Burleigh et al. forthcoming).

Imported pottery, brooches and coins

Besides the evidence discussed above for a nucleated pre-Roman settlement at Baldock, centred on a junction of tracks and defined by the positions of tracks and cemeteries (the latter phenomenon itself perhaps suggesting a semi-urban development), the evidence of material wealth and trade from the finds made in the settlement could be used to argue for oppidum status for the settlement. Valery Rigby places Baldock sixth for its collection of Gallo-Belgic fine-ware imports after the oppida at Camulodunon, Verlamion, Braughing, Silchester and Chichester (Stead & Rigby 1986, 224). This is indeed exalted company and perhaps gives an indication of Baldock's actual status in the late Iron Age. Further finds of Gallo-Belgic wares have been made during the more recent excavations.

Baldock has produced a large number of pre-Conquest brooches (Stead & Rigby 1986, 109-25), and the recent excavations have more or less doubled the number found by Stead. Don Mackreth, who is studying the recently found brooches, is of the opinion that the collection indicates a very strong pre-Conquest presence, especially in the first century BC. He has formed the impression that the population grew and the site became progressively more intensively settled during the 50-70 years before the Roman Conquest (D. Mackreth, pers. comm.). Again, this evidence might suggest that Baldock was approaching ur-

ban status. The manufacture of brooches on the site (Stead & Rigby 1986, 122-3) might be an activity which was controlled by a local authority; certainly it is an industrial activity which might indicate a semi-urban environment.

There are c.140 Celtic coins recorded now from the Baldock settlement. Most, of course, are issues of Tasciovanus and Cunobelin, or related types, but there are also a few types from further afield, including coins from the territories of the Corieltauvi and Durotriges. All these coins may be taken as an indication of Baldock's wealth and status, and of its position as a trading centre. Finds of Gallo-Belgic, early British and potin types help to suggest that an early high-status settlement was developing at Baldock throughout the first century BC. Interestingly, there seems to be a difference emerging in the record between coins found on Walls Field and those found on Upper Walls Common, that is between those west of the pit alignment in the original settlement area and those east of the pit alignment: the cemetery area into which the settlement expanded from the last quarter of the first century BC. Issues of Cunobelin predominate on Walls Field while Upper Walls Common has a normal coin profile for the region, although with a slight bias towards developed issues of Cunobelin. This could be taken to reflect a greater coin loss of Cunobelin types on Upper Walls Common, suggesting that the settlement was expanding there in the later period, as is known to have occurred from other evidence. What is surprising is the Walls Field profile, due to its having yielded three times as many later issues of Cunobelin as it has coins of the time of Tasciovanus (C. Haselgrove, pers. comm.). Haselgrove has suggested that there is an element of deliberate coin deposition on Walls Field either late in the Iron Age or early in the Roman period, perhaps indicating the existence of a temple. The area where these coins have been recovered is too far from the known later temple site (over 200 m) for there to be an association.

Boundary dykes

Looking beyond the settlement area itself to the surrounding landscape, it has become apparent from the study of aerial photographs taken over the last 30 years that there is an unusual concentration of boundary features in the vicinity of Baldock, and apparently dating to the Iron Age. There is a significant number of multiple dykes running parallel to the line of the Icknield Way between Baldock and Deadman's Hill, in effect making a third group of Chilterns dykes (Bryant & Burleigh this volume). As far as is known, dykes parallel with the Icknield Way only occur over this limited area immediately to the east of Baldock. Moreover, there are also multiple dykes running across the Icknield Belt in this same area, forming small sub-divisions which again are not apparent in any other part of the Chilterns. In addition, although only few in number, there are more pit alignments in this area than are known so far in any comparable stretch of the Icknield Belt. Taken with other single ditch boundaries, the concentration and layout of all these features in this one relatively small area is quite remarkable. It really does look as if there was a system of dykes related to the late Iron Age settlement at Baldock, forming the core territory of a minor oppidum.

It is possible to suggest that in the Bronze Age the area was divided up with barrow cemeteries acting as boundaries and sub-divisions on a rather different layout to that which evolved in the Iron Age. The linear barrow cemeteries on Deadman's Hill and on the ridge to the south-east of Baldock indicate a landscape with major boundaries on an east-west alignment, while the pit alignments east of Arbury Banks, if early, suggest further divisions north-south. By the end of the Bronze Age and beginning of the Iron Age, the landscape became divided up by a combination of pit alignments and single banks and ditches, the major boundaries running approximately north-west to south-east across the Icknield Belt, forming one of the territories of the eastern Chilterns, in this case apparently centred by the early to middle Iron Age on Arbury Banks.

Other settlements

Another important settlement at this period was that at Blackhorse Road, Letchworth (Moss-Eccardt 1988), where a number of farmsteads existed, some within ditched enclosures although not necessarily all contemporary. In the early Iron Age the settlement was sub-divided by a pit alignment (Matthews & Burleigh, forthcoming). The settlement was occupied throughout the Iron Age, although apparently declining in importance towards the end of the period, coinciding with the growth of the Baldock settlement. Nevertheless, at least one D-shaped enclosure was occupied between the second and late first centuries BC by someone with certain material wealth, including a bronze cauldron with an iron rim and collar (Moss-Eccardt 1965). This suggests that although the oppidum was becoming nucleated at Baldock by the second half of the first century BC, some of the outlying farmsteads, whether earlier in origin or not, continued to be occupied by people of some status. At this point it is perhaps of interest to note the situation at Welwyn in the late pre-Roman Iron Age (LPRIA). There, a nucleated settlement has been identified at Welch's Farm which may prove to be an oppidum (Rook 1974, 170). It lies close to the find-spot near Mardleybury of a rich burial containing amphorae (Andrews 1905; 1911). Other settlements in the vicinity are high-status enclosed farmsteads, at least one of which, Grub's Barn, appears to be associated with a Welwyn-type "chieftain's" burial (Rook 1970b). The two "chieftain's" burials from Welwyn itself are not as yet associated with any definite LPRIA settlement site; however, it may be significant that a Romano-British settlement developed in the locality. Apart from the nucleated settlement at Welch's Farm, there is a pattern of high-status enclosed farmsteads on the plateaux overlooking the rivers Mimram and Lea (Rodwell 1976, 337; Burleigh et al. 1990).

Another similar area of intense late Iron Age activity lies in the Broomhall Farm-Staples Farm-Hookscross Farm vicinity, near Aston. A massive ditch, c.8 m wide and 2.5 m deep, has apparently been traced for c.400 m forming three sides of an enclosure, and probably first dug towards the end of the late Iron Age. A cremation burial was found which was probably associated with the discovery nearby of a decorated bronze mirror; a high status site thus appears to be likely. There are apparently several centres of activity in the vicinity, but another site of the oppidum class is a possibility (Rook 1982; S. Bryant, pers. comm.).

What the relationship was to the area of the early Iron Age unenclosed hilltop settlement at Jack's Hill, sited about 3.5 km south of Baldock, is unclear since too little is as yet known about it (Tebbutt 1932; Burleigh 1976; Barrett 1980; Matthews & Burleigh 1988). Clearly, Arbury Banks was a major defended settlement in the early to middle Iron age and, presumably, at least until the growth of Baldock, was the foremost settlement in the area. It is noticeable that there are similar, though smaller, enclosed settlements of Arbury type in the surrounding landscape, for example on Deadman's Hill and possibly at three other locations south of Arbury Banks (Fig. 44, 1-4). How many are contemporary is unknown since none has been excavated. Only Arbury itself has been the subject of any excavations and they were in the nineteenth century (Beldam 1859). Finds from the site include early and middle Iron Age material as well as Romano-British pottery, and it is possible that the site was still a high-status farmstead in the late Iron Age, even if losing its pre-eminence to Baldock.

The Baldock settlement is in fact equidistant between the hillforts of Arbury Banks and Wilbury

Hill. Wilbury seems to have a similar history and development to Arbury, coming to prominence as a defended site in the early Iron Age, although possibly with late Bronze Age antecedents. Wilbury has produced considerable evidence of LPRIA occupation and seems still to have been at least a farmstead in the Romano-British period. Like Arbury, it appears to have been the dominant settlement in one of the Chilterns territories defined by dykes crossing the Icknield Belt. What its relationship to Baldock was is as yet unclear. However, Baldock's major relationship appears to be with Arbury because, as discussed, it seems to succeed the latter as the principal settlement in a territory defined by a system of dykes situated to the south of Arbury and to the east of Baldock.

Numerous other settlements and enclosures are apparent on figure 44. That at Blackhorse Farm (Fig. 44, 10), known from surface finds, was occupied in the late Iron Age and Romano-British periods. The settlement and field system at Norton (Fig. 44, 11) looks of Iron Age type, as do a number of features around Bygrave (Fig. 44, 12). The settlement at Slip End, lying between the main line of the Icknield Way and a multiple dyke, is known to have been occupied throughout the Romano-British period. Recent excavation of late Iron Age inhumations under an early Roman cremation cemetery (Burleigh *et al.* 1993), as well as the appearance of features on the aerial photographs, indicate that the settlement may well have originated during the Iron Age. The underlying presence here of a Bronze Age barrow cemetery may have further implications for the origins and development of both the settlement and land boundary.

Multiple dykes

The evidence from Dray's Ditches suggests that at some time from the early Iron Age onwards the major cross-ridge dykes, originally apparently pit alignments and/or single banks and ditches, were elaborated by the addition of further banks and ditches. Without further excavations, we cannot be sure when this happened in each case, and it may be that it was a gradual transformation. At the Mile Ditches a radiocarbon date from a horse's jaw-bone 2,040 $\pm$ 80 bp (HAR-3485) found in the base of the western ditch, which was possibly the earliest of the three here, indicates that the ditch was open during the second century BC; but if the dyke was being maintained and the ditch kept clean, there is no way at the moment of knowing how long prior to that the ditch had been in use; nor do we know when the two eastern ditches were added to the system. All that is

known about the Mile Ditches is that they were silting up from the early Roman period.

The major territorial boundary on Deadman's Hill, for instance, also had two additional banks and ditches added to the apparently original western bank and ditch. In a later phase, a dyke aligned parallel with the Icknield Belt and consisting of five banks and ditches cuts across the main dyke, forming a junction on the crest of the ridge. Like other multiple dykes, this dyke might also have had more than one phase of construction.

What is apparent from this information is that by the later pre-Roman Iron Age, an area *c.*6 km from west to east by *c.*2 km north to south had been defined by a dyke system, thus enclosing *c.*12 km^2, with the main route of the Icknield Way running through the long axis of the area: in effect a defined and controlled corridor. The system of boundary dykes thus defines an apparent estate lying between the springs of the Ivel and the stream known as the Cat Ditch, with the nucleated late Iron Age settlement of Baldock at the west end of the estate and the smaller settlement of Slip End at the east end. Baldock developed into a Romano-British small town while the settlement at Slip End developed into what might be termed a 'village'.

It has already been suggested that in the early and middle Iron Age, Arbury Banks was the controlling settlement of a double territory defined by cross-ridge dykes athwart the Icknield Way at Wilbury and the Mile Ditches, with a major subdivision at Deadman's Hill. At some time in the later Iron Age the centre of local power seems to have shifted to Baldock. Elements of the dykes which it is here proposed formed Baldock's core estate already existed from the early Iron Age or before, for example Deadman's Hill and possibly the pit alignment at Baldock, as well as the single bank and ditch which continues the latter's line to the east. The alignment of this particular boundary seems to reflect the earlier alignment of the linear barrow cemeteries. Whether the dykes defining this proposed oppidum's core estate were originally constructed as multiple banks and ditches or whether they evolved from single banks and ditches is not as yet known. However, it is likely that it was a complex development over time, as there do appear to be several phases of development and sub-division. Within the estate defined by the dykes, besides the settlements at Baldock and Slip End, other small settlements may well have been occupied in the late Iron Age (e.g. Fig. 44, 12-14 at Bygrave). The settlements at Blackhorse Road and Norton were probably just outside the defined oppidum whereas that at

Blackhorse Farm would be just inside. Recent fieldwalking on the latter site has produced evidence for intense activity in the late Iron Age.

To re-cap then, the oppidum was defined by the dykes apparent on figure 44 at Deadman's Hill, Slip End, Mitchell Hill (15), and Bygrave (16-17). At the west end the Ivel formed the boundary; there may have been further dykes south of the springs but this area has the medieval and modern town of Baldock overlying it. South-east of Baldock the boundary is defined by a succession of pit alignments and single and multiple dykes (Fig. 44, 18-20). In this vicinity a large square-ditched enclosure (Fig. 44, 21) overlies the main pit alignment. This enclosure might be very late Iron Age or even Romano-British in date. In this vicinity also, it is interesting to see two short lengths of pit alignments (Fig. 44, 22) running parallel with the main one and, just to the east, a possible double ditched dyke or trackway (Fig. 44, 23).

Possible defensive ditches at Baldock

A short length of dyke (Fig. 44, 24), consisting of at least a 60 m stretch of three major ditches, has recently been revealed by geophysics only c.150 m south-east of the Baldock nucleated settlement, apparently straddling the trackway from Braughing and aligned approximately at right-angles to the pit alignment. These particular ditches were in fact sectioned during trial trenching in 1968 when, within the space of 22 m, at least nine major ditches, including re-cuts, were recorded (Stead 1975, 127). The south-eastern ditch, with at least five re-cuts, suggests that the monument was a major feature whose function needed to be maintained, and which was possibly in use over a long period. The largest of these ditches were c.3 m wide by 2.25 m deep. Although Stead (1975, 127) was able to write that "this is the nearest approach to defences yet found at Baldock", their significance as part of a triple dyke system was not appreciated. There was evidence that they were being filled in from the early second century AD (Stead & Rigby 1986, 431 & Fig. 7). This might well be expected from a feature that retained little importance for the expanding Romano-British town and it compares with the silting of the Mile Ditches from the later first century AD (see below).

Moreover, it is possible that another but earlier phase of dyke existed defining and protecting the south-eastern boundary to the settlement. On the edge of the settlement area, c.150 m north-west of the previously mentioned dyke, Stead's trial trenches found several substantial parallel ditches, including some re-cuts, which were being in-filled during the first century BC and early first century AD. These ditches (Fig. 44, no. 25), the largest of which was c.2.25 m wide and 1.5 m deep, marked the edge of intensive late Iron Age occupation, including pits and possible enclosure ditches. Again, the latest geophysical survey appears to show these boundary ditches heading in the direction of the pit alignment for a distance of at least 110 m, perhaps constituting another dyke c.35-40 m in width; with banks and possibly palisades this would have been another impressive and formidable barrier. Approximately 60 m still further to the north-west, and again straddling the track entering the settlement from the Braughing direction, the geophysical survey indicates yet another triple ditch feature which may prove to be another even earlier dyke, perhaps from a phase when the settlement was smaller in extent. This particular length of possible dyke (Fig. 44, 31) is known for a distance of 60 m but would be only about 15 m in width. On a similar alignment, but c.70 m west, Stead's trial trenches recorded a large ditch which was c.4 m wide by 2 m deep, and which was becoming in-filled in the first quarter of the first century AD. This could be a continuation of the same dyke.

Another 50 m again to the north-west, the trial trenches revealed a large ditch, c.2.5 m in width and 1.5 m in depth, which subsequently had a massive post-hole, c.1 m deep by 0.35 m across, inserted on its northern edge, perhaps for a palisade; 1 m to the north of the ditch edge a second smaller post-hole could indicate another palisade. The ditch filling was dated to the second quarter of the first century AD. This ditch (Fig. 44, 32) can be seen on the geophysical survey heading north-east for a distance of 100 m, until it makes a junction with another ditch running for c.100 m in a north-westerly direction; the ditches perhaps formed two sides of a major late Iron Age settlement enclosure, probably the core of the oppidum. It is perhaps significant that it is in this area of the later town that a Romano-Celtic temple was erected and a small house of winged type. It is interesting that the site notebook from the 1968 trial trenching actually concluded that the evidence of this sequence of large Iron Age ditches, and probable palisade, together with the evidence for contemporary settlement, suggested the existence of a defended "oppidum".

There were other dykes forming the outer limit of the oppidum further to the south-east (Fig. 44, 20) and east (Fig. 44, 26), protecting the approaches from those directions. In fact, one of the purposes of at least some of the short lengths of dykes would appear to be to control trackways approaching Baldock and the Icknield Way.

At present there is a gap in the evidence between Wallington and Deadman's Hill, but this may well be rectified in time by future aerial photography. There are sub-divisions across the long axis of the estate at Slip End (Fig. 44, 27), Mitchell Hill (Fig. 44, 15) and in two places south-east of Baldock itself (Fig. 44, 26 & 28). An apparent short length of triple dyke by the Cat Ditch (Fig. 44, 29) to the west of Arbury may indicate that the situation was even more complicated than is being suggested here. Certainly recent work has located a single linear ditched boundary (Fig. 44, 30) of several Iron Age phases running south-east from Arbury Banks into an area later occupied by an extensive Romano-British villa (Richmond & Burleigh 1993).

Purpose and character of the Dykes

From the manner in which the lengths of dykes are arranged along the line of the Icknield Way, it seems probable that part of the purpose of the dykes was to channel this cross-country route and control movement, and thus trade, along it during the late Iron Age. As detailed above there is evidence from Baldock for trade and contacts over regional and wider spheres; control of the major east-west route, the Icknield Way, may have been a primary factor in the rise and development of the Baldock oppidum from the first century BC. It is accepted that the routeway known as the Icknield Belt was perhaps as much as 5 km broad in this area, stretching from the chalk ridge in the south to the edge of the Gault Clay in the north, and that it comprised several parallel trackways, not all of which are contemporary. Nevertheless, archaeological evidence from this area, including excavated evidence from Blackhorse Road and Baldock, demonstrates that, as in later periods, the line indicated on figure 44 was in fact the main branch in the late Iron Age and Romano-British periods.

The best evidence for the original size and scale of the Baldock dykes when they were in use and for their date comes from analogy with the cross-ridge dykes of the Mile Ditches and Dray's Ditches. The former survived as earthworks until the early 1940s, and fortunately were photographed from the air by Major Allen in 1934, while the latter are still extant in part as earthworks. All those in the immediate Baldock area have long since been ploughed flat and only the in-filled ditches are visible on aerial photographs.

Dyer's work (1961) on Dray's Ditches shows that

at their most elaborate, apparently from the early Iron Age, the earthworks consisted of three ditches, the largest perhaps originally c.5 m wide and 2 m in depth with three banks, perhaps originally c.2 m in height. There were also three lines of palisades, represented by post-holes, running between two of the ditches. The total width of the monument may have been in excess of 35 m, assuming that all the elements were part of the final form. This would have presented a formidable barrier, especially if the top of the banks, now lost to erosion, had also been surmounted by palisades.

The Mile Ditches in final form consisted of three ditches running between four banks. The largest ditch may originally have been c.3.5 m wide and 1.5 m in depth, and the banks may originally have been c.2 m in height. There was no evidence in the 1978 excavations (Burleigh 1980) for palisades between the ditches, but there could have been palisades on top of the banks. The total width of this multiple dyke was c.30 m, which again would have presented a formidable boundary.

The dykes east of Baldock defining the proposed oppidum, in their final form, consist mainly of three and four ditched monuments which could have had up to five associated banks. The dyke widths seem to vary between c.15 m and 50 m. If it is assumed that their ditches and banks were of a similar scale to those of Dray's and Mile Ditches, they would also have provided impressive barriers, especially if they included palisades.

The strength of these multiple ditched and banked dykes was not in the depth or width of their ditches, nor in the height of their banks; these were relatively slight, and in their earliest phases they would therefore have been simple boundaries. However, in their final form, presenting a succession of banks and ditches, and maybe palisades, they would have represented considerable obstacles; literally strength in depth. On the other hand, what detracts from their effectiveness as barriers or defences is their apparently discontinuous nature; although some lengths could have been longer than they look at present, and they might have been linked by other features such as hedging or fencing, but these certainly would not have been defensive. Was part of their function in the late Iron Age as much to impress as anything else?

Dykes associated with other oppida

By comparison, the well-known dykes at such territorial oppida as Camulodunon, Selsey, Silchester and Bagendon usually consisted of massive single banks and ditches. There is a triple dyke at Camulodunum but this has been shown to belong to the Roman military occupation apparently (Rodwell 1976, 348). Not only are the dykes at these sites far more massive in scale than those associated with Baldock, with deep ditches and very high banks, but they also occur as very long continuous stretches and they are therefore much more convincing as defences as well as boundaries.

In a sense, a better comparison with Baldock is provided by the oppidum at Verlamion where the occupation of the plateau above the river Ver in the area of Prae Wood was at its zenith, as indicated by finds of imported pottery, in the first half of the first century AD. The boundaries of this oppidum did not comprise massive earthworks, but instead consisted of relatively slight ditches with palisades. Cunliffe (1991) classifies Verlamion as an 'open' oppidum, although this is debatable, whereas the proposed Baldock oppidum, with $c.12$ km^2 apparently enclosed by dykes must surely count as a small territorial type. It could be argued that in fact the Verlamion oppidum is a territorial one also, of at least 12 km^2, defined to the north by Devil's Dyke and Beech Bottom Dyke, thus enclosing a length of the Ver valley. Within this area late Iron Age occupation has been found widely spread, but also with centres under the later Roman city, at Gorhambury and at Prae Wood. The enclosed area at Prae Wood may then be seen as only one element, although the most extensive, in a complex pattern of settlement involving several centres. A major cemetery was situated at King Harry Lane (Stead & Rigby 1989), on one interpretation possibly in use from $c.15$BC to $c.$AD45 (D. Mackreth, pers. comm.), and a "chieftain's" burial of great significance has recently been excavated on the opposite side of the Ver valley at Folly Lane (Niblett 1992; this volume), probably dating to just after the Conquest.

There may, in fact, even be an outer limit to the Verlamion territorium much further to the north. North of Redbourn, aerial photographs have revealed a triple ditched dyke, visible for more than 600 m cutting across the valley of the Ver, and enclosing two successive Romano-Celtic temples, as well as a ring-ditch which may be an earlier Iron Age shrine, all within a ditched temenos (Edwards & Partridge 1978, pl. xx; C. Saunders, pers. comm.). Another large enclosed site was recorded in the same vicinity (Edwards & Partridge 1978, 44). So far, this site is the only place in Hertfordshire where a multi-ditched dyke has been recorded away from the chalk ridge of the Chilterns. The site may eventually prove to be of considerable significance in the LPRIA of the area; it could possibly be yet another minor oppidum.

Indeed, the situation is much more involved even than this. There are extensive sites apparently of oppida class, interspersed with numerous farmsteads, many of high status, situated on the plateaux between the various streams flowing south-east from the Chilterns chalk ridge. Travelling in a north-easterly direction from Verlamion which lies in and above the valley of the Ver, there is Wheathampstead above the Lea valley, which was possibly linked to Verlamion by a dyke; between the Lea and the Mimram numerous farmsteads of the period are known, with concentrations around Welwyn Garden City and Welwyn, either or both of which might prove to be oppida; crossing the Mimram, there is the probable oppidum at Welch's Farm with its substantial ditches; and only $c.3$ km to the north east again is the possible oppidum in the vicinity of Broom Hall and Staples Farms, above the valley of the Beane, and again with a substantial ditched enclosure. This raises the possibility of other significant LPRIA settlements existing between the rivers Beane and Rib, in the valley of which lies Braughing. The plateaux and valleys around the Old Bourne and the Dane End tributary might produce interesting results from fieldwork. A study of the valleys and plateaux south-west from Verlamion might also be enlightening in this respect. Indeed, west of Verlamion, a major LPRIA settlement which devloped into a significant Romano-British settlement is already known. At Cow Roast, in the valley of the Bulbourne, there exists a LPRIA settlement of some importance, perhaps of minor oppidum status, which developed into a nucleated Romano-British settlement (see Morris & Wainwright this volume).

It is of interest that the aristocratic burials from the Welwyn area, Verlamion and Camulodunum all appear to be later in date than the "chieftain's" burials from Baldock, perhaps suggesting that the latter site came to prominence earlier than the others. Also of interest perhaps is the fact that, as yet, there are no known aristocratic burials from either Braughing or Cow Roast, and no known dyke system associated with Braughing despite its undoubted importance as a trading emporium. The point being that although all the sites discussed, and no doubt others in the region, were important in the LPRIA, they were not necessarily all important for the same reasons; hence they may each have had at least some different functions one from another, and thus perhaps different characteristics.

Conclusion

To summarise, therefore, the dykes defining the proposed oppidum at Baldock had a number of functions. They helped to define and provide visibly impressive boundaries to a core estate which consisted of the nucleated settlement at Baldock itself, with a smaller centre at Slip End, and a number of other farmsteads. Within this 12 km² territory there was also a linear arrangement of burial enclosures and cemeteries on a low ridge immediately to the east of the Baldock settlement, with at least one other cemetery at Slip End. The area enclosed by the dykes, which themselves undoubtedly represent several phases of development, included one stream and bordered another, thus ensuring a plentiful water supply, although it is known from excavations that wells were being dug also on the higher ground at Baldock away from the springs of the Ivel by the end of the Iron Age. This estate would have included many acres of arable and grazing land for the stock represented by the bones of cattle, sheep, pig and horse found within the main nucleated settlement. The dykes would have had a role in the protection of both people and stock from raiders, but it is difficult to envisage them having a very significant military function. One of the main purposes of these dykes may have been to control the movement of people and stock, and thus trade, along the Icknield Way and other tracks, as well as the junction of routes which met the Way at Baldock from the contemporary centres at Braughing, Welwyn/Verlamion, Sandy and beyond.

Unlike the massive single dyke systems at the other major oppida in south-east England, which tend to be constructed at a very late date in the pre-Roman Iron Age, the Baldock dykes were multiple and apparently reached their utmost complexity by the mid-first century BC, having developed from earlier single boundaries. The Baldock dykes appear to have a more complex history than the much more massive dykes of the major oppida, with perhaps different origins. The origins of the Baldock settlement perhaps lie in the middle Iron Age, while the origins of the postulated related estate with its defining dykes are perhaps even earlier.

In 1975 Stead was able to write "Baldock is significant as an Iron Age oppidum, established certainly by the first century BC" (Stead 1975, 128). Although that view at the time was formed on more limited evidence, and it was a view that was not developed in Stead's final publication (Stead & Rigby 1986), nevertheless it was prescient. It is hoped that this paper, based as it is on the further extensive investigations completed at Baldock during the 20 years since Stead's work there, has provided some additional evidence to the view of the settlement as an oppidum. The archaeological evidence from the settlement itself, including finds such as coins, brooches and imported pottery, the layout of the related dykes system and the fact that the settlement developed very quickly into a small town after the Conquest, all indicate that the LPRIA settlement was not only nucleated but also perhaps semi-urban in character by the second quarter of the first century AD.

THE MEDIEVAL CHAPELS OF THE CHILTERNS:
THE EVIDENCE FROM SOUTH-WEST HERTFORDSHIRE

Nicholas Doggett

Introduction

The aim of this contribution is to examine the manorial chapels and chapels-of-ease of south-west Hertfordshire. From this it may be possible to extrapolate wider trends which occurred across the Chiltern region in the medieval period.

Although some of the chapels may be pre-conquest origin and their distribution may reflect earlier, more dispersed settlement patterns, particular attention is paid here to the twelfth and thirteenth centuries, a period of increasing population and recolonisation of the waste and the time when the majority of the chapels were founded. The chapels provide a useful indicator to the spread of settlement and the location of manors.

Little is known of the physical appearance of many of the chapels and most did not survive the medieval period: their existence, however, is significant and shows that this part of the Chilterns was far more heavily churched, and presumably populated, than the evidence of the surviving parish churches suggest.

Description of the area

After 1066 south-west Hertfordshire lay in the secular administrative unit of the Hundred of Dacorum. This area forms a typical Chiltern landscape of hill, river valleys and low-lying pasture and arable. In the north west, the parish of Puttenham and part of Tring are flat clayland, part of the Vale of Aylesbury. This provides a striking contrast in land use and settlement pattern with the Chiltern Hills, which run from south west to north east across the area , covering much of the parishes of Wigginton, Aldbury, Northcurch, Berkhamstead, Great and Little Gaddesden, Studham and Kensworth. Two important ancient routes cross the area: the Icknield Way and Akeman Street, the Roman road from St Albans to Cirencester.

South-east of the Chilterns the land begins to fall in height and is intersected by the valleys of the Bulborne, Gade and Ver. Further still to the south and east the land is even flatter as the London Clay is reached. In this area are the four detached parishes of Aldenham, Bushey, North Mimms and Shenley. Some of the region is now heavily urbanised as a result of the growth of Hemel Hempstead and Watford.

The selection of a secular administrative area such as Dacorum for a study of parish churches or chapels is open to criticism (Stocker 1990, 141), and at first sight it may not seem as appropriate as that of an ecclesiastical unit. There are, however, important reasons why this particular area has been chosen. Firstly, there have been numerous changes in the ecclesiastical organisation of this part of Hertfordshire, making the selection of an area more difficult. Most of the churches and chapels in Dacorum (part of which now lies in Bedfordshire) were in the rural deanery of Berkhamsted in the archdeaconry of Huntingdon, which until 1845 formed part of the vast diocese of Lincoln, but if this deanery alone had been selected for study, the number of parishes would have been too small for any quantitative analysis. Secondly, and perhaps more importantly, all boundaries are to some extent arbitrary and there is no reason why the natural and topographical features, which to a large degree dictate the location of churches and chapels, should either influence or respect ecclesiastical administrative boundaries any more than they do secular ones. As an area of varied geology, landscape and topography, typical of the Chilterns, the area covered by the medieval Hundred of Dacorum therefore seems to be a suitable candidate for a study of this sort.

The colonisation of the waste and the provision of chapels

To take a relatively well-documented period as a starting point, the later twelfth and thirteenth centuries are often cited as a time of increasing population, with the clearance of woodland and expansion onto marginal land (Postan 1972, 5; Hallam 1981, 94-103), and Dacorum appears to be no exception to this pattern. One consequence of this demographic growth and the reclamation of uncultivated land was the proliferation of chapels. The building of chapels-of-ease is chiefly characteristic of the twelfth century, while in the thirteenth century the founding of private manorial chapels became more common. In both cases the rise of population and the establishment of new settlements, either of village communities or of individual manorial complexes, meant that the existing parish churches could no longer meet all the needs of the local people. In both circumstances the mother church would be very anxious to guard its rights over the newly-established dependent chapels. Thus the new chapels were not originally granted the rights of baptism, marriage and burial with their accompanying dues, although many of the chapels were to obtain these rights and in some cases to achieve parish status themselves before the end of the Middle Ages.

It was probably in the mid- to late twelfth century that the large parishes of Tring and Wheathampstead acquired the chapels-of-ease at Long Marston and Harpenden respectively. It is not known exactly how long these chapels remained fully dependent on their mother churches but in 1319 Pope John XXII granted the inhabitants of Harpenden licence to receive the sacraments and to have the right of burial in the chapel and chapel-yard. It is possible, however, that the people of Harpenden had enjoyed the right of baptism from rather earlier than this as the font currently in the church dates to c.1200. The font, though, may have been transferred from Wheathampstead in c.1320 as it was about this time that the latter church acquired its present fine font; in this case it would seem more likely that Harpenden did not obtain the right of baptism until this time, as suggested by Pope John's grant. Tring also had two other dependent chapels: one at Tiscott, demolished in 1661, and the other at Wilstone, the location of which is probably marked by Chapel Field on the south side of the village.

Just as Tring and Wheathampstead acquired parochial chapels in the twelfth century, so did the parishes of Berkhamsted St. Mary (Northchurch) and Berkhamsted St. Peter (themselves formerly one large parish) in the thirteenth century, although in this case the chapels were manorial. To take the situation in St Peter's first, apart from at least three chapels in the castle, William de Berkhamsted was given land by the Earl of Cornwall in 1235 on which to build a chapel, presumably for his private use. Its exact site is unknown but the ruins of a chapel at Maudelyns (now Marlin Chapel Farm) in Northchurch, founded about the same date by the lord of that manor, can still be seen alongside the farmhouse, which now occupies the moated platform of the former manor itself. Indeed, according to Chauncy (1700: reprinted 1975, 552) there were formerly several other chapels in Northchurch which by his day had been demolished or converted into barns.

Much better documentation attaches to the chapels in the parish of Hemel Hempstead. The chapels of Bovingdon and Flaunden, both in heavily wooded areas and serving settlements not recorded as place names until the thirteenth century, were both in existence by 1235 when it was ordered that the vicar of Hemel Hempstead must provide them with chaplains. The vicar was also responsible for the upkeep of the chapels' books and ornaments and the maintenance of their chapel-yards; he was, however, granted 20s towards the support of the chaplain at Bovingdon (Davis 1914, 292). Despite the mention of the chapel-yards in this document it was not until 1478 that a bull authorised burials at Flaunden, since it was five miles away from the parish church. Indeed, distance from the parish church and the difficulty of getting there in bad weather was the main reason cited by Robert de Hagh in 1238 when he successfully petitioned the Bishop of Lincoln for licence to have a chapel in his court of Haya, without font or bells or right of burial. Such stipulations against the ringing of bells were a frequent condition when permission was granted for a chapel as it was feared, probably with some justification, that the sound of bells would attract passers-by and possibly dissuade them from making the often arduous journey to the parish church. The main reason, of course, that the mother church wished people to attend its own services was for the gifts and offerings that this would bring in, thus the demand that those who usually used the chapels would still have to attend the mother church on the principal saints' days. The desire to retain the payment of mortuary dues and other fees was also the main reason why chapels-of-ease and manorial chapels were not originally given rights of baptism, marriage or burial (Cutts 1898, chapter 8), although in due course such rights were frequently obtained by the chapels in the later Middle Ages. Other chapels in the parish of Hemel Hempstead were at Westbrook Hay, where John de La Hay was allowed to celebrate divine service in 1325, and at unspecified locations in the manor where similar licences were granted to Walter la Enneysi and Sir William La Zouche in 1323/4 and 1332 respectively.

One of the earliest-known manorial chapels in Dacorum was at Broad Colney in the parish of Shenley. Its origins are unknown but in the twelfth century Avelina de Somery endowed it with 20 acres of land. After a change of ownership, it revenues were considerably augmented in 1191 by Henry Fitz Reiner who, in return for permission to celebrate divine service there, granted to the parson of the mother church at Shenley all the land held of him in Shenley plus one pound of cumin to be paid at the feast of St. Botolph, the patron saint of the parish church. Under the terms of Henry's refoundation charter it was ordained that there should be two chaplains with their ministers and for a time at the end of the thirteenth/beginning of the fourteenth century the chapel was governed by a warden and may have been collegiate in status. It seems to have fallen into disuse in the fifteenth century, the last reference to a chaplain there being 1446, and shortly afterwards became ruinous. Another chapel in Shenley was at Titburst, which was in the patronage of the lords of Salisbury Hall in the thirteenth and fourteenth centuries. Its precise location is unknown but it was probably in the detached piece of Shenley between the detached parts of Aldenham and Ridge.

In other parishes chapels were also established in the twelfth and thirteenth centuries. In Caddington the dean and canons of St Paul's had a manorial chapel at Caddington Bury, because of the distance from the parish church which they also held. A survey of 1181 shows that close links were maintained between the church and chapel: in return for one third of the rectorial tithes the minister from the church was to serve the chapel three days a week when the lessee of the manor or his steward was present and required this of him (Coleman 1985, 44; Hale 1858, 147). There was also a chapel at the prebendal manor of Caddington Major, described as destroyed and profaned by 1458. In Aldbury a chapel at *Hamelden* is mentioned in 1297 but the whereabouts of this place are unknown. At Wheathampstead in 1297 William Inge, chief justice of the king's bench, was granted a licence by the Bishop of Lincoln to found a chantry chapel in his house, which was described as being distant both from the parish church and the chapel at Harpenden, while in 1428 there is mention of a chapel at the manor of Herons. The chapel at Nettleden was probably not built until after 1291, as it is not mentioned in Pope Nicholas IV's *Taxatio Ecclesiastica* of that year, but it was in existence by 1381 when it is referred to as a chapel annexed to Pitstone, Bucks. Even in the fifteenth century manorial chapels continued to be built when the circumstances dictated: thus early in the century John de Dyrham was granted licence by Bishop Repingdon of Lincoln (1405-19) to celebrate divine service in his private oratory at North Mimms (Archer 1963, 87). However, the last chapel known to have been built before the reformation in Dacorum was that dedicated to St. Mary and St. George at Copthorne Hill in Aldenham, erected "for the consolation of Christ's faithful,

and especially for the infirm, and for men and women broken with age, and women who have infants, and who dwell far from the parish church." This building was consecrated for the celebration of the eucharist and baptisms in 1520. The founder was Sir Humphrey Coningsby but the original inspiration seems to have come from the will of Ralph Penne (d. 1483/4), who directed his trustees to build a chapel (VCH 1908, 160-1). Although the chapel does not seem to have served as a chantry, it was nevertheless closed under the 1547 act for the dissolution of the chantries: its site is unknown but is thought to be in the immediate vicinity of the Victorian church of Radlett. Finally, in this section, reference should be made to a chapel at Wigginton, described as ruind in 1587/8 (VCH 1908, 317). Nothing further is known of this chapel but it is likely to have been of medieval origin.

Possible pre-conquest origins and the implications for settlement patterns

The model of chapels proliferating as population increased and new settlements were established is frequently backed up by documentary evidence: there were numerous petitions to the bishop, dating to all centuries of the medieval period, complaining about the difficulties of getting to the mother church from far-flung parts of the parish in bad weather, a problem often made worse by the deplorable state of the roads. Sometimes, though, such written evidence may obscure the original reason for the existence of more than one church or chapel in a particular parish. Such a case may be provided by the situation at Studham, where in 1236 William De Eltesdon was granted the right to found a chantry in his manorial chapel at Barworth, on condition that it did not interfere with the rights of the mother church at Studham (Fowler 1926, 152). This chantry was short-lived but the apparently dependent status of Barworth may be misleading. The church mentioned in a charter of 1064 is usually assumed to be the predecessor of the church at Studham but the priest recorded in Domesday is listed under Barworth. This suggests that there may have been two churches in the parish of Studham in the late eleventh century and that only in the twelfth century did the one at Studham become a parish church, this dominance leading some commentators to believe that the chapel at Barworth was founded as a dependent chapel of Studham. It is worth noting here that the Priory of Dunstable, which had been granted Studham in the twelfth century, would naturally have defended this church's "rights" over Barworth when it gave William de Eltesdon permission to found his chantry, thus helping confirm

Fig. 45. a. Upper: south-west view of Long Marston in 1832 (Buckler Drawings, vol. 1 fol. 161);
b. lower: south-east view of Wigginton in 1832 (Buckler Drawings, vol. 1 fol. 189).
Reproduced by kind permission of Hertfordshire Record Office.

the impression that Studham was the more important church which by this date it certainly had become.

A similar model for there originally being more than one church in a parish in the pre-conquest period, with only one becoming dominant and then surviving into the late medieval period, has been postulated for Wharram Percy (Bell 1984), while in Worcestershire there are several examples of "the ancient church (being) superseded as the parochial centre by one of its own chapels"

(Bond 1988, 138). Certainly, there are frequent instances of churches changing status in the medieval period: in Dacorum itself Wigginton, apparently once an independent church, became a chapel of Tring in 1328, although it retained rights of baptism.

Whatever the origins of these chapels, and most probably truly are foundations of the twelfth and thirteenth centuries, they do show that even a relatively poor area like Dacorum was heavily churched in the Middle Ages. There are only 24 churches or chapels, excluding the ruins at Marlin Chapel Farm, of medieval origin remaining in Dacorum but if this chapel and the others for which there is now only documentary evidence are included, and there were possibly more for which no written proof survives, this total (excluding the chapels in Berkahamsted Castle and Chauncy's unsubstantiated reference to former chapels in Northchurch) increases to 43, although admittedly not all were in existence at the same time. This astonishingly high figure puts a totally different complexion on the picture of church provision in the area and suggests a considerably higher population than might otherwise be postulated.

The architecture of manorial chapels and chapels-of-ease

Generally, very little is known about the physical appearance of these buildings. Some were quite substantial but others seem to have been very small indeed. Not surprisingly, the chapels-of-ease rather than the manorial chapels tended to be bigger buildings, suggesting that the architecture of chapels-of-ease may have been more similar to that of parish churches than manorial chapels.

Some of the chapels-of-ease were relatively large buildings, as the drawings of late eighteenth-century and early ninetenth-century artists like H.G. Oldfield and J.C. Buckler show. Perhaps the most impressive chapel was at Harpenden which, before its rebuilding in 1862 (said to have been modelled on its previous architecture) was an early twelfth-century cruciform building, originally with a central tower but replaced by a western tower of c.1470 which still survives today. Also dating from the twelfth century was the chapel at Long Marston (Fig. 45), rebuilt on a new site in 1882. The chapel here consisted of an aisleless nave and chancel with a west tower added in the fifteenth century, all that now survives of the medieval building. The chapel at Wigginton (Fig. 45) also originated as an aisleless nave and chancel with a western chamber, added as a separate structure in the fifteenth century but now incor-porated in the body of the church. Bovingdon and Nettleden were almost entirely rebuilt in the nineteenth century, although the lower parts of the tower at Bovingdon date from the fifteenth century and the tower at Nettleden is still largely an early sixteenth century structure. The chapels at Flaunden and Marlin Chapel Farm are now little more than heaps of rubble, although the former retained most of its unusual Greek cross plan, dating from c.1230, albeit in ruinous form until earlier this century (RCHM 1910, 89-90).

Only documentary evidence survives for the chapels at Caddington Bury and Copthorne Hill, Aldenham. The former, last mentioned in a survey of 1499, is described in 1299 as stone built, roofed with tiles and with a cellar beneath; the Aldenham chapel is known to have been a brick building with a tiled roof and a porch covered with lead. In 1888 Canon Davys (1888, 13-4) discovered what he thought were the remains of a roadside chapel converted into a cottage (since demolished) at Gustard Wood in Wheathampstead, which the *VCH Hertfordshire* has equated with the chapel of Herons mentioned in 1428. However, from Davys's description of the building which had a crown-post roof, it sounds equally likely to have been an open-hall house of relatively high status. Further research into such chapels, both through documents and in the field, is likely to prove a fruitful area for study (Blair 1988, 15).

Note. All unreferenced dates are taken from *VCH Hertfordshire*.

EARTHWORK ENCLOSURES IN THE BUCKINGHAMSHIRE CHILTERNS

Andrew Pike

High up in the Buckinghamshire Chilterns is a number of earthwork enclosures, each consisting of a bank and ditch. Some have been known about for many years and are recorded in early volumes of the *Records of Buckinghamshire*, Lipscomb's *History* (1847) and the Royal Commission on Historical Monuments (England) volume for the area, published in 1912. Others have been discovered at different times - one as recently as 1982.

The average size and shape of these enclosures resembles a largish moat - about 150 x 75 m. None has been excavated and their function must remain conjectural. Inevitably, Victorian writers described them as Roman camps, but this interpretation is unlikely. All the enclosures are situated at a height of between 155 m and 190 m OD and all are located in woodland.

All the enclosures lack documentary evidence. In contrast, the relatively few moated sites in the Chilterns can usually be equated with known manors, as recorded by *VCH Buckinghamshire* in the relevant parish. This suggests that the enclosures did not have an administrative function but that the banks and ditches had some sort of defensive purpose rather than the mainly "decorative" status of moats. Many of the enclosures contain subsidiary enclosures either within the principal one or alongside it, suggesting a house site. Interestingly, at least three of the enclosures have produced iron slag, indicating industrial activity. Also, as mentioned above, all the known enclosures are situated in woodland. This may account for their survival but it also points to some form of activity associated with the famous Chiltern beechwoods. One possibility is that the enclosures were connected with the chase and that they contained dwellings used as hunting lodges or lived in by game-keepers.

In short, these enclosures can perhaps be interpreted as the centres of small woodland settlements, with the principal dwelling and outbuildings situated within the smaller enclosure, where there is one. The larger "bailey enclosure" would have, perhaps, afforded protection to a small domestic herd from wild animals such as deer and wild boar which were prevalent in Buckinghamshire in the medieval period. It would doubtless be the deer and boar which were the principal animals that were hunted. Fieldwork in some of the enclosures has produced small quantities of medieval pottery so, despite the lack of documentary evidence, a date in the medieval period for these structures may be suggested. As well as the industrial activity suggested by the slag, it may be significant that saw-pits exist in the woods close to many of these enclosures.

Gazetteer of Chilterns' enclosures

1. The Lee (Brays Wood) SP915049: an irregularly-shaped enclosure, 150 x 80 m, with a smaller enclosure, 50 m square, against its eastern edge. A fairly dense flint scatter is visible in the smaller enclosure, suggesting a building. Slag is also evident in the enclosure.

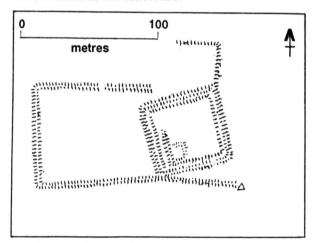

Fig. 46. No. 1 The Lee (Brays Wood). After Allcroft 1908, 473.

2. Great Missenden (The Castle) SP909004: a roughly square enclosure, 80 x 80 m with a substantial external ditch and causeway across it to an entrance on the north-east side. Slag and a small quantity of medieval pottery have been found within the enclosure.

3. Great Missenden (Jenkins Wood) SP904022: a low bank and ditch surrounds the wood, enclosing a triangular-shaped area about 200 x 140 m. In the south-west corner is a smaller subrectangular enclosure measuring about 80 x 50 m.

4. Little Missenden (Coleman's Wood) SU913981: a nearly square enclosure, about 90 x 90 m. There is a possible entrance by the north-west angle. A straight bank continues south from the

west side for about 15 m. There is a substantial external ditch and a slight opposing bank on three sides. Large flints and slag were found in the south-east corner. Saw-pits and the probable site of a building are visible in the vicinity.

5. Amersham/Little Missenden (Brays Wood) SU933997: an irregular bank and ditch encloses an area measuring about 90 x 60 m. A quantity of roofing tiles and medieval pottery was found within the enclosure in the 1930's (Cockburn 1937) and the foundations of three buildings were noted in 1968 when further thirteenth-fourteenth century 'sherds were found (Gowing 1969, 331).

6. Stokenchurch (Dells Wood) SU788943: a small banked enclosure 90 m long by 30 m wide. Surface finds include thirteenth-fourteenth century 'sherds and a quantity of roof tiles, indicating a possible building (Easterbrook 1978).

Possible sites

7. Hughenden (Naphill Common) SU838968: three sides of a ditched enclosure, measuring approximately 150 x 50 m. Iron slag has been found within the enclosure.

8. Great Missenden (Bury Farm) SP907023: a possible enclosure, measuring about 150 x 50 m, defined by a slight bank and external ditch. A second, smaller enclosure may have lain to the south, now mutilated by farm buildings. This site does not lie in woodland and may simply represent an early field enclosure.

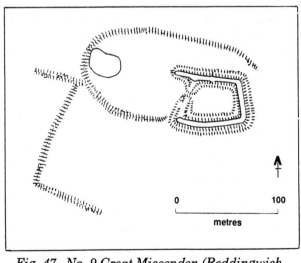

Fig. 47. No. 9 Great Missenden (Reddingwick Wood). After Allcroft 1908, 472.

9. Great Missenden (Reddingwick Wood) SP916020: this is primarily a moated site, perhaps representing the chapel and chantry of Robert de Wymberville at "La Rudinge" recorded in 1233 (Jenkins 1938). The moat, of which three sides

remain, measures 60 x 40 m, but lies within a much larger enclosure comprising a substantial bank and external ditch. Only two-and-a-half sides remain but its original size would have been about 170 x 40 m.

It should also be noted that there is a number of other enclosures in the Chilterns. These are generally accepted as being ringworks and include Hawridge (SP950058), Desborough (SU847933), Fillington (SU798948) and Frith Hill (SP900013) - the last identified by M.E. Farley after woodland clearance in 1991.

THE A41 BY-PASS PROJECT, HERTFORDSHIRE ARCHAEOLOGICAL TRUST

Tom McDonald

The A41 Berkhamsted and Kings Langley By-passes represent a substantial road building scheme, totalling 19 km (11.3 miles) and dual carriagewayed for their entire length. The western end will be linked to the Tring By-pass, from there it will pass south of Berkhamsted, Hemel Hempstead and Kings Langley, to connect with the M25.

The road scheme provided the first major opportunity within the region to observe an entire section cut through a chalk valley, and therefore obtain evidence for the long term settlement and exploitation of a distinct geographical area.

The entire lengths of the by-passes were evaluated in advance of road construction. Largescale trial trenching, as opposed to fieldwalking, was undertaken on the basis that the former will reveal a wider spectrum of archaeological sites, particularly those of prehistoric date. The trenches were 30 m long and 2 m wide, and were laid out at close-set intervals (30 m apart).

Access for the Kings Langley By-pass evaluation was largely obtained by the Hertfordshire Archaeological Trust following lengthy negotiations with numerous landowners, tenants and their agents. Access to the route of Berkhamsted By-pass was not obtainable because of the conditions set by the landowners and agents, principally the payment of legal fees, agents fees and aggravation fees. In addition the Trust was required to take indemnity for the land. Access to the Berkhamsted By-pass was arranged by the Department of Transport who arranged entry ahead of the start of works. This provision coincided almost precisely with the Minister of Transport's statement (August 1991) regarding archaeological evaluations in advance of roadschemes and was made possible partly because of that statement. Time was available for the evaluation of the route (c.2 months), but not for the ensuing excavations. The Department of Transport agreed to delay the awarding of the Berkhamsted contract, and a 6-month programme of excavation was incorporated into the programme of road construction.

Archaeological investigations

The only known site to be affected by the scheme was Grim's Ditch, but since the road was to pass near several Iron Age and Romano-British sites, the discovery of contemporary sites was anticipated. The evaluations, in fact, revealed eight new sites located along the southern plateau edge of the Bulbourne and Gade valleys. Although considerable Iron Age and Romano-British evidence was identified, there was also an unexpectedly high incidence of neolithic and Bronze Age material. The site locations are significant since they are the first of prehistoric date to be found in the county on Clay-with-flints overlying chalk. The overall number and concentration of these sites is unique in the region, and probably reflects not only the exploitation of a favourable settlement zone, but also the enhanced level of information retrieval provided by systemmatic evaluation of a large landscape area.

Stony Lane. This site is located c. 5 km southwest of Hemel Hempstead (TL011059). Roman pottery, tile and animal bone were found in prolific quantities and the pottery assemblages include fine table wares and Samian ware. The finds were derived from pits and ditches within a small enclosure. The nucleus of the site is probably c.100-200 m from the road corridor on an adjacent area of high ground.

Hamberlins Wood. The first site to be excavated on the Berkhamsted By-pass was a length of Grim's Ditch, adjacent to Hamberlins Wood, c.3 km west of Berkhamsted (SP 960088). The bank is actually preserved within the wood and the new road will be diverted to avoid this uncommon feature. Machine and hand dug trenches were cut across the line of the ditch during December 1991. The steep V-profile of the ditch (maximum depth 1.8 m) was recorded and Iron Age pottery was recovered from the basal fill. The majority of the sections through the ditch and adjacent areas revealed ploughed-out bank material on the north side. This material was traceable in section for some 15 m, and in area excavation was recorded sealing small shallow features. It is possible that the features were contemporary with two substantial, subcircular, shaft-like pits which were comparable in size and depth to the neolithic flint shaft mines excavated in the north of the county. Worked flint was recovered during the excavations. Numerous features were revealed in the vicinity of the monument, including pits and

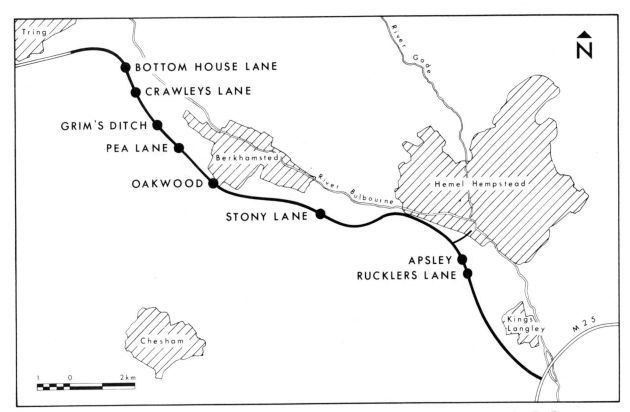

Fig. 48. Location of sites investigated on the A41 Berkhamstead and King's Langley By-Passes.

ditches containing later Iron Age, Romano-British and medieval pottery, indicative of unexpected activity post dating the monument.

Bottom House Lane. This site lies on a terrace of the Bulbourne Valley (132 m OD), *c.*0.5 km from the river (now canalised: SP951105). The natural soil comprises glacially deposited Clay-with-flints, overlying Cretaceous Chalk. The site was substantial; an area 300 m by 60 m was opened using D6 and D8 boxscrapers and a 360 degree mechanical excavator (Figs. 49-50).

Approximately 40 ditches, all aligned east/west, were excavated within a 50 m length of the site. A least six phases of ditch digging and remodelling were identified, including the blocking of a causeway. It seemed that three ditches were most commonly open at any one time, and that they represent either enclosure ditches or, more likely, relate to a linear monument. It is proposed that geophysical surveying is undertaken outside the roadline to resolve the course of the ditches. The earlier phases of ditch digging pre-date a pit which contained substantial fragments of a late neolithic Peterborough Ware pot. Substantial evidence of multi-phased activity was recorded in the vicinity of the ditches dating from the early neolithic to the Iron Age. This evidence will be phased during post excavation. Six- and eight-post structures represented the final phase of occupation (late Bronze Age/Iron Age) and provided

a useful *terminus post quem.*

Crawleys Lane. This site is located 0.6 km south of the Bottom House excavations (SP 955098) and the Cow Roast site (Morris & Wainwright this volume) is nearby to the east. The natural soil comprises glacially deposited Clay-with-flints overlying Cretaceous Chalk. The chalk outcrops within the site and the excavated evidence indicates that it was quarried in the Romano-British period. An area 270 m by 25 m was stripped of topsoil and excavated. Over much of the site the features revealed consisted of dispersed pits and gullies.

The site can be divided into two periods of occupation. To the south of the upland slope, there was a high concentration of prehistoric features, including a round house comprising 21 post- and stake-holes, diameter 5 m. The central and northern areas of the excavation revealed evidence of Romano-British activity in the form of quarrying. A supine inhumation with a late Romano-British beaker and an area of metalling and associated ditches were excavated. The metalling sealed a large fluvial channel which was later re-used as a hollow way.

Pea Lane. This site (SP 964083) occupies a crest (176.95 m OD) which slopes away northwards to the River Bulbourne, *c.* 50 m below. The subsoil comprises Clay-with-flints overlying chalk.

Fig. 49. Excavation in progress of the large neolithic site at Bottom House Lane (photo: Bruce Sampson, Hertfordshire Archaeological Trust).

Fig. 50. Excavation of later neolthic ditches at Bottom House Lane (photo: Bruce Sampson, Hertfordshire Archaeological Trust).

The main features revealed comprise three circular buildings of Bronze Age/Iron Age date enclosed by a boundary ditch. The latest structures were four-post buildings similar to those found at Bottom House Lane. Coarse pottery was retrieved from the post bases. A possible long house structure of later Bronze Age/Iron Age date was revealed within the central area of the site measured 18 m by 11 m and was aligned north/south. Its main components consisted of subcircular post pits and slots and it appeared that a least one phase of alteration had been undertaken.

Oakwood. This site is located on the south west side of Berkhamsted (SP 974072). It was the most extensive site with features occurring throughout 570 m of road corridor. Grim's Ditch and Pea Lane are located less than 0.50 km to the north.

The evaluation revealed a large number of dispersed features (pits, gullies, ditches) truncated by ploughing. Few finds were retrieved but those that were date from the neolithic/Bronze Age and Iron Age. Three areas, each 50 m by 50 m, were stipped and excavated. The northernmost area revealed evidence of middle to late Iron Age oc-

cupation and produced a large quantity of finds. The southern areas revealed evidence of earlier activity, principally a large circular building of probable neolithic date.

Magnotometer surveys were undertaken on the Pea Lane and Oakwood sites prior to their excavation and the results will be directly compared to the excavated evidence.

Further considerations

The construction of the Kings Langley and Berkhamsted By-passes necessitates the disposal of several 100,000 tons of excess soil and most will be deposited on land adjacent to the by-passes. The scale of the operation is such that the amount of land required for dumping is comparable to that purchased for the roads. Planning permissions included provisions for archaeological evaluations prior to dumping, and also provided protection for the archaeological sites which were identified.

At Boxmoor Common, Hemel Hempstead (TL 038059) the evaluation revealed peat deposits (up to 2 m deep) infilling periglacial features known as pingos. These are formed by subterranean ice action: on melting, the ice can leave behind water-filled hollows surrounded by a ring of soil and/or rock. The archaeological evaluations revealed four pingos. Little is known of early post-glacial woodland development in southern England and these are the only known post-glacial peat deposits in the Chilterns immediately north of London. The location of these features therefore offers a rare opportunity to study the early Flandrian vegetation history of the area.

FIELD WORK BY THE CHESS VALLEY ARCHAEOLOGICAL AND HISTORICAL SOCIETY (CVAHS) IN THE BUCKINGHAMSHIRE CHILTERNS

Bambi Stainton

Introduction

The Chess Valley Archaeological and Historical Society (CVAHS) was founded in 1963 and its work falls into three periods. For some years field walking and surface observations were carried out by a few knowledgeable members in their own time and in areas of their choice. Finds were recorded, but fields with no finds were not, and this negative evidence is not recoverable. In 1969 a *First Report of Field Work by the CVAHS*, including evidence from others, was compiled.

In 1975 an organised field survey of the Chess Valley was launched. Initially this was taken to be the river valley sides from crest to crest, but its scope was widened with time as discussed below. All available fields under plough were systematically walked in line abreast approximately 10m apart, depending on the requirements of the survey and the expertise of the members. Being a voluntary society this varies widely and must be taken into account when assessing results. Finds were bagged at appropriate intervals along a strip and recorded on a plan of the field. Hedges, soil type, etc. were also noted. When closer examination was necessary an area was gridded in 10 m squares. Significant excavations have been carried out following field observations. Pasture and woodland were also examined and surveys of earthworks were carried out. Field Group members also observed surface finds in their own areas, i.e. walking, gardening, etc., as well as systematic field walking. These are mostly beyond the scope of the survey area shown in figure 51 but their general area is indicated in figure 52. The CVAHS Records Group undertook research into documents and old maps which might assist the work of the Field Group.

By 1984 all active Field Group members also belonged to the County Museum Archaeological Group (CMAG) and field work is now done in conjunction with the Museum's field survey and excavation programme. Members organise some of the Museum field walks, and specialised research projects are carried out by experienced members. A watching brief is kept on road-works and developments (small works in this part of Bucks.) by members. All finds are recorded in the Society's card index and passed to the Aylesbury Museum as part of their County Museum Antiquities Survey. The drawing and analysis of pottery and flint artefacts is part of the CVAHS programme.

Topography

The Chiltern Plateau in south Buckinghamshire slopes gently from north-west to south-east, parallel to the underlying chalk. The landscape is untypical of a chalk region since the Chilterns are capped largely with Clay-with-flints: an apt description as any local person with a garden will know. This fact, exploited by prehistoric flint knappers, makes life very difficult for the field walkers. There is, however, some evidence from at least one excavation that they may have had access to flint nodules within the chalk, while a flint mine was noted near High Wycombe at the beginning of the century.

The plateau is cut by rivers running down the dipslope, some of which are now dry. The river Chess and the river Misbourne are two of these flowing into the river Colne. The valley sides rise fairly steeply from the valley floor (100 m OD) at Chesham and Amersham, with a wide ridge between them rising to over 165m OD. The whole area is under cultivation, some of it grassland, with patches of secondary woodland. In the early days of the CVAHS we had almost unlimited access throughout the winter to available arable fields. The change in farming techniques to winter wheat has much curtailed field walking since there is so little time between harvesting and replanting.

Archaeological evidence

Sporadic finds of all periods have been made in the Chilterns for many years, as recorded in Jack Head's (1955) *Early Man in South Bucks*. He talks about the "lightness of prehistoric occupation as indicted by the distribution maps" and, twenty years later, it was possible for Dr. J. Evans (1975, 64 & 138), based on available information, to write that "evidence of prehistoric and early settlement in the Chilterns is sparse". Also that "the paucity of Neolithic and Bronze Age settlements in these

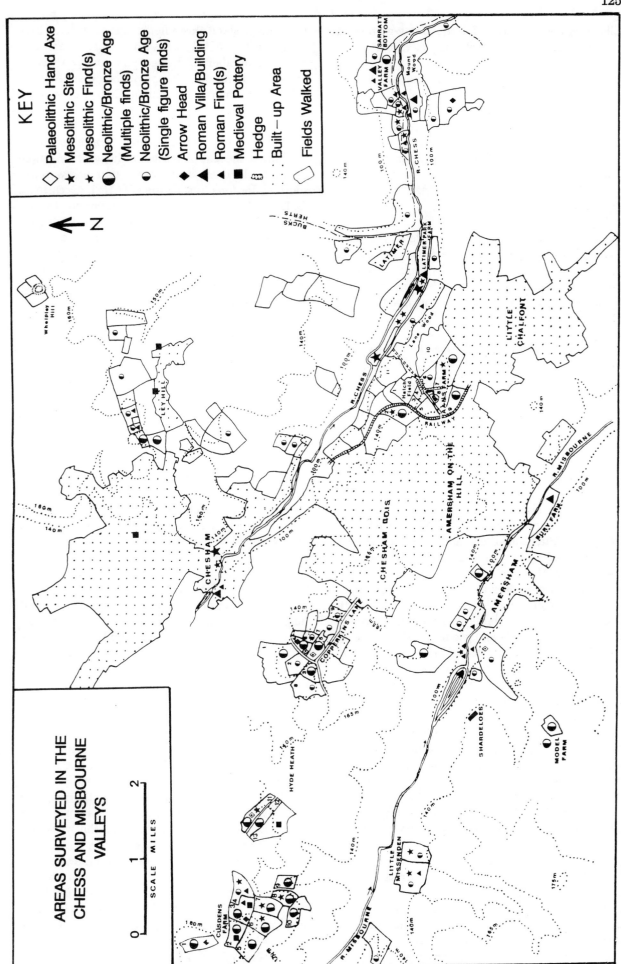

Fig. 51. Areas surveyed in the Chess and Misbourne valleys.

hills is almost certainly due to . . . clay-with-flints . . . tenacious and intractable for cultivation".

It is now equally obvious in 1992 that what were sparse were archaeologists. A discussion on the finds made by the CVAHS and their period and possible significance is given below though, as is so often the case, new information only brings new questions and the true settlement pattern is far from clear.

Palaeolithic period

Evidence for the presence of people in the Chilterns during the palaeolithic periods relies on the chance finds of hand axes. Two mid-Acheulian ovates have been found by members in the valley of the river Misbourne at Amersham and Chalfont St Peter.

Two roughly ovate middle Acheulian hand axes were found on the ploughed surface of two fields on the high ground south of Chesham at Copperkins Lane, ocherous and weathered but unrolled (Stainton 1991), and one was found, equally ocherous, during CMAG and CVAHS field walking at Hyde Heath (Field 11).

Mesolithic period

A mesolithic site with flint working, flora and fauna has been excavated by the CVAHS at Chesham (Stainton 1989) and one with similar finds located by field walking was excavated by the County Museum (Farley 1983) with CMAG and CVAHS members at Gerrards Cross, where the M25 would cross the river Misbourne. Both sites were dated to the late mesolithic period by their microliths, rods and geometric shapes of the late mesolithic 'narrow blade industry' and confirmed by radiocarbon dating of their animal bones. Field walking along the river Chess at Latimer Park Farm discovered a concentration of flint working on a dark area on the river flood plain. Later, gridding yielded eight late mesolithic microliths, cores and core debris and 750 flakes and blades. Further flakes were noted in worn patches among the grass for the next half mile downstream as far as cultivation and trout hatchery tanks. A few fine blades and one piece of bone were found in a dark layer showing in the side of a new hatchery tank.

Further down the river Chess to Sarratt Bottom occasional flint flakes and blades were found beside the path and in molehills. Though one cannot assume that all the flakes were mesolithic it seems reasonable that late mesolithic occupation extended along much of the river Chess.

Members walked three fields along the river Misbourne with CMAG in the Little Missenden area, where a number of blades and snapped blades were found and mesolithic evidence was recorded during the Amersham Romano-British excavation (Yeoman 1985).

No finds in our area have been attributed so far to the earlier mesolithic period, although two simple broad blade microliths were found a few miles south at Jordans (not by the CVAHS). Occasional finds of blades and cores, attributed to the mesolithic period, have been found on the higher ground. Two blades at Raans Farm, five blades (one obliquely truncated) at Copperkins Lane, sixteen blades, one core and obliquely truncated pieces from six of the eleven fields walked at Hyde Heath (CMAG and CVAHS).

Neolithic period - Bronze Age

Forcing archaeological periods and finds into labelled pigeon holes is no longer acceptable, though the terminology is still useful. The interface is nowhere more indistinct than between the neolithic period and the Bronze Age.

In any field walking in this part of the Chilterns the most frequent finds are waste flint flakes, always notoriously difficult to date. The colour of nearly all the flakes ranges from light honey colour to the majority in various shades of mottled grey with cherty inclusions. Their quality varies widely, from finely made flakes from soft hammer technique to flakes of unbelievable crudity, using surface pebbles, much flawed and the poor knapping showing in multiple points of percussion and hinge and plunging fractures. These flakes are often short and squat, or wider than long, with wide striking platforms. They are generally considered late neolithic-Bronze Age when flint was no longer respected as the only tool material.

Figure 51 shows a scatter of neolithic-Bronze Age flakes on most of the fields walked, a fact noted in field work in many other areas. At Ley Hill on the high ground to the north east of Chesham, over six wide-spaced fields, four scrapers, one core and 103 fairly crude flakes were found, the majority from Field 1. Figure 51 also shows three concentrations of neolithic-Bronze Age flintwork but only at Copperkins Lane has it been possible to cover enough area to partly delineate the site.

For various reasons some of the Copperkins Lane fields were walked more than once, which partly accounts for the high flake count. Even so, it appears to be a major site with two leaf arrowheads, 14 scrapers, one pick, 21 cores and 672 flakes.

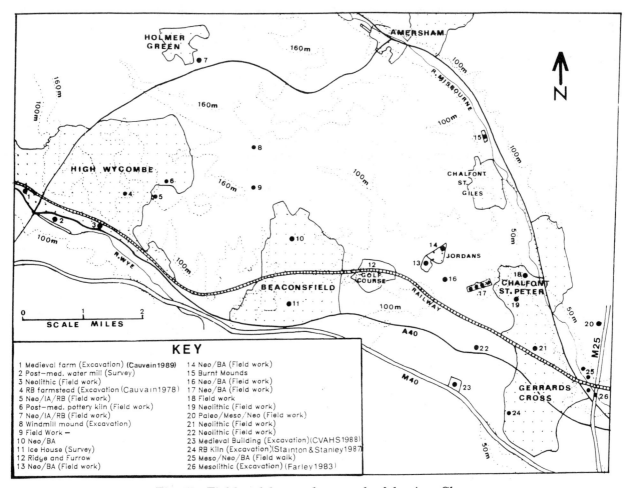

Fig. 52. Fieldwork by members south of the river Chess.

The presence of arrowheads need only indicate the presence of arrows but the other artefacts suggest occupation as well as flint working.

Burnt flints, so-called pot-boilers, are also found in most fields. One cannot be certain how many of these are of prehistoric origin but at the Copperkins Lane site burnt flints in Field 4 occur in a discrete area: within that of the flint finds and so likely to relate to it. The fields at Hyde Heath were walked by mem-bers with CMAG to a different pattern, but the total of one leaf and one transverse arrowhead, one possibly neolithic flaked axe, 19 and possibly more scrapers and 365 flakes indicate a definite working and possibly occupation site. A smaller site was found at Raans Farm, producing nine possible scrapers, one fabricator, three cores and 180 flakes, most of them of the crude variety. The general scatter of indeterminate flakes continues down the Chess to Sarratt Bottom and up the hillsides above Latimer Park Farm and Mount Wood: all indicting the fields then available for walking. This scatter occurs along the Misbourne, 28 flakes from Field (a), seven flakes from Fields B1 and B2, and in Field (c) three scrapers, three cores and 85 flakes, the majority from the 140 m contour line with a

few having tumbled down the slope.

On the south side of the Misbourne one polished axe, one round scraper and 28 crude chunky waste flakes were found in Field (d). Further up the hillside, at and near Model Farm, were found one pick, one pick rough out, two large borers, two scrapers, three cores and 127 very crude flakes, some very large. Further upstream, in the three fields in the Little Missenden area mentioned above, a light scatter of flakes were found in each field. The spread of burnt flints at Copperkins Lane had direct relationship to the flint flakes but much greater concentrations of burnt flints were noted along the side, and even in, the river Chess. Each grouping of the burnt flints seemed similar in size. At Latimer Park Farm, some 20 m from the mesolithic area mentioned above, a discrete oval some 10 m across, of fine pieces of burnt flint about the size of a thumbnail, enough to make the whole feature appear grey, was recorded in 1976. There were other, smaller patches of burnt flint down-stream, some obviously from dredging the long lake, and patches of burnt flints occurred at intervals along the Chess as far as the CVAHS field walking ended, at the Bucks./Herts. boundary below Sarratt Bottom, where burnt flints could be seen on the bed of the Chess.

In 1984 members assisted the County Museum in surveying two Bronze Age Burnt Mounds beside the river Misbourne at Chalfont St Giles (Fig. 52, 15: Smithson 1984). In 1990 two members attended the International Burnt Mound Conference in Birmingham. It now seems possible that the large quantity of burnt flints along the river Chess could be the remains of such mounds, in which case they are rare concrete evidence of Bronze Age occupation.

Iron Age

With flint no longer used as a tool material, finding evidence of late prehistoric occupation in our area has been very unsuccessful. There are no Iron Age earthworks and the late prehistoric pottery seldom survives the rigours of plough soil. The presence of Iron Age hill forts on the Chiltern escarpment, as well as plateau forts in other areas, indicates an Iron Age population we can only imagine from the 'sherds of late pre-Roman Iron Age (Belgic) pottery found. Some of the 'sherds from field walking in the vicinity of the Sarratt Roman villa appear to be of hand-made Belgic ware. 'Sherds of Belgic pottery have also been found at Holmer Green and in the High Wycombe area.

Romano-British period

The evidence for Romano-British villa sites along the rivers of the Chilterns is well known. Latimer was excavated in 1964-71 under Professor Keith Branigan by the CVAHS (Branigan 1971). CVAHS members assisted the County Museum in their excavation of the farm area of the Amersham villa 1982-84 (Yeoman 1985). It was instructive that field walking the remaining unexcavated portion of that site yielded only prehistoric flakes and burnt flints. A few Romano-British 'sherds were found upstream in two of the Little Missenden fields. Romano-British 'sherds, however, abound in the lower part of Shardeloes estate on the south side of the Misbourne, and municipal work trenches dug along the road uncovered Romano-British sherds. The villa itself is know to have been cut into when the ornamental lake was dug in 1751.

A watching brief on a new sewer pipe along the Misbourne noted stone footings, roofing material and Romano-British 'sherds at Bury Farm, and a small excavation was carried out by CVAHS ahead of the pipe work (CVAHS 1985). A few Romano-British 'sherds were found by field walk-

ing near the Latimer villa, while extensive field work around Valley Farm between 1969 and 1972 collected a very large quantity of Romano-British sherds and building materials. Coins and jewellery were found by metal detector in the Valley Farm area. Field walking at Mount Wood resulted in the excavation ahead of deep ploughing of a Roman farm building, malting kiln and infant burial (Dunnett 1985). Some Romano-British 'sherds were found by field walking at Ley Hill, and several were found over fields 3 and 4 at Hyde Heath, possibly the result of manuring of Romano-British fields.

There is much more Romano-British evidence undiscovered. At one time there were nine metal detector groups working the Chess Valley, "the best area for Roman coins they had ever found". Some of these have co-operated with the CVAHS and their coins and jewellery finds are reported, recorded and published (CVAHS 1987).

Post Romano-British period

No pottery of Saxon origin has been found in our area so far. Medieval 'sherds are found on field walks: faint scatters probably indicating no more than manuring fields, with little pottery thrown on middens, but the more than 288 medieval sherds found at Hyde Heath, on Fields 2, 3, 4 and 7, suggest an early date for settlement in the Cudsden Farm area.

The CVAHS did an in-depth study of Raans Farm, which is on record as having been a manor in 1166. Documents (the earliest 1322) and estate maps (from 1733) were studied and many of the earlier estate boundaries recovered. Hedge dating confirmed a very early origin for the remains of what was once a main trackway from the Chess valley to Amersham Common, going through Lane Wood (on an early map "Old Lane Wood"). The name Hatchfield Headland on an estate map suggested that the faint undulations in the present Field 4 should be surveyed, which revealed the first headland known in the Chilterns. Careful observation during a snowfall revealed ridge and furrow (rare and very shallow in the Chilterns) in the grass portion at the west end of Field 7, and further ridge and furrow was noted in Field 5, clearly showing at dusk with buttercups along the ridges.

It is a matter of some thought that the Raans Farm field walks found no medieval 'sherds, although the surveyed areas were peripheral to the central farm area. The CVAHS also surveyed, drew and photographed very finely built channels beneath a barn floor at Raans Farm, considered to be an early corn-drying floor. Other slight earth works were surveyed, including possible medieval fish ponds (David Neal) near Valley Farm and a water meadow and sluice at Latimer.

Figure 52 shows the golf course at Beaconsfield, where a member observed and recorded areas of ridge and furrow, which showed clearly in melting snow. The tumulus of unknown date within a wooded area on the golf course was also surveyed (Fig. 52, 12).

The fields south of Ley Hill show evidence of pits. These may relate to the finds of medieval and post-medieval pottery and tile found at Ley Hill (CVAHS 1989). One kiln was excavated there by the County Museum, assisted by CVAHS (Farley 1988). Field work ahead of development at Emmanuel Church, Chesham, in 1972 yielded an area of post-medieval 'sherds and a large pit of pottery and wasters. Further field work in 1989 located and excavated two early seventeenth century kilns (Cauvain 1989). A member of the CVAHS carried out a watching brief in 1987 and 1988 of a watermain pipeline betwen Hedsor and Bourne End, Bucks.; two other members gave assistance. Late neolithic/Bronze Age flints were found, a Romano-British site was identified and medieval Wooburn north-east of the church was defined (Chaffey 1990).

Discussion

Field work by the CVAHS over the past 30 years has proved, like field work elsewhere, that prehistoric remains are widespread.
The few hand axes of Palaeolithic date found in river valleys cannot confirm a human presence on that spot but the hand axes found on high ground in the Chilterns are considered to be of special significance. It is believed that ice sheets did not override the Chiltern Escarpment in glacial times and that hand axes found on high ground, i.e. Copperkins Lane and Hyde Heath, are virtually *"in situ"*, although their original land surface has long weathered away.

The presence of mesolithic occupation along the Chess and the Misbourne valleys confirms their known preference for waterside sites. The occasional presumed mesolithic blade found away from the rivers could be the result of forays with some flint working into the higher wooded areas. Or if clearance had already started, they could be the remains of greater concentrations that have eroded away.

The concentrations of evidence of neolithic-Bronze Age flint working on the higher ground appears to represent another preference for occupation on those soils. Whether the occupation was continuous or intermittent, they suggest a considerable population. They also indicate areas that were cleared of woodland. It is more difficult to interpret the widespread appearance of slight scatters of waste flakes. Can so much have been cleared? Were there large, or small, scattered clearances?

The present woodland in this part of the Chilterns is of no great antiquity. Areas of marginal land such as hill tops and ridges and areas of poorer soil have been tree planted. If these were areas of preferred occupation in earlier times, we now lose the opportunity of examining and defining areas of prehistoric importance. The concentration of flakes and artefacts found during replanting at Crutches Wood, Jordans, is an example (Fig. 52, 13). The interchange of climate, human activity, land clearance and use is very complicated. Finds cannot be analysed only in relation to present day conditions (see Simmons & Tooley (1981) for a discussion of these perplexing problems).

The CVAHS Romano-British finds follow closely the known pattern of Romano-British occupation sites, although further field work could fill out the picture and finds of more areas of Belgic pottery would help to bridge the late prehistoric settlement gap.

The only medieval finds shown on figure 51 are in the Hyde Heath area where their quantity indicates nearby medieval occupation. Occasional single medieval and thirteenth and fourteenth century 'sherds have been found but do not indicate any definite site. This dearth of medieval evidence is puzzling. It could reflect only the availability of fields for observation, or that the extensive built up areas could mask their earlier beginnings (Fig. 52, 8: Cauvain 1989). Research into the early history of local farms may help to suggest earlier settlements, as would further study of field names. From the example of Raans Farm, one should examine the immediate area around older farms.

Future programme

The above reflections will direct our future programme. With so many fields yielding prehistoric evidence, negative evidence which could delineate sites becomes equally important.

Not only winter wheat now makes large attended field walks difficult to organise but also the recession. Many of our once active wives now work (no weekday field walks) and week-ends are therefore doubly precious for family affairs. We need to be more project orientated, so as to make best use of our resources.

It is hoped to carry out an examination of the river banks, in view of the quantity of burnt flints already noted, in the hope of pin-pointing further burnt mounds. Geophysical surveys are another fruitful field, along with close study of soil types and contour-related areas to suggest further areas for field work.

FIELDWALKING IN SOUTH BEDFORDSHIRE, 1988-91

R.E.T. Hudspith

Introduction

This is an interim report on survey work which is currently still in progress. The maps illustrating the survey (Figs. 53-57) indicate areas fieldwalked up to November 1991. Since December 1988 fieldwalking, i.e. surface collection survey, has been carried out on arable land around Caddington, Houghton Regis, Sundon, Streatley, Chalgrave and Toddington. This survey has been co-ordinated by the writer, working alone and with the Manshead Archaeological Society of Dunstable (Hudspith 1990; 1991a; 1991b; 1992) covering an area of approximately 16 km². The aim of this survey has been to try and recover the evidence for, and pattern of, settlement in this area from the mesolithic to medieval periods.

Location

Caddington is situated on a Clay-with-flints covered chalk plateau at 150-200 m OD on the edge of the Chilterns. There are steep scarp slopes north and west with a more gentle slope to the south east. The plateau is dissected by dry river valleys running north west-south east. The Icknield Way runs along the foot of the chalk scarp to the north of Caddington on an east-west route, crossing the Roman Watling Street at Dunstable.

The village of Houghton Regis to the north of Dunstable is situated on a chalk ridge at 125 m OD. Several streams rise from the area around Houghton Regis, mainly draining to the south east on gently sloping chalk loam soils as tributaries of the river Lea. A tributary of the Ouzel brook rises to the north of Houghton Regis and flows westward over chalk loam and clay soils along a broad valley. To the north of the Ouzel brook the land rises to a Boulder Clay covered ridge (at height 130 m OD) running from Chalton to Wingfield. The high clay-covered land continues in an undulating fashion from Wingfield to Toddington. From the hill spur at Chalgrave church, height 140 m OD, the land slopes eastward to the chalk marl drainage basin of the river Flitt. Sundon, another chalk ridge site (at height 160 m OD), has steep scarp slopes to the north and clay-covered ridges to south and east. Most of the area covered by fieldwalking is at a height of above 100 m OD.

Archaeological background

Previous fieldwork in the south Bedfordshire area has been carried out by the antiquarian W.G. Smith (1904), fieldwalking around Dunstable and investigating brickearth pits in the vicinity of east Luton, Caddington, Gaddesden Row and Whipsnade. F.G. Gurney (1920) walked and wrote about the ridgeway route known as the Theedway (Thiedweg: The Highway), as well as investigating the area to the north-west of Dunstable.

The Manshead Society has recovered much information on the archaeology of Dunstable and its surrounding area, mainly from rescue excavations over the past forty years (Matthews & Schneider 1989). The Society carried out limited fieldwalking around the the two small excavation sites of Chalton and Bidwell (Matthews 1962a; 1962b, 12; 1986: Fig. 56, 1 and 2). D. Hall and R. Fowler fieldwalked the parish of Sundon in 1977 (Hall 1991), whilst land at Zouches Farm, Caddington, outside the survey area has been walked by M. Wilmot (Holgate 1991a). The identification of several previously unrecorded sites during the present survey suggests that much of the area has not been extensively fieldwalked in the past.

Method

The method of survey was walking lines spaced 25 m apart and collecting artefacts lying on the field surface along these lines. Finds were identified, recorded and mapped on site. The results were then abstracted to give the visual summary shown in figures 53-57. The method used meant only a small proportion (4%) of the total area was surveyed. How much that sample is representative of the area's archaeology is a matter of inference. A brief discription and discussion of finds, by period, is given below.

The mesolithic period (Fig. 53)

A large flintworking area has been discovered on the ridgetop near Chalton (Fig. 53, 1: TL0226), extending down into the valley along the course of the Ouzel brook. Other isolated finds and small scatters of flints occurred elsewhere along the ridge and valley floor. The finds consisted mainly of broken blades and unretouched flakes, along

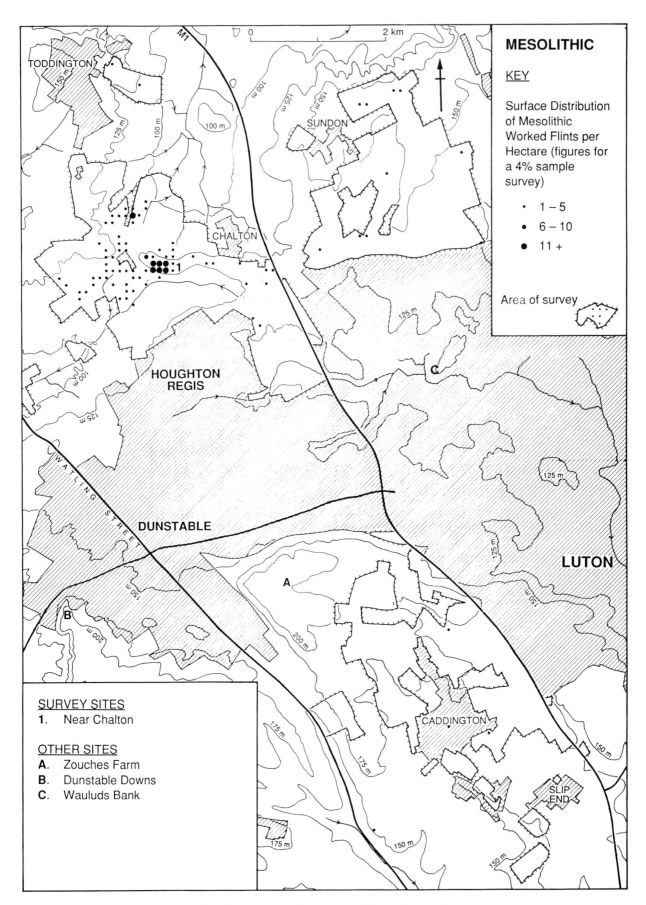

Fig. 53. Distribution of mesolithic flintwork.

with a few cores, and have been identified as mesolithic in date (R. Holgate, pers. comm.). A

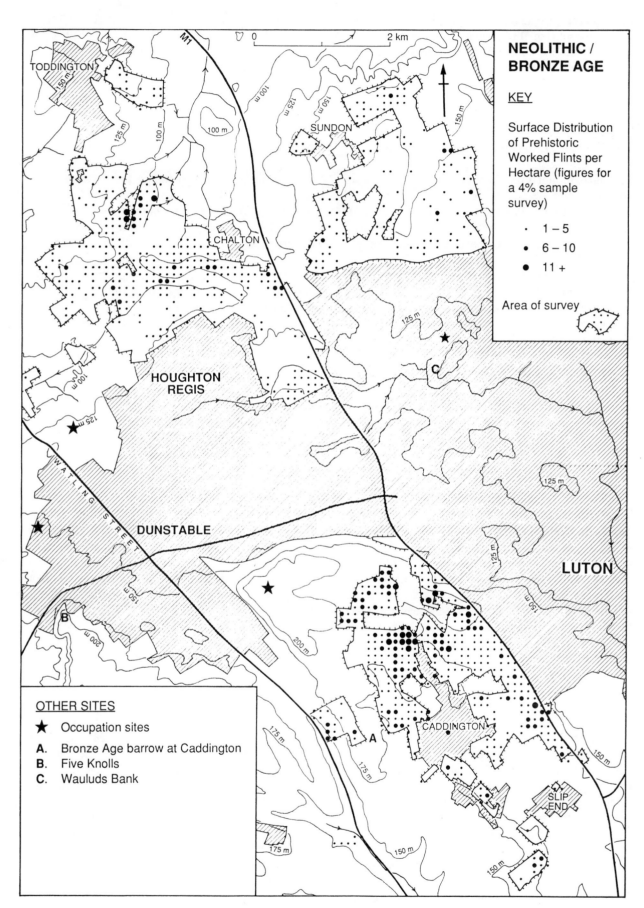

Fig. 54. Distribution of neolithic-Bronze Age flintwork.

smaller concentration of mesolithic flintwork was   found on a low ridge at Chalgrave to the north of the Chalton site (Fig. 53). Other upland areas where mesolithic flints have been found include the scarp slopes at Sundon and Caddington, and three known flintworking sites at Zouches Farm, Caddington (Fig. 53, A: Holgate 1991a, 83-4), Dunstable Downs (Fig. 53, B: Holgate 1991b) and Waulud's Bank (Fig. 53, C: Holgate 1988b, 215).

The neolithic period and Bronze Age (Fig. 54)

Prehistoric activity across the landscape is demonstrated by the widespread distribution of worked flints (cf. Shennan 1985, 47 & 70). Although a general scatter ("background noise") was noted some areas, particularly the ridgetops, did account for greater concentrations of finds. This suggests that the flintworkers of the neolithic and Bronze Age, although exploiting the landscape, still concentrated occupation or activity sites along the ridges, much as in the mesolithic period. However, the effects of erosion and colluviation must be taken into consideration as they may well be distorting the overall picture of prehistoric activity and settlement (Holgate 1988b, 30).

The apparent preference for the upland, Clay-with-flints covered area in terms of activity or settlement sites may be because these areas were used as surface quarries or were intensively cultivated for short periods before the original loess or brown soils eroded away (Shennan 1985, 54). This observation is supported by the results of recent excavation along the line of the A41 Bypass at King's Langley (McDonald this volume). Most of the worked flints had been hard hammer-struck and were mainly unretouched flakes (debitage) with occasional finds of retouched and notched flakes, cutting pieces, scrapers and piercers. A concentration of worked flint finds from Chalgrave (Fig. 54: TL0127) may represent a late neolithic-early Bronze Age occupation or activity site (it overlies a mesolithic site). The range of implements present included cutting flakes, end scrapers and piercers. Nearby was found a polished flint axe fragment, reworked for re-hafting, and 500 m to the east a Beaker period flint dagger, perhaps originally part of a funerary deposit. Some areas yielded very few flint finds; this may be because these were once densely wooded or marshy, or it may reflect differences in land use, for example extensive pasture, where flint was not widely used and discarded.

The ridgeway route known as the Theedway, on the Boulder Clay ridge to the north of Houghton Regis, is indicated by the flint finds as a broad band of passage across the countryside (Fig. 54). No neolithic pottery was found in the survey area. Some fragments of possible late Bronze Age or,

more likely, Iron Age pottery were found, probably indicating occupation sites. Surviving remains of monuments of these periods include Waulud's bank, a low-lying henge monument at the source of the river Lea (Fig. 54, C: Dyer 1964a), and round barrows on Dunstable Downs (Fig. 54, B: Dyer 1991).

The Iron Age (Fig. 55)

A few 'sherds of flint-gritted pottery possibly indicate sites of early Iron Age occupation (cf. Shennan 1985, 76). Several areas produced such finds: along the Theedway at Chalton (TL0325) and Wingfield (Fig. 55, 8: TL0026) and along the ridges at Sundon and Sundon Park (Fig. 55, 4: TL0626). A large scatter of Belgic (late pre-Roman Iron Age) pottery was found on the slope at Wingfield, representing the remains of an extensive occupation site here (Fig. 55, 8). Other smaller scatters of Belgic pottery were found around Grove Farm (Fig. 55, 2: TL0125), Chalgrave (TL0126), Ouzel Brook (north of Houghton) (Fig. 55, 1: TL0325), Houghton Park (TL0324), Sundon (Fig. 55, 4: TL0626; Fig. 55, 5: TL0427), Sundon Park (Fig. 55, 3: TL0626), Inions Farm, Caddington (Fig. 55, 6: TL0720) and Gatehouse Field (Fig. 55, 7: TL0419). These were found mainly in association with Romano-British potsherds and probably indicate a continuity of settlement on these sites.

The distribution of the Iron Age sites suggests the ridgeway route, or the Theedway, was of considerable importance during this period, with settlement alongside or within a short distance of the trackway and by the Romano-British period it may also have acted as a fixed boundary between land holdings.

The Romano-British period (Fig. 56)

The survey identified several previously unrecorded occupation sites: Wingfield (Fig. 56, 7: TL0026), Chalgrave (Fig. 56, 8: TL0126), Houghton Park (Fig. 56, 4: TL0324), Chalton Cross (Fig. 56, 3: TL0325), Sundon Park (Fig. 56, 11: TL0626), Inions Farm, Caddington (Fig. 56, 10: TL0720) (near a possible villa site: Simco 1984, 110) and Gatehouse Field (Fig. 56, 9: TL0419). In addition, a re-assessment was made of the extent of several known sites: Bidwell (Fig. 56, 1: TL0125), Chalton (Fig. 56, 2: TL0226) and the sites recorded at Sundon by D. Hall (1991). The occupation sites were generally marked by scatters of tile, pottery and stone with occasional finds of quernstone fragments, bone and iron slag. The only identifiable piece of Roman metalwork was a barrel lock found near the site at Chalgrave

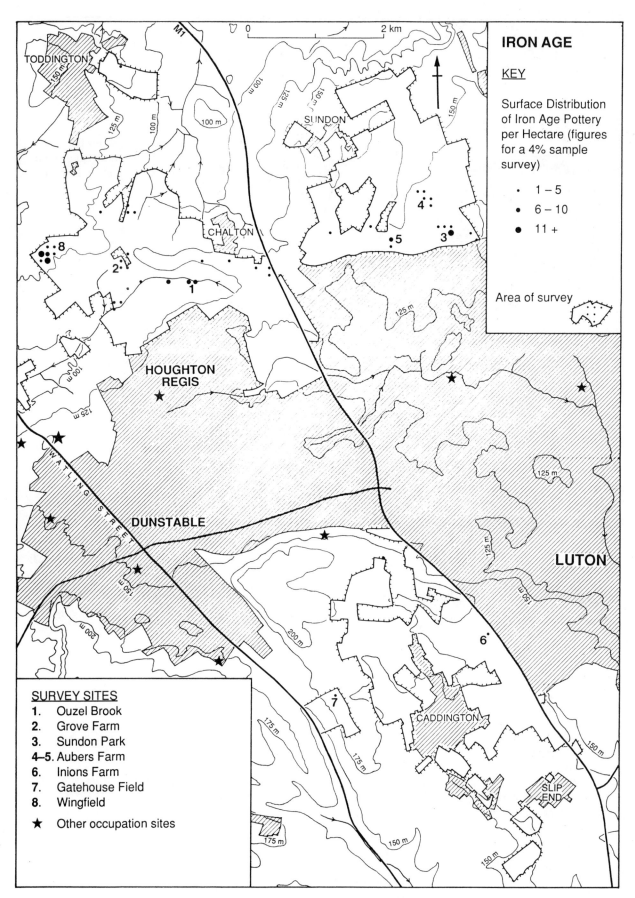

Fig. 55. Distribution of Iron Age pottery.

(Fig. 56, 8). The scatters of pot and tile fragments around each site suggests intensive infield cultiva-

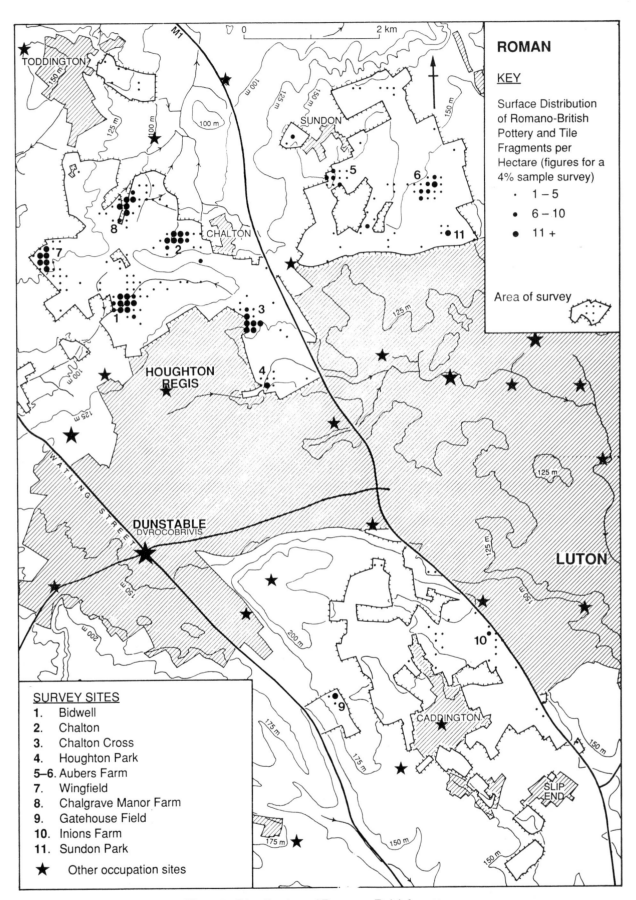

Fig. 56. Distribution of Romano-British pottery.

tion covering a few hectares, with perhaps much   of the land given over to pasture or managed

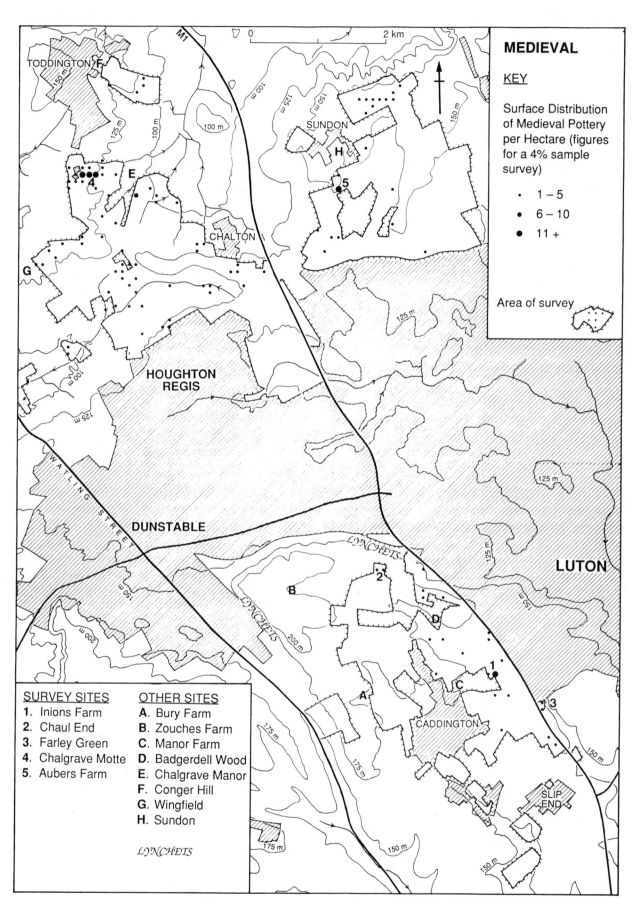

Fig. 57. Distribution of Medieval pottery.

woodland.   There appears to be a significant overlap or continuity of settlement from the late pre-Roman Iron Age through into the Romano-British period. The inhabitants at most of these farmsteads, in time, adopted Romano-British style pottery and building methods of using tile and stone. Finds of flue and hypocaust tiles suggest a degree of affluence by the late Romano-British period at many of these sites, unless they were all re-using building materials from demolished villas. The farmsteads may in part resemble the site at Odell, north Beds. (Simco, 1984, 24) or Chells, Stevenage (Hunn, forthcoming).

The character of the settlement pattern in the Romano-British period seems to be one of dispersed farmsteads of late Iron Age origin. Each of these farmsteads appears to have been within a land unit of approximately 1 km², although the main occupation site may have shifted over time as appears to have been the case at Sundon, where the farmstead site apparently moved location along the ridgetop. These farms may have represented individual landholdings or have been units within a larger estate. The relative closeness of each settlement, regardless of surface geology, suggests a period of maximum landscape exploitation probably not repeated until the later medieval or post-medieval period.

The medieval period (Fig. 57)

To date, no early or mid-Saxon pottery has been recovered from the survey area and only a few possible 'sherds of late Saxon pottery have been found. Rescue excavations at Puddlehill and Sewell Lane by the Manshead Archaeological Society (Matthews & Hawkes 1985, 59) have indicated several Saxon occupation sites along the chalk ridge. These appear to follow on from the established pattern of Iron Age and Romano-British farmsteads, a situation which may also have occurred at Wingfield, where the medieval village (Fig. 57, G) lies close to an Iron Age and Roman site. Whether the Saxon settlement of the lowland followed that of the Romano-British period is unclear.

Figure 57 illustrates finds of the periods c. eleventh-fifteenth centuries. Two main observations can be made from this information. Firstly, the overall quantity of medieval pottery recovered was low, excluding the two occupation sites at Chalgrave and Wingfield, suggesting broken pottery was not readily thrown on the muckheap and transferred to the land by manuring. Secondly, most of the pottery found was in distinct scatters, frequently with building materials, suggesting domestic occupation sites and ploughed out refuse pits, as indicated by the former motte site at

Chalgrave (Pinder & Davison 1988: Fig. 57, 4: TL0027). Finds at Chalgrave and Wingfield of developed St Neots type pottery and local greywares suggest a twelfth-thirteenth century date range. Other possible domestic sites were found at Sundon (Fig. 57, 5: TL0427) and Caddington, indicated by spreads of flint and tile (including Roman tile). These Caddington sites were at Inions Farm (a cropmark site; Fig.57, 1: TL0720), Farley Green (Fig. 57, 3: TL0719) and Chaul End (Fig. 57, 2: TL0521). A medieval building has been excavated in Badgerdell Wood by D. Warren (pers. comm.: Fig. 57, D).

More tangible evidence can be seen in the form of manorial earthworks at Caddington (Fig. 57, A: TL0519; Fig. 57, B: TL0321, Fig. 57, C: TL0620), Chalgrave (Fig. 57, E: TL0228), Conger Hill motte (Fig. 57, F: TL0127) and earthworks at Sundon village (Fig. 57, H: TL0427). Strip lynchets can be seen along the scarp slopes at Caddington.

The post-medieval period

A general scatter of post-medieval pottery, glass, tile and other materials confirms widespread arable cultivation over the past four hundred years. Finds of late medieval transitional wares were particularly apparent around Houghton Regis and Caddington. Dense scatters of post-medieval potsherds alongside trackways indicates the long history of fly tipping in the area.

Conclusions and future work

The surveys have identified previously unrecorded domestic sites of the mesolithic, later prehistoric, Romano-British and medieval periods. As well as suggesting areas of cultivation in the later prehistoric and Romano-British periods, and indicating the antiquity of the ridgeway route known as the Theedway. Some general conclusions can be put forward, for example the visible relationship of Iron Age and Romano-British settlement sites to the Theedway and that, in some local areas at least, the ridgetops were preferred occupation sites for several millennia. However, these should be seen as observations of very localised settlement trends, based on topography, geology and probably innate conservatism, and within a few kilometres very different trends can be observed. Some of these differences between localised areas have been highlighted by recent survey work at Totternhoe (Hudspith 1991b; 1993a) and north-east of Luton (Hudspith 1991c; 1993b). At Totternhoe, prehistoric activity is indicated by large scatters of worked and fire-fractured flints along the valley floor, related to an available water source and close to the Icknield

Way. To the north-east of Luton, the flint scatters tended to occur along the Clay-with-flints covered ridges up to 1 km from the Icknield Way.

The evidence of late Iron Age and Romano-British settlement at Totternhoe, including the villa site, suggests a similar pattern to that noted elsewhere in the survey area, whereas to the north-east of Luton the settlement evidence found so far occurs mainly along the ridge tops and appears to be more widely dispersed. A general scatter of medieval 'sherds was found in most fields around Totternhoe, probably evidence of medieval manuring, unlike most of the survey area where medieval 'sherds were few and mainly limited to apparent occupation sites.

The survey work reported here has already been extended to include neighbouring parishes and may tie in with other field survey work being carried out in surrounding counties. Further fieldwork in surrounding areas is essential to increase knowledge of this part of the Chilterns and, by comparison, to show how the past settement patterns in this area differ from that in other parts of the country.

FIELD WALKING IN MID HERTFORDSHIRE:
CROSS FARM, HARPENDEN

Roger Miles

Introduction

The Archaeology Group of the St Albans and Hertfordshire Architectural and Archaeological Society (SAHAAS) has been undertaking fieldwork in the St Albans area for some 15 years, much of it effectively as a volunteer arm of the Verulamium Museum. This is distinct from participation in Museum excavations and, in the more distant past, undertaking Society excavations.

The Group's fieldwork around St Albans has until recently been confined to two activities, surveying and fieldwalking, with suitable sites and areas for surveying or prospecting being suggested by Museum staff. Four earthwork sites surviving within woodland have been surveyed; we intend to report these as a group once the fourth is complete. The third and fourth lie within the area which is the subject of this short report and will be referred to briefly.

Work was begun in 1987 on a survey of known but unrecorded earthwork features within a wood on Cross Farm, Harpenden. What, however, started as purely another site survey evolved fairly rapidly into a wider study of the archaeology of a landscape, fieldwalking being a part of it.

Cross Farm and Thames Wood

Cross Farm lies on the southern edge of Harpenden, immediately to the east of the London-Bedford railway line, and extends eastward as far as Nomansland Common. The farm (located at TL151129) has a number of older buildings, most notable of which is the farmhouse itself, a fifteenth century timber-framed house, much modified and extended, with brick cladding added in the seventeenth century. The farm and lands were in the ownership of Westminster Abbey for several hundred years.

Thames Wood, believed to derive its name from ownership in the fourteenth century by a Robert de Thame (Feet of Fines 1358: Page 1908, 307), is one of a number of woods on the farm.

Topology and geology

The land is, typically for this part of Hertfordshire, a drift covering of clay, sandy clay and Clay-with-flint on Chalk (Institute of Geological Sciences 1981). Gravels mark a dry valley which runs from northwest to southeast. The highest point is at 126 m OD, the bottom of the valley at 95 m, this change of elevation occurring over a distance of approximately 1 km. Exploitation of the clays is marked by several clay pits (all within woods) and there were brickworks in the south Harpenden area into this century, one just on the border of the farm itself (OS 6" 1879; marked BW on Fig. 58). The underlying chalk is only in evidence where rabbits have burrowed in the side of one of the clay pits mentioned. The clay soils are acid to a greater or lesser extent, necessitating treatment with chalk or lime, particularly for the calcium-depleting grain crops which have predominated for many years. However, there is no obvious evidence of marl pits for chalk extraction for this purpose on the farm itself.

Thames Wood lies very close to, and only a few metres lower than, the highest part of the farm, which is some 200 m to the north-east of it. Part way down the slope into the valley is Clappers Wood, similar to Thames Wood in that there are coppiced trees of some antiquity and earthworks in evidence (this is the fourth site being surveyed).

Although the farmhouse and buildings lie in the valley bottom, sheltered from south-westerly winds, in the vicinity of Thames Wood on the rise above the farm and in the fields beyond exposure to winds is unimpeded for several kilometres. Those engaged in the studies of the farm will attest to the unpleasant conditions for fieldwork that this can bring at times. Maps of the last century and earlier show greater woodland coverage and more fields with attendant hedges which would have had a mollifying effect on the wind.

Archaeological background

The County Archaeological Record shows a large number of sites of various periods in the Sandridge-Wheathampstead-Harpenden area, with the farm, which covers some 200 ha, including three: the farmhouse itself, Thames Wood and Clappers Wood (Herts. SMR 2874, 2669 & 6198).

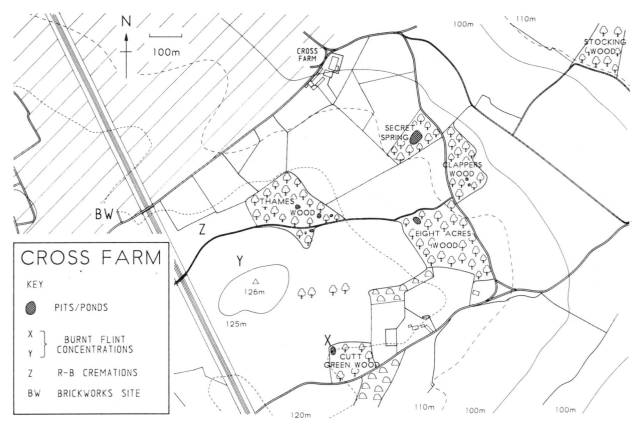

Fig. 58. Cross Farm: location of survey area and archaeological features.

Both the woods are noted because of the earthworks within them.

Fragments of Hertfordshire greyware pottery found while surveying Thames and Clappers Woods indicate a possible medieval date for the earthwork features that they contain, but this cannot be conclusive on that evidence alone. Each of the two woods has in addition to the earthwork banks and ditches what appear to be single, isolated dumps of building demolition material. These consist of flints, fragments of Romano-British brick and roof tile and clay peg tile with large amounts of decayed mortar. Both are surmounted by large tree stumps. Distribution of material is tight and not extensive enough to resemble that from a collapsed building. A sondage in the Thames Wood feature yielded in addition to the material already mentioned a fragment of part-glazed peg tile and a fragment of glazed medieval floor tile of the series from St Albans Abbey Chapter House. The Clappers Wood feature appears from superficial examination to contain similar building material. The source, or sources, of the material in both woods has yet to be identified. The mix of materials must suggest re-use of Romano-British materials in a medieval or later structure that has in turn been intentionally demolished and dispersed.

No previous fieldwalking is known to have been done on Cross Farm. As far as we know the nearest was carried out by Verulamium Museum in 1986-1987, at Sandridge, some 2.5 km away.

Fieldwalking method

The Group has consistently used a 100% sample method, both for Cross Farm and for the locations worked on previously. Strips 30 m in width are walked, lengths varying according to the size and shape of the fields, but not normally exceeding 250 m. Rough sorting is done on the spot, all further examination taking place after washing. Consistency of coverage is recognized not to be very high, with varying numbers of personnel with varying experience. For numbers between six and ten, strips are walked full width; four or five people walk in half widths. Because of this variability in prospecting effort, the results should be regarded as something less than truly quantitative, but better than only qualitative. The area covered so far (autumn 1992) is approximately 45 ha.

In order to assess the effectiveness of the fieldwalking and obtain some 'absolute' figures for finds content in the soil, a series of sondages are being made over the whole area. A 1 m square trench is excavated to the base of the ploughsoil, with total recovery of artefact content by (dry) sieving. This work is not complete yet, but we in-

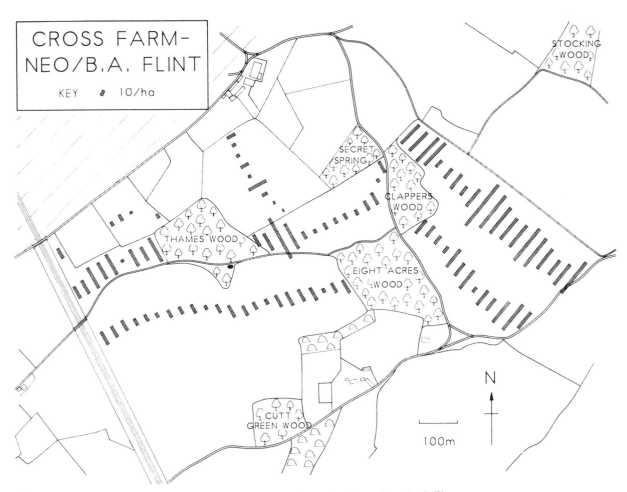

CROSS FARM-
NEO/B.A. FLINT
KEY ▮ 10/ha

STOCKING WOOD

SECRET SPRING

CLAPPERS WOOD

THAMES WOOD

EIGHT ACRES WOOD

CUTT GREEN WOOD

N

100m

Fig. 59. Cross Farm: distribution of worked flint.

tend to look at most of the walked fields in this way. Preliminary results show the large quantities (tonnage in some cases) of artefact material residing in areas of agricultural land.

Fieldwalking results

The distribution density values are plotted as bars, centred on and aligned with the fieldwalking strips (Figs. 59 & 60).

Worked flints

More than 1,000 worked flints have been recovered from the area walked so far. An overwhelming proportion of them date are of neolithic/ Bronze Age date. Only three could be ascribed to the mesolithic with certainty and a single flake was possibly palaeolithic in date. The breakdown by type is shown in Table 9.

About 1.3% showed varying degrees of patination. A not-insignificant number of worked flints has been found casually, during the course of other fieldwork, and also by the farm owners. These have not been included in the figures given above.

Table 9. Flints from the survey.

Flakes	89.0%
Tools	6.4%
Blades	2.4%
Cores	1.1%
Scrapers	0.7%
Hammerstones	0.2%
Core tools	0.1%

The distribution plot (Fig. 59) shows a background level of around 15 flints per hectare, with a maximum of 80-90 per ha. There are areas of concentration on the higher ground, with a more marked general increase towards the valley bottom, where the maximum values occur. This latter could be attributable to soil migration downslope or might indicate that the now dry valley had a stream at some time in the past that could have been a focus for human activity.

Burnt flint

Fieldwalking by the group over many years, as described in the introduction, has shown the widespread occurrence of burnt flint in the St Al-

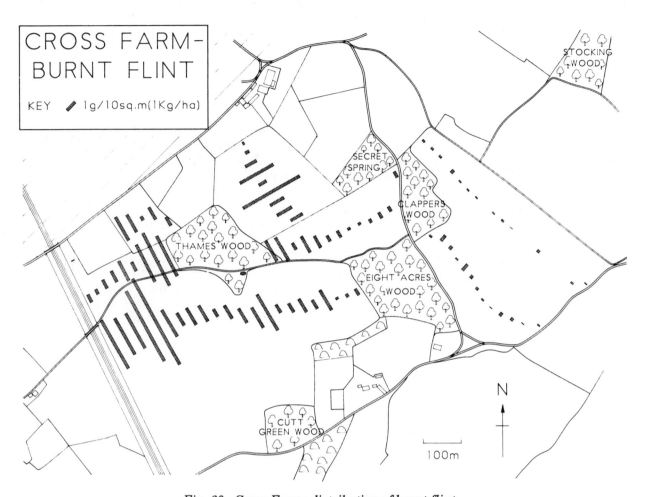

Fig. 60. Cross Farm: distribution of burnt flint.

bans district. Cross Farm proved to be no exception to this and in fact proved to be notable in one particular area. The distribution of burnt flint is shown in Fig. 60. Density ranged from zero to 8 g/10 m2 (8 kg/ha) with low values downslope to the valley bottom and larger amounts to be found on the highest ground. The area of maximum density lies very close to a shallow depression in the field (Y in Fig. 58), approximately 15 m diameter by 1 m deep. There is no direct indication of whether this is natural or man-made, but a tithe map of 1840 showing the fields now amalgamated into that concerned names one as Brickfield and another as Great Brickfield. Hence the depression may be a remnant of a filled-in clay pit, which might be significant in view of what will be described below. During survey work in Thames Wood burnt flint was found with little difficulty in many parts and is present in other woods on the farm.

The owners of Cross Farm brought to our attention the fact that appreciable amounts of burnt flint were to be found in Cutt's Green Wood, in the vicinity of a (presumed) clay pit (X on Fig. 60). Investigation showed this observation to be true

to the extent that in places the topsoil consisted of a mixture of just leafmould, stones and burnt flint. The ground was systematically sampled and in one place yielded over 2 kg of burnt flint in the top centimetre of a 1 m^2 area. The general and particular occurrence of burnt flint on Cross Farm, and in other areas covered by the SAHAAS Archaeology Group, has prompted a detailed study of this material, in an attempt to explain its source or sources. Research has consisted of both field and laboratory experiments and general research, the full results of which will be reported elsewhere. One finding, in brief, however, is that there seems to have been a practice, not as far we can discover yet recorded, of using crushed, calcined flint to 'dress' the surfaces of bricks before firing. Examples can be seen in many older buildings in Hertfordshire, but its wider occurrence has yet to be ascertained. The burnt flint in the vicinity of the clay pit is apparently wastage from the production of the material from flints dug out with the clay.

Pottery

Pot (disregarding the ubiquitous post-medieval

144

and modern material) was scarce, the few pieces found being of either Roman or medieval date. The former were represented most notably by a fragment of plain Samian ware and a piece of mortarium rim from adjacent fields at the high end of the farm. 'Seeing' conditions for fieldwalking were extremely bad when the Samian ware was found and the field was rewalked several seasons later. This resulted in the discovery of a cremation burial, followed by a further five in close proximity (Z on Fig. 58). A second-century cemetery is indicated and awaits excavation by Verulamium Museum. The inferred existence of an associated occupation site is reinforced by the mortarium fragment.

Medieval pot was represented by a few fragments of Hertfordshire greyware. A larger quantity of greyware has been found, both casually and as a result of sampling, within Thames and Clappers Woods. These fragments are at present the best indication of the date of the earthworks in the woods.

Building material

The occurrence of Romano-British brick and roof tile in at least one of the presumed dumps (i.e. that in Thames Wood) has already been described. Similar material was found in virtually all areas fieldwalked, but very thinly spread and not indicative of any building. In the almost certain knowledge that a post-Roman building in the vicinity had incorporated re-used Romano-British material and then been demolished, all the material found might be explained by the normal dispersal processes operating on agricultural land.

Other work

Another recently started fieldwork project is a study of the hedgerows on the farm, but this is not yet complete.

All of the pits or ponds (nine) lying within the area so far studied on the farm have been tested by coring the bottoms. Without exception they consist of solid clay, of more than adequate quality for brickmaking. This finding led to the comment on the absence of marlpits made earlier. It is possible that a disused pit excavated into the hillside, close to the farmhouse, may have been for chalk extraction.

Conclusions

The amount of worked flint, while apparently large, is not exceptional for this type of landscape in this part of the British Isles. This might be in part attributable to differences in skill between amateur and professional fieldwalkers. Such limitations have been commented on above.

Clearly the discovery of the Romano-British cemetery is notable and alone would justify the work put in to fieldwalking on Cross Farm. The full significance of the find awaits excavation. Small-scale rural cemeteries and burial grounds of the Romano-British period have been found and excavated very infrequently, in contrast with those associated with towns and cities, which can be large and easily located. There is the additional prospect that the settlement which the cemetery indicates may be located.

Although explanations for the origin of burnt flint did not arise directly from consideration of its distribution as shown by fieldwalking, there was some corroboration of association with clay extraction for brickmaking. It should be emphasized, however, that this local explanation may be only one of several accounting for the widespread occurrence of burnt flint.

It is hoped that the results of the fieldwalking in the restricted area described in this report will be incorporated with those obtained in other parts of the St Albans district, in a wider-ranging study in the future.

I took the opportunity to explore the use of computer-aided draughting (CAD) in producing maps and other graphical presentations arising from the Cross Farm work. For the record, and for those interested, the maps in this report were produced using FastCAD software on an IBM-compatible PC.

CHEMICAL ANALYSIS OF MEDIEVAL CERAMICS FROM SOUTH BUCKINGHAMSHIRE

Stanley P. Cauvain

Introduction

The production of pottery and tiles in medieval and later periods in south Buckinghamshire is noted in both historical and archaeological records. Centres of medieval ceramic production include Brill (Ivens 1981), Boarstall (Farley 1982), Potters Row, Great Missenden (Ashworth 1983), Denham (Farley and Leach 1988), Ley Hill (Farley 1988) and Penn (Hohler 1941; 1942). The initial interest in medieval ceramics made at Penn centred on the production of decorated floor tiles (Hohler 1941; 1942; Eames 1980), many of which were sold to Windsor Castle and churches in the south-east Midlands in the fourteenth century AD. More recent fieldwork around the villages of Tylers Green and Penn (Buckinghamshire County Museum 1983; Farley and Hutchings 1989; Cauvain et al. 1989) has revealed that in addition to decorated floor tiles, production of plain floor tiles, roof tiles and pottery was taking place around the two villages between the fourteenth and sixteenth centuries AD.

While it is relatively easy to distinguish the ceramic products of particular kiln groups through distinctive shapes, patterns or glazes, it is more difficult to separate visually the unglazed pottery and tiles which form a large, if not the major, part of medieval kiln products. The chemical compositions of fired ceramics mostly reflect the compositions of their parent materials and processing techniques, though other factors undoubtedly affect the composition at the moment of analysis (Stewart et al. 1990). Thus, providing ceramic production centres are exploiting different and relatively local raw materials, individual centres have potential 'chemical fingerprints' which can be used to distinguish one production centre from another. The reader is referred elsewhere for general literature on the subject of chemical analysis of ceramics (Wilson 1978; Parkes 1986; Rice 1987).

This study describes an investigation of the potential of chemical analysis in characterising unglazed pottery and tiles produced at four medieval ceramic production centres in south Buckinghamshire and examines the techniques which can be used to distinguish the products of one centre from another.

Materials and methods

Sample selection

The four medieval ceramic production centres providing unglazed pottery samples for this study were Boarstall (site code CAS5211 in Farley 1982), Joiners Close, Ley Hill (Farley 1988), Rush Green southern kilns, Denham (Farley and Leach 1988) and Tylers Green/Penn (Fig. 61). Samples collected from these centres were given the prefix codes BOA (Boarstall), LEY (Joiners Close), DEN (Rush Green) and TG (Tylers Green/Penn).

Five of the possible medieval pottery and tile production areas which have been identified in the vicinity of the villages of Tylers Green and Penn provided samples for this study (Fig. 62); four areas were identified from recent fieldwork and one (TGD) from a Buckinghamshire County Museum collection of tiles. Samples from Tylers

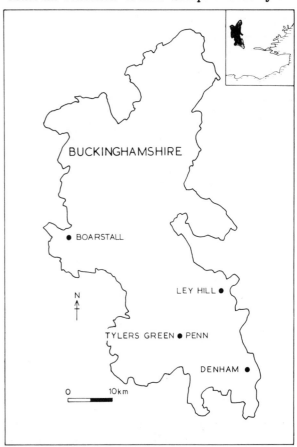

Fig. 61. Location of Medieval ceramic production centres providing samples for this study.

Green/Penn were given the general prefix code TG followed by individual site codes from A through to E. The underlying geology of the Tylers Green/Penn area is mapped as three slightly different clay types overlying Chalk (Geological Survey 1974). At least one of the Tylers Green/Penn production areas is located on each of the clay types (Fig. 62). Not all of the Tylers Green/Penn sites appear to have been producing the same range of ceramic types; however, samples of pottery, tiles and local clays were collected for a more detailed study of this particular medieval ceramic industry.

While the study was underway a sample of a possible Penn tile from the English Heritage excavations at Windsor Castle (Kerr pers. comm.) became available and this was used to test the hypothesis that the Tylers Green/Penn chemical fingerprints could be used to establish the origin of tiles ascribed to Penn on purely stylistic considerations. This sample was coded WIN.

Sample preparation

Fired ceramics, and tiles in particular, have heterogeneous structures, in part because of the clay source and in part because of manufacturing

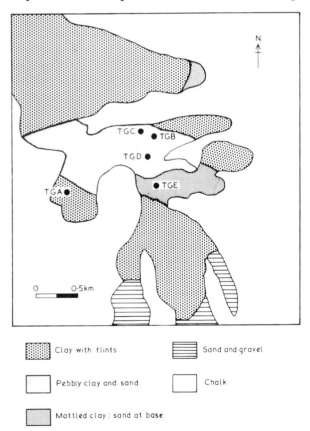

Fig. 62. Location of sampling sites around Tylers Green and Penn (based on the Geological Survey). Each letter code refers to an individual medieval ceramic production area.

techniques. For example, sand or calcined flint may be added to the clay by the potter to modify its handling characteristics. Such additions create variability within fired ceramics and will affect the reliability of the small samples (typically 10-100 mg) needed for chemical analyses.

In an attempt to minimise problems of ceramic heterogeneity about 10 g of each sample were ground by hand to a fine powder with an agate pestle and mortar, and sub-samples for chemical analysis were removed from this mass. In the case of unglazed tiles special care was taken to ensure that the full cross-section was represented because of their much greater thickness compared with that of the pottery. The ground ceramics were stored in glass containers until required for analysis.

Chemical analysis

Both atomic absorption spectroscopy (AAS) and neutron activation analysis (NAA) were used to establish chemical compositions of the unglazed ceramics.

Samples were prepared for AAS by heating between 10 and 15 mg of each sample with approximately 100 mg lithium metaborate in an electrically heated furnace. The resulting fused mixture was dissolved in dilute nitric acid (3% v/v) and element concentrations were measured using a Perkin-Elmer series 560 AA spectrometer. The particular elements measured are given in Table 10.

Table 10. Elements measured by AAS.

Element	Gas mixture
Aluminium	Nitrous oxide/acetylene
Calcium	Nitrous oxide/acetylene
Iron	Air/acetylene
Magnesium	Air/acetylene
Sodium	Air/acetylene
Potassium	Air/acetylene

Approximately 100 mg samples of ceramics from each of the five TG production areas were irradiated in the reactor of Imperial College at Silwood Park, Ascot. The irradiation time was a few minutes less than seven hours. Individual samples were counted with a germanium-lithium detector coupled to a Canberra series 35 multichannel analyzer about 100 and 400 h after irradiation. This procedure enables both short and longer-lived isotopes to be evaluated in turn. Counting times were 2-3000 and 6000 sec respectively, as suggested by Leese *et al.* (1986). The elements identified and measured by NAA common to all samples are given in Table 11.

Table 11. Elements identified and measured in NAA common to all samples.

Isotope	Half-life
Potassium 40	12.4h
Sodium 24	15.5h
Lanthanum 140	40.2h
Samarium 153	47.0h
Lutetium 177	6.7d
Arsenic 76	26.5d
Chromium 51	27.8d
Cerium 141	32.5d
Hafnium 181	42.5d
Iron 59	45.0d
Cobalt 60	58.0d
Scandium 46	83.9d
Manganese 54	310.0d
Thorium 228	1.9y
Caesium 134	2.0y
Europium 152	12.0y

Multivariate statistical analysis

Hierarchical cluster analysis (Gordon 1981) using Genstat 5 (release 1.3) was applied to the data. The general idea behind such methods of analysis is to produce a dendrogram, which is a sort of family tree, of ceramic samples. In the dendrogram, similar ceramic groups appear on close branches, and dissimilar groups on widely separated branches. The mean values of the ceramic groups are used with weighting according to the variability within the group. A basic assumption in this method of statistical analysis is that there are no significant correlations between the measured elements.

Results and data analysis

Differences in pottery composition between production centres

Mean values for the AAS data for the four production centres covered in this study are given in Table 12. Initially the pottery data for the TG areas were grouped together and treated as being derived from a single pottery population. Visual inspection of the results in Table 12 reveals several clear differences between the four centres, such as a lower iron value for BOA, higher magnesium for LEY and lower aluminium for DEN. The relevance of some of these observations are further discussed below. Statistical analysis confirmed that there were some significant differences between the centres for each of the elements measured but no single element could be used to separate the four centres.

Table 12. AAS mean compositions (%) for pottery samples.

Element	Production centre			
	LEY	DEN	BOA	TG
n =	6	6	6	20
Aluminium	8.88	3.01	7.88	8.31
Calcium	0.33	0.10	0.14	0.84
Iron	4.93	4.75	2.02	4.74
Magnesium	1.34	1.02	0.53	0.62
Sodium	0.21	0.15	0.09	0.19
Potassium	2.59	1.93	1.92	1.92

n = number of pottery samples analysed

Mean concentrations of each element for each production centre were plotted against one another. The pair of elements which appeared to offer the best possibility for discriminating between centres was calcium and magnesium, and the binary plot for these two elements is illustrated in figure 63. There is little overlap in the data between production centres for the ± one standard deviation range, but the grouped TG data covers a wide range of calcium values and reduces the overall potential for using this combination of elements as site discriminators.

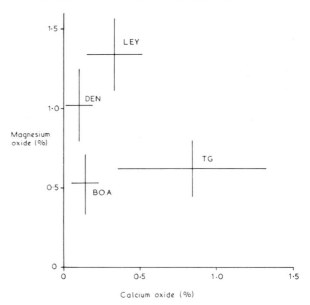

Fig. 63. Mean concentrations of magnesium and calcium for all centres. Error bars indicate +/- one standard deviation of the appropriate mean.

The dendrogram obtained from complete linkage cluster analysis of the pottery data is illustrated in figure 64. The results clearly show the low level of similarity between the centres since the first cluster to form, that between LEY and DEN, does not do so until above the 50% dissimilarity level. Samples from BOA are clearly different from the rest because of the the low iron concentration noted above.

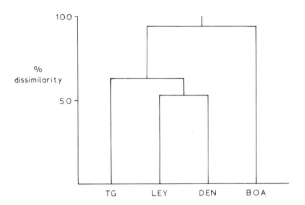

Fig. 64. Dendrogram derived by complete linkage cluster analysis of pottery data.

Differences between TG ceramics

Within this study the possibility exists for evaluating the potential of the data in identifying differences between the five TG production areas. It is uncertain whether all five TG sites were manufacturing a mixture of pottery and tile but this does not necessarily restrict the potential of the data. All the TG tile AAS data were combined as a single group and subjected to complete linkage cluster analysis, along with the pottery data from all four production centres. The results illustrated in figure 65 show that the TG pottery and tile data very quickly form a single TG cluster which is quite different from the other three production centres. Thus, we can see that TG pottery and tile compositions are more like one another than other centres, though differences in chemical composition between individual TG areas may still be significant.

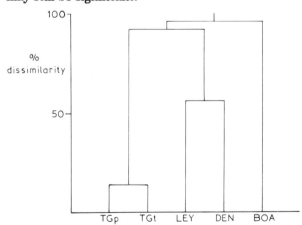

Fig. 65. Dendrogram derived by complete linkage cluster analysis of ceramic data (TGp = grouped TG pottery, TGt = grouped TG tile).

The mean AAS values obtained by treating all twenty TG and eight TG tile sherds as two separate groups are given in Table 13. There are some differences between the two profiles with the tiles having higher concentrations for five out of the six measured elements, the exception being

calcium. Statistically the tiles had significantly higher levels of sodium, magnesium and potassium. There were only a small number of samples from each of the three mixed ceramic production areas and ranges of values were so large for the elements that it was not possible to examine sites individually for significant differences between pottery and tile composition.

Table 13. AAS mean composition (%) for TG pottery and tile.

Element	Pottery	Tiles
n =	20	8
Aluminium	8.31	9.21
Calcium	0.84	0.80
Iron	4.74	5.56
Magnesium	0.62	0.77
Sodium	0.19	0.40
Potassium	1.92	2.35

n = number of samples analysed

Each of the three clay types local to the Tylers Green/Penn area (Fig. 62) was sampled within one of the defined production areas. A sample from TGA was chosen to represent the 'clay with flints', one from TGB to represent the 'pebbly clay and sand' and one from TGE to represent the 'mottled clay'. A comparison of AAS data for the clay samples and the means of the ceramics from the three sites is given in Table 14. In many cases measured element concentrations in the clays were significantly different from the means of the ceramic samples. No clear pattern of differences emerged with only the clay sample from TGA being a fairly good match with its ceramic group.

The composition of Tylers Green/Penn tiles

Tile samples were analysed using both AAS and NAA. Mean values for AAS data are given in Table 15. If we assume that all eight TG results are representative of all unglazed tiles made at Tylers Green/Penn it is possible to calculate an overall mean and standard deviation for this group. These values were used to present the results for all TG sites in diagrammatic form in figure 66 where the width of the band defined by the solid lines represents +/- one standard deviation about the mean for a particular element. The dotted line in figure 66 represents the WIN tile sample profile which mostly fits comfortably within the +/- one standard deviation band, the exception being for potassium which lies just beyond the + one standard deviation value of the grouped data. Statistical significance testing based on the six elements measured by AAS confirmed that Tylers Green/Penn was a likely source

Table 14. Comparison of Tylers Green/Penn clays and ceramics.

Element	TGA		TGB		TGE	
(%)	clay	ceramic	clay	ceramic	clay	ceramic
Aluminium	11.86	7.81	nd	9.35	5.35	8.83
Calcium	0.77	1.31	0.13	0.96	0.74	0.30
Iron	7.73	4.87	3.17	5.64	4.35	4.80
Magnesium	0.48	0.53	0.43	0.74	0.28	0.70
Sodium	0.08	0.20	0.17	0.26	0.43	0.31
Potassium	0.97	1.91	0.93	2.28	3.96	2.02
Mg/Ca ratio	0.62	0.40	3.31	0.77	0.38	2.33

nd = not determined

of the WIN sample.

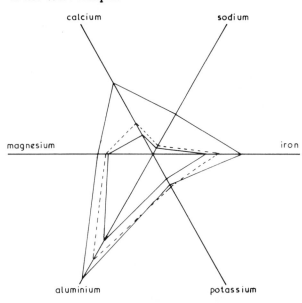

Fig. 66. Comparison of AAS tile data for TG and WIN. Solid line indicates +/- one standard deviation of TG mean tile data and broken line the WIN sample. For calcium, magnesium and sodium 1 mm = 0.035% and for iron, potassium and aluminium 1 mm = 0.17%.

Table 15. Composition (%) of TG tiles.

Element	TGA	TGB	TGD	TGE
n =	2	3	2	1
Aluminium	8.07	9.75	10.08	8.11
Calcium	0.97	1.07	0.46	0.35
Iron	6.76	5.99	5.17	2.63
Magnesium	0.73	0.78	0.84	0.70
Sodium	0.24	0.25	0.46	1.10
Potassium	2.36	2.46	2.36	2.01

n= number of samples measured

On first analysis the NAA data revealed six points of dissimilarity between the WIN and grouped TG tile sample (Table 16). Closer examination of the data suggests that the WIN sample profile is very

similar to that of the mean TG and that much the of difference between the two profiles arises from differences in overall element concentrations. One of the points of statistically significant dissimilarity is for the element scandium. Several workers (Aspinall 1977; Leese *et al.* 1986) have recommended recalculating other element concentrations as ratios of scandium and if such a procedure is carried out on the tile data given in Table 16 the WIN sample becomes a much closer fit to the mean TG data.

Table 16. Element concentrations (ug/g) by NAA for TG and WIN samples.

Element	TG mean	WIN	WIN rescaled
Samarium	8.90	11.80	9.20
Lanthanum	43.60	56.10	43.80
Arsenic	12.90	17.70	13.80
Scandium	15.90	20.50	15.90
Cerium	113.50	138.50	108.00
Europium	1.50	2.50	2.00
Lutetium	0.50	0.60	0.50
Thorium	12.10	16.00	12.50
Chromium	128.10	185.20	111.50
Cobalt	65.00	93.50	72.90
Sodium (%)	0.16	0.20	0.20
Potassium (%)	2.96	3.74	2.92
Iron (%)	4.89	5.22	4.07

The number of samples analyzed by NAA was too small to draw specific conclusions about the similarities between the WIN sample and individual TG sites. Analysis of individual site data suggested that combinations of plots for the elements cobalt, lanthanum and cerium might be useful as site discriminators. The binary plot for lanthanum and cerium is given in figure 67 and shows that the WIN sample was closer in composition for these two elements to TGA and TGD than either TGB or TGE. This affinity was also suggested for binary plots for cobalt and cerium, and lanthanum and cobalt.

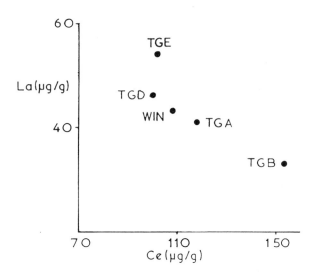

Fig. 67. Binary scatter plot for lanthanum and cerium concentrations for tile samples.

Archaeological implications

The characteristics of the ceramic groups

Some of the chemical charcteristics of the individual ceramic groups are worthy of discussion because they may provide further information on parent materials, production techniques or weathering histories. At first sight the low iron values for BOA samples are surprising since within 2 km there are low hills overlooking the production areas at Boarstall and they are known to have ironstone deposits. Microscopic analysis of the BOA pottery fabric showed a larger number of quartz grains are present in this pottery than the pottery from the other production centres covered in this study. The effects of the high level of silicon in the quartz grains will be to reduce the concentration of all other elements present and indeed some of the other elements, for example sodium, are lower in BOA samples than for other sites. It may be that the clays local to BOA have naturally high levels of quartz grains present or it may be that large quantities of quartz were deliberately added to local Boarstall clays to modify their character during manufacture. Field studies around the BOA site suggest that the local clays derive from low lying, relatively wet areas. The mobility of iron depends on its valency state and it is relatively soluble in waterlogged or reduced soils. Thus, the local BOA clay may have a naturally depressed iron concentration. Weathering of the clay before use will also contribute to low iron concentrations, as will weathering of the sherds on the field surface after firing.

The ceramic production areas at Rush Green, Denham, lie adjacent to a small river, the Alderbourne, and the surrounding area has a tendency to become waterlogged. Size and density sorting of rock minerals during the physical movement of water is a common geological phenomenon. As the result of water sorting, aluminium tends to be concentrated in the fine-grain clays and the topography around the DEN production areas is likely to provide such deposits. Indeed a clay-pit (?) adjacent to the southern kilns had been dug into alluvial clays in antiquity (Farley and Leach 1988). It is interesting then that the aluminium levels in the DEN ceramic are the lowest of all the centres examined in this study. Within the DEN fabrics potentially silicon rich inclusions were identified as forming between 10 and 35% of the matrix (Farley & Leach 1988). This deliberate modification of the alluvial clay is undoubtedly the main cause for the depleted aluminium concentration in the DEN samples.

Although the clays in the Tylers Green/Penn area overly Chalk, the ease with which calcium is removed by translocation processes during weathering makes the high calcium value for TGA samples hard to understand. Chalk is not commonly deliberately added to ceramics, nor is it likely to migrate into ceramic sherds as they weather on the field surface. Magnesium is less mobile than calcium because of its ability to be fixed in secondary clay minerals by exchange and adsorption, so the high magnesium concentration in LEY samples would appear to be a characteristic of clays local to the Ley Hill kiln.

Separating ceramic groups

The potential for using chemical analysis to characterise ceramic groups is well established and many examples can be seen in the archaeological literature. Often the objective of such studies is to establish the basis for determining the geochemical source of the ceramics by matching clay and ceramic profiles. There have been few such studies of medieval ceramics in the British Isles (Aspinall 1977; Hughes *et al.* 1982; Kilmurry 1982; Leese *et al.* 1986) and there is no published data for medieval ceramics from Buckinghamshire, though some analyses have been carried out for the products of Brill kilns (R. Ivens, pers. comm.).

The chemical compositions of fired ceramics mostly reflect the compositions of their parent materials, e.g. clay and temper, but other factors undoubtedly influence the composition at the moment of analysis. Stewart *et al.* (1990) expressed the variance in the chemical composition of a ceramic data set using the "simple" equation:

$$G = f (P, W, T, H, A, L, e)$$

where the value of a geochemical data point (G) is a function (f) of the parent rock materials (P), the weathering history (W), the transportation and deposition history (T), the human manipulation history (H), the archaeological history (A), the analytical history (L) and the anlytical error (e). Some of these sources of variance may be identified, for example (P), and others controlled, for example (e), but most remain unknown. It is clear from such an equation that each single sherd selected for analysis, even those derived from similar environments, will have a unique value for (G).

From the foregoing considerations it is inevitable that there will be a spread of values for any given kiln group. Sometimes the spread may be so large as to make separation of one group from another difficult, if not impossible. Many studies of ceramic groups involve one or more forms of multivariate statistical analysis and one such methods, cluster analysis, has been used successfully in this study to distinguish between four major centres of ceramic production in south Buckinghamshire in the medieval period. Multivariate statistical methods need not be the automatic choice in compositional studies, indeed in this study simple binary plots have proved relatively effective in separating the four pottery production centres.

Tylers Green/Penn ceramics

The Geological Survey places the clays of the Tylers Green and Penn area into three separate categories. The five potential production areas cover all three clay types, with TGB, TGC and TGD being situated on the same clay type (see Fig. 62). Ceramic samples from the sites TGA and TGE were largely different from one another but the large range of values for the TGB/C/D 'group' has considerable overlap with the other two sites. This overlapping of TG site data is not surprising considering the close proximity of the sites to one another on the ground. It is possible that the overlapping values are influenced, at least in part, by the use of a common raw material source, such as sand.

The reader is referred elsewhere for a comprehensive review of the difficulties of matching archaeological ceramics with their clay sources (Rice 1987) though some comments will be made on the attempts to match TG ceramics and clays in this study. Three samples of clay were collected adjacent to three relatively well defined TG production areas. The samples were judged as having potential for ceramic production though not necessarily without further modification

(P.M.Cauvain, pers. comm.).

In general, attempts to match TG ceramic and clay profiles met with limited success. A good match was obtained for the TGA site where the clay sample was taken from what appears to be an abandoned clay-pit a few metres from the production area, but the other matches were less conclusive. Since the compositions of clays are commonly modified for ceramic manufacture inconclusive matches must be expected. The ceramics from the TG sites have significant quantities of quartz grains present, especially the tiles, and chemical analysis of local sand deposits might provide the additional data needed to improve attempts to match TG ceramics and clays.

The potential of chemical analysis for provenanccing 'Penn' tiles

Previous studies on the distribution of the products of the Tylers Green/Penn kilns have largely been based on a range of distinctive patterns pressed onto floor tiles. In some cases the distances over which large quantities of these weighty tiles (individual weight about 0.5 kg) appear to have been transported are not inconsiderable for the medieval period, up to 40 or 50 km. There have been suggestions that it was not the individual tiles that were transported but rather the stamps or other devices used to produce the designs. These designs being the property of an itinerant potter/tiler who then manufactured 'Penn' tiles from clay sources near to the local market for such tiles.

The results presented in this study show the immediate potential of chemical analysis in augmenting stylistic analyses of decorated, and indeed all medieval tiles, with potential for providing specific 'chemical fingerprints' for medieval tile production areas. Given a sufficiently large data base it may be possible to more accurately provenance so-called Penn tiles and to provide information on the true distribution of the products of the Tylers Green/Penn ceramic industry.

Conclusions and scope for future work

This study has presented preliminary findings on the chemical analysis of unglazed medieval pottery which show that it is possible with the aid of complete linkage cluster analysis, and other statistical techniques, to distinguish chemically between four production centres in south Buckinghamshire.

A more detailed study of medieval ceramics from production areas around Tylers Green and Penn has revealed some potential for using chemical analysis to discriminate between the individual production areas, and between groups of unglazed pottery and tile. 'Chemical fingerprints' from Tylers Green/Penn kilns have been used to confirm that they were the likely source of a sample of suspected Penn tile from excavations at Windsor Castle.

Further sampling of individual production areas at each of the major centres considered in this study and other medieval ceramic centres in the south-east Midlands will be needed to establish definitive 'chemical fingerprints' before they can be used to provenance pottery of unknown origin with any degree of certainty. It is intended to continue using chemical analysis to study the manufacture of Penn tiles by extending the work to include analysis of glazes and slips used on patterned tiles.

POTTERY STUDIES IN BEDFORDSHIRE

A.M. Slowikowski

Introduction

Over the past five years, with the establishment of an expanded Archaeology Service within Bedfordshire County Council and the greater number of excavations carried out, the ceramic data for the county have increased. This contribution outlines briefly the work on ceramics that has been carried out in Bedfordshire in that period, and points to gaps in our knowledge where future study may be directed profitably. The sites mentioned here are illustrated in figure 21.

Type Series, the basis of all pottery studies, have been established for all ceramics excavated in Bedfordshire. These Type Series consist of fabric descriptions accompanied by physical examples of the type, and a corpus of forms arranged by fabric type. The Type Series are based on excavated material and are therefore biased according to where these excavations have taken place. Gaps in the record can be glaring but, as excavations are gradually spread into unknown regions of the county, the Type Series are ever expanding. Examples of kiln material (so far only of medieval or post-medieval date) have been sent to the British Museum to be included in their National Type Series.

Pottery is not just a tool for dating archaeological sites. It is the primary evidence for the function and status of the site; it can pinpoint patterns of trade and contact; it puts the site into its context temporally and spacially. This is a view espoused by most pottery researchers but it is not always possible to put into practice. Constraints of time and resources frequently limit what can be done. Dependence upon project funding has meant that there is a lack of synthetic work on pottery of all periods, and not just in Bedfordshire. It is the aim of all pottery researchers to gather together all the data and eventually produce a model for the ceramics in their area; not only what was happening, but why. Not enough data have been gathered yet in Bedfordshire but a broad outline can be made and gaps can certainly be pinpointed.

The prehistoric period

With the exception of the neolithic and Bronze Age pottery from the henge site at Bury Farm, Goldington, and the pottery from peripheral features of the late Iron Age village of Salford, studies of the ceramics of the prehistoric period have concentrated on the later prehistoric period, especially the Iron Age. Bedfordshire lies at the edge of the distribution of 'Belgic' pottery and, although the types are well known (Thompson 1982), the relationship with the earlier and/or contemporary native wares is unclear. Preliminary scans of the large assemblages from the Iron Age village at Salford, as well as the work in progress on the Iron Age pottery from Chamberlains Barn and the smaller assemblages recovered from Willington Quarry, show distinct regionality at least in terms of pottery fabric. Further analysis of both fabric and forms from these sites, and a comparison with those further west into the Chilterns, will perhaps clarify the distribution.

The Romano-British period

The study of the Romano-British pottery is well advanced if looked at from the point of view of the fine wares, but rather backward when it comes to the coarse wares. The fine wares are well known and much work has been done on them elsewhere in the country. The major industries of Much Hadham, Hertfordshire, Oxfordshire, the Nene valley and the Verulamium region all supplied sites in Bedfordshire. The local coarse wares are less well known, and this remains one of the major gaps in Romano-British pottery studies. It appears from the survey of Romano-British pottery studies that this situation pertains to other counties, not just Bedfordshire (Fulford & Huddleston 1991). This situation needs remedying and inroads into this black hole will be made with the keenly awaited publication of the kilns at Harrold (Brown 1994).

Two recent discoveries will add greatly to our knowledge of the distribution and marketing of Romano-British coarse wares in the county. The first is a kiln producing a variety of forms in both reduced and oxidised sandy fabric (Fig. 68), excavated at Warren Villas Quarry, Caldecote, 1 km from the Romano-British town at Sandy (Slowikowski & Dawson 1994). The wasters were abandoned within the remains of the kiln after the final disasterous firing. The kiln is of sunken type, described by Swan (1984, 55-6). The forms indicate an early Roman date, perhaps sometime in the early second century. The pottery was in a

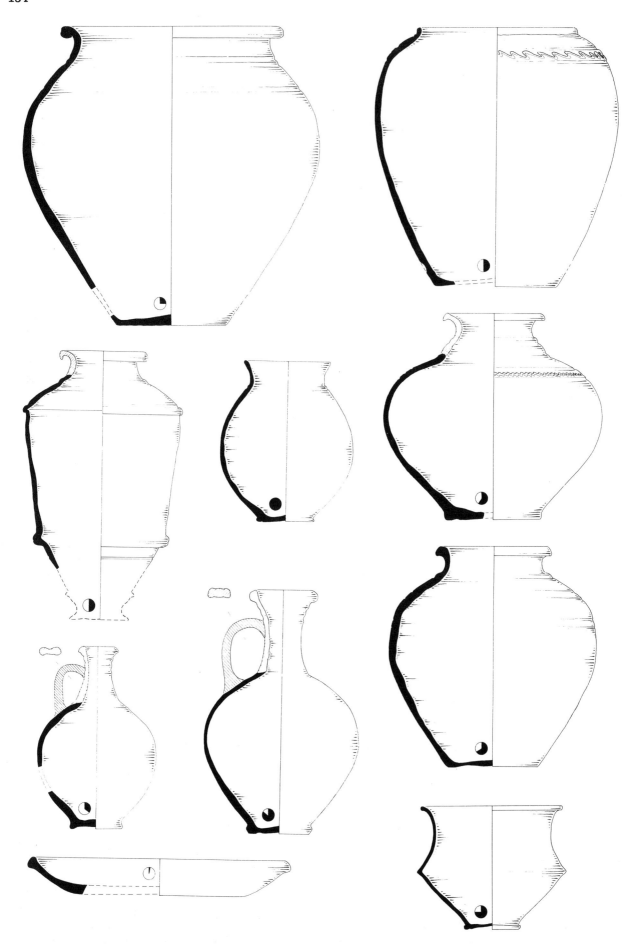

Fig. 68. Romano-British pottery from the final firing of the kiln at Warren Villas (scale 1:4).

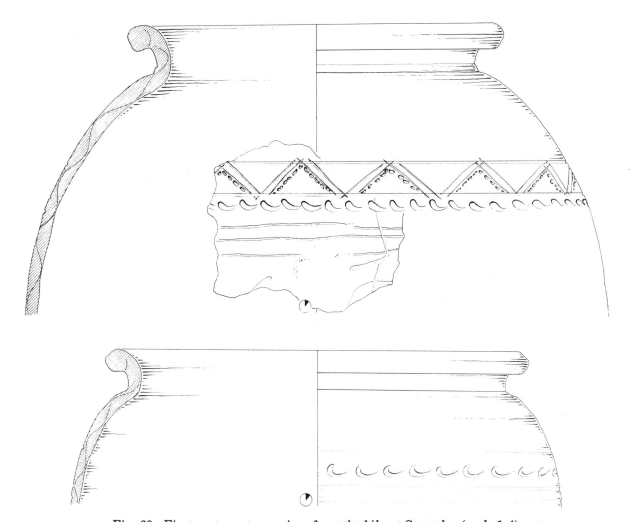

Fig. 69. First century storage jars from the kiln at Stagsden (scale 1:4).

substantially reconstructable state. The air bubbles in the walls and the spalling clearly seen on most of the vessels, as well as the incomplete firing of the whole batch, suggests that the weather conditions were unsuitable or the pottery had not dried out sufficiently before firing, causing an explosion in the kiln. The firing was abandoned and any vessels surviving the explosion would not have been fired to a sufficient temperature to be usable. When the pottery from the excavations at Sandy has been analysed, the question of marketing and supply may be answered: was the Warren Villas potter supplying the town of Sandy, or some other settlement or villa nearby? Only the one kiln was found, suggesting a small-scale industry. The decoration on the pottery, all made by a left-handed potter, suggests that the last batch, at least, was produced by one individual.

The second discovery is of four kilns, at Stagsden, north Bedfordshire, near to a late Iron Age and early Romano-British settlement. An archaeomagnetic date of cal. AD40-110 has been obtained for one of these kilns (measurement ref.

AJC-102). The pottery is in a shelly fabric, and can be dated, from the forms, to the first century, perhaps just before or about the time of the Conquest. In Bedfordshire, shelly fabrics were in use in the late Iron Age and continued in use throughout the Romano-British period. The industry at Stagsden appears to have been specialising in large storage jars (Fig. 69), comparable to those produced by the first-century Caldecotte kilns in Buckinghamshire (Marney 1990, 97, Fig. 38 no. 2). In addition, smaller jars were made in the same fabric. Both types of jar were being supplied to the near-by settlement.

A number of other kiln sites is known in the county (Simco 1984, 39-41), but few have produced a quantity of pottery together with evidence of the kiln structure. The Harrold kilns have been mentioned above and the grey ware producing kilns at Mile Road, Bedford, await full publication (Dring 1971, 69-71; Swan 1984, 63 & 65); all other sites have produced scant evidence in the form of wasted pottery or fragments of kiln furniture. The analysis of the pottery and its distribution particularly from these four kiln sites

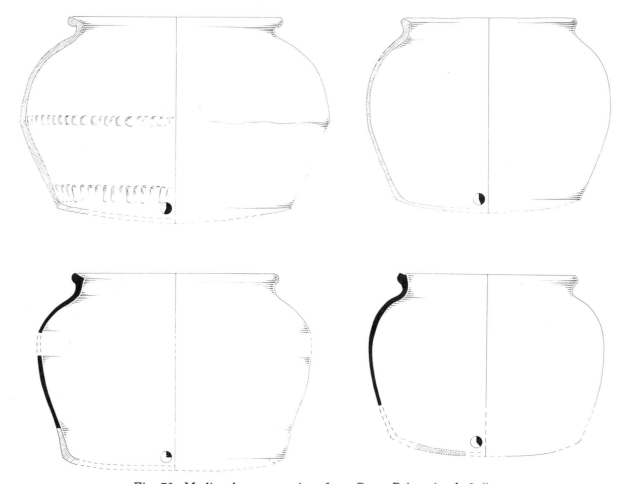

Fig. 70. Medieval grey ware jars from Grove Priory (scale 1:4).

(Harrold, Mile Road, Stagsden and Warren Villas) should add greatly to our knowledge of the local coarse ware industry in Bedfordshire.

The medieval period

The study of medieval pottery has been well established, at least for the town of Bedford, with the publication of the pottery from excavations in the town (Baker & Hassall 1979, 147-240). Of the other major urban centres in the county, only Dunstable has produced a quantity of medieval pottery. The pottery from recent excavations at the Friary is still to be analysed, but the pottery from earlier excavations at the Friary published by the Manshead Archaeological Society of Dunstable (Green & Horne 1991) goes some way in laying the foundations for the study of the ceramics of the town.

Elsewhere in the county the pottery available for study has been predominantly from rural sites. There has been a concentration of work in recent years in the south-west of the county. The pottery from the sites at Grove Priory, near Leighton Buzzard (Slowikowski, in prep.), and the motte and bailey castle at Chalgrave (Brine 1988, 40-46), only 9 km from each other, form the basis for

ceramic study in this part of the county. The earliest medieval pottery comes from Chalgrave, dated to the tenth or eleventh century. It is a mixture of shelly St Neots types, early medieval sandy wares and part hand-made grey wares. The sandy and the grey wares are also found in the earliest phase at Grove Priory, in the fill of a ditch and pits that pre-date the construction of the main range of buildings. Here, however, they are found in association with Hertfordshire grey wares, all in a substantially complete if shattered state and probably deposited at the same time. It would appear that these types continued for a long time; the conservative nature of pottery industries is well known (Arnold 1989, 220-4).

In the thirteenth century, the Hertfordshire grey wares form the major part of the domestic coarse ware assemblage in this part of the county, with jars (both storage and cooking pots) predominating (Fig. 70). Bowls, jugs and dripping pans form a less important element. Fineware jugs were imported from outside the county, particularly the Brill-Boarstall pottery manufacturing area in Buckinghamshire (Ivens 1982), and the Potterspury kilns in Northamptonshire (Mynard 1970). The pottery is of a distinctly local nature with few vessels travelling long distances, although examples are known to have come from Stamford, London and as far away as Laverstock, near Salisbury; these are, however, exceptional. The shelly wares appear to make few inroads into the south of the county, although they are present at Chalgrave at about the time of the Conquest. By the thirteenth century, the Harrold and Olney Hyde industries are supplying predominantly the north of the county (Hall 1972; Mynard 1984). The sites in the south are turning to Hertfordshire for their pottery supplies.

With the exception of Bedford, few sites have been excavated in the north of the county. The Biggleswade area, in particular, was a gap in our knowledge. This picture is about to change with the excavations now underway at the deserted medieval village of Stratton, Biggleswade. These excavations have produced a large quantity of St Neots type wares, together with previously unknown sandy wares, possibly of local manufacture. They may be contemporary with the St Neots ware, or perhaps slightly later. The presence of eighth-ninth century Maxey-type shelly wares in one area of the site suggests an occupation of the site immediatly preceding that evidenced by the presence of St Neots types. The full analysis of this pottery has yet to begin but it will go a long way to fill in the gaps in our knowledge of this area.

In the later medieval period, greater uniformity of pottery manufacture led to the widespread distribution of the late medieval reduced wares, first described by Moorhouse (1974), and it is this type that dominates both the north and south of the county. The waster heap from Church End, Flitwick, published by Mynard, Petchey and Tilson (1983, 75-84), contained these types, as did the waster heap from Water Lane, also in Flitwick, excavated by Bedfordshire County Council's Archaeology Service in 1984. The associated kilns were never found, although the presence of waster heaps at two ends of the town indicates more than just a minor industry. In the north of the county a kiln and its waster pit recently excavated by Bedfordshire County Council's Archaeology Service at Everton has confirmed Hassall's suggestion of a reduced ware industry in this area (Hassall 1976, 69). The pottery from this kiln site has been found at the village of Stratton, about 5 km away, less than a day's walking distance. The full distribution of the Everton pottery awaits the excavation of more sites in this part of the county.

Conclusion and future work

Considerable advances have been made in our knowledge of the pottery of all periods in Bedfordshire in the last five years. There are questions still to be answered and new questions will, no doubt, be posed in the future. It is already possible to outline what was happening ceramically at this northern end of the Chiltern region, perhaps with more certainty for some periods than others. There is, however, the need for more data, as well as the analysis and publication of that already collected, before our knowledge can be drawn together to form a synthetic picture of the wheres, the hows and the whys of pottery production, distribution and use.

Note

The following conventions have been used to illustrate the pottery: hand-made vessels are differentiated from wheel-thrown vessels by their hatched section; applied parts to a vessel (e.g. handles, separately attached necks, bases, etc.) have their sections hatched; coil-built vessels are indicated by a wavy line within the section; the proportion of the vessel surviving is indicated by the pie diagram at the base of each drawing.

RECORDING ARCHAEOLOGY IN BUCKINGHAMSHIRE

Andrew Pike

Interest in local archaeology and making provision for its preservation and recording can be seen to have threads going back many years. Henry VIII's historian, Leland, commented on the countryside he visited on his travels; in Buckinghamshire he described the recent desertion of villages like Burston, the Greyfriars at Aylesbury just before its dissolution and the towns of Buckingham and Newport Pagnell. 1586 saw the publication of the first edition of William Camden's *Britannia* which contained many observations on the history of the towns he travelled to. Thus of Buckingham he wrote "The chief town of the county which Edward the Elder in 915 fortified with a rampart and turrets on both sides of the bank against the incursions of the Danes. The castle is seated in the middle of the town on a great mount".

In 1755 Browne Willis published the first part of what was intended to be a major county history. Although born in Dorset, Willis was soon to inherit estates in Buckinghamshire where he spent most of his life - first at Beachampton, then at Whaddon. Only the Hundred and Deanery of Buckingham was ever published; notes for the remainder of the county (the Hundreds of Newport and Cottesloe were almost completed) survive in a large series of manuscript notes now in the Bodleian Library, Oxford. Willis' main interests were churches and monasteries - his surveys of cathedrals and mitred abbeys in England are still regarded as important sources - and much of his wealth was spent on the restoration of Buckinghamshire's churches. Buckingham old church was one such; the preservation of the tower of St Mary Magdalene's church, Stony Stratford was entirely due to Willis's efforts after the rest of the building was destroyed by fire. When he does comment on archaeological sites his observations are as often as not very accurate. He describes the Roman barrows at Thornborough, near Buckingham, thus: "Two remarkable tumuli, which I judge were raised in the time when the Romans possessed this island, on account of some battle fought here. The vulgar have several old traditions about their being inhabited by fairies" (Willis 1755, 290).

The early nineteenth century saw an increased interest in things classical, which spawned such bogus antiquities as the Egyptian Spring at Hartwell. "Ruined" follies and grottoes featured in many a landscape garden. In the 1830s we see a renewed interest in archaeology with the founding of several national and local societies. In 1839-1840 one of the earliest recorded excavations in Buckinghamshire took place on the site of the Roman villa at Foscott, near Buckingham, followed by an excavation of the Thornborough Mounds. It is interesting to read the account of the latter: "A trench was cut through the centre which displayed the stratification consisting of alternate layers of clay and mould, until the workmen had cut down to the level of the contiguous ground where a large and long layer of rough limestone was disclosed on which were found many bronze ornaments" (Lipscomb 1847, 115).

1847 was an important year for Buckinghamshire archaeology. George Lipscomb's four-volume county history was published and the Buckinghamshire Archaeological Society was founded. In his inaugural address to the new Society, the Bishop of Oxford said "We have, as archaeologists, a speculative, and as architects a practical character: we study the past that we would the present; we seek to call up out of the grave that old bygone time; we bid it yield to us the knowledge of its buried wealth and hoarded treasures; we patiently unwind its cere-cloths and look upon the calm or mouldering features of the dead, that we may reproduce the old life which slumbers in that death, in order to learn its secrets and profit by its wisdom" (Wilberforce 1848, 3). Excavations of various earthworks in the Chilterns and elsewhere feature in the pages of the early volumes of the Society's journal *Records of Buckinghamshire*, which also contain carefully surveyed plans of moats and enclosures and other sites.

In 1908 Hadrian Allcroft published his *Earthwork of England*. One of the unsung heroes of archaeology, he was amongst the first to sort out the various classes of earthworks, using examples in the Chilterns to illlustrate his comments. He was probably the first person to appreciate the structure of a motte and bailey castle. "In scores of villages and towns", he wrote: "the mounds and trenches which alone mark the sites of British forts and Roman stations and Norman castles still retain fragmentary existence, but they are so obvious, so much a part of the recognized features of the spot that they excite no remark. Year by year they are being slowly levelled down and in the end they mostly perish utterly without ever having been remarked at all" (Allcroft 1908, 22-3).

Influenced, no doubt, by Allcroft and also by the great General Pitt Rivers and his work in Dorset and Wiltshire, the Royal Commission on Historical Monuments produced its volumes for Buckinghamshire in 1912 and 1913. Though mainly concerned with standing buildings, the Commission did include several major earthworks and other archaeological sites in its inventories. The *Victoria County History for Buckinghamshire* was also published at about the same time. From 1912 to 1914 A.H. Cocks carried out the first major excavation in Buckinghamshire at Hambleden Roman villa, particularly noteworthy for the systematic recording of features and finds.

In the 1920s, O.G.S. Crawford's appointment to the Ordnance Survey led to the creation of the "Archaeological Correspondent" system. In Buckinghamshire, the curator of the County Museum received each year a set of 6-inch maps on which he was asked to mark all archaeological discoveries made that year. The information was then collated by the Ordnance Survey onto cards, thus forming the basis for the current National Archaeological Record. The County Museum itself was instrumental in organising several excavations between the wars, such as J.F. Head's work on various sites in the Bledlow area, and in the 1950s and 1960s, including areas being developed for the expanding town of Aylesbury. In 1957 responsibility for funding and staffing the Museum passed from the Archaeological Society to the Buckinghamshire County Council. For much of its existence, the Buckinghamshire Archaeological Society has been the only major such society in the county. The burgeoning interest in archaeology in the 1950s and 1960s, doubtless fuelled by such personalities as Sir Mortimer Wheeler on radio and television, led to the founding of several local societies in the county including the Wolverton, Bletchley, Buckingham, Chess Valley and Middle Thames archaeological societies. In their early days these societies carried out fieldwork and excavation. Nowadays the Chess Valley probably remains the most active (Stainton this volume), whilst others such as the North Buckinghamshire Archaeological Society have more recently appeared on the scene.

In 1967 the Milton Keynes New City Designation Order was approved by parliament. The County Museum, together with other interested bodies, responded by setting up the Milton Keynes Research Committee which was soon to give birth to the Milton Keynes Archaeology Unit. Over a period of 20 years the Unit undertook an intensive programme of research, fieldwork and excavation throughout the area of the new city. Sadly the Unit is being wound up, the remaining staff being occupied in writing up and publishing the results of its work.

The County Museum has always remained at the forefront of archaeological provision in Buckinghamshire. As well as liaising with the Archaeological Division of the Ordnance Survey, the curator organised excavations and fieldwork. In 1969 the Museum's first Field Archaeologist was appointed. Since then an extensive programme of archaeological work has been carried out, including major excavations at Walton (Aylesbury) in 1973 and 1974, Amersham (Mantles Green Roman site) from 1982 to 1984 and excavation and survey at Missenden Abbey. From 1985 to 1988 the Aylesbury Past Project, a Community Programme funded by the Manpower Services Commission and based at the County Museum, undertook extensive survey, fieldwalking and excavation in the Aylesbury area.

The county Sites and Monuments Record was initiated in 1972; this was put on a firm footing with the appointment of an Archaeological Records Officer in 1976. At the same time, archaeology began to be seen as a consideration in planning decisions. Nowadays the Museum has close links with the Planning and Engineering departments of the County Council as well as the planning officers in each of the five district councils. A large number of applications is also received for commment from the Forestry Authority and various statutory undertakings. There is no doubt that the Department of the Environment's circular Archaeology and Planning (PPG 16) has put the whole issue of archaeology in the county on a much stronger foundation. The field side remains active in carrying out evaluations and watching briefs throughout the county. In 1972 the County Museum Archaeological Group was formed. This remains a vital volunteer force available to help at excavations and process finds, as well as undertaking a systematic programme of fieldwork throughout the county and carrying out a number of research projects aimed at enhancing the Sites and Monuments Record. As for the Sites and Monuments Record itself, it has grown to some 6000 sites, represented by nearly 40,000 records on the County Council's mainframe computer. Still expanding, it reflects the ever changing interests of archaeologists locally and nationally and forms the first line of defence in the preservation of the county's heritage.

ARCHAEOLOGICAL CONSERVATION WORK IN HERTFORDSHIRE:
A COUNTY COUNCIL PERSPECTIVE

Mike Daniells

As with most counties, provision for archaeology in Hertfordshire has developed organically, with the result that numerous bodies and organisations are involved. These currently include at least nine museums with archaeological collections, three professional organisations concerned with fieldwork (Heritage Network, based at Hitchin; the Field Archaeology Department of St Albans Museums (St Albans District Council; and the Hertfordshire Archaeological Trust) and the County Council's Archaeology Section, based within the County Planning and Environment Department.

Local societies

The local societies have, by and large, long recognised - and it is to their credit- that they do not have the resources that are required to respond to all the demands of modern fieldwork, especially 'rescue' excavation. They have thus mostly restricted their recent roles to modest fieldwork, especially surveys; the provision of a local focus for the interested public; and support for their local professional organisations. These latter roles should not be underestimated. The existence of a support group and, if necessary, a pressure group is a vital provision in a time of static or decreasing public resources.

There are eight local archaeological societies in the county: Berkhamsted and District Archaeological Society, Bishops Stortford and District Local History Society, East Hertfordshire Archaeological Society, North Hertfordshire Archaeological Society, St Albans and Hertfordshire Architectural and Archaeological Society, South West Hertfordshire Archaeological and Historical Society, the Stevenage Archaeological Group and the Welwyn Archaeological Society. Four of these have recently been involved in fieldwork, e.g. the St Albans and Hertfordshire Architectural and Archaeological Society (Miles this volume).

Professional bodies

The museums, with the exception of North Hertfordshire and Verulamium, have mainly restricted their specifically archaeological roles to that of curating their collections. This fundamental archaeological provision is also too often under-

valued by fieldworkers.

The County Council's role is essentially 'curatorial' and involves two main areas of work. The first and most important of these is the identification and conservation of the surviving resource. This is currently being addressed in two principal ways: through the 'Monuments Protection Programme' (MPP), in conjunction with English Heritage, and through the 'Countryside Heritage Project', a County Council initiative. Depending on the pace of MPP, it is envisaged that all the known sites in Hertfordshire that are worthy of protection and, realistically, can be protected, will be formally designated by the end of the decade.

The other principal area of the County Council's work is that of 'development control'. This includes advising eight of the ten District and Borough Planning Authorities in Hertfordshire, and all planning applications are routinely screened on a daily basis, in addition to the perusal of the weekly lists of such applications. In this way all notifiable development likely to have archaeological implications is picked up. After due consideration and, if necessary, discussion with the various parties involved, a formal recommendation for appropriate action is made to the Local Planning Authority. The applicant is also informed of this recommendation.

The District Planning Authorities at St Albans and North Hertfordshire District Councils receive archaeological advice from their own professional archaeologists. In the case of North Hertfordshire this is based at the Field Archaeology Section of the Museum Service, and with St Albans the archaeologist is based within the Planning Department itself.

Summing up

The above is necessarily a simplification of the situation that currently prevails in Hertfordshire and it should not be read as a comprehensive account. In particular, it is important to realise that the division of responsibilities outlined is not as rigid as it might appear and that, for instance, the 'curatorial' role is by no means exclusively the preserve of the County Council. Provision for archaeology varies widely in Britain, and the hallmark of the Hertfordshire arrangements is also variety. Nevertheless, this has not prevented the development of a significant degree of unity of direction and purpose and provides a model that seems to meet the county's requirements. It will doubtless evolve further as circumstances and requirements change.

THE COUNTY ARCHAEOLOGICAL SERVICE OF OXFORDSHIRE: CONSERVING THE RESOURCE

Paul S. Smith

Evolution of the service

For many years an integral part of the County Museum at Woodstock, the County Council's archaeology section evolved under the influence of that environment, and developed a pro-active stance in important areas of work. Around 1965 it was responsible for producing the first local authority-based Sites and Monuments Record which became the model for most SMRs in both Britain and abroad. In the 1970s the museum's archaeologist carried out a broad spectrum fieldwork including set-piece excavations, while the 1980s saw the continuance of the Field Section's role with an increased emphasis on the recording of standing buildings. By 1990 the County Museums Service had become part of a fully integrated Department of Leisure and Arts, and its archaeology section was adopting a more tightly defined curatorial role in line with national guidelines and local needs. In 1991 County Archaeological Services moved from Woodstock Museum to become part of the newly created Centre for Oxfordshire Studies: the Department of Leisure and Arts' multi-disciplinary resource centre based in Oxford.

The post-PPG16 environment

In its capacity as curator, Oxfordshire's County Archaeological Service currently delivers an integrated archaeological resource management service to all four rural District Councils, its own departments including W.S.Atkins-Oxford, and to all other organisations and individuals concerned with the development or conservation of the cultural landscape.

In Oxfordshire competitive tendering has proven to be a very suitable and effective model. Six professional archaeological organisations (including some of the most highly experienced and respected units in the country) regularly compete for work within the county. This provides a large, flexible force of skilled field archaeologists and gives the developer greater confidence as to the impartiality of the curator, and the cost effectiveness of the project. While this system still generates considerable debate within the profession, it is difficult to see how contracting archaeology can avoid competitive tendering when most commercial companies, local planning authorities and Crown Agencies are creating strict policies requiring the tendering of all contracts.

Rigorous curatorial influence and support throughout the whole process is, however, essential: to ensure that approved practices and standards are maintained; that developers (especially in the early stages of the process) are provided with all necessary information and assistance; and that all steps are taken to achieve a suitable and practical mitigation strategy. The County Archaeological Officer and his staff are responsible for producing briefs, validating project designs/specifications, and monitoring of the progress and standard of the archaeological work. In Oxfordshire this model has the support of all concerned, not least the developers.

Since the adoption of PPG16 procedures, the number of field evaluations carried out in the county has increased dramatically. During the period April 1991 to March 1993 for example, Oxfordshire's County Archaeological Service advised the local planning authorities and major utility companies of the need for nearly 200 field evaluations/watching briefs. While the Chilterns is not itself a zone of high development activity, except in those settlements that lie on its fringe in the Thames Valley, a number of investigations have taken place prior to development that provide important new evidence on the archaeology of the Chilterns area.

Local archaeological groups

The work of professional units in the Chilterns area of South Oxfordshire, generated mainly through development control procedures, has also been augmented by the work of local amateur groups, notably the South Oxfordshire Archaeological Group (SOAG) and the Henley Archaeological and Historical Group (HAHG). These groups, while recognizing the limitations placed upon them by the increasingly complex and resource-demanding discipline of modern archaeology, have carried out invaluable work in field survey, modest excavations, and documentary research. Their continuing work, incorporated within the County Sites and Monuments Record, will provide positive support for the future management of the archaeological resource in this region of Oxfordshire.

Some recent work in and around the Oxfordshire Chilterns

Recent examples include work by the Trust for Wessex Archaeology (TWA) at Windmill Hill, Nettlebed, where an evaluation produced evidence of an homogeneous mesolithic worked flint assemblage in remarkably fresh condition, which comprised pieces from all stages of manufacture. The character and distribution of the assemblage suggested that the material represents the product of a single phase of activity, probably a seasonal Mesolithic camp established near a spring (TWA 1994). At Bell Street, Henley-on-Thames the Oxford Archaeological Unit (OAU) carried out investigations which revealed the first substantial stratigraphic evidence for Roman activity within the town's historic core. Important evidence of the medieval frontage of Bell Street was also recovered (Maloney 1994).

Also in Henley, the Henley Archaeological & Historical Group (HAHG) carried out modest, but important, excavations in the Stable behind the King's Arms Public House in the Market Place. The fieldwork in conjunction with well researched documentary evidence, provides valuable information on the evolution and use of this burgage plot over eight centuries (Kendal & Cottingham 1994). The South Oxfordshire Archaeological Group (SOAG) has been continuing its long-term project at Gatehampton Farm, Goring. A magnetometer survey carried out in conjunction with surface collection suggested the presence of Romano-British features. Subsequent limited excavations revealed ditches, pits and the possible destruction layer of a Roman building. This provides further valuable data on the intensive exploitation of this area over many millennia, and SOAG is currently working on the production of a strategic overview that will aid the future management and research of this important cultural landscape (Graham-Kerr 1993).

PREHISTORIC AND ROMANO-BRITISH BEDFORDSHIRE: RESEARCH PRIORITIES AND PRACTICAL OPPORTUNITIES

Angela Simco

Summary

The relevance of archaeological considerations within the planning system has been increasingly recognised over the last 20 years. The development of the principle of environmental assessment, and the publication of Planning Policy Guidance Note 16 in November 1990, have been fundamental to this. At the same time, it is widely felt that archaeological work funded as part of development schemes should still be undertaken within a broad research framework. This section looks at the benefits and limitations of existing planning legislation, policies and practices, and examines how far it is possible to tackle broader research objectives within their framework.

Archaeology and planning: a brief history

During the 1970s, recognition was given to the fact that archaeology could be treated as a material consideration in the determination of planning applications, for example the Department of the Environment Circular 11/72, 'Field Monuments and Local Authorities'. In practice, this generally meant that in the case of important monuments, development proposals could be turned down or modified in the interests of archaeological preservation. Recommendations could only be made in the light of existing information, and there was no framework for requiring investigation in advance of a planning decision. Where archaeology was known to exist, but there was insufficient information to warrant a recommendation for refusal on archaeological grounds, there was no precedent in planning law to require that what might be destroyed in the course of development should be recorded.

Section II of the Ancient Monuments and Archaeological Areas Act (1979) introduced a new archaeological designation, the Area of Archaeological Importance. In areas so designated, it became a requirement that a period of time be allowed for archaeological investigation between planning permission and the start of development. It did not address the question of who was to pay. In practice, it has been implemented for only a few major historic urban areas.

The same Act introduced the scheduled monument consent procedure for works affecting scheduled ancient monuments, but again there was no reference to the provision of resources for any consequent archaeological recording.

The Department of the Environment's Circular on Planning Conditions, issued in 1985 (Circular 1/85) included two model conditions relating to archaeology. These dealt with the erection of fencing to safeguard known ancient monuments from accidental damage, and with the provision of access for archaeological recording during development. It emphasised that "conditions should not require work to be held up while archaeological investigation takes place." The underlying assumption, as with earlier guidance and legislation, was that finance would be available from other sources than the developer, and again no provision was made for investigation before a planning decision was made.

Growing concern for the environment generally, particularly in the 1970s and early 1980s, led to a recognition of the importance of identifying the environmental impact of development schemes before they are implemented. A European Community Directive of 1985 (85/337/EEC) laid down the principles of environmental assessment, which was to cover, among other things, "the direct and indirect effects of a project on . . . material assets and the cultural heritage" (Article 3). It was implemented in England and Wales under the Town and Country Planning (Assessment of Environmental Effects) Regulations 1988, but the explanatory circular on Environmental Assessment (DoE Circular 15/88) recommended that it should only be applied in the case of major, or particularly sensitive, projects. However, the principle of assessment before a planning decision is made was generally established, and became increasingly used where development proposals affected areas of known archaeological interest.

Archaeological assessment (more commonly referred to as evaluation) was formally recognised in the Department of the Environment's Planning Policy Guidance note 16, issued in November 1990. It is now standard practice for many development schemes. It enables planning decisions to take full account of archaeological factors, from a position of reasonable knowledge. It also allows the planning and realistic costing of subsequent recording action, which is the responsibility of the developer (paragraph 30: "No development shall take place . . . until the applicant has secured the implementation of a programme of archaeological work").

The present situation: benefits and limitations

Where archaeological deposits are known to exist on a proposed development site, for example through cropmarks, surface scatters or previous finds, evaluation in advance of a planning decision should clarify whether there are grounds for refusal of the application; or whether excavation before development is more appropriate and, if so, how it is to be undertaken. Evaluation can also be justified where there is reason to believe there may be archaeological interest, for example below alluvial deposits near rivers or close to known areas of interest. Some would advocate routine evaluation of all green field, i.e. previously undeveloped sites, though PPG 16 (paragraph 22) requires there to be "good reason to believe there are remains of archaeological importance".

The main benefit of the evaluation process is that planning decisions can be taken from a position of knowledge, whether that decision is for full or partial preservation or development after an appropriate scheme of investigation. With well-defined or definable 'sites' this can be a relatively straightforward process.

The system does however have some weaknesses. It reinforces the 'site' concept, favouring the preservation of well-defined areas or features of interest, and thus inevitably increasing the development pressure on the wider archaeological landscape. For example, clearly identified prehistoric or Romano-British settlement complexes can be more easily protected from development pressures, simply because they are so obviously there and may deter a potential developer from even considering an application.

Evaluation is usually limited to the application area, whereas the wider landscape context of a particular site may have a major bearing on its importance. Resources can also still be an issue: some developments, for example charitable institutions, will not have the profit margin generated by a commercial housing development, but the scale of necessary archaeological work may well be as large.

Changes in agricultural land-use, or an increase in ploughing depth, are of course still outside planning controls, and therefore do not require evaluation in advance or generate any resources through developer funding.

The need for a research framework

The changes in the field of archaeology and planning, marked by PPG 16, have led to a large increase in archaeological funding. The allocation of that funding may often be determined by the nature and location of development schemes, and not by the archaeological priorities set by broader research frameworks. The problems this generates can be highlighted by reference to a selection of current research questions relevant to prehistoric and Romano-British archaeology in Bedfordshire.

Palaeolithic period. The identification of surviving in situ deposits is a major research need, both in the Chilterns area of the county and in the river valleys in the north. This would require detailed analysis of the circumstances of previous discoveries, geological survey, and historical research into quarry pit locations. All these are likely to be beyond the justifiable scope of a single site-specific evaluation programme.

Early prehistoric period. Areas of 'ritual landscape' have been identified on gravel terraces in the Ouse valley, initially through identification of the individual monuments within them. Investigation of the spatial, temporal and functional relationships between their component parts involves looking at their wider landscape context and topographical setting. This may generate research questions in a wider area than that covered by development proposals.

Early prehistoric settlement archaeology (mesolithic period to Bronze Age) has received much less attention than the 'ritual' archaeology of the same periods. Settlements are more difficult to locate, as they rarely appear as cropmarks, and surface scatters of lithic material require intensive survey under the right conditions to be identified. In areas of intensive agriculture, evidence may be limited to the plough-zone; full recovery of habitation evidence, and evidence for exploitation of the surrounding landscape, would require several seasons of intensive field-walking and/or gridded removal and sieving of ploughsoil. Neither of these processes fit comfortably within a normal development timetable.

Environmental studies, particularly the analysis of colluvial/alluvial deposits and waterlogged remains, can be served well by gravel extraction adjacent to water-courses. There will, however, be diminishing returns in this area of research if the context for the examined deposits cannot also be explored, and the use of the wider landscape analysed. This will tend to happen if mineral extraction is steered away from good agricultural land and therefore away from areas of past agricultural exploitation.

Late prehistoric/Romano-British period. Late prehistoric and Romano-British settlements are more easily definable than those from earlier periods. They have therefore tended to receive greater attention as individual sites. It is now important to explore the differences and relationships between settlements in varied geological and topographical areas, and over time. Modern development pressures (mainly mineral extraction) have inevitably led to a concentration on settlements on a limited range of soils and geologies. In Bedfordshire, settlements on the clay uplands are under-represented in the archaeological record, and are likely to continue to be so, simply because the major development pressures are elsewhere.

As for earlier periods environmental studies continue to be a priority, particularly the investigation of waterlogged deposits in river valleys, but the same need for establishing the wider landscape context remains.

Soil exhaustion during the Romano-British period, and its effect on economy and settlement over time, again demonstrates the need for the exploration of the wider landscape, and not just individual settlements. This may require detailed investigation of field boundaries and land divisions (particularly deep ditches with waterlogged deposits) away from settlements and their infields. These are precisely the areas, perhaps containing intermittent and poorly understood cropmarks, which are likely to be at risk because of the tendency to preserve discrete definable complexes from development.

The way forward

As the procedures in PPG 16 become common practice, accommodation between the realities of modern development and the requirements of archaeological research could be approached through implementing the following principles.

1.   In considering the appropriate response to development threats, preservation should continue to be the first option, even for site types which are thought to be comparatively well-understood. This approach has been challenged in recent years, on the grounds that archaeology as an academic discipline, will fossilise if it is deprived of a major research technique, namely excavation. On the other hand, there are more than enough developments where the full preservation option cannot be implemented, for the profession's existing capacity.

2.   Pressure must be maintained to require evaluation where archaeological research priorities can justify it, such as the landscape between known activity locations (whether settlement or ritual), and possible habitation areas where archaeology may only survive in the ploughsoil. When this type of evaluation is required, it must be supported by a clear academic framework in order for it to be defended, if necessary, at a planning appeal. (It may not be sufficient to argue that all developments areas should be evaluated 'just in case'.)

3.   There should be a higher profile for archaeological research on linear developments, involving detailed evaluation, to build up case-histories in which evaluation results are compared with the results of the full investigation. In this way, it should be increasingly possible to predict how far the results of non-destructive survey techniques reflect the character of buried archaeological deposits in any given geological and topographical setting. The advantage of using linear developments for this research is that a given area of land will cover a wider range of geological and topographical situations than the same area on a discrete development site.

4.   It must be acknowledged that developer funding will not be sufficient to support all archaeological research, even in the rescue context, and that some public money must continue to be available. The survey of palaeolithic deposits is a prime example of this, recognised by English Heritage through its funding of the Southern Rivers Palaeolithic Project (Wymer 1991; 1992). Other survey projects, such as monitoring of plough damage to known sites through periodic examination of surface scatters, may never be in a position to attract private sector funding. Where research needs and development pressures do not coincide, an element of public money must be available to ensure that research needs are not neglected.

REFERENCES

Ager, B.M. 1989 The Anglo-Saxon cemetery. In Stead, I. & Rigby, V. *Verulamium. The King Harry Lane site.* English Heritage Archaeol. Rep. 12, 219-39.

Allcroft, A.H. 1908 *Earthwork of England.* London: MacMillan.

Allen, D. 1986 Excavations in Bierton 1979: a late Iron Age 'Belgic' settlement and evidence for a Roman villa and a twelfth to eighteenth century manorial complex. *Rec. Buckinghamshire* 8, 1-162.

Allen, M. 1991 The vegetational history at Barton. In Clark, R. Excavations at Barton ring ditches: landscape history and archaeology. *Bedfordshire Archaeol.* 19, 20.

Andrews, R.T. 1900 Romano-British remains in Bury Field. *Trans. East Hertfordshire Archaeol. Soc.* 1 (ii), 187.

Andrews, R.T. 1905 Roman remains in Welwyn. *Trans. East Hertfordshire Archaeol. Soc.* 3, 32-3.

Andrews, R.T. 1911 A Late Celtic Cemetery at Welwyn, Herts. *Antiq.* 47, 53-4.

Anthony, I.E. 1960 Rural Hertfordshire in the Iron Age and Roman period. *Hertfordshire's Past and Present* 1, 2-9.

Anthony, I.E. 1968 Excavations in Verulamium Hills Field, St Albans 1963-64. *Hertfordshire Archaeol.* 1, 9-65.

Anthony, I. E. 1970. St Michael's, St Albans, excavation, 1966. *Hertfordshire Archaeol.* 2, 51-61.

Applebaum, E.S. 1934 An Early Iron Age Site at Holwell Hertfordshire. *Antiq. J.* 14, 383-8.

Applebaum, E.S. 1949 Excavations at Wilbury Hill, an Iron Age Hillfort Near Letchworth, Hertfordshire. *Archaeol. J.* 106, 12-45.

Applebaum, E.S. 1972 The boundaries of the Ditchley Villa estate, Oxfordshire. In Finberg, H.P.R. (ed.) *The Agrarian History of England and Wales, AD43-1042.* I(ii). Cambridge: Univ. Press, 266-7.

Applebaum, E.S. 1975 Some observations on the economy of the Roman villa at Bignor, Sussex. *Britannia* 6, 118-32.

Appleton, G. & Dawson, M. forthcoming. A large stone relief from the Roman small town of Sandy, Bedfordshire. *Britannia.*

Archer, M. (ed.) 1963 The Register of Bishop Philip Repingdon, 1405-19, I. *Lincolnshire Rec. Soc.* 57.

Arnold, C.J. 1984 *Roman Britain to Saxon England: an Archaeological Study.* London: Croom Helm.

Arnold, D.E. 1989 *Ceramic Theory and Cultural Process.* Cambridge.

Ashworth, H. 1983 Evidence for a Medieval pottery industry at Potter Row, Great Missenden, Buckinghamshire. *Rec. Buckinghamshire* 25, 153-59.

Aspinall, A. 1977 Neutron activation analysis of Medieval ceramics. *Med. Ceramics* 1, 5-16.

Aubrey, J. 1668 Monumenta Britannica. Collected mss, unpublished, Bodleian Lib., Oxford.

Avery, M. 1976 Hillforts of the British Isles: A Students Introduction. In Harding, D.W. (ed.) *Hillforts: Later Prehistoric Earthworks in Britain and Ireland.* London: Academic Press, 1-56.

Bailey, G.N. & Davidson, I. 1983 Site exploitation territories and topography: two case studies from Palaeolithic Spain. *J. Archaeol. Sci.* 10, 87-115.

Baker, A.R.H. 1983 Discourse on British Field Systems. *Agricultural Hist. Rev.* 31(2), 149-55.

Baker, D. 1971 Excavations at Elstow Abbey, Bedfordshire, 1968-1970, third interim report. *Bedfordshire Archaeol. J.* 6, 55-7.

Baker, D., Baker, E., Hassall, J. & Simco, A. 1979 Excavations in Bedford 1967-77. *Bedfordshire Archaeol. J.* 13.

Baker, D. & Simco, A. 1982 The archaeology of Bedfordshire. *Archaeol. J.* 139, 1-68.

Baker, E. 1985 Report of Bedfordshire County Planning Department 1984: excavation. *South Midlands Archaeol.* 15, 15-16.

Baker, E. 1986 Note on King William's Close, Kempston. *South Midlands Archaeol.* 16, 26.

Baker, E. & Hassall, J. 1979 The pottery. In Baker, D., Baker, E., Hassall, J. & Simco, A., Excavations in Bedford 1967-1977. *Bedfordshire Archaeol. J.* 13, 147-240.

Barker, G. & Webley, D. 1977 An Integrated Economy for Gatecombe. In Branigan, K. (ed.) *Gatecombe: The Excavation and Study of a Romano-British Villa Estate 1967-76.* Brit. Archaeol. Rep. Brit. Ser. 44, 198-211.

Barrett, J. 1978 The EPRIA prehistoric pottery. In Hedges, J. & Buckley, D. Excavations at a Neolithic causewayed enclosure, Orsett, Essex, 1975. *Proc. Prehist. Soc.* 44, 219-308.

Barrett, J. 1980 The pottery of the Late Bronze Age in Lowland England. *Proc. Prehist. Soc.* 46, 297-320.

Barrett, J. & Bradley, R. (eds.) 1980 *Settlement and Society in the British Later Bronze Age.* Brit. Archaeol. Rep. Brit. Ser. 83, i-ii.

Bartlett, A. 1974 Unpublished report from the Ancient Monuments Laboratory: Geophysics 4/74

Bedfordshire SMR Archaeology Section, Planning Department, County Hall, Bedford MK42 9AP.

Beldam, J. 1859 Memoir on Excavations at Arbury Banks. *Proc. Soc. Antiq.* 1st ser. 4, 285-90.

Bell, R.D. 1984 The development of the parish of Wharram Percy, Yorkshire. Paper delivered at a conference on the Anglo-Saxon Church, Rewley House, Oxford.

Biddle, M. 1977 Alban and the Anglo-Saxon church. In Runcie, R. (ed.) *Cathedral and City. St Albans Ancient and Modern.* London, Martyn Assoc., 23-42.

Biddle, M. 1986 Archaeology, Architecture, and the cult of saints in Anglo-Saxon England. In Butler, L.A.S. & Morris, R.K. (eds.) *The Anglo-Saxon church: papers on history, architecture, and archaeology in honour of Dr H.M. Taylor.* Counc. Brit. Archaeol. Res. Rep. 60, 1-31.

Bilikowska, K. 1980 The Anglo-Saxon settlement of

Bedfordshire. *Bedfordshire Archaeol. J.* 14, 25-38.

Birchall, A. 1965. The Aylesford-Swarling culture: the problem of the Belgae reconsidered. *Proc. Prehist. Soc.* 31, 241-367.

Birley, M. 1988 The Iron age Pottery. In Moss-Eccardt, J. Archaeological Investigations in the Letchworth Area, 1958-1974. *Proc. Cambridge. Archaeol. Soc.* 87, 79-84.

Blagg, T.F.C. 1984 *Military and civilian in Roman Britain.* Brit. Archaeol. Rep. Brit. Ser. 136.

Blair, W.J. 1988 Introduction: from Minster to Parish Council. In Blair, W.J. (ed.) *Ministers and Parish Churches. The Local Church in Transtition 950-1200.* Oxford Univ. Comm. for Archaeol. Monograph 17, 1-19.

Bloemers, J.H.F. 1983. Acculturation in the Rhine-Mease basin in the Roman period: a preliminary survey. In Brandt, R. & Slofstra, J. (eds.) *Roman and native in the Low Countries.* Brit. Archaeol. Rep. Supp. Ser. 184.

Bolton, J.L. 1980 *The Medieval English economy 1150-1500.* London: J. M. Dent & Sons.

Bond, C.J. 1979 The reconstruction of the medieval landscape: the estates of Abingdon Abbey. *Landscape Hist.* 1, 59-75.

Bond, C.J. 1988 Church and parish in Norman Worcestershire. In Blair, J. (ed.) *Minsters and Parish Churches. The local church in transition 950-1200.* Oxford Univ. Comm. for Archaeol. Monograph 17, 119-58.

Bradley, R.J. 1969 The South Oxfordshire Grim's Ditch and its significance. *Oxoniensia* 33, 1-13.

Bradley, R.J. 1984 *The Social Foundations of Prehistoric Britain.* London: Longmans.

Bradley, R. & Chambers, R. 1988 A new study of the Cursus Complex at Dorchester on Thames. *Oxford J. Archaeol.* 7(3), 271-89.

Bradley, R. & Gardiner, J. (eds.) 1984 *Neolithic Studies: a review of some current research.* Brit. Archaeol. Rep. Brit. Ser. 133.

Bradley, R.J., Lobb, S., Richards, J. & Robinson, M. 1980 Two late Bronze Age settlements on the Kennet Gravels: excavations at Aldermaston Wharf and Knight's Farm, Burghfield, Berkshire. *Proc. Prehist. Soc.* 46, 217-96.

Branigan, K. 1967 Romano-British rural settlement in the eastern Chilterns. *Archaeol. J.* 124, 129-59.

Branigan, K. 1977 *Gatecombe: The excavation and study of a Romano-British villa estate 1967-1976.* Brit. Archaeol. Rep. Brit. Ser. 44.

Branigan, K. 1985 *The Catuvellauni.* Gloucester: Alan Sutton.

Brine, G. 1988 The pottery. In Pinder, A. & Davison, B. The excavation of a motte and bailey castle at Chalgrave, Bedfordshire, 1970. *Bedfordshire Archaeol.* 18, 40-6.

Brooks, H. & Bedwin, O. 1989 *Archaeology at the Airport: The Stanstead Archaeological Project 1985-89.* Essex County Council.

Brown, A.E. & Taylor, C. 1989 The Origins of Dispersed settlements, some results from fieldwork in Bedfordshire. *Landscape Hist.* 2, 61-82.

Brown, A.E. 1994 A Romano-British shell-gritted pottery and tile manufacturing site at Harrold, Bedfordshire. *Bedfordshire Archaeol.* 21, 19-107.

Brown, A.G. & Edmonds, M.R. (eds.) 1987 *Lithic analysis and later British prehistory: some problems and approaches.* Brit. Archaeol. Rep. Brit. Ser. 162.

Bruneaux, J. 1986 *Les Gaulois, sanctuaires et rites.* Paris: Collection des Hesperides.

Bryant, S.R. 1994 Whiteley Hill, near Royston: a late Bronze Age ringwork? *Hertfordshire Archaeol.* 11, 26-9.

Bryant, S.R. & Niblett, R. forthcoming The late Iron Age in Hertfordshire and the north Chilterns. In Gwilt, A. & Haselgrove, C. (eds.) *Time, space and culture in Iron Age Britain.*

Buckinghamshire County Museum, 1983. Unpublished observations at 'The Orchard', Penn, Buckinghamshire.

Buckinghamshire SMR County Museum. Technical Centre, Tring Road, Halton, Aylesbury HP22 5PJ.

Buckley, D.G. & Hedges, J.D. 1987 *The Bronze Age and Saxon Settlements at Spingfield Lyons, Essex: an Interim Report.* Essex County Council Occ. Pap. 5.

Burleigh, G.R. 1976 Pipeline archaeology. *Hertfordshire's Past* 1, 17-18.

Burleigh, G.R. 1980 Excavations at the Mile Ditches, near Royston, 1978. *Hertfordshire's Past* 8, 24-9.

Burleigh, G.R. 1982 Excavations at Baldock, 1980-81. *Hertfordshire's Past* 12, 3-18.

Burleigh, G.R., Atkinson, M. & Richmond, A.D.W. 1991 Archaeological investigations on the Slip End, Ashwell, to Wicker Hall, Royston, water pipeline. North Hertfordshire District Council Museums unpublished archive report.

Burleigh, G.R., West, D. & Matthews, K. 1990 An archaeological evaluation at Hollard's Farm, Codicote, Herts. North Hertfordshire District Museums Field Archaeol. Rep. 5.

Burleigh G. & Matthews, K. forthcoming Excavations at Jack's Hill, 1988. *Hertfordshire Archaeol.*

Burleigh, G.R. et al. forthcoming *Excavation at Baldock, Hertfordshire 1978-1989.* Hertfordshire Archaeol. Monograph.

Burnham, B.C. & Wacher, J. 1990 *The 'Small Towns' of Roman Britain.* London: Batsford.

Busby, J.H. 1954 Rothamsted: Roman Shrine Excavation, 1936. *Trans. East Hertfordshire Archaeol. Soc.* 13(2), 209.

Cambridgeshire SMA Dept. of Lands and Buildings, Cambridgeshire County Council, Shire Hall, Castle Hill, Cambrdge CB3 0AP.

Campbell, J.B. & Hubbard, R.N.L.B. 1978 Biological investigations of the Rackley site. In Sampson, C.G. (ed.) *Paleoecology and Archeology of an Acheulian Site at Caddington, England.* Southern Methodist Univ., 47-60.

Campbell, J. (ed.) 1982 *The Anglo-Saxons.* Oxford: Phaidon.

Catt, J.A. 1978 The contribution of loess to soils in lowland Britain. In Limbrey, S. & Evans, J.G. (eds.) *The effect of man on the landscape: the lowland zone.* Counc. Brit. Archaeol. Res. Rep. 21, 12-20.

Cauvain, P., Cauvain, S. & Green, M. 1989 Prehistoric, Romano-British and fourteenth-century activity at Ashwells, Tylers Green, Bucks. *Rec. Buckinghamshire* 31, 111-19.

Cauvain, S. & Cauvain, P. 1978 A Romano-British Site at Micklefield, High Wycombe. *Rec. Buckinghamshire* 20, 828-34.

Cauvain, S. & Cauvain, P. 1987 Romano-British finds in the area of Mount Wood and Sarratt. *CVAHS J.*, 12-22.

Cauvain, S. & Cauvain, P. 1989a A medieval site in Priory Road, High Wycombe, Bucks. *Rec. Buckinghamshire* 31, 33-6.

Cauvain, S. & Cauvain, P. 1989b Prehistoric, Romano-British and fourteenth century activity at Ashwells, Tylers Green, Bucks. *Rec. Buckinghamshire* 31, 111-19.

Cauvain, S. & Cauvain, P. 1989c Excavations at Emmanuel Church, Chesham. *CVAHS J.*, 12-24.

Chaffey, J. & Wells, M. 1989 Distribution of medieval and post-medieval pottery in the Ley Hill area of Buckinghamshire. *CVAHS J.*, 27-9.

Chaffey, J. 1990 Hedsor Reservoir and Wycombe Slough Link main. *CVAHS J.*, 26-31.

Champion, T.C. 1980 Settlement and Environment in Later Bronze Age Kent, in Barrett, J.C. & Bradley R.J. (eds.) *Settlement and Society in the British Later Bronze Age.* Brit. Archaeol. Rep. Brit. Ser. 83, 223-46.

Chauncy, H. 1700, reprinted 1975 *The Historical Antiquities of Hertfordshire, II.*

Childe, V.G. & Smith, I.F. 1954 Excavation of a neolithic barrow on Whiteleaf Hill, Bucks. *Proc. Prehist. Soc.* 20, 212-30.

Chisholm, M. 1979 *Rural Settlement and Land Use. An essay in location.* London: Hutchinson Univ. Lib.

Clark, A. 1992 Stagsden bypass, Bedfordshire: archaeomagnetic dating AJC 102. Unpublished report.

Clarke, D.L. 1972 *Models in Archaeology.* London: Methuen.

Clark, R. 1991 Excavations at Barton ring ditches: landscape history and archaeology. *Bedfordshire Archaeol.* 19, 4-24.

Cockburn, R.W.T. 1937 Note. *Rec. Buckinghamshire* 13, 300.

Coleman, S. 1985 *Caddington and Kensworth.* Bedfordshire Parish Surveys 4.

Collins, D. & Lorimer, D. (eds.) 1989 *Excavations at the mesolithic site on West Heath, Hampstead 1976-1981.* Brit. Archaeol. Rep. Brit. Ser. 217.

Collis, J. 1984a *The European Iron Age.* London.

Collis, J. 1984b *Oppida: earliest towns north of the Alps.* Sheffield: Univ. of Sheffield.

Cotton, J. 1991 Prehistory in Greater London. *Curr. Archaeol.* 124, 151-4.

Cotton, M.A. & Frere, S.S. 1968 Ivinghoe Beacon Excavations, 1963-5. *Rec. Buckinghamshire.* 18, 187-260.

Couchman, C.R. 1980 The Bronze Age in Essex, in Buckley,

D.G. (eds.) *Archaeology in Essex to AD 1500.* Counc. Brit. Archaeol. Res. Rep. 34, 40-6.

Cra'ster, M.D. 1961 The Aldwick Iron Age Settlement, Barley, Hertfordshire. *Proc. Cambridge Antiq. Soc.* 57, 22-46.

Cra'ster, M.D. 1965 Aldwick, Barley: Recent Work at the Iron Age Site. *Proc. Cambridge. Antiq. Soc.* 58, 1-11.

Crawford, O.G.S. 1931 The Chiltern Grim's Ditch. *Antiq.* 5, 161-71.

Crawford, O.G.S. 1936 Field Archaeology of the Royston District. *Proc. Prehist. Soc.* 2, 97-105.

Crummy, P. 1993 Aristocratic graves at Colchester. *Curr. Archaeol.* 132, 4-6.

Cunliffe, B. 1968 Early Pre-Roman Iron Age Communities in Eastern England. *Antiq. J.* 48, 175-91.

Cunliffe, B. 1978 *Iron Age Communities in Britain.* London: Routledge & Kegan Paul, 2nd edition.

Cunliffe, B.W. 1988. *Greeks, Romans and Barbarians.* London: Batsford.

Cunliffe, B.W. 1991 *Iron Age communities in Britain.* London: Routledge & Kegan Paul, 3rd edition.

Cunliffe, B. & Miles, D. 1984 *Aspects of the Iron Age in Central Southern Britain.* Univ. Oxford Comm. Archaeol. Monograph 2.

Cutts, E.L. 1898 *Parish Priests and their People in the Middle Ages in England.*

CVAHS 1985 A Report on Excavations at Bury Farm, Amersham. *Rec. Buckinghamshire* 27, 119-28.

CVAHS 1987 *CVAHS J.*

CVAHS 1989 *CVAHS J.*

CVAHS & Hedgerley Historical Society 1988 Excavations at Moat Farm, Hedgerley. *Rec. Buckinghamshire* 30, 183-87.

Dalwood, H. & Platell, P. 1988 Note on Coldharbour Farm Saxon site in Aylesbury Field Survey. *South Midlands Archaeol.* 18, 36-7.

Davis, F.N. (ed.) 1914 Rotuli Roberti Grossetest and Rotulus Henrici de Lexington. *Lincolnshire Rec. Soc.* 11.

Davis, J. 1981 Grim's Ditch in Buckinghamshire and Hertfordshire. *Rec. Buckinghamshire* 23, 23-31.

Davis, J. & Evans, J.G. 1984 Grim's Ditch, Ivinghoe. *Rec. Buckinghamshire* 26, 1-10.

Davies, W. & Vierck, H. 1974 The contexts of the Tribal Hidage: social aggregates and settlement patterns. *Fruhmittelalterliche Studien* 8, 223-93.

Davey, N. 1932 Roman Tile and Pottery Kiln at "Black Boy" Pits, St Stephens, near St Albans. *Trans. St Albans Architect. Archaeol. Soc.*, 212-4.

Davey, N. 1935 Romano-British cemetery at St Stephens Hill. *Trans. St Albans Architect. Archaeol. Soc.*, 243.

Davys, W.O. 1888 Notes on the Remains of a Medieval Wayside Chapel at Gustard Wood. *Trans. St. Albans Archit. Archaeol. Soc.* 13-14.

Dawson, M. 1988 Sandy, Bedfordshire. In Bedfordshire County Planning Department, Conservation and Archaeology Section. *South Midlands Archaeol.* 18, 14.

Dawson, M. 1994. *A late Roman cemetery at Bletsoe.* Bedfordshire Archaeol. Monograph 1.

Dawson, M. & Slowikowski, A.M. 1988. A Romano-British cemetery at Warren Farm, Deepdale. Sandy. *Bedfordshire Archaeol.* 18, 25-32.

Day, I. 1980a Excavations at Brayfields. *Hertfordshire's Past* 8, 29-37.

Day, I. 1980b Rush Green Lodge, Amwell. *Hertfordshire's Past* 9, 38-40.

Devoy, R.J. 1980 Post-glacial environmental change and man in the Thames estuary: a synopsis. In Thompson, F.H. (ed.) *Archaeological change and coastal change.* Soc. Antiq. London Occ. Paper 1, 134-48.

Dix, B. 1983 An Excavation at Sharpenhoe Clappers. Beds. *Bedfordshire Archaeol.* 16, 65-74.

Dix, B. 1985 Report on excavations at Odell, Bedfordshire. Unpublished draft report and site archive at Bedford Museum, acc. no. 1985/18.

Dring, G.J. 1971 Romano-British pottery kiln site near Elstow. *Bedfordshire Archaeol. J.* 6, 69-71.

Drury, P.J. 1978 *Excavations at Little Waltham 1970-71.* Counc. Brit. Archaeol. Res. Rep. 26.

Drury, P.J. 1980 The Early and Middle Phases of the Iron Age in Essex, in Buckley, D.G. (ed.) *Archaeology in Essex to AD 1500.* Counc. Brit. Archaeol. Res. Rep. 34, 47-54.

Dunnett, B.R.K. 1972 Report on the trial excavations at Wards Coombe, Ivinghoe 1971. *Rec. Buckinghamshire* 19, 141-55.

Dunnett, R. 1985 Excavations at Mount Wood, Chenies. *Rec. Buckinghamshire* 27, 107-18.

Dunning, G.C. & Wheeler, R.E.M. 1931 A barrow at Dunstable, Bedfordshire. *Archaeol. J.* 116, 1-24.

Dyer, C. 1990 Dispersed settlements in medieval England. A case study of Pandock, Worcestershire. *Medieval Archaeol.* 34, 97-121.

Dyer, J.F. 1960 Barrows of the Chilterns. *Archaeol. J.* 116, 1-24.

Dyer, J.F. 1961 Dray's Ditches, Bedfordshire, and Early Iron Age Territorial Boundaries in the Chilterns. *Antiq. J.* 118, 32-42.

Dyer, J.F. 1962 Neolithic and Bronze Age sites at Barton Hill Farm, Bedfordshire. *Bedfordshire Archaeol. J.* 1, 1-24.

Dyer, J. 1963 The Chiltern Grim's Ditch. *Antiq.* 37, 46-49.

Dyer, J.F. 1964a A secondary neolithic camp at Waulud's Bank, Leagrave. *Bedfordshire Archaeol. J.* 2, 1-15.

Dyer, J.F. 1964b A Rectilinear Enclosure at Maulden Firs, Barton. *Bedfordshire Archaeol. J.* 2, 47-9.

Dyer, J.F. 1974 The excavation of two barrows on Galley Hill, Streatley. *Bedfordshire Archaeol.* 9, 13-34.

Dyer, J.F. 1976 Ravensburgh Castle, Hertfordshire. In Harding, D.W. (ed.) *Hillforts: Later Prehistoric Earthworks*

in Britain and Ireland. London: Academic Press, 153-9 & 421-3.

Dyer, J.F. 1978 Worthington George Smith. In Worthington George Smith and other studies presented to Joyce Godber, *Bedfordshire Hist. Rec. Soc.* 57, 141-79.

Dyer, J.F. 1991 The Five Knolls and associated barrows at Dunstable, Bedfordshire. *Bedfordshire Archaeol.* 19, 25-9.

Dyer, J.F. & Hales, A.J. 1961 Pitstone Hill - A Study in Field Archaeology. *Rec. Buckinghamshire* 17, 49-56.

Eagles, B.N. & Evison, V.I. 1970 Excavations at Harrold, Bedfordshire, 1951-53. *Bedfordshire Archaeol. J.* 5, 17-56.

Eames, E., 1980 *Catalogue of lead glazed earthernware Medieval tiles in the Dept. of Medieval and Later Antiquities.* London: British Museum, 2 vols.

Easterbrook, B.D. 1978 A medieval earthwork at Stokenchurch. *Rec. Buckinghamshire* 20, 667-8.

Edwards, D. & Partridge, C. (eds.) 1978 Recent work in Hertfordshire. *Aerial Archaeol.* 1, 44.

Ellis, W. 1732 *The Practical Farmer or Hertfordshire Husbandman* London.

Esmonde Cleary, A.S. 1991 *The Ending of Roman Britain.* London: Batsford.

Evans, J.G. 1972 *Land Snails in Archaeology.* London: Seminar Press.

Evans, J. 1975 *The Environment of Early Man in the British Isles.* London: Paul Elek.

Evans, J.G. & Valentine, K.W.G. 1974 Ecological change induced by prehistoric man at Pitstone, Bucks. *J. Archaeol. Sci.* 1, 343-51.

Farley, M. 1976 Saxon and medieval Walton and Aylesbury: excavations 1973-74. *Rec. Buckinghamshire* 20(2), 153-290.

Farley, M. 1978 Excavations at Low Farm, Fulmer, Bucks. 1: the mesolithic occupation. *Rec. Buckinghamshire* 19, 344-51.

Farley, M. 1982 A Medieval pottery industry at Boarstall, Buckinghamshire. *Rec. Buckinghamshire* 24, 107-17.

Farley, M. 1983a A mirror burial at Dorton, Buckinghamshire. *Proc. Prehist. Soc.* 9, 269-302.

Farley, M. 1983b Archaeological Notes from the County Museum. *Rec. Buckinghamshire* 25, 169.

Farley, M. 1986a Aylesbury. *Curr. Archaeol.* 101, 187-9.

Farley, M. 1986b Excavations at the Prebendal Court, Aylesbury 1985. *South Midlands Archaeol.* 16, 37-8.

Farley, M. 1988 A late Medieval kiln at Ley Hill, Latimer, Bucks. *South Midlands Archaeol.* 18, 30.

Farley, M. 1991 Coldharbour farm, Aylesbury. *South Midlands Archaeol.* 21, 39.

Farley, M. & Browne, S. 1983 A prehistoric crouched burial at Princes Risborough. *Rec. Buckinghamshire* 25, 142-7.

Farley, M. & Leach, H. 1988 Medieval pottery production areas near Rush Green, Denham, Buckinghamshire. *Rec. Buckinghamshire* 30, 53-102.

Faull, M. & Moorhouse, S.A. (eds.) 1981 *West Yorkshire: an Archaeological Survey to AD 1500.* 4 vols., Wakefield: West Yorkshire Metropolitan County Council.

Finberg, H.P.R. 1955 *Roman and Saxon Withington: a Study in Continuity.* Univ. of Leicester: Dept. of English Local Hist. Occ. Pap. 8.

Foard, G. 1978 Systematic fieldwalking and the investigation of Saxon settlement in Northamptonshire. *World Archaeol. 9,* 357-74.

Ford, S. 1982 Fieldwork and Excavation on the Berkshire Grim's Ditch. *Oxoniensia 47,* 13-36.

Ford, S. 1987 Flint scatters and prehistoric settlement patterns in south Oxfordshire and east Berkshire. In Brown, A.G. & Edmonds, M.R. (eds.) *Lithic analysis and later British prehistory: some problems and approaches.* Brit. Archaeol. Rep. Brit. Ser. 162, 101-35.

Fowler, G.H. (ed.). 1926 A digest of Charters Preserved in the Cartulary of the Priory of Dunstable. *Bedfordshire Hist. Rec. Soc.* 10.

Fox, C. 1924 A Settlement of the Early Iron Age at Abington Pigotts, Cambs. *Proc. Prehist. Soc. East Anglia* 4, 211-33.

Fox, C. & Clarke L.G.C. 1925 Excavations in Bulstrode Camp. *Rec. Buckinghamshire* 1, 283-8.

Frere, S.S. 1967 *Britannia.* London: Routledge & Kegan Paul.

Frere, S.S. 1983 *Verulamium Excavations Volume 2.* Soc. Antiq. London Res. Rep. 41.

Frere, S.S. 1984 *Verulamium Excavations Volume III.* Oxford Univ. Comm. Archaeol. Monograph 1.

Frere, S.S. (ed.) 1984 Roman Britain in 1983: sites explored. *Britannia* 15, 304.

Frere, S.S. 1987 Roman Britain in 1986. *Britannia* 18, 301-59.

Frere, S.S. 1991 *Britannia.* London: Routledge & Kegan Paul, 2nd edition.

Fulford, M.G. & Huddleston, K. 1991 *The Current State of Romano-British Pottery Studies.* English Heritage Occ. Pap. 1.

Gaffney, V. & Tingle, M. 1989 *The Maddle Farm Project.* Brit. Archaeol. Rep. Brit. Ser. 200.

Garmonsway, G.N. 1955 *The Anglo-Saxon Chronicle.* London: J.M.Dent.

Gent, H. 1983 Centralised Storage in Later Prehistoric Britain. *Proc. Prehist. Soc.* 49, 243-67.

Geophysical Surveys of Bradford 1991 Report 91/29 Cardington, Bedford. Unpublished report.

Gibbard, P.L. 1985 *The Pleistocene history of the Middle Thames Valley.* Cambridge: Univ. Press.

Girling, M. & Greig, J. 1977 Palaeoecological investigations of a site at Hampstead Heath, London. *Nature* 268, 45-7.

Girling, M.A. & Greig, J. 1985 A first fossil record for *Scolytus scolytus* (F.) (Elm Bark Beetle): its occurrence in Elm Decline Deposits from London and the implications for Neolithic elm disease. *J. Archaeol. Sci.* 12, 347-51.

Going, C.W. 1987 *The Mansio and other sites in the south eastern sector of Caeseromagus: the Roman pottery.* Counc. Brit. Archaeol. Res. Rep. 72 & Chelmsford Archaeol. Trust Rep. 3.2.

Goodburn, R. 1976 Roman Britain in 1975. *Britannia* 7, 338-9.

Goodburn, R. 1978 Roman Britain in 1977. *Britannia* 9, 444.

Gordon, A.D., 1981 *Classification : methods for the exploratory analysis of multivariate data.* London: Chapman and Hall.

Gover, J.E.B., Mawer, A. & Stenton, F.M. 1970 *The Place-names of Hertfordshire.* English Place Name Society 15.

Gowing, C.N. 1969 Archaeological notes from the Buckinghamshire County Museum. *Rec. Buckinghamshire* 18, 331-6.

Graham Kerr, C. 1988 Gatehampton Farm - stop press. *South Oxfordshire Archaeol. Gp. Bull.* 44, 12-15.

Graham Kerr, C.A. 1993 SOAG Site at Gatehampton. *South Midlands Archaeology* 23, 86-8.

Green, H.M.J. 1975. Roman Godmanchester. In Rodwell, W. & Rowley, T. (eds.) *The small towns of Roman Britain.* Brit. Archaeol. Rep. Brit. Ser. 15, 183-210.

Green, H.S. 1981 The Dating of Ivinghoe Beacon. *Rec. Buckinghamshire* 23, 1-3.

Green, M. & Horne, B. 1991 Analysis of the medieval pottery from Friary Field, Dunstable. *The Manshead Magazine* 31, 1-31.

Greenfield, E. 1961 The Bronze Age round barrow on Codicote Heath, Hertfordshire. *Trans. St Albans Architect. Archaeol. Soc.,* 5-20.

Greig, J. 1989 From lime forest to heathland - five thousand years of change at West Heath Spa, Hampstead, as shown by the plant remains. In Collins, D. and Lorimer, D. (eds.) *Excavations at the mesolithic site on West Heath, Hampstead 1976-1981.* Brit. Archaeol. Rep. Brit. Ser. 217, 89-99.

Gregory, A. 1991 *Excavations in Thetford, 1980-82, Fison Way.* East Anglian Archaeol., 2 vols.

Grigson, C. 1976 The animal bones from pit 6. In Matthews, C.L. *Occupation sites on a Chiltern Ridge: excavations at Puddlehill and sites near Dunstable, Bedfordshire.* Brit. Archaeol. Rep. Brit. Ser. 29, 11-18.

Gurney, F.G. 1920 Yttingaford and the 10th century bounds of Chalgrave and Linslade. *Bedfordshire Hist. Rec. Soc.* 5.

Haddon-Reece, D. 1976 Unpublished report from the Ancient Monuments Laboratory: Geophysics G 20/76

Hagen, R. 1971 Anglo-Saxon burials from the vicinity of Biscot Mill, Luton. *Bedfordshire Archaeol. J.* 6, 23-6.

Haggett, P. 1968 *Locational Analysis in Human Geography.* London: Edward Arnold.

Hale, W.H. (ed.) 1858 The Domesday of St Paul's of the year 1222. *Camden Soc.* 1st Ser., 69.

Hall, D.N. 1972 A thirteenth century pottery kiln at Harrold, Beds. *Milton Keynes J.* 1, 23-32.

Hall, D. 1981 The changing landscape of the Cambridgeshire

Fens. *Landscape Hist.* 3, 37-49.

Hall, D. 1985 Late Saxon topography and early medieval estates. In Hooke, D. (ed.) *Medieval Villages.* Oxford Univ. Comm. for Archaeol. Monograph 5, 61-9.

Hall, D. 1987 *The Fenland Project No.2: Fenland Landscapes and Settlement between Peterborough and March.* East Anglian Archaeol. 35 & Fenland Project Comm. & Cambridge Archaeol. Comm.

Hall, D. 1991 Field Surveys in Bedfordshire. *Bedfordshire Archaeol.* 19, 51-6.

Hall, D.N. & Hutchins, J.B. 1972. The distribution of archaeological sites between the Nene and the Ouse valleys. *Bedfordshire Archaeol.* 7, 1-16.

Hall, D.N. & Nickerson, N. 1966 Sites on the North Bedfordshire and South Northamptonshire border. *Bedfordshire Archaeol.* 3, 1-6.

Hallam, H.E. 1970 In Phillips, C.W. (ed.) *The Fenland in Roman times.* Roy. Geog. Soc. London Res. Ser. 5.

Hallam, H.E. 1981 *Rural England, 1066-1348.*

Hammond, F.W. 1978 Regional Survey Strategies: a simulation approach. In Cherry, J.F., Gamble, C. & Shennan, S. (eds.) *Sampling in Contemporary British Archaeology.* Brit. Archaeol. Rep. Brit. Ser. 50, 67-85.

Harding, D.W. 1974 *The Iron Age in Lowland Britain.* London: Routledge & Kegan Paul.

Harding, D.W. (ed.) 1976 *Hillforts: later prehistoric earthworks in Britain and Ireland.* London: Academic Press.

Harding, P., Bridgland, D., Keen, D. & Rogerson, R. 1991 A Palaeolithic site rediscovered at Biddenham, Bedfordshire. *Bedfordshire Archaeol.* 19, 87-90.

Hartley, B.R. 1957 The Wandlebury Iron Age hill-fort, excavations of 1955-56. *Proc. Cambridge Antiq. Soc.* 50, 1-27.

Haselgrove, C. 1987 *Iron Age Coinage in South-East England.* Brit. Archaeol. Rep. Brit. Ser. 174, i.

Haselgrove, C. 1988 The Archaeology of British Potin Coinage. *Archaeol. J.* 145, 99-122.

Haselgrove, C. 1990 The later Iron Age in Southern Britain and beyond. In Todd, M. (ed.) *Research on Roman Britain 1960-89.* Britannia Monograph 11, 1-18.

Haselgrove, C. Millett, M. & Smith, I. (eds.) 1985 *Archaeology from the Plough Soil. Studies in the Collection and Interpretation of Field Survey Data.* Sheffield: Dept. of Archaeol. & Prehist.

Hassall, J. 1976 Medieval pottery and a possible kiln site at Everton. *Bedfordshire Archaeol. J.* 11, 69-75.

Hawkes, C.F.C. 1940a A site of the late Bronze Age - early Iron Age transition at Totternhoe, Beds. *Antiq. J.* 20, 487-91.

Hawkes, C.F.C. 1940b The Excavations at Bury Hill, 1939. *Proc. Hampshire Fld. Club Archaeol. Soc.* 14, 136-94.

Hawkes, C.F.C. 1962 Early Iron Age Pottery from Linford Essex. In Barton, K.J. (ed.) Settlements of the Iron Age and Pagan Saxon Periods at Linford Essex. *Trans. Essex Archaeol. Soc.,* 57-104.

Hawkes, S.C. 1982 The archaeology of conversion: cemeteries. In Campbell, J. (ed.) *The Anglo-Saxons.* Oxford: Phaidon 48-49.

Hayfield, C. 1987 *An Archaeological Survey of the Parish of Wharram Percy, East Yorkshire.* Brit. Archaeol. Rep. Brit. Ser. 172.

Head, J.F. 1955 *Early Man in South Buckinghamshire: an introduction to the archaeology of the region.* Bristol.

Head, J.F. 1974 An important early route through the Chilterns. *Rec. Buckinghamshire* 9, 422-8.

Head, J.F. & Piggot, C.M. 1946 An Iron Age Site at Bedlow, Buckinghamshire. *Rec. Buckinghamshire* 14, 189-209.

Herne, A. 1988 A time and a place for the Grimston bowl. In Barrett, J.C. & Kinnes, I.A. (eds.) *The archaeology of context in the neolithic and Bronze Age: recent trends.* Sheffield: Dept. of Archaeol. & Prehist., 9-29.

Hertfordshire SMR Planning & Environment Dept., County Hall, Hertford SG13 8DN.

Hingley, R. 1989 *Rural Settlement in Roman Britain.* London: Seaby.

Hingley, R. & Miles, D. 1984 Aspects of Iron Age settlement in the Upper Thames valley. In Cunliffe, B. & Miles, D. (eds.) *Aspects of the Iron Age in Central Southern Britain.* Univ. Oxford Comm. Archaeol. Monograph 2.

Hinchliffe, J. 1975 Excavations at Grim's Ditch, Mongewell, 1974. *Oxoniensia* 40, 122-35.

Hodder, I. 1972 Locational models and the study of Romano-British settlement. In Clarke, D.L. (ed) *Models in Archaeology.* London: Methuen, 887-909.

Hodder, I. & Orton, C. 1976 *Spatial Analysis in Archaeology.* Cambridge: Univ. Press.

Hodder, I. & Millett, M. 1980 Romano-British Villas and Towns. A Systematic Analysis. *World Archaeol.* 12(1), 69-76.

Hohler, C., 1941 Medieval paving tiles in Buckinghamshire. *Rec. Buckinghamshire* 14, 1-49.

Hohler, C., 1942 Medieval paving tiles in Buckinghamshire. *Rec. Buckinghamshire* 14, 99-132.

Holgate, R. 1988a A review of neolithic domestic activity in southern Britain. In Barrett, J.C. and Kinnes, I.A. (eds.), *The Archaeology of Context in the Neolithic and Bronze Age: recent trends.* Sheffield: Dept. of Archaeol. & Prehist., 104-12.

Holgate, R. 1988b *Neolithic settlement of the Thames Basin.* Brit. Archaeol. Rep. Brit. Ser. 194.

Holgate, R. 1991a Luton Museum. In Wingfield, C. & Holgate, R. Acquisitions, enquiries, research on collections and fieldwork at Bedford and Luton Museums, 1988-89. *Bedfordshire Archaeol.* 19, 79-86.

Holgate, R. 1991b The prehistoric pottery and flint. In Dyer, J.D. The Five Knolls and associated barrows at Dunstable, Bedfordshire. *Bedfordshire Archaeol.* 19, 28-9.

Holmes, 1954 Ermine Street at Ware. *Trans. East Hertfordshire Archaeol. Soc.* 13(ii), 156.

Holmes, J. & Frend, W. 1959 A Belgic Chieftain's Grave at Hertford Heath. *Trans. East Hertfordshire Archaeol. Soc.* 14,

1-19.

Hoskins, W.G. 1967 *Field work in local history*. London: Faber & Faber.

Hudspith, R.E.T. 1990 Caddington fieldwalking survey. *Manshead Magazine* 30, 37-45.

Hudspith, R.E.T. 1991a Fieldwalking at Caddington 1991. *Manshead Magazine* 31, 39-43.

Hudspith, R.E.T. 1991b Fieldwalking at Houghton Regis 1989-90. *Manshead Magazine* 31, 44-51.

Hudspith, R.E.T. 1991c Fieldwork in north-east Luton 1989-90. *Manshead Magazine* 31, 52-55.

Hudspith, R.E.T. 1991d Fieldwalking at Houghton Regis and Caddington, South Bedfordshire 1988-90. *Bedfordshire Archaeol.* 19, 57-64.

Hudspith, R.E.T. 1992 Fieldwalking. *Manshead Magazine* 32, 11-23.

Hudspith, R.E.T. 1993a Fieldwalking at Houghton Regis and Tottemhoe 1991-92. *Manshead Magazine* 33, 32-40.

Hudspith, R.E.T. 1993b Fieldwalking at Streatley, Lilley and north Luton 1991-92. *Manshead Magazine* 33, 22-31.

Hughes, M.J., Cherry, J., Freestone, I.C. & Leese, M. 1982 Neutron activation analysis and petrology of medieval English decorated floortiles from the Midlands. In Freestone, I., Johns, C. & Potter, T. (eds.) *Current Research in ceramics: thin section studies*. Brit. Mus. Occ. Pap. 32, 113-22.

Hunn, J.R. 1981 A note on the Medieval defences of St Albans. *Hertfordshire's Past* 11, 2.

Hunn, J.R. 1990 Reconstruction and Measurement of Landscape Change: a study of six parishes in the St Albans area. Unpublished PhD thesis, Univ. of Southampton.

Hunn, J.R. 1992 The Verulamium oppidum and its landscape in the late Iron Age. *Archaeol. J.* 149, 39-68.

Hunn, J.R. forthcoming The excavation of a Romano-British farmstead at Boxfield Farm, Stevenage, 1988-89. Hertfordshire Archaeol. Trust.

Hunn, J.R. & Blagg, T.F.C. 1984 Architectural Fragments from the Vicinity of Verulamium. *Antiq. J.* 64(2), 362-5.

Hussen, C-M. 1983 *A Rich Late La Tene Burial at Hertford Heath, Hertfordshire*. Brit. Mus. Occ. Pap. 44.

Hutchings, N. & Farley, M. 1989 A fifteenth-sixteenth century pottery industry at Tylers Green, Penn, Buckinghamshire. *Rec. Buckinghamshire* 31, 105-10.

Hyslop, M. 1963 Two Anglo-Saxon cemeteries at Chamberlains Barn, Leighton Buzzard, Bedfordshire. *Archaeol. J.* 120, 161-200.

Institute of Geological Sciences 1981 *Mineral Assessment Report* 69.

Ivens, R.J., 1981 Medieval pottery kilns at Brill, Buckinghamshire. *Rec. Buckinghamshire* 23, 102-6.

Ivens, R.J. 1982 Medieval pottery from the 1978 excavations at Temple Farm, Brill. *Rec. Buckinghamshire* 24, 144-170.

Jacobi, R.M. 1973 Aspects of the "Mesolithic Age" in Great Britain. In Kozlowski, S.K. (ed.) *The mesolithic in Europe*.

Warsaw: Univ. Press, 237-65.

Jacobi, R.M. 1975 *Aspects of the post-glacial archaeology of England and Wales*. Unpublished Ph.D. thesis, Univ. of Cambridge.

Jacobi, R.M. 1980 The upper palaeolithic of Britain with special reference to Wales. In Taylor, J.A. (ed.) *Culture and environment in prehistoric Wales*. Brit. Archaeol. Rep. Brit. Ser. 76, 15-100.

Jarman, M.R. 1972 A Territorial Model for Archaeology; a behaviourable and geogrphical approach. In Clarke, D.L. (ed.) *Models in Archaeology*. London: Methuen, 705-33.

Jenkins, J.G. 1938 The Cartulary of Missenden Abbey, part 1. *Rec. Branch Buckinghamshire Archaeol. Soc.* 2, 32, 84 & 186.

Johnson, D.E. 1974. The Roman settlement at Sandy Bedfordshire. *Bedfordshire Archaeol.* 9, 35-54.

Jones, A.H.M. 1964 *The Later Roman Empire 284-602*. Oxford: Blackwell.

Jones, M. 1986 Towards a model of the villa estate. In Miles, D. *Archaeology at Barton Court Farm, Abingdon, Oxon*. Counc. Brit. Archaeol. Res. Rep. 50, 38-42.

Jones, M.U. & Bond, D. 1980 Later Bronze Age Settlement at Mucking, Essex. In Barrett, J.C. & Bradley, R.J. (eds.) *Settlement and Society in the Later British Bronze Age*. Brit. Archaeol. Rep. Brit. Ser. 83, 471-82.

Jope, E.M. 1951 Medieval and Saxon finds from Felmersham, Bedfordshire. *Antiq. J.* 31, 45-50.

Keeley, H. 1987 *Environmental Archaeology: A regional review II*. English Heritage Occ. Pap. 1.

Keevill, G.D. & Campbell, G.E. 1991 Investigations at Danesfield camp, Medmenham, Buckinghamshire. *Rec. Buckinghamshire* 33, 87-99.

Kendal, R.J. & Cottingham, A.H.G. 1994 Excavations at the Stable at the rear of Nos.32-36 Market Place, Henley-on-Thames, Oxfordshire. *Henley Archaeological and Historical Group Report* no. HY 93 1.

Kennard, A.S. 1938 Report on the non-marine mollusca. In Head, J.F. The excavation of the Cop Round Barrow, Bledlow. *Rec. Buckinghamshire* 13, 347-51.

Kennett, D.H. 1970 Pottery and other finds from the Anglo-Saxon cemetery at Sandy, Bedfordshire. *Medieval Archaeol.* 14, 17-33.

Kennett, D.H. 1972a An um from Moggerhanger and Panel Style at Kempston. *Bedfordshire Archaeol. J.* 7, 39-44.

Kennett, D.H. 1972b Seventh century finds from Astwick. *Bedfordshire Archaeol. J.* 7, 45-51.

Kennett, D.H. 1973a Some Anglo-Saxon pottery from Luton. *Bedfordshire Archaeol. J.* 9, 93-98.

Kennett, D.H. 1973b Seventh century cemeteries in the Ouse Valley. *Bedfordshire Archaeol. J.* 8, 99-108.

Kennett, D.H. 1986 Recent work on the Anglo-Saxon cemetery found at Kempston. *South Midlands Archaeol.* 16, 3-14.

Kilmurry, K., 1982 The manufacture of Stamford ware: an application of thin-sectioning and neutron activation analysis. In Freestone, I., Johns, C. & Potter, T. (eds.) *Current research in ceramics: thin section studies.* Brit. Mus. Occ. Pap. **32**, 105-11.

Kiln, R.J. 1970 An Early Iron Age Site at Moles Farm, Thunderidge. *Hertfordshire Archaeol.* **2**, 10-22.

Kiln, R.J. 1973 Ware. *Hertfordshire Archaeol. Rev.* **7**, 123-4.

Kiln, R.J. 1986 *The Dawn of History in East Hertfordshire.* Hertford.

Kimball, D. 1933 Cholesbury Camp. *J. Brit. Archaeol. Assoc.* n.s. 39(1), 187-208.

King, D.W. 1969 *Soils of the Luton and Bedford District: A Reconnaissance Survey.* Agricultural Research Council Soil Survey, Special Survey No. 1.

Knight, D. 1984 *Late Bronze Age and Iron Age settlement in the Nene and Great Ouse basins.* Brit. Archaeol. Rep. Brit. Ser. 130, i-ii.

Lacaille, A.D. 1963 Mesolithic industries beside Colne Waters in Iver and Denham, Buckinghamshire. *Rec. Buckinghamshire* **17**, 143-81.

Lambrick, G. & Robinson, M. 1978. *Iron Age and Roman riverside settlements at Farmoor, Oxfordshire.* Counc. Brit. Archaeol. Res. Rep. 32.

Leese, M.N., Hughes, M.J. & Cherry, J., 1986 A scientific study of N. Midlands medieval tile production. *Oxford J. Archaeol.* **5**, 355-70.

Lethbridge, T.C. & Palmer, W.M. 1929. Excavations in the Cambridgeshire Dykes. *Proc. Camb. Antiq. Soc.* 30.

Levett, A.E. 1938 *Studies in the Manorial Court.* Oxford: Univ. Press (reprinted 1962).

Lewis, J.S.C., Wiltshire, P.E.J. & Mcaphail, R. 1992 A late Devensian/early Flandrian site at Three Ways Wharf, Uxbridge: environmental implications. In Needham, S. & Machlin, M.G. (eds.) *Alluvial Archaeology in Britain.* Oxbow Monograph 27, 235-47.

Lipscomb, G. 1847 *History and Antiquities of the County of Buckingham.* Vols. 1-4. London: J.B. Nichols.

Longley, D. 1980 *Runneymead Bridge 1976: Excavations on the Site of a Late Bronze Age Settlement.* Res. Vol. Surrey Archaeol. Soc.

Longworth, I 1989 The Late Prehistoric Pottery. in Stead, I. & Rigby V. 1989 *Verulamium: the King Harry Lane Site.* English Heritage Archaeol. Rep. 12, 53-8.

Loveday, R. 1989 The Barford Ritual Complex: further excavations (1972) and a regional perspective. In Gibson, A. (ed.) *Midlands Prehistory: some recent and current researches into the prehistory of central England.* Brit. Archaeol. Rep. Brit. Ser. 204, 51-84.

Lowther, A.W.G. 1937 Excavation of the Roman structure at Rothamsted, Harpenden. *Trans. St Albans Architect. Archaeol. Soc.*, 108-14.

Luard, H.R (ed.) 1882 *Matthaei Parisiensis Chronica Majora.* 4, 1240-1247 (Rolls Series). London.

Maloney, C. 1994 Henley-on-Thames. *Oxford Archaeol. Unit Ann. Rep. 1993-94,* **32**.

Manby, T.G. 1980 Bronze Age Settlement in Eastern Yorkshire. In Barrett, J.C. & Bradley, R.J. (eds.) *Settlement and Society in the Later British Bronze Age.* Brit. Archaeol. Rep. Brit. Ser. 83, 307-70.

Manning, W.H. & Scott, I.R. 1979 Roman military timber gateways. *Britannia* 10, 19-62.

Marney, P.T. 1990 *Roman and Belgic Pottery from Excavations in Milton Keynes 1972-82.* Buckinghamshire Archaeol. Soc. Monograph 2.

Matthews, C.L. 1962a Current excavations. *Manshead Magazine* 9, 143-4.

Matthews, C.L. 1962b The Anglo-Saxon cemetery at Marina Drive, Dunstable. *Bedfordshire Archaeol. J.* 1, 25-47.

Matthews, C.L. 1963 The current excavations. *Manshead Magazine* 10, 6-15.

Matthews, C.L. 1976 *Occupation sites on a Chiltern Ridge. Excavations at Puddlehill and sites near Dunstable, Bedfordshire. Part 1: Neolithic, Bronze Age and Early Iron Age.* Brit. Archaeol. Rep. Brit. Ser. 29.

Matthews, C.L. 1986 Possible late Roman temple, Bidwell, nr. Dunstable, South Bedfordshire. *S. Midlands Archaeol.* 16, 29-34.

Matthews, C.L. 1989 *Ancient Dunstable.* Manshead Archaeol. Soc. of Dunstable, 2nd edition.

Matthews, C.L. *et multi alli.* 1981 A Romano-British Inhumation Cemetery at Dunstable. *Bedfordshire Archaeol. J.* 15.

Matthews, C.L. & Hawkes, S.C. 1985 Early Saxon settlements and burials on Puddlehill, near Dunstable, Bedfordshire. In Hawkes, S.C., Campbell, J. & Brown, D., *Anglo-Saxon Studies in Archaeology and History 4.* Oxford Univ. Comm. for Archaeol. 4, 59-115.

Matthews, C.L., Schneider, J. & Horne, B.J. 1992 A Roman villa at Totternhoe. *Bedfordshire Archaeol.* 20, 41-95.

Matthews, K. & Burleigh, G.R. 1988 Archaeological evaluation of an early Iron Age site at Jack's Hill, Graveley, Hertfordshire. North Hertfordshire District Council Museums unpublished archive report.

Matthews, K. & Burleigh, G. in prep. Early Iron Age Settlements in North Hertfordshire. *Hertfordshire Archaeol.*

Meaney, A.L. 1964 *A Gazetteer of Early Anglo-Saxon Burial Sites.* London: George Allen & Unwin.

Merriman, N. 1990 *Prehistoric London.* London: HMSO.

Miles, D. 1986 *Archaeology at Barton Court Farm, Abingdon, Oxon.* Counc. Brit. Archaeol. Res. Rep. 50.

Millett, M. 1990 *The Romanisation of Roman Britain.* Cambridge: Univ. Press.

Mitchell, C.W. 1973 *Terrain Evaluation.* London: Longman.

Morrill, R.L. 1970 *The spatial orgainisation of society.* Belmont, California: Wadsworth.

Morris, J. 1962 The Anglo-Saxons in Bedfordshire. *Bedfordshire Archaeol. J.* 1, 58-76.

Morris, J. (ed.) 1976 *Domesday Book.* Chichester: Phillimore.

Morris, J. 1987 *The Age of Arthur. A history of the British Isles from AD350-650.* Chichester: Phillimore.

Morris, R.K. 1985 The Church in the Countryside: two lines of inquiry. In Hooke, D. (ed.) *Medieval Villages: a review of current work.* Oxford Univ. Comm. for Archaeol. Monograph 5, 47-60.

Moorhouse, S. 1974 A distinctive type of late medieval pottery in the eastern Midlands: a definition and preliminary statement. *Proc. Cambridge Antiq. Soc.* 65, 46-59.

Moss-Eccardt, J. 1964 Excavations at Wilbury Hill, an Iron Age Hillfort Near Letchworth, Hertfordshire. *Bedfordshire Archaeol. J.* 2, 34-46.

Moss-Eccardt, J. 1965 An Iron Age Cauldron-rim from Letchworth, Hertfordshire. *Antiq. J.* 45, 173-7.

Moss-Eccardt, J. 1971 Anglo-Saxon cemetery at Blackhorse Road, Letchworth, Bedfordshire. *Bedfordshire Archaeol. J.* 6, 27-32.

Moss-Eccardt, J. 1988 Archaeological investigations in the Letchworth area, 1958-1974. *Proc. Cambridge Antiq. Soc.* 77, 35-103.

Munby, L.M. 1964 *Hertfordshire Population Statistics 1563-1801.* Hertfordshire Loc. Hist. Counc.

Munby, L.M. 1977 *The Hertfordshire Landscape.* London: Hodder & Stoughton.

Mustoe, R.S. 1988 Salvage excavation of a neolithic and Bronze Age ritual site at Goldington, Bedford: a preliminary report. *Bedfordshire Archaeol.* 18, 1-5.

Mynard, D.C. 1970 Medieval pottery of Potterspury type. *Bull. Northamptonshire Fed. Archaeol. Socs.* 4, 49-55.

Mynard, D.C. 1984 A medieval pottery industry at Olney Hyde. *Rec. Buckinghamshire* 26, 56-85.

Mynard, D.C., Petchey, M.R. & Tilson, P.G. 1983 A medieval pottery at Church End, Flitwick, Bedfordshire. *Bedfordshire Archaeol. J.* 16, 75-84.

Naroll, R. 1961 Floor area and settlement population. *American Antiq.* 27, 587-8.

Neal, D.S. 1974 *The Excavation of the Roman Villa in Gadebridge Park, Hemel Hempstead 1963-1968.* Comm. Soc. Antiq. London Res. Rep. 31.

Neal, D. 1977 Northchurch, Boxmoor and Hemel Hempstead Station: the excavation of three Roman buildings in the Bulbourne Valley. *Hertfordshire Archaeol.* 4, 1-135.

Neal, D. 1978 The growth and decline of villas in the Verulamium area. In Todd, M. (ed.) *Studies in the Romano-British Villa.* Leicester, 33-58.

Neal, D.S. 1984 A sanctuary at Wood Lane End, Hemel Hempstead. *Britannia* 15, 193-215.

Neal, D.S. 1987 Excavations at Magiovinium, Buckinghamshire, 1978-1980. *Rec. Buckinghamshire* 29, 1-124.

Neal, D.S., Wardle, A. & Hunn, J. 1990. *Excavation of the Iron Age, Roman and Medieval Settlement at Gorhambury, St Albans.* English Heritage Archaeol. Rep. 14.

Needham, S. & Burgess, C. 1980 The Late Bronze Age in the Lower Thames Valley: The metalwork evidence. In Barrett, J.C. & Bradley, R.J. (eds.) *Settlement and Society in the British Later Bronze Age.* Brit. Archaeol. Rep. Brit. Ser. 83, 437-68.

Needham, S. & Longley, D. 1980 Runnymead Bridge, Egham: a Late Bronze Age riverside settlement. In Barrett, J.C. & Bradley, R.J. (eds.) *Settlement and Society in the British Later Bronze Age.* Brit. Archaeol. Rep. Brit. Ser. 83, 397-436.

Niblett, R. 1990a Interim report on archaeological excavations at Old Parkbury, Colney Street, Herts. Typescript report, St Albans Museums.

Niblett, R. 1990b Verulamium. *Current Archaeol.* 120, 410-17.

Niblett, R. 1992 A Catuvellaunian chieftain's burial from St. Albans. *Antiq.* 66, 917-29.

Niblett, R. 1993. *Verulamium* since the Wheelers. In Greep, S.J. (ed.) *Roman Towns: the Wheeler inheritance. A review of 50 years' research.* Counc. Brit. Archaeol. Res. Rep. 93, 78-92.

Niblett, R. & Reeves, P. 1992. A wealthy grave from Verulamium. *Antiq. J.* 70(ii), 441-6.

O'Donoghue, K. 1980 The Saxon cemetery of Luton 1, Bedfordshire. Unpublished dissertation, Univ. of London.

O'Neil, H.E. 1945 The Roman villa at Park Street, near St Albans, Hertfordshire: report on the excavations of 1943-45. *Archaeol. J.* 102, 21-109.

Page, W. 1906 Kingsbury Castle. *Trans. St Albans Architect. Archaeol. Soc.*, 149-57.

Page, W. 1917 The origins and forms of Hertfordshire towns and villages. *Arch.* 69, 53.

Parkes, P.A. 1986. *Current scientific techniques in archaeology.* Beckenham: Croom Helm.

Parry, S. & Webster, M. 1991 Raunds survey. *South Midlands Archaeol.* 21, 39.

Partridge, C. 1975 A corn dryer at Foxholes. *Curr. Archaeol.* 52, 152-3.

Partridge, C. 1979 Excavations in Ware. *Hertfordshire Archaeol.* 7, 135-58.

Partridge, C. 1980a Late Bronze Age artifacts fromHertford Heath, Hertfordshire. *Hertfordshire Archaeol.* 7, 1-9.

Partridge, C. 1980b Excavations at Puckeridge and Braughing 1975-79. *Hertfordshire Archaeol.* 7, 28-132.

Partridge, C. 1981a *Skeleton Green. A late Iron Age and Romano-British site.* Britannia Monograph 2.

Partridge, C. 1981b Prehistoric and Romano-British settlement in Ware. *Hertfordshire's Past* 10, 28-33.

Partridge, C. 1989 *Foxholes Farm. A multi-period gravel site.* Hertfordshire Archaeol. Trust Monograph.

Pautreau, J. 1991 Sepulture aristocratique Augusteenne à Antran (Vienne) - note preliminaire. *Archaologisches Korrespondenzblatt* 21. Mainz: Romisch Germanischen Zentralmuseums, 271-81.

Percival, J. 1976. *The Roman Villa.* Oxford: Univ. Press.

Phillips, C.W. (ed.) 1970 *The Fenland in Roman times.* Roy. Geog. Soc. London Res. Ser. 5.

Pickering, J. 1978 The Jurassic spine. *Curr. Archaeol.* 64, 140-3.

Pinder, A. & Davison, B. 1988 The excavation of a motte and bailey castle at Chalgrave, Bedfordshire, 1970. *Bedfordshire Archaeol.* 18, 33-56.

Pitkin, D.S. 1962 Partible Inheritance and the Open Fields. *Agricultural History* 35-6, 65-9.

Postan, M.M. 1972 *The Medieval Economy and Society.*

Proudfoot, L.J. 1983 The Extension of Parish Churches in Medieval Warwickshire. *J. Hist. Geog.* 9(3), 231-46.

Pryor, F., French, C. & Taylor, M. 1986 Flag Fen, Fengate, Peterborough I: discovery, reconnaissance and initial excavation (1982-85). *Proc. Prehist. Soc.* 52, 1-24.

Rankov, N.B. 1982 Roman Britain in 1981: sites explored. *Britannia* 13, 369.

Rawlins, B.F. 1970 A Roman tile kiln at Park Street near St Albans. *Hertfordshire Archaeol.* 2, 62-5.

RCHM 1910 *Hertfordshire.* London: HMSO.

RCHM 1912 *An Inventory of the Historic Monuments in Buckinghamshire: Volume I.* London: HMSO.

Reece, R. 1982 The coins from the Cow Roast, Herts. - a commentary. *Hertfordshire Archaeol.* 8, 60-6.

Reece, R. 1984. The coins. In Frere, S.S. *Verulamium Excavations Volume III.* Oxford Univ. Comm. Archaeol. Monograph 1, 3-18.

Rees, Y.F. 1937 Romano-Briitish cemetery of St Stephens Hill. *Trans. St Albans Architect. Archaeol. Soc.*, 151.

Reed, M. 1979 *The Buckinghamshire Landscape.* London: Hodder & Stoughton.

Rice, P.M. 1987 *Pottery analysis: a sourcebook.* London: Univ. of Chicago Press.

Richardson, K.M. & Young, A. 1951 An Iron Age Site on the Chilterns. *Antiq. J.* 31, 132-48.

Richmond, A.D.W. & Burleigh, G.R. 1992 Archaeological investigations on the Norton, Hertfordshire, to Morden Grange, Cambridgeshire, gas pipeline. North Hertfordshire District Council Museums unpublished archive report.

Riley, H.T. (ed.) 1867a *Gesta Abbatum Monasterii S. Albani.* 1, Rolls Series. London.

Riley, H.T. (ed.) 1867b *Gesta Abbatum Monasterii S. Albani.* 2, Rolls Series. London.

Roberts, E. 1981 St Albans Borough Boundary and its significance in the Peasants Revolt. In *The Peasants Revolt in Hertfordshire in 1381.* Stevenage: Hertfordshire Publications.

Robinson, B. 1992. Excavations at Brent Ditch 1992. *Cambridgeshire C.C. Archaeol. Section Rep.* 68.

Roden, D. 1966 Field systems of the Chiltern Hills and of parts of Kent from the late 13th to the early 17th century. *Trans. Inst. Brit. Geog.* 38, 73-88.

Roden, D. 1969a Demesne Farming in the Chiltern Hills. *Agricultural Hist. Rev.* 17, 9-23.

Roden, D. 1969b Fragmentation of Farms and Fields in the Chiltern Hills, thirteenth century and later. *Medieval Stud.* 31, 225-38.

Roden, D. 1970 Enclosure in the Chiltern Hills. *Geografiske Annaler ser. B* 52, 115-26.

Roden, D. 1973 Field systems of the Chiltern Hills and their environs. In Baker, A.R.H. & Butlin, R.A. (eds.) *Studies of Field Systems in the British Isles.* Cambridge: Univ. Press, 325-76.

Rodwell, W. & Rowley, T. (eds.) 1975 *The small towns of Roman Britain.* Brit. Archaeol. Rep. Brit. Ser. 15.

Rodwell, W. 1976 Coinage, oppida and the rise of Belgic power in S.E. Britain. In Cunliffe, B. & Rowley, T. (eds.) *Oppida: the beginnings of urbanisation in Barbarian Europe.* Brit. Archaeol. Rep. Supp. Ser. 11, 181-366.

Rodwell, W. 1984 Churches in the Landscape: Aspects of Topography and Planning. In Faull, M. (ed.) *Studies in late Anglo-Saxon settlement.* Oxford Univ. Dept. of Ext. Stud., 1-25.

Rodwell, W.J & Rodwell, K.A. 1986 *Rivenhall: Investigation of a villa, church, and village 1950-1977.* Chelmsford Archaeological Trust & Counc. Brit. Archaeol. Res. Rep. 55.

Roe, D.A. 1968 *A gazetteer of British lower and middle palaeolithic sites.* Counc. British Archaeol. Res. Rep. 8.

Roe, D.A. 1981 *The Lower and Middle Palaeolithic Periods in Britain.* London: Routledge & Kegan Paul.

Roffe, D. 1984 Pre-Conquest Estates and Parish Boundaries. A discussion with examples from Lincolnshire. In Faull, M. (ed.) *Studies in Late Anglo-Saxon settlement.* Oxford Univ. Dept. of Ext. Stud., 115-22.

Rook, A.G. 1968 Investigation of a Belgic Occupation Site at Crookhams, Welwyn Garden City. *Hertfordshire Archaeol.* 1, 51-65.

Rook, A.G. 1970a A Belgic and Roman Site at Brickwall Hill, Welwyn Garden City. *Hertfordshire Archaeol.* 2, 23-30.

Rook, A.G. 1970b Investigation of a Belgic Site at Grubs Barn, Welwyn Garden City. *Hertfordshire Archaeol.* 2, 31-36.

Rook, A.G. 1974 Welch's Farm. *Hertfordshire Archaeol. Rev.* 9, 170.

Rook, A. 1976 Cow Roast. *Hertfordshire Archaeol. Rev.* 10, 199.

Rook, A.G. 1982 An Iron Age Bronze Mirror from Aston, Hertfordshire. *Antiq. J.* 62, 18-34.

Rook, A. 1986 The Roman site at Dicket Mead, Lockleys, Welwyn. *Hertfordshire Archaeol.* 9, 79-175.

Rutherford Davis, K. 1982. *Britons and Saxons. The Chiltern Region 400 -700.* Chichester: Phillimore.

Salter, C. & Ehrenreich, R. 1984 Iron Age metallurgy in central southern Britain. In Cunliffe, B. & Miles, D. (eds.) *Aspects of the Iron Age in Central Southern Britain.* Oxford Comm. for Archaeol. Monograph 2, 146-61.

Salway, P. 1986 *Roman Britain.* Oxford: Clarendon Press.
Saunders, A. 1963 Excavation at Park Street 1954-57. *Archaeol. J.* 118, 100-35.

Sampson, C.G. (ed.) 1978 *Paleoecology and archaeology of an Acheulian site at Caddington, England.* Dallas: Southern Methodist Univ.

Saunders, C. 1972 The Pre-Belgic Iron Age of the Central and Western Chilterns. *Archaeol. J.* 128, 1-30.

Saunders, C. 1982 Some thoughts on the oppida at Wheathampstead and Verulamium. *Hertfordshire Archaeol.* 8, 31-9.

Saunders, C. & Havercroft, A.B. 1977 A kiln of the Potter Oastrius and related excavations at Little Munden Farm, Bricket Wood. *Hertfordshire Archaeol.* 5, 109-56.

Saunders, C. & Havercroft, A.B. 1982a Excavations on the line of the Wheathampstead By-Pass 1974 and 1977. *Hertfordshire Archaeol.* 8, 11-39.

Saunders, C. & Havercroft, A. 1982b Excavations at St Helen's Church, Wheathampstead. *Hertfordshire Archaeol.* 8, 102-11.

Saville, A. 1981 The flint assemblage. In Mercer, R.J. *Grimes Graves excavations 1971-72.* London: DoE Archaeol. Rep. 11 vol. 2.

Schofield, A.J. (ed.) 1990 *Interpreting Artefact Scatters.* Oxbow Monograph.

Selkirk, A. 1972 Waulud's Bank. *Curr. Archaeol.* 30, 173-6.

Selkirk, A. 1983 Baldock. *Curr. Archaeol.* 86, 70-4.

Shennan, S. 1985 *Experiments in the collection and analysis of archaeological survey data: the East Hampshire survey.* Sheffield: Dept. of Archaeol. & Prehist.

Simco, A. 1973 The Iron Age in the Bedford Region. *Bedfordshire Archaeol. J.* 18, 5-22.

Simco, A. 1984 *Survey of Bedfordshire: the Roman Period.* Bedfordshire County Council & RCHM(E).

Simmons, I. & Tooley, M. 1984 *The Environment in British Prehistory.* London: Duckworth.

Slowikowski, A.M. & Dawson, M. 1994 An early Roman period pottery kiln at Warren Villas Quarry, Upper Caldecote, Bedfordshire. *J. Roman Pottery Stud.* 6, 37-49.

Smith, I.F. 1974 The Neolithic. In Renfrew, C. (ed.) *British Prehistory: a new outline.* London: Duckworth, 100-36.

Smith, R.A. 1919 The palaeolithic 'floor' at Whipsnade, Bedfordshire. *Proc. Soc. Antiq.* 2nd ser. 312, 39-50.

Smith, R.F. 1987 *Roadside Settlements in Lowland Roman Britain: a gazetteer and study of their origins, growth, decline, property boundaries and cemeteries.* Brit. Archaeol. Rep. Brit. Ser. 157.

Smith, T.P. 1973 *The Anglo-Saxon churches of Hertfordshire.* Hertfordshire Local History Council: Phillimore.

Smith, W.G. 1904 *Dunstable: its history and surroundings.* London.

Smith, W.G. 1916 Notes on the palaeolithic floor near Caddington. *Arch.* 67, 49-74.

Smithson, S. 1984 The burnt mounds of Chalfont St. Giles: a survey. *Rec. Buckinghamshire* 15, 113-16.

Spratt, D. 1989 *The Linear Earthworks of the Tabular Hills, North Yorks.* Sheffield: Dept. of Archaeol. & Prehist.

Stainton, B. & Stanley, C. 1987 A Romano-British Pottery Kiln at Gerrards Cross. *Rec. Buckinghamshire* 29, 160-9.

Stainton, B. 1989 Excavation of an early prehistoric site at Stratfords Yard, Chesham. *Rec. Buckinghamshire* 31, 49-74.

Stainton, B. 1990 Two palaeolithic hand axes. *CVAHS J.*, 24-5.

Stamp, D.L. (ed.) 1941 *The Land of Britain. The Report of the Land Utilisation Survey of Britain. Hertfordshire pt. 80.* London: Geographical Publications Ltd.

Stanford, S.C. 1974 *Croft Ambrey.* Hereford.

Stanford, S.C. 1981 *Midsummer Hill: an Iron Age Hillfort of the Welsh Marches.* Leominster.

Stead, I. 1967. La Tene III burial at Welwyn Garden City. *Arch.* 101, 1-62.

Stead, I.M. 1969 Verulamium 1966-68 *Antiq.* 43, 45-51.

Stead, I.M. 1975 Baldock. In Rodwell W. & Rowley, T. (eds.) *Small Towns of Roman Britain* Brit. Archaeol. Rep. Brit. Ser. 15, 125-9.

Stead, I.M. & Rigby, V. 1986 *Baldock: the excavation of a Roman and pre-Roman settlement, 1968-72.* Britannia Monograph 7.

Stead, I.M. & Rigby, V. 1989 *Verulamium. The King Harry Lane Site.* English Heritage Archaeol. Rep. 12.

Stenton, F.M. 1971 *Anglo-Saxon England.* Oxford: Clarendon Press.

Stevenson, M.D. 1980 An Initial Survey of Prehistory in the Royston Area. Unpublished dissertation, Univ. of Southampton Dorest Institute of Higher Education.

Stewart, D. 1983 Half Hide Lane Turnford. Unpublished typescipt held in Herts. SMR.

Stewart, J.D., Fralick, P., Hancock, R.G.V., Kelly, J.H. & Garrett, E.M. 1990 Petrographic analysis and INAA geochemistry of prehistoric ceramics from Robinson Pueblo, New Mexico. *J. Archaeol. Sci.* 17, 601-25.

Stocker, D.A. 1990 Review of Minsters and Parish Churches, the Local Church in Transition 950-1200 (ed. Blair, W.J. 1988). *J. Brit. Archaeol. Assoc.* 143, 140-3.

Stopford, J 1987 Danebury: an Alternative View. *Scottish Archeaol. Rev.* 4, 70-5.

Swann, V. 1984 *The pottery kilns of Roman Britain.* RCHME Supp. Ser. 5

Taylor, A.F. & Woodward, P.J. 1985 A Bronze Age barrow cemetery, and associated settlement at Roxton. *Bedfordshire Archaeol.* 14, 73-149.

Tebbutt, C.F. 1932 Early Iron Age Settlement on Jack's Hill, Great Wymondley, Herts. *Proc. Prehist. Soc. East Anglia* 31, 371-4.

Thomasson, A.J. 1964 *The Soils and Land Use of the District around Aylesbury and Hemel Hempstead.* London: HMSO.

Thomasson, A.J. 1969 *Soils of the Saffron Walden District: A Reconnaissance Survey.* Agricultural Research Council Soil Survey, Special Survey No. 2.

Thomasson, A.J. & Avery, B.W. 1970 *The Soils of Hertfordshire.* Agricultural Research Council Soil Survey, Special Survey No. 3. Harpenden.

Thompson, A. & Holland, E. 1977 Excavation of an Iron Age Site at Dellfield, Berkhamsted. *Hertforshire Archaeol.* 4, 137-48.

Thompson, I. 1982 *Grog-tempered 'Belgic' pottery of Southeastern England.* British Archaeol. Rep. Brit. Ser. 108, i-iii.

Tilson, P. 1973. A Belgic and Romano-British site at Bromham. *Bedfordshire Archaeol. J.* 8, 23-67.

Trust for Wessex Archaeology Ltd 1994 Nettlebed Reservoir, Nettlebed, Henley-on-Thames, Oxfordshire Archaeological Evaluation. *Trust for Wessex Archaeol. Rep.* W663a.

VCH 1905-27 *Buckinghamshire.* Volumes 1-4. London: A. Constable/St Catherine Press.

VCH 1908 *Hertfordshire,* II. London: A. Constable/St Catherine Press.

VCH 1971a *Hertfordshire,* 2. London: Dawsons of Pall Mall.

VCH 1971b *Hertfordshire,* 4. London: Dawsons of Pall Mall.

Vince, A. 1990 *Saxon London: an archaeological Investigation.* London: Seaby.

Vita-Finzi, C. & Higgs, E.S. (eds.) 1970 Prehistoric Economy in the Mt Carmel area of Palestine. Site Catchment Analysis. *Proc. Prehist. Soc.* 36, 1-37.

Wade Martins, P. 1980 *Village sites in Launditch Hundred.* East Anglian Archaeol. Rep. 10.

Wait, G.A. 1991. Fleam Dyke 1991 - Interim Report. *Cambridgeshire C.C. Archaeol. Section Rep.* 49.

Wait, G.A. 1992. Devils' Dyke Excavations 1991. *Cambridgeshire C.C. Archaeol. Section Rep.* 52.

Wardle, A. 1982 Kings Langley Roman villa. *Hertfordshire's Past* 13, 20-2.

Ward-Perkins, J.R. 1938 Romano-British Villa at Lockleys. *Antiq. J.* 18, 339-76.

Warren, S.H., Clark, J.G.D., Godwin, M.E. & Macfayden, W.A. 1934 An early mesolithic site at Broxbourne sealed under Boreal peat. *J. Roy. Anthropol. Inst.* 64, 101-28.

Waton, P.V. 1982. Land snail evidence of Post-Glacial environmental change on the Hertfordshire chalklands. *Trans. Hertfordshire Nat. Hist. Soc.* 28, 63-75.

Watts, D.J. 1989 Infant burials and Romano-British Christianity. *Archaeol.* 146, 372-83

Welch, M.G. 1984 Saxon Sussex. *Current Archaeol.* 92, 280-2.

Waugh, H. 1968 Pottery from Pitstone Hill. In M.A. Cotton & S.S. Frere, Ivinghoe Beacon Excavations, 1963-5. *Rec. Buckinghamshire* 18, 235-49.

West, S. 1992 Excavations at Redbourn. St Albans Museums evaluation report.

West, S. 1993a Aldwickbury Golf Course (B93). St Albans Museums evaluation report.

West, S. 1993b Friar's Wash A93. St Albans Museums evaluation report.

Westall, W.P. 1937 Romano-British occupation site at Wymondley. *Trans. East Hertfordshire Archaeol. Soc.* 10(i), 11-15.

Wheeler, R.E.M. & Wheeler, T.V. 1936 *Verulamium: a Belgic and two Roman cities.* Soc. Antiq. London Res. Rep. 11.

Whittock, M.J. 1986 *The origins of England. 410-600.* Beckingham: Croom Helm.

Wilberforce, S., Bishop of Oxford 1848 *An Inaugural Address...to the Architectural and Archaeological Society for the County of Buckingham.* Aylesbury: J. Pickburn.

Wilkerson, J.C. & Cra'ster, M.D. 1959 Excavations at Whiteley Hill, Barley, Herts. *Proc. Cambridge Antiq. Soc.* 52, 2-5.

Williams, R.J. 1985 Note on other sites and finds in Milton Keynes Archaeology Unit, Bucks. County Council, Annual Report 1984. *South Midlands Archaeol.* 15, 60.

Williams, R.J. 1986 Bancroft 'Mausoleum'. In Mynard, D.C. Milton Keynes Archaeology Unit, Buckinghamshire County Council, Annual Report 1985. *South Midlands Archaeol.* 16, 43-9.

Williams, R.J. 1989 Wavendon Gate - Iron Age, Roman and Saxon Settlement, interim report. *South Midlands Archaeol.* 19, 18-21.

Williamson, T. 1984 Roman and Medieval Settlement in N.W. Essex. Unpublished Ph.D. theses, Univ. of Cambridge.

Williamson, T.M. 1984 The Roman Countryside: settlement and agriculture in N.W. Essex. *Britannia* 15, 225-30.

Williamson, T.M. 1985 Sites in the landscape: approaches to the post-Roman settlement of S. E. England. *Archaeol. Rev. Cambridge* 4 (1), 51-64.

Williamson, T.M. 1986 Parish boundaries and early fields: continuity and discontinuity. *J. Hist. Geog.* 12, 241-48.

Williamson, T.M. 1988 Explaining regional landscapes: woodland and champion in southern and eastern England. *Landscape Hist.* 10, 5-14.

Willis, B. 1755 *The History and Antiquities of the Town, Hundred and Deanery of Buckingham.* London: B. Willis.

Wilson, A.L., 1978 Elemental analysis of pottery in the study of its provenance: a review. *J. Archaeol. Sci.* 5, 219-36.

Wilson, D.R. 1975a Roman Britain in 1974. I. Sites Explored. *Britannia* 6, 220-83.

Wilson, D.R. 1975b Some pitfalls in the interpretation of air photographs. In Wilson, D.R. (ed.) *Aerial reconnaissance for archaeology.* Counc. Brit. Archaeol. Res. Rep. 12, 59-69.

Wingfield, C.R. 1991 Bedford Museum. In Wingfield, C.R. & Holgate, R. Acquisitions, enquiries, research on collections and fieldwork at Bedford and Luton Museums, 1988-89, *Bedfordshire Archaeol.* 19, 65-79.

Woodward, P.J. 1978 Flint distribution, ring ditches and Bronze Age settlement patterns in the Great Ouse Valley. *Archaeol. J.* 135, 32-56.

Woodward, P.J. 1986 Ring-ditch sites in the Great Ouse valley: notes relating to the Bronze Age burial sites at Roxton, Radwell and Willington with specific reference to double ring-ditches. *Bedfordshire Archaeol.* 17, 7-9.

Wright, T. 1849 On some early notices to the antiquities of St Albans. *Arch.* 33, 262-68.

Wymer, J. 1968 *Lower Palaeolithic Archaeology in Britain as represented by the Thames Valley.* London: John Baker.

Wymer, J. 1991 The Southern Rivers Palaeolithic Project. *Lithics* 12, 21-3.

Wymer, J. 1992 The Southern Rivers Palaeolithic Project. *PAST* 13, 6-8.

Yelling, J.A. 1977 *Common Field and Enclosure in England 1450-1850.* England: Macmillan Press.

Yeoman, P.A. 1985 Mantles Green Farm, Amersham, summary report. *South Midlands Archaeol.* 15, 25-6.

Young, A. 1971 *General View of the Agriculture of the County of Hertfordshire (1804).* Newton Abbot: David & Charles.

INDEX

182

Books Published by
THE BOOK CASTLE

JOURNEYS INTO HERTFORDSHIRE: Anthony Mackay.
Foreword by The Marquess of Salisbury, Hatfield House.
Nearly 200 superbly detailed ink drawings depict the towns, buildings and landscape of this still predominantly rural county.

JOURNEYS INTO BEDFORDSHIRE: Anthony Mackay.
Foreword by The Marquess of Tavistock, Woburn Abbey.
A lavish book of over 150 evocative ink drawings.

CHILTERN ARCHAEOLOGY: RECENT WORK:
A Handbook for the Next Decade: edited by Robin Holgate.
The latest views, results and excavations by twenty-three leading archaeologists throughout the Chilterns.

COUNTRYSIDE CYCLING IN BEDFORDSHIRE,
BUCKINGHAMSHIRE and HERTFORDSHIRE: Mick Payne.
Twenty rides on- and off-road for all the family.

LOCAL WALKS: South Bedfordshire and North Chilterns:
Vaughan Basham. Twenty-seven thematic circular walks.

LOCAL WALKS : North and Mid-Bedfordshire: Vaughan Basham.
Twenty-five thematic circular walks.

CHILTERN WALKS: Hertfordshire, Bedfordshire and
North Buckinghamshire: Nick Moon.

CHILTERN WALKS: Buckinghamshire: Nick Moon.

CHILTERN WALKS: Oxfordshire and West Buckinghamshire:
Nick Moon. A trilogy of circular walks, in association with the Chiltern Society.
Each volume contains thirty circular walks.

OXFORDSHIRE WALKS:
Oxford, the Cotswolds and the Cherwell Valley: Nick Moon.

OXFORDSHIRE WALKS:
Oxford, the Downs and the Thames Valley: Nick Moon.
Two volumes that complement Chiltern Walks: Oxfordshire and complete coverage of the county, in association with the Oxford Fieldpaths Society. Thirty circular walks in each.

FOLK: Characters and Events in the History of Bedfordshire and
Northamptonshire: Vivienne Evans. Anthology about people of yesteryear — arranged alphabetically by village or town.

LEGACIES:
Tales and Legends of Luton and the North Chilterns: Vic Lea.
Twenty-five mysteries and stories based on fact, including Luton Town Football Club. Many photographs.

ECHOES: Tales And Legends of Bedfordshire and Hertfordshire:
Vic Lea. Thirty, compulsively retold historical incidents.

MYTHS and WITCHES, PEOPLE and POLITICS:
Tales from Four Shires: Bucks., Beds., Herts., and Northants.:
John Houghton.
Anthology of strange but true historical events.

ECCENTRICS and VILLAINS, HAUNTINGS and HEROES.:
Tales from Four Shires: Northants., Beds., Bucks. and Herts.: John Houghton.
True incidents and curious events covering one thousand years.

THE RAILWAY AGE IN BEDFORDSHIRE: Fred Cockman.
Classic, illustrated account of early railway history.

JOHN BUNYAN: HIS LIFE AND TIMES: Vivienne Evans.
Foreword by the Bishop of Bedford. Preface by Terry Waite.
Bedfordshire's most famous son set in his seventeenth century context.

SWANS IN MY KITCHEN: The Story of a Swan Sanctuary: Lis Dorer.
Foreword by Dr Philip Burton. Updated edition.
Tales of her dedication to the survival of these beautiful birds through her
sanctuary near Hemel Hempstead.

WHIPSNADE WILD ANIMAL PARK: 'MY AFRICA': Lucy Pendar.
Foreword by Andrew Forbes. Introduction by Gerald Durrell.
Inside story of sixty years of the Park's animals and people – full of anecdotes,
photographs and drawings.

DUNSTABLE WITH THE PRIORY, 1100–1550: Vivienne Evans.
Dramatic growth of Henry I's important new town around a major crossroads.

DUNSTABLE DECADE: THE EIGHTIES:
A Collection of Photographs: Pat Lovering.
A souvenir book of nearly 300 pictures of people and events in the 1980s.

DUNSTABLE IN DETAIL: Nigel Benson.
A hundred of the town's buildings and features, plus town trail map.

OLD DUNSTABLE: Bill Twaddle.
A new edition of this collection of early photographs.

BOURNE AND BRED: A Dunstable Boyhood Between the Wars:
Colin Bourne.
An elegantly written, well-illustrated book capturing the spirit of the town over
fifty years ago.

ROYAL HOUGHTON: Pat Lovering.
Illustrated history of Houghton Regis from the earliest times to the present.

BEDFORDSHIRE'S YESTERYEARS Vol. 1:
The Family, Childhood and Schooldays: Brenda Fraser-Newstead.
Unusual early 20th century reminiscences, with private photographs.

BEDFORDSHIRE'S YESTERYEARS Vol 2:
The Rural Scene: Brenda Fraser-Newstead.
Vivid first-hand accounts of country life two or three generations ago.

BEDFORDSHIRE'S YESTERYEARS Vol 3:
Craftsmen and Trades People: Brenda Fraser-Newstead.
Fascinating recollections over several generations practising many vanishing
crafts and trades.

PUBS and PINTS:
The Story of Luton's Public Houses and Breweries: Stuart Smith.
Three hundred rare photographs illustrate this detailed account of the town's
important brewing industry and retail beer outlets, past and present.

THE CHANGING FACE OF LUTON: An Illustrated History:
Stephen Bunker, Robin Holgate and Marian Nichols.
Luton's development from earliest times to the present busy industrial town.
Illustrated in colour and monochrome. The three authors from Luton Museum are
all experts in local history, archaeology, crafts and social history.

THE MEN WHO WORE STRAW HELMETS:
Policing Luton, 1840–1974: Tom Madigan.
Meticulously chronicled history; dozens of rare photographs; author served Luton
Police for nearly fifty years.

BETWEEN THE HILLS:
The Story of Lilley, a Chiltern Village: Roy Pinnock.
A priceless piece of our heritage – the rural beauty remains but the customs and
way of life described here have largely disappeared.

GLEANINGS REVISITED:
Nostalgic Thoughts of a Bedfordshire Farmer's Boy: E W O'Dell.
His own sketches and early photographs adorn this lively account of rural
Bedfordshire in days gone by.

FARM OF MY CHILDHOOD, 1925–1947: Mary Roberts.
An almost vanished lifestyle on a remote farm near Flitwick.

THE TALL HITCHIN SERGEANT:
A Victorian Crime Novel based on fact: Edgar Newman.
Mixes real police officers and authentic background with an exciting storyline.

THE TALL HITCHIN INSPECTOR'S CASEBOOK:
A Victorian Crime Novel based on fact: Edgar Newman.
Worthies of the time encounter more archetypal villains.

LEAFING THROUGH LITERATURE:
Writers' Lives in Hertfordshire and Bedfordshire: David Carroll.
Illustrated short biographies of many famous authors and their connections with
these counties.

THROUGH VISITORS' EYES:
A Bedfordshire Anthology: edited by Simon Houfe.
Impressions of the county by famous visitors over the last four centuries,
thematically arranged and illustrated with line drawings.

THE HILL OF THE MARTYR:
An Architectural History of St. Albans Abbey: Eileen Roberts.
Scholarly and readable chronological narrative history of Hertfordshire and
Bedfordshire's famous cathedral. Fully illustrated with photographs and plans.

SPECIALLY FOR CHILDREN

VILLA BELOW THE KNOLLS: A Story of Roman Britain: Michael Dundrow.
An exciting adventure for young John in Totternhoe and Dunstable two thousand
years ago.

ADVENTURE ON THE KNOLLS: A Story of Iron Age Britain:
Michael Dundrow.
Excitement on Totternhoe Knolls as ten-year-old John finds himself back in those
dangerous times, confronting Julius Caesar and his army.

THE RAVENS: One Boy Against the Might of Rome: James Dyer.
On the Barton Hills and in the south-east of England as the men of the great fort
of Ravensburgh (near Hexton) confront the invaders.

Further titles are in preparation.
All the above are available via any bookshop, or from the publisher and bookseller

THE BOOK CASTLE
12 Church Street, Dunstable, Bedfordshire, LU5 4RU
Tel: (01582) 605670